ANSON COUNTY, NORTH CAROLINA: ABSTRACTS OF EARLY RECORDS

Compiled by
MAY WILSON McBEE

Baltimore
GENEALOGICAL PUBLISHING CO., INC.

Originally Published: Greenwood, Mississippi, 1950
Reprinted: Genealogical Publishing Co., Inc.
Baltimore, 1978, 1980
Library of Congress Catalogue Card Number 77-88217
International Standard Book Number 0-8063-0790-0
Made in the United States of America

PREFACE

The fire of April 2nd, 1868 destroyed most of Anson County's records but it is, by no means, what genealogists call "a burned county," for the fundamental wills and deeds remain. There were, also, some charred pages of the minutes of the Court of Common Pleas and Quarter Sessions, 1771-1777, which have been made available by Mr. R. E. Little, of Wadesboro, who, during his tenure as Clerk of the Superior Court, 1930-1942, had these records copied and indexed. These minutes are mines of information, the proving of the deeds, alone, being practically a list of real estate transfers for that period. Unfortunately there are a few gaps, which, however, make us more grateful for the exceptional data preserved in these Court Orders.

Another source of valuable information is several hundred pages of probate reports in the back of Will Book 1, dating from 1749 through 1789, but not entered chronologically, as if copied from a lot of loose papers. These have been indexed through the late Mr. W. K. Boggan's appreciation of their genealogical value. Mr. Boggan was Clerk of the Superior Court from Dec. 10,1910 to Dec. 1, 1930.

Until 1760 letters of administration were granted and wills probated at the Office of the Secretary of State. However, there are on record in Anson County a number of administration papers before that date and five wills. Anson was a large county at the time of its organization, practically all of the "back country." Two of these wills were of men who lived on the Catawba which was "a far piece" from Anson Court House and too far from Wilmington, the Capitol of the Province.

The deeds are nice and meaty. Only a few have a beginning or an ending missing. It is regrettable not to have been able to abstract the first twenty volumes straight through since all of the other early records of the county are abstracted in this collection. For the 500 deeds selected, the basis is those originally chosen for genealogical use and added to as the family groups expanded. When it was decided to share these records by publishing them, the deeds were supplemented by paging the early volumes and adding abstracts of those deeds giving the most genealogical information.

In an effort to have all of our Anson ancestors who were there before 1790 somewhere in these records, a number of petitions from Anson County to the General Assembly are included. There are no qualifications to signing most petitions, so these should, to a large extent, show who lived in the county in the years covered, 1770-1789, many of whom are not in the minutes of the County Court. However, the most famous Anson petition is not included as it is published elsewhere. It is that of the Regulators in 1769, one of the first demonstrations by Colonists against the Crown. It was the back country voicing loudly its complaints against the Government and its agents. Only the first page of the original petition remains (Dept. of Archives and History, Raleigh) and none of the signatures, but is preserved to us in full in the North Carolina Colonial Records, Vol. 8, 75-80.

The list of Anson County Land Grants is from the index file of grants in the Office of the Secretary of State at Raleigh. Except in a few instances, there is only one listing to a name and an effort was made to give the first grant in each case, with an asterisk to denote other grants to the same person. Besides the name and the date the grant was issued, the number of the grant is given and the general location. In the abstracts of Land Grant Surveys, is shown the information that may be obtained by an examination of the papers in the files, which the excellent force in this department is ready to furnish on request. The genealogical value of land patents is inestimable.

In February 1779, Montgomery County was formed from the northern part of Anson and in October of the same year Richmond County was organized from the section east of the Peedee. The inhabitants of the two newly-created counties were so much a part of Anson County that, in order to follow up some records of the mother county, the few available records of Montgomery,

PREFACE

which had a disastrous fire about 1835, and some of the pertinent deeds and wills of Richmond, which has all its records intact, are also given. All the records of Montgomery are from the Department of Archives and History, at Raleigh, without whose help these abstracts of early records would have been sadly deficient. Grateful acknowledgment is made to the Department for the use of their excellent material and to the members of the staff who have patiently assisted in making it available. Most of the deeds, wills and probate records were copied in the Anson Courthouse at Wadesboro; some of them and all of the County Court Minutes were taken from the Anson County microfilms in the Archives. Microfilms of the older counties of North Carolina have been made by the Genealogical Society of Utah and duplicates presented to the State Department of Archives and History, for the privilege of filming the records. They are a valuable addition to the Department.

The offices of the Clerk of the Superior Court and the Register of Deeds in Wadesboro are pleasant places to work and the officials and their staffs courteous and helpful. Thanks especially to Miss Hazel Tice, the deputy Register of Deeds. She has been patient and gracious as well as efficient. Acknowledgments, too, to Mr. Isaac London, editor of the Rockingham Post-Dispatch, for the privilege of using his collection of historical and genealogical material. His habit of lending a helping hand is well-known. Mrs. DeVogt, in the Secretary of State's Office, at Raleigh, with other members of the Land Grant Division, was of much assistance.

To the many who have encouraged the publication of these records, the compiler is also indebted, especially to George W. Glass who urgently suggested it.

May Wilson McBee

August 1950
Greenwood, Mississippi.

TABLE OF CONTENTS

Preface iii

List of Land Grants 1

Abstracts of Land Grant Surveys 23

Abstracts of Deeds 26

Abstracts of County Court Minutes, 1771-1777 69

Anson Civil Suits in Salisbury District Superior Court 112

Abstracts of Wills 114

Abstracts of Probate Reports, 1749-1789 126

Petitions, 1770-1789 133

List of Major James Cotton's Accts, 1776 141

Montgomery County Records 142

Richmond County Records 149

Index 157

ABBREVIATIONS

a - acre

apptd - appointed

beg - beginning

bond - bondsmen

ch - chain-carriers (in surveying)

con - consideration

ent - entered

est - estate

gdn - guardian

gr - granted

iss - issued

ord - ordered

pr - proved

prob - probated
       probably

relinq - relinquished

sd - said

surv - surveyed or surveyor

w - wife

*in List of Land Grants - other grants to same name.
[ ] - not in text, supplied by compiler from records.

LAND GRANTS

*Acre, Christian #1476 - 10 Apr. 1761 - br. of Long Cr.
*Acre, Peter #1986 - 10 Apr. 1761 - Indian Cr. [S.C.]
*Adams, Richard #2106 - 20 Apr. 1763 - Mountain Cr.
Adams, Thos. #3458 - 23 July 1774 - Mountain Cr.
*Adams, Wm. #3470 - 23 July 1774 - Mountain Cr.
*Adair, Wm. #2144 - 27 Mch. 1755 - Long Cr.
{ Adcock, James
  Crawford, John } #3848 - 4 Mch. 1775 - Peedee River.
  Adcock, Henry
*Adcock, Henry #3637 - 25 July 1774 - Hitchcock Cr.
Adcock, James #2593 - 16 Dec. 1769 - Solomon's Cr.
Addams, John #4394 - 14 Oct. 1782 - SW of Peedee R., Ray's Fk.
Akers, Christian #2165 - 31 Mch. 1755 - Beaver Dam Cr.
*Alexander, Benj. #1215 - 24 Sept. 1754 - Saluda Path [S.C.]
*Alexander, Ezekiel #112 - 6 Apr. 1753 - Sugar Cr.
*Alexander, James #02 - 7 Apr. 1750 - both sides of Rocky River.
*Alexander, John #939 - 22 Feb. 1754 - Broad R., Thicketty Cr. [S.C.]
*Alexander, Nathaniel #698 - 29 Mch. 1753 - north of Catawba [S.C.]
Alexander, William #976 - 25 Mch. 1752 - adj. John Peterson.
Allen, Chas. #2689 - 24 Dec. 1770
*Allen, Darling #5735 - 20 Dec. 1803 - Cribs Cr.
Allen, Gabriel #5026 - 27 June 1793 - Gould's 3rd corner
{ Allen, James
  Burford, Daniel } #051 - 21 May 1773
*Allen, James #3345 - 4 Mch. 1775
*Allen, John #1625 - 17 May 1754 - N of Catawba R. [S.C.]
*Allen, Joseph #03 - 3 Apr. 1752 - S of Cape Fear R., Bear Cr.
Allen, Mark #2935 - 22 Jany. 1773 - Cheek's Cr.
Allen, Samuel #2028 - 24 Apr. 1762 - East of Catawba [S.C.]
Allen, Wm. #6859 - 2 Apr. 1752 - adj. Geo. Stegall.
*Alley, James #2237 - 26 Nov. 1757 - NE of Peedee R.
*Allison, Andrew #975 - 25 Mch. 1752 - Catawba River [S.C.]
*Allison, James #973 - 24 June 1751 - Crane Cr.
*Allison, Robert #427 - 15 Oct. 1755 - Fishing Cr., S of Catawba
Almond, Edward #2567 - 16 Dec. 1769 - NE Peedee R. Hitchcock Cr.
*Alred, John #3850 - 4 Mch. 1775 - Buffalo Cr.
Alton, John #3042 - 24 May 1773 - NE Peedee
*Ambrose, Phillip #498 - 1 Mch. 1758 - SW Peedee
*Ancrum, John #2009 - 10 Dec. 1761 -
*Anderson, John #1894 - 26 Nov. 1757 - NE S Fk of Catawba [S.C.]
*Anderson, John #3823 - 3 Mch. 1775 - NE Peedee R.
*Anderson, Thos. #1467 - 10 Apr. 1761 - Leonard Sealor's Cr.
Andrews, George #4060 - 3 Sept. 1779 - SW Peedee, Buffalo Cr.
Armour, Andrews #1463 - 10 Apr. 1761 - Catawba
Armstrong, Isaac #2505 - 22 Dec. 1768 - E of Little R, Buffalo Cr.
*Armstrong, James #06 - 20 Feb. 1754 - Beaverdam Cr. S Fk of Catawba
Arnett, John #5488 - 27 Dec. 1799 - Cribs Cr.
Arnett, Wm. #3632,- 25 July 1774 - Cribbs Cr.
Arrenton, James #4080 - 3 Sept. 1779 - SW of Peedee, Jones Cr.
Arrinton, Thos. #1595 - 20 Apr. 1762 -
Adenton, John #01 4 Apr. 1752 King's Cr.
*Adkins, Wm. #608 - 7 Apr. 1749 - SW Peedee Jones Cr.
*Arthaud, Isaac #395 - 3 Oct. 1755 - Thompson's Cr.
*Ashley, John #016 - 25 Sept. 1766 - Richardson's Cr.
Ashley, Nath'l #3551 - 23 July 1774 - Brown Cr. Flat Fk.
*Ashley, Wm. #3484 - 23 July - Naked Cr.
*Ashmore, Wm. #3051 - 23 May 1773 - SW Peedee, Island Cr.
Ashmore, Wm. #3092 - 24 May 1773 - Dutchman's Cr. Uwary R.
Auld, John #4843 - 16 Nov. 1790 -
*Auld, James #3058 - 24 May 1773 - SW Peedee
Auld, Michael #4771 - 16 Nov. 1790 - Ratcliff's line
Atkins, Lewis #4549 - 14 Oct. 1783 - SW Peedee, Buffelow Cr.
Aulquire, Abraham #2947 - 22 Jany 1773 - SW Peedee
*Austin, John #4344 - Oct. 1783 - S side Rocky R.

*More than one land grant for this name; the one given the earliest.

LAND GRANTS

*Austin, Michael #5138 - 10 July 1797 - N of Richardson's Cr.
*Austin, Richard #4398 - 14 Oct. 1783 - Rocky R.
Averitt, John #1756 -   - NE Peedee
Ayer, Hartwell #4707 - 7 Aug. 1787 - adj. James Jones
Babock, Wm. #014 - 20 Feb. 1754
Badgitt, James #4176 - 30 Mch. 1780 - NE Peedee, Mark's Cr.
*Bagby, Geo. #3573 - 25 July 1774 - waters of Rockhole
*Bagby, Geo. Jr. #2531 - 21 Oct. 1767 - SW Yadkin, Long Cr.
Baggett, James, Jr. #4145 - 30 Mch. 1780 - NE Peedee Solomon's Cr.
Baggett, Shadrack #4227 - 30 Mch. 1780 - NE Peedee
*Baggott, Abraham #043 - 1 July 1758 - NE Peedee
Bailes, Jesse #2680 - 11 Dec. 1770 - br of Thompson's Cr.
*Bailey, Jacob #5407 - 6 Dec. 1799 - Jones Cr.
Bailey, Lidia #4798 - 16 Nov. 1790 - adj. Thos. Bailey
*Bailey, Mathew #3241 - 4 Mch. 1775 - Jones Cr.
*Bailey, Thomas #3048 - 24 May 1773 - SW Peedee
Bailey, Adam #1902 - 27 May 1760 - SW Peedee
*Bailey, Andrew #1393 - 27 May 1760 - SW Peedee
Bailey, Thos. #1447 (ent. 1756) - 5 Dec. 1760 - SW Peedee
Bailes, Fereby #5096 - 8 Dec. 1794 - N of Brown Cr.
Baird, Benj. #3563 - 25 July 1774 - Dison's Cr.
Baird, Benj. #3567 - 25 July 1774 - SW Peedee, Jones Cr.
{Baird, Benj.   } #3553 - 23 July 1774 - West
{Smith, John [S.H.]} of Little R.
{Baird, Benj.   }
{Smith, John [S.H.]} #3929 - 11 March 1775 - West
{Smith, David [S.H.]} of Little R.
*Baird, Wm. #010 - 4 Apr. 1752 - N of Catawba, Waxhaw Cr.
Baker, Aaron #4673 - 25 Aug. 1786 - SW Peedee
*Baker, Francis #5467 - 18 Dec. 1786 - SW Peedee
Baker, James #4924 - 16 Nov. 1790
Baker, Samuel #012 - 11 May 1753 - Golden Grove Cr.
Baker, Samuel #1177 - 20 May 1754 - SW br NW br Cape Fear
*Baker, Wm. #4358 - 14 Oct. 1783 Lane's Cr.
Bankston, Andrew #2746 - 18 Apr. 1771 - S of Yadkin
Barber, Abraham #4787 - 16 Nov. 1790
Barkley, John #1674 - 17 May 1754 - S of Bear Cr.
Barnes, John #020 - 14 Oct. 1752 - N fork Fishing Cr. [S.C.]
*Barnes, John #832 - 30 Aug. 1753 - S side of Catawba [S.C.]

Barnes, Thomas #4822 - 16 Nov. 1790
Barnes, Wm. #2634 - 9 Apr. 1770 - Clark's Cr.
*Barnet, John #2484 - 22 Dec. 1768 - Yadkin R.
*Barnet, Wm. #1530 - 24 Apr. 1762 - N fork of Steel Cr.
Barr, John #679 - 28 Mch. 1753 - Catawba
Barrett, Thos. #022 - 20 Oct. 1767 - Thompson's Cr.
Barriner [Barringer] Paul #021 - 2 Apr. 1751
Barrintine, Jacob #4036 - 3 Sept. 1779 - adj. Rice Henderson
Bass, Frederick #4299 - 24 Oct. 1782 - Flat Fk of Brown Cr.
Bawen [Bowen] Joseph #4342 -   - NW Rocky River
*Baxley, Aaron #4359 - 14 Oct. 1783 - Brown Cr.
Beacham, Aleck #5071 - 9 July 1794
Beacham, Wm. #4948 - 20 Dec. 1791
Beard, John #2759 - 18 Apr. 1771
Beard, Wm. #930 - 25 Feb. 1754 - N side of Catawba
*Beason, Samuel #1696 - 20 May 1754 - Clark's Cr.
Beatey, Francis #2218 - 26 Sept. 1757 - Long Cr.
*Beatey, Chas. & Thos. #708 - 31 Mch. 1753 - Stoney br of Catawba
Beck, John #3998 - 3 Sept. 1779 - SW Peedee, Cedar Cr.
*Becton, Frederick #2006 - 8 Jany 1760 - SW Lynches Cr.
Bedinfield, Henry #034 - 7 Apr. 1750 - Little R. of Peedee
Bedinfield, Henry #035 - 5 Apr. 1749 - N side of Peedee
*Bedinfield, Wm. #897 - 23 Feb. 1754 - N side of Peedee
Beggar, Matthew #2024 - 24 Apr. 1762 - McAlpine's Cr.
*Bell, Joseph #4150 - 3 Sept. 1779 - Huwary River
Bell, Thomas #037 - 3 Apr. 1752
Belew, George #3435 - 16 Mch. 1775 - Flat Fk of Brown Cr.
Belew, Hanry #3026 - 24 May 1774 - SW Peedee
*Belew, Abraham #2406 - 6 Apr. 1765 - Cedar Cr.
*Bennet, Joseph #3323 - 4 Mch. 1775
Bennet, Nevel #4899 - 16 Nov. 1790
*Bennet, Wm. #2828 - 22 Nov. 1771 - NE Peedee
*Bennett, Wm. Jr. #031 - 5 Apr. 1770 - S side of Peedee
Benson, Wm. #2944 - 22 Jany. 1773 - NE Peedee
Benton, Chas. #4583 - 23 Sept. 1785
*Benton, James #4626 - 23 Sept. 1785
Benton, James #2982 - 22 Jany. 1773 - SW Peedee
Benton, Job #3085 - 24 May 1773 - SW Peedee
*Benton, Benton #3611 - 25 July 1774
*Berringer, Paul #1327 - 27 Sept. 1756 - SW Peedee
*Berry, Andrew #293 - 23 Feb. 1754 - McDowell's Cr., Catawba

LAND GRANTS 3

*Berry [Barry], Hugh #1482 - 14 Apr. 1761 - Harden's Road
*Best, Bolston #1652 - 16 May 1754 - Leepers Cr.
*Bettis, Elijah #011 - 24 Oct. 1765 - Brown Cr.
Bettis, Ensient #2836 - 14 May 1772 - Rushing's Cr. of Thompson's
*Beverly, John #5355 - 9 Mch. 1799 - Lane's Cr.
Beverly, John #4804 - 16 Nov. 1790 - N side of Meadow Br.
*Beggar, James #0539 - 20 Apr. 1762
Beggar, Matthew #1529 - 24 Apr. 1762 - McAlpin's Cr.
*Biggleston, James #038 - 13 Jany. 1773 - Little Brown Cr.
*Billingsley, Sias #3066 - 24 May 1773 - Dutchman's Cr., Uwarry R.
*Bingham, Thos. #1367 - 25 May 1757 - SW of Peedee
Bingham, Wm. #1961 - 10 Apr. 1760 - Cow Cr.
*Birmingham, Chas. #2927 - 22 Jany. 1773 - SW Peedee
Bird, John #3966 - 3 Sept. 1779 - Gum Swamp
Bivins, Abel #5095 - 8 Dec. 1794 - Richardson's Cr.
Black, Archibald #1553 - 24 Apr. 1762 - NE Peedee
Black, Kenneth #3009 - 22 Jany. 1773 - Cypress Pond
Blackford, Samuel #5341 - 9 Mch. 1799
Blakeney, Wm. #5468 - 18 Dec. 1799 - Thompson's Cr.
{Blewett, Wm. } #2259 - 1 July 1758 - NE
{Cartledge, Edmond} Peedee
*Blewett, Wm. #1386 - 6 Mch. 1759 - NE Peedee
Bloodworth, John #4742 - 7 Aug. 1787 - adj. Thos. Bailey
Bloodworth, Samuel #3878 - 4 March 1775 - Buck Br of Brown Cr.
Blount, James #4956 - 20 Dec. 1791 - Richardson Cr.
Blount, Reuben #4988 - 27 Nov. 1792
Boatright, Thos. #5389 - 26 July 1799 - Thompson's Cr.
*Boggan, James #3967 - 23 Sept. 1799 - SW Peedee, Gould's Fk.
*Boggan, Patrick #4268 - 24 Oct. 1782
*Boggan, Wm. #4013 - - Gold's Fk of Brown Cr.
*Bole, Elisha #2131 - 28 Mch. 1755 - Catawba
*Bole, Susanna #934 - 23 Feb. 1754 - Broad Riv. Turkey Cr.
*Bolin, John #1427 - 5 Dec. 1760 - Little River of Peedee
{Bolton, William } #3541 - 23 July 1774 - Mill Br.
{Slaughter, Owen}
Bond, Elisha #2928 - 22 Jany. 1773 - SW Peedee
*Bond, Nicholas #2514 - 23 Dec. 1768 - Cypress Pond

*Bond, Richard #3923 - 11 Mch. 1775 - Cedar Cr.
Bond, (Bone), John #044 - 10 Oct. 1749 - Drowning Cr.
Booth, Charles #2543 - 4 May 1769 - Thompson's Cr. Rushing's br
*Booth, John #4749 - 7 Aug. 1787 - adj. own land
Booth, John #2850 - 19 May 1772 - SW Peedee, Cedar Cr.
Booth, Wm. #2851 - 19 May 1772
*Bostick, Abitha (Tabitha) #3963 - 4 Mch. 1775 - NE Peedee
*Bostick, Eliz. #3339 - 4 Mch. 1775 - Hamer's Cr.
Bostick, Ezra #2749 - 18 Apr. 1771 - NE Peedee
{Bostick, James} #3880 - 4 Mch. 1775 - Lick Cr.
{Scott, John   }
Bostick, John #2747 - 18 Apr. 1771 - NE Peedee
*Bound, James Sr. #2332 - 9 Nov. 1764 - Hitchcock's Cr.
*Bound, James #3473 - 23 July 1774 - Coe br of Hitchcock's Cr.
*Bound, Jesse #2917 - 22 Jany. 1773 - NE Peedee Cow Br
Bound, John #2854 - 19 May 1772 - NE Peedee
Bowing, Joseph #3989 - 3 Sept. - SW Peedee
*Bowling, John #462 - 26 Nov. 1757 - NE Peedee
*Bowman, Wm. #4694 - 30 July 1784 - Lane's Cr.
Boyd, Abraham #046 - - S side of Peedee
Boyd, Robt. #2426 - 25 Sept. 1766 - Jones Cr.
Boyle, Edw. #047 - 28 Mar. 1753 - Catawba
*Brasewell, Richard #3187 - 22 Nov. 1771 - Little River
Bracken, William #4035 - Crib's Cr.
Bradford, Richard #1800 - 15 Mar. 1756 - Thos. Stafford's corner
Bradly, Hobbs #4949 - 20 Dec. 1791
*Branch, John #4723 - 7 Aug. 1787 - Province line
Branderway, Robt. [Broadaway] #4360 - 14 Oct. 1783 - Lanier Cr.
*Brandon, John #048 - 28 Sept. 1750 - S side of Yadkin
Brandon, Richard #978 - 25 Mar. 1752 - Grant's Cr.
Brandon, William #992 - 25 Mar. 1752
Brantley, James #2839 - 15 May 1772 - SW Peedee
Brasswell, Benj. #4547 - 14 Oct. 1783 - SW Peedee
Brasswell, Nathan #4356 - 14 Oct. 1783 - SW Peedee
Brasswell, William #4571 - 14 Oct. 1783 - SW Peedee
*Brevard, John #997 - 25 Mar. 1752 - Rocky River
Brevard, Robt. #961 - 20 Feb. 1754 - Reedy River
*Braswell, Richard #3769 - 29 Feb. 1775 - Dry Cr. (Leap Year?)
*Brewer, George #4309 - 24 Oct. 1782
*Brigham, Isaac - 26 Oct. 1767 - Little River of Peedee
Brigham, Joshua #3995 - 3 Sept. 1779 - SE Peedee
*Brigham, Thomas #058 - 27 Sept. 1766 - NE Peedee

LAND GRANTS

*Brigham, Wm. #059 - April 1762
Bringham, Joshua #4759 - 27 Nov. 1789 - SW Peedee
*Bringham, Thos. #1876 - 25 May 1789 - SW Peedee
Briley, George #4604 - 23 Sept. 1785
Brinkley, Robt. #057 - 6 April 1750 - Jones Cr.
*Broadaway, Robt. #055 - 27 Sept. 1756 - NE Peedee Buffalo Cr.
Brooks, Eliz. #4117 - 3 Sept. 1779 - SW Peedee
*Brooks, James #2790 -   - Leveretts Cr.
*Brooks, John #1559 - 24 Apr. 1762
*Brooks, William #1558 - 24 Apr. 1762 - Rocky River
Brooler, Elisha #4798 - 16 Nov. 1790 - adj. Nathl. Morgan
Brown, Augustus #052 - 4 Apr. 1753 - Brown Cr.
*Brown, Edward #4869 - 16 Nov. 1790
Brown, Jesse #3931 - 11 March 1775 - Rocky Fk of Jones Cr.
*Brown, John #1547 - 24 Apr. 1762 - NE Peedee
*Brown, Morgan #454 - 26 Nov. 1757 - NE Peedee
*Brown, Neil #3023 - 25 Jany. 1773 - Mountain Cr.
Brown, William #870 - 17 Nov. 1753 - beg. Great Fall of Peedee
Brown, William #248 - 17 Nov. 1753
{Brownlow, James} #0380 - 23 Sept. 1766 - Brown
{Lyon, John } Cr.
Bruff, John #3311 - 4 Mar. 1667 - NE Peedee
*Brumlow (Brownlow), David #4927 - 16 Nov. 1790
*Brumlow, James and John #2483 - 22 Dec. 1768 - Gould's Fork
Bruton, Samuel #2840 - 15 May 1772 - Miry Branch
*Bryan, Morgan #983 - 27 Oct. 1752 - north of Yadkin
Bryant, David #4334 - 14 Oct. 1783 - Rocky River
Bucher, Joseph #4572 - 14 Oct. 1783 - Chinkerpin Cr.
Burcham, John #3502 - 23 July 1774 - NE Peedee
Burcham, Henry #2887 - 22 May 1772 - Little River
Burford, Daniel #3213 - 4 Mar. 1775 - NE Peedee Mark's Cr.
{Burford, Daniel}
{Allen, James } #051 - 21 May 1773
*Burlyson, David #4422 - 14 Oct. 1780 - south of Peedee
Burnett, Charles #996 - 25 March 1762
Burnett, John #995 - 24 June 1751 - Crane Cr.
Burnett, Samuel #1110 - 20 May 1750 - Joseph White's line
Burnett, Samuel #1624 - 20 May 1754 - Joseph White's line
*Burns, William #3701 - 24 Feb. 1775 - NE Peedee
Burris, Joshua, Jr. #4134 - 3 Sept. 1779 - SW Peedee, Island Cr.

Burris, Joshua, Sr. #3987 - 3 Sept. 1779 - SW Peedee, Jones Cr,
*Burt, Wm. #2869 - 20 May 1772 - Drowning Cr.
Burtin, Richard #1544 - 24 Apr. 1762 - Drowning Cr.
Bush, Richard #4935 - 20 Dec. 1791
Butler, Christopher #2910 - 22 Jany. 1773 - Bear Cr.
Butler, Elisha #4347 - 30 March 1780 - SW Peedee
Butler, John #1943 - 5 Dec. 1760 - NE Peedee
Butnell, Joseph #4511 - Oct. 1783 - Savannah Cr.
Calwell, Robert #876 - 23 Feb. 1754 - Waxhaw Cr.
Calloway, Job. #0136 -   - SW Yadkin
{Campbell, Archibald}
{McArthur, Neil   } #2895 - 22 May 1772
*Campbell, Archibald #3509 - 23 July 1774 - Naked Cr.
*Campbell, Charles #5335 - 9 Mch. 1799 - Savannah Cr.
Campbell, Farquard #5427 - 6 Dec. 1799 - Jones Cr.
*Campbell, James #3471 - 23 July 1774 - Little River
Camble, James #3052 - 24 May 1773 - Thompson's Cr.
Canady, Felix #735 - 5 April 1753
*Cannon, John #1432 - 5 Dec. 1760 - NE Peedee
Capper, Robert M. #594 - 4 Oct. 1751 - Catawba
*Care, Robert #1243 - 25 Sept. 1754 - Little River
*Carr, John #727 - 2 Apr. 1753
*Carr (Ker), Patrick #0178 - 3 Oct. 1755
Carr, Robt. #2792 - 18 Nov. 1771
*Carral, Torance #2058 - 24 Apr. 1762 - NE Peedee
Carruth, John #4112 - 3 Sept. 1779 - west of Peedee
Carruth, Walter #2159 - 28 March 1755 - Enoree River
*Carter, George #0129 - 18 April 1763 - Hitchcock's Cr.
Carter, Jacob #3679 - 25 July 1774 - Mountain Cr.
Carter, Joshua #4063 - 3 Sept. 1779 - Mountain Cr.
Carter, Joshua #3579 - 25 July 1774 - SW Yadkin
*Carter, William #435 - 26 May 1757 - SW Peedee
*Cartledge, Edmond #1323 - 27 Sept. 1756 - N side of Peedee
Calloway, Job #2900 - 23 Jany. 1773 - SW Yadkin
Caudle, Jesse #4661 - 25 Aug. 1786 - Lane's Cr.
Chambers, Maxwell #4747 - 7 Aug. 1787
Chambers, Edward #2517 - 4 May 1769 - Cheeks Cr.
Chamness, Anthony #1007 - 24 June 1751 - Cane Cr.
*Cheek, Elizabeth #2353 - 30 Oct. 1765 - Hurricane Br. Brown Cr.
*Cheek, Hannah #2355 - 30 Oct. 1765 - Hurricane Br. Brown Cr.
*Cheek, John #3680 - 25 July 1774 - SW Peedee Davis Cr.

Cheek, John #2173 - 3 Oct. 1755
*Cheek, Randolph #4343 - 14 Oct. 1783 - SW Peedee
*Campbell, Malcolm #3052 - 24 May 1773 - Thompson's Cr.
Cheek, Sarah #2354 - 30 Oct. 1765 - Flat Fk of Brown Cr.
Chevers, Thomas #0122 - 24 Oct. 1765 - SW Peedee
Chevers, Thomas #2665 - 25 Aug. 1786 - Negro Head Cr.
Chewing, Bartholomew #4536 - 16 Nov. 1790
*Chiles, John #0124 - 21 May 1773 - Island Fish Trap and Ferry.
Chiles, John #3433 - 1775 - at Grassy Island Ford
*Chiles, Thos. #4226 - 30 March 1780 - Little River N of Peedee
*Chivers, Joel #3141 - 26 Oct. 1767 - Lane's Cr.
Christian, Christopher #0123 - 16 May 1772 - East of Litcle Riv.
Christian, Nicholas #4253 - 30 Mch. 1780 - West of Little Riv.
Christian, Nicholas #3828 - 3 Mch. 1775 - Little Rocky Creek
Christian, Nicholas #3271 - 4 Mch. 1775 - Little Rocky Creek
Christian, Nicholas #3829 - 3 Mch. 1775 - Little Town Creek
Christian, Nicholas #3272 - 4 Mch. 1775 - Little Town Creek
Clark, Chas. #2981 - 22 Jany. 1773 - SW Peedee
*Clark, Christopher #3137 - 26 Oct. 1767 - Watery Br.
Clark, Cornelius #5109 - 8 Dec. 1784 - Crooked Br.
Clark, Francis #2886 - 22 May 1772 - Solomon's Cr.
{ Clark, Francis
Crawford, John
Moorman, Thos.
Hailey, Isham } #2535 - 4 May 1769 - an island and shoal in Peedee
*Clark, John #607 - 13 Apr. 1749 - S of Peedee
Clark, Nevan #0119 - 16 Jany 1773 - Mountain Cr.
*Clark, Thos. #4696 - 21 Mch. 1789 - Jones Cr.
Clements, George #1 - 4 Apr. 1750 - west of Little River
Clements, Matt. #676 - 31 Mch. 1753 - Fishing Cr.
Clenachan [McClenachan], Robert #950 - 25 Feb. 1754 - west of Catawba
Clenachan, Robert #317 - 25 Feb. 1754
Clenachan, Robert #951 - 20 Feb. 1754
McClenachan, Robert #318 - 20 Feb. 1754
*Clerk, Isaac #4281 - 24 Oct. 1782 - Richardson Cr.
*Clifton, Salathiel #4077 - 3 Sept. 1779 - 7 July 1778 - Brown Cr.
Clinton, John #3997 - 3 Sept. 1779 - Cribbs Cr.

Coburn, Jacob #1132 - 20 May 1754 - Catawba
*Coburn, John #212 - 30 Aug. 1753 - Catawba
Coburn, Judith #189 - 31 Aug. 1753 - Catawba
Coburn, Judith #811 - 30 Aug. 1753 - Catawba
*Coburn, Samuel #35 - 29 Sept. 1750 - Catawba
Coburn, Samuel #79 - 31 March 1753 - on Indian Path
*Cockerham, Abraham #3783 - 29 Feb. 1775 - Grim's Cr.
*Cockerham, Jacob #2462 - 21 Oct. 1758 - NE Peedee
*Cockerham, Thos. #3219 - 4 Mch. 1775 - Mountain Cr.
Cockran, John #2754 - Apr. 1771 - NE Peedee
Codil, Lewis #4423 - 14 Oct. 1783 - NE Peedee
Cohan, William #1803 - 13 Mar. 1756 - N side of Peedee
*Cole, John #0112 - 18 Apr. 1767 - Raiford bridge to Jno Crawford
Cole, Stephen #0111 - 3 May 1769 - Davis Mill Branch
{ Cole, Stephen
Coleman, William } #3082 - 24 May 1773 - west of Huwarry River
Cole, William #3121 - 27 Apr. 1767 - on Yadkin Rd.
*Coleman, John #0113 - 15 Dec. 1769 - NE Peedee
{ Coleman, William
Pickett, James } #0494 - 21 May 1773 - Jones Cr.
Coleman, Wm., Thos. & John #1827 - 27 Sept. 1752 - NE Peedee
{ Coleman, Wm.
Cole, Stephen } #3082 - 24 May 1773 - west of Huarry
*Coleman, William #3415 - 11 Mch. 1775 - on Crawford's Road
*Coleson (Collson), John #1438 - 5 Dec. 1760 - SW Peedee
*Coleson, Joseph #4650 - 23 Sept. 1785
*Coleson, William #2919 - 22 Jany. 1773 - Bet. Peedee & Rocky Rivers
*Collins, George #3310 - 4 Mar. 1775
Collins, Joshua #3158 - 29 Apr. 1768 - Mountain Cr.
*Conelly, Thomas #1930 - 5 Dec. 1760 - N of Peedee River
Conner, Edward #4701 - 7 Aug. 1787 - adj Robt. Jarman
Conner, Thomas #3972 - 3 Sept. 1779 - SW Peedee, Bailey's Cr.
*Cook, Chas. #4891 - 16 Nov. 1790
*Cook, Isaac #1644 - 17 May 1754 - Broad River
Cooper, John #0144 - 24 May 1773 - Long Cr.
Copeland, Isaac #3885 - 4 Mch. 1775
Copeland, Peter #3540 - 23 July 1774 - Drowning Cr.
Corbo, John #527 - 23 July 1774 - Jones Cr.
Cornwell, Edward #3517 - 23 July 1774 - NE Peedee

*Corry, John #3084 - 24 May 1773 - NE Peedee
*Cossart, Henry #1004 - 12 Nov. 1754 - Yadkin River
Costillon, Edward #4969 - 27 Nov. 1792 - Lane's Cr.
Costly, Michael #5217 - 12 Oct. 1794 - Lane's Cr.
Cotton, Alicia #3088 - 24 May 1773 - NE Peedee
*Cotton, James #0139 [n.d.] NE Peedee Denson's Fork
*Cotton, James #0142 - 16 May 1772 - in Anson & Cumberland, Cabbin Cr.
Cotton, John #3584 - 25 July 1774 - SW Peedee
{Cotton, James / Neale, Christopher} #3706 - 4 March 1775
*Courtney, Wm. #1399 - 21 Oct. 1758 - Codale Cr.
*Covington, Benj. #2801 - 6 Apr. 1770 - Jones Cr.
Covington, Henry #2611 - 7 Apr. 1770 - Naked Cr.
Covington, John Jr. #3964 - 3 Sept. 1779 - Gum Swamp
Covington, Matthew #3507 - 23 July 1774 - NE Peedee
Covington, Nath'l. #4229 - 30 Mar. 1780 - NE Peedee
Covington, Simon #4214 - 29 Jany. 1779 - Cattail Branch
*Coward, James #1324 - 27 Sept. 1756 - N of Peedee
Cox, Adam #4300 - 24 Oct. 1782
Cox, Avington #4089 - 3 Sept. 1779 - SW Peedee N prong of Jones Cr.
Cox, William #2766 - 18 April 1771 - Jones Cr.
Crane, William #2951 - 22 Jany. 1773 - SW Peedee Peedee
Crawford, Edward #3591 - 25 July 1774 - Savannah Branch
*Crawford, John #589 - 4 Apr. 1750 - Hitchcock's Cr.
Crawford, John Jr. #2104 - 20 Apr. 1763 - NE Peedee
Crawford, Michael #4179 - 30 Mar. 1780 - SW Peedee Jones Cr.
Crawford, Oliver #236 - 30 Aug. 1753 [S.C.]
Covington, William #3000 - 22 Jany. 1773 - SW Peedee
*Crawford, Thomas #4049 - 3 Sept. 1779 - SE Peedee Dees Cr.
*Creel, Thomas #2852 - 19 May 1762 - SW Peedee
*Crittenden, Wm. #431 - 25 May 1757 - NE Peedee
*Cross, Thomas #3071 - - NE Peedee
*Crouch, John #1272 - 23 Dec. 1754 - N of Buffalo Cr.
Crowson, Jehucal ? #4061 - 3 Sept. 1779 - NE Peedee, Wooten's Br.
Culp, Casper #331 - 20 Feb. 1754 - west of Catawba
Culp, Casper #1230 - 25 Sept. 1754 - west of Catawba
*Culpepper, John #4341 - 14 Oct. 1783 - S of Rocky River

*Culpepper, Samson #2457 - 21 Oct. 1758 - SW Peedee
Culpepper, William #3397 - 11 March 1775 - Rock Rocky River
Cumbo, Cannon #3015 - 22 Jany. 1773 - Drowning Cr.
*Cunningham, Hugh #960 - 20 Feb. 1754
Cunningham, Thos. #1162 - 18 May 1754
Cunningham, Walter #3400 - 11 Mch. 1775 - Thompson's Cr.
Curbow #4113 - SW Peedee
Curby, William #5048 - 8 July 1794
Curlee, William #3990 - 3 Sept. 1779 - Lane's Cr.
Curry, Samuel #0116 - 26 Apr. 1768 - Mill Cr.
Curtis, Blundle #4192 - 29 Mch. 1780 - SW Peedee, Talton Cr.
Curtis, Samuel #4885 - 16 Nov. 1790
*Dabbs, Geo. #512 - 13 Apr. 1749 - S of Peedee
Dabbs, Nath'l. #2515 - 4 May 1769 - Davis Branch
Davenport, Francis #456 - 26 Nov. 1757 - NE Peedee
Davenport, William #4997 - 27 Nov. 1792
Davidson, David #5087 - 8 Dec. 1794
*Davidson, George #1013 - 25 Mar. 1752 [S.C.]
*Davidson, George #4269 - 24 Oct. SW Peedee
*Davis, Arthur #4285 - 24 Oct. 1782 - Rocky River
*Davis, Benjamin #99 - 4 Apr. 1753
*Davis, Christopher #4293 - 24 Oct. 1782 - Lane's Cr.
*Davis, David #096 - 28 Sept. 1750
Davis, Gabriel #945 - 23 Feb. 1754
*Davis, John #2204 - 25 May 1757 - SW Peedee
Davis, Joseph #1680 - 17 May 1757 - [S.C.]
*Davis, Samuel #1014 - 20 Sept. 1748 - NE Yadkin
*{Davis, Samuel / Carter, James} #139 - 9 Apr. 1753
*Davis, Walter #0558 - 20 Apr. 1762 - Steel Cr.
Dawson, James #105 - 17 Nov. 1753 - N of Peedee, Mountain Cr.
Dearman, Solomon #3676 - 25 July 1774 - Gum Branch
*Dearman, Richard #1311 - 27 Sept. 1756 - N of Peedee
Deason, Benj. #4419 - 14 Oct. 1783 - SW Peedee
*Deason, Enoch #4519 - 14 Oct. 1783 - Lane's Cr.
Deason, James #1010 - 25 June 1751 - at David Fullerton's
Deason, John #4420 - 14 Oct. 1783 - Richardson Cr.
Deason, Wm. Shepard #4325 - 14 Oct. 1783 - SW Peedee
Dees, Benj. #3017 - 22 Jany. 1773 - Gum Branch
*Dees, James #1552 - 24 Apr. 1762 - Leeth's Cr.
*Dees, Mark #3250 - 4 Mch. 1775
DeJernett, John #4573 - 14 Oct. 1783
Dellinger, Henry #0560 - 20 Apr. 1762 - Rudisles Cr.
*Demery, Allen #4395 - 14 Oct. 1783 - SW Peedee
*Denson, James #243 - 15 Nov. 1753

LAND GRANTS

Denson, Richard #0109 - 5 Oct. 1751
{ Denson, Shadrack } #0106 - 20 Apr. 1768 - Great
{ Neale, Christopher } Buffalo Cr.
*Denson, Shadrack #3183 - 22 Nov. 1771 - Cedar Cr. of Peedee
Derinson, Geo. #0108 - 11 Apr. 1749 - Branch of Rocky Cr.
*Dick, John #262 - 25 Feb. 1754
Dick, Matthias #094 - 26 Sept. 1751
Dickinson, Leonard #4791 - 16 Nov. 1790 - Hadley's line.
*Dickson, John #102 - 6 Apr. 1753
Dickson, Michael #0562 - 19 Oct. 1762 - Bullock Cr.
*Dickson, Thos. #076 - 24 Oct. 1765 - SW Peedee, Huckleberry Cr.
Diggs, Solomon #2577 - 16 Dec. 1769 - Jones Cr. & Mill Cr.
Diggs, William #2557 - 16 Dec. 1769 - Jones Cr.
Dill, Phillip #073 - 26 Oct. 1767 - Lane's Creek
*Dinkins, John #4276 - 23 Oct. 1782
Dinkins, Thos. #1771
Dinkins, William #1320
Dixon, David #1151 [S.C.]
Dobbs, George #569 - 13 Apr. 1749
*Dockery, Thomas #093 - 14 Dec. 1769 - NE Peedee
*Dodd, George #4574 -   - adj. John King Hutchinson
*Donahoe, John #1586 - 22 Apr. 1763 - Cabin Creek
Donaldson, John #1631 - 16 May 1754
Donaldson, William #071 -   - 12-Mile Cr. [S.C.]
Donham (Dunham) Joseph #2684 - 24 Dec. 1770 - Bailey's prong of Jones Cr.
Douglass, John #3760 - 29 Feb. 1775 - Savannah Cr
Douglass, John #3193 - 4 March 1775 - Savannah Cr.
Duthett, David #1901 - 27 May 1760 - SW Peedee
{ Dowd, Wm. } #0276 - 17 Mch. 1756 - N of
{ Franks, Edward } Peedee
Dowland, Henry #1011, - 25 March 1752
*Downer, John #3566 - 25 July 1774 - Jones Cr.
*Downs, Henry #444 - 26 May 1757 - SW Peedee
Downing, James #2980 - 22 Jany. 1773 - Hamor's Cr.
*Downing, Renatus #3855 - 4 Mch. 1775 - Wm. Smith's corner
*Dowse, Joseph } #3845 - 4 Mch. 1775 - NE
*Graham, Richard } Peedee
*Dry, William #091 - 19 Oct. 1762 - Catawba
*Dry, William #590 - 5 Oct. 1751 - S of Great Peedee
Duffett, David #0428 - 27 Sept. 1756 - SW Peedee
*Dumas, Benj. #088 - 20 Feb. 1754 - Brown Cr.
*Dumas, David #3641 - 25 July 1774 - Dry Cr.
*Dumas, Jeremiah #1407 - 5 Dec. 1760 - NE Peedee

Duncan, Alexander #092 - 14 Apr. 1761 - NE Peedee
*Duncan, Alexander #1573 - 22 Oct. 1762 - Richardson Cr.
Duncan, John #4921 - 16 Nov. 1790
Dunn, Aaron #5362 - Nov. 26, 1799 - Cribbs and Lane's Crs.
Dunn, John #3422 - 14 Mch. 1775
Durham, Thos. #4021 - 3 Sept. 1779 - Mountain Cr.
Downer, Thos. #2691 - 24 Dec. 1770 - SW Peedee
Eaves, Benj. #3031 - 24 May 1773
Edens, John #4543 - 14 Oct. 1783 - SW Peedee
Edwards, John Colo. #1016 - 5 March 1752
Edwards, Robert #3174 - 29 Apr. 1768 - Jones Creek
*Elkins, John #1900 - 6 March 1759 - NE Peedee
Ellis, William #3609 - 25 July 1774 - NE Peedee Long Cr.
Elmore, James #4197 - 29 March 1780 - NE Peedee
Englis, Thomas #065 - 27 Sept. 1766 - Richardson Cr.
Eppes, Daniel #4011 - 3 Sept. 1779 - Yadkin
Ethridge, James #4749 - 7 Aug. 1787
*Evans, Ann #5114 - 8 Dec. 1794 - Richardson Cr.
*Evans, David #1919 - 5 Dec. 1760 - SW Peedee
*Evans, Jonathan #1804 - 17 Mch. 1756 - N of Peedee
*Evans, Mary #3354 - 11 Mch. 1775 - Town Cr.
Everet, Benj. #062 - Oct. 1752
Everet, Henry #4959 - 27 Nov. 1792
Everett, John #1321 - 27 Sept. 1756 - NE Peedee
*Fanner [Tanner?] Thos. #1546 - 24 Apr. 1762 - NE Peedee
*Fanning, Edmund #2405 - 6 April 1765 - both sides of Little Riv.
*Fanning, Hannah #3275 - 4 Mch. 1775 - Gould's Fk of Brown Cr
Fanning, Richard #2607 - 16 Dec. 1769 - Brown Cr.
*Fanning, Thomas #3108 - 21 July 1774 - bet. Sampson Williams, Arrington's and Luke Robinson
Farr, James #3429 - 14 March 1775 - crossroad Mecklenburg and Healy's
Farr, Richard #3313 - 4 March 1775 - SW Peedee
Farrell, Thos. #694 - 31 Mar. 1753
Faulkner, Nathan #4875 - 16 Nov. 1790
Fenner, Richard #1398 - 21 Oct. 1758 - SW Peedee
Ferguson, Donald #3495 - 23 July 1774
Ferguson, John #3454 - 23 July 1774 - Dry Fk Mountain Cr.
Ferrell, Charles #4840 - 16 Nov. 1790
*Ferrill, William #1824 - 27 Sept. 1756 - N of Peedee
*Ferry [Terry], William #872 - 9 Mch. 1754
Fielding, William #2624 - 9 Apr. 1770 - Jones Cr.
Fields, John #4387 - 14 Oct. 1783 - adj. John Ham

LAND GRANTS

Fields, Smith #0270 - 20 Oct. 1767 - Jones Cr.
Flake, Samuel #2814 - 22 Nov. 1771 - SW Peedee
Flanagan, John #4565 - 14 Oct. 1783 - adj. Samuel Thomas
Fletcher, James #3623 - 25 July 1774 - Cribbs Cr.
Flinton, John #2974 - 22 Jany. 1773 - NE Peedee
Flippens, Henry #2361 - 30 Oct. 1765 - Mountain Cr.
Flowers, John #2782 - 18 Nov. 1771 - SW Peedee
*Folds, George #1419 - 5 Dec. 1760 - NE Peedee
Ford, Edward #2812 - - NE Peedee
*Ford, Thos. #0271 - 21 Dec. 1768 - Island Cr. of Peedee
Ferguson, Alexander #1303 - 13 Mch. 1756 - Little River
*Forman, Mary #1550 - 24 Apr. 1762 - NE Peedee
*Forster, Henry #418 - 3 Oct. 1755 - Mitchell's Cr.
*Fowler, John #2907 - 22 Jany. 1773 - NE Peedee
*Foy, James #3586 - 25 Jany. 1774 - Jones Cr.
*Frazier, William #2365 - 23 Sept. 1766 - Drowning Cr.
Fleming, Edward #908 - 23 Feb. 1754 - Hickory Cr.
*Frances, John #2250 - 1 July 1758 - NE Peedee
Franklin, Lawrence #2722 - 18 Apr. 1771 - SW Peedee
Franks, Samuel #1877 - 25 May 1757 - SW Peedee
Freeland, Eliz. #1451 - 10 Apr. 1761 - Beaver Dam Cr.
French, James #0277 - 26 Apr. 1768 - Savannah Cr.
Fronaberger #359 - 28 Mch. 1755
Fry, Joseph #3602 - - NE Yadkin
Fry, James #3267 - 4 Mch. 1775 - SW Peedee
Fry, Thomas #3063 - - NE Yadkin
Fullerton, Hugh #2271 - 1 July 1758 - SW Peedee
Goad, Joseph #3531 - 23 July 1774 - Dry Cr.
Gad, Joseph Sr. #4417 - 14 Nov. 1783 - NE Peedee
Gaddy, Thos. #2997 - 22 Jany. 1773 - Drowning Cr.
Garland, David #4588 - 23 Sept. 1785
*Garret, Daniel #1019 - 25 Mch. 1752 - Yadkin
Garret, John #1020 - 25 Mch. 1752 - Yadkin
Garratt, James #4772 - 16 Nov. 1790
Gatewood, Griffin #4913 - 16 Nov. 1790
Gathings, Phillip #4860 - 16 Nov. 1790
Geyst, John #3644 - 25 July 1774 - Drowning Cr.
Gibson, Gideon #1548 - 24 Apr. 1762 - Falling Cr.
Gibson, John #2327 - 2 Nov. 1764 - N of Peedee
*Gibson, Jordan #481 - 1 July 1758 - fork of Little Peedee
*Gibson, Nelson #3061 - 24 May 1773 - Hitchcock's Cr.
*Gibson, Thomas #2524 - 4 May 1769 - Hitchcock's Cr.
*Gibson, Walter #1415 - 5 Dec. 1760 - SW Peedee
*Gilbert, Jesse #4355 - 14 Oct. 1783 - SW Peedee
Gilbert, Thos. #4339 - 14 Oct. 1783 - Rocky River
Gill, Thos. #741 - 6 Apr. 1753
Gill, Thos. Shaw #0279 - 4 Sept. 1753
*Gilespy, James #543 - - S of Peedee
*Gilespy, Thos. #1025 - 24 June 1751- N of 3rd Creek
Gilespy #4857 - 23 Mar. 1785 - SW Peedee (Thomas)
*Gingles, Sam'l #1762 - 24 Sept. 1754 - Rocky River
*Givans, Edward #1534 - 24 Apr. 1762 - Davidson's Cr.
*Givans, William #1509 - 15 Nov. 1766 - 12-Mile Cr. [S.C.]
*Gleghorn [Cleghorn], William #2022 - 24 Apr. 1762 - Catawba
Glenn, Duke #4312 - 24 Oct. 1782
Goldsbee, James #2450 - 21 Oct. 1758 - NE Peedee
Goodale, Abraham #4086 - 3 Sept. 1779 - SW Peedee
Goodman, Christopher #4842 - 16 Nov. 1790
Goodwin, George #4346 - - SW Peedee
*Gordon, Alex #0282 - - NE Peedee
*Gordon, Frederick #0522 - 6 Dec. 1794 - adj. own and Isaac Nicolas land
*Gordon, James #0284 - 15 Mch. 1756 - N of Peedee
*Gordon, John #1201 - 24 Sept. 1754 - head of Little River
*Gordon, Thos. #1114 - 20 May 1754 - Long Lick
Gower, Thos. #3237 - 4 Mch. 1775 - Batt Dickson's Branch
Graham, Richard #3302 - 4 Mch. 1775 - NE Peedee
Granard, John #4156 - 3 Sept. 1779 - SW Peedee
Granade, John #4273 - 24 Oct. 1782
Grande, Martin #4460
Graves, Thomas #2030 - 24 Apr. 1762 - Long Cr.
*Greathouse, Jacob #479 - 1 July 1758 - SW Peedee
*Green, Gideon #4324 - 14 Oct. 1783 - Rocky River
Green, James #1373 - 26 May 1757 - SW Peedee
Green, Joseph #1402 - 21 Oct. 1758 - Beaver Dam
Green, Richard #3466 - 26 July 1774 - Denson's Fork of Little R.
Gregory, Willis #5036 - 9 July 1794 - Savannah Cr.
*Grice, Christopher #1851 - 13 Oct. 1756 - adj. own improvement
*Grice, John #0552 - 14 May 1772 - SW Drowning Cr.

LAND GRANTS 9

Grice, Joiner #4644 - 23 Sept. 1785
Griffin, David #4769 - 16 Nov. 1790
Griffin, Edward #630 - 3 Apr. 1752
*Griffin, Richard #4918 - 16 Nov. 1790
*Griffin, Thos. #4923 - 16 Nov. 1790
*Grimes, Archibald #429 - 25 May 1757 - NE Peedee
*Gross, Solomon #3355 - 11 Mch. 1775 - Thickety Cr.
Guin [Gwin], Christopher Jr. #0287 - 27 Nov. 1762 - Brown Cr.
Guin, Hardy #4737 - 7 Aug. 1787
Gullege, Jeremiah #3010 - 22 Jany. 1773 - SW Drowning Cr.
*Gullege, William #3360 - 11 Mch. 1775 - SW Drowning Cr.
*Gullick, John #1306 - 13 Mch. 1756
Gurley, Jacob #4962 - 27 Nov. 1792
Hadley, John #3075 - 24 May 1773 - NE Peedee
Hogan, John #1458 - 10 Apr. 1761 - adj. Jas. Lin, Jas, Miller.
*Hogan, William Griffin # - 16 Nov. 1764 - SW Peedee
Hager, George # - 30 Aug. 1753
Hagin, John #1049 - 25 Mch. 1752
Hagler, John #4007 - 3 Sept. 1779 - SW Peedee
Haley, Isham #3526 - 23 July 1779 - SW Peedee
⎧Haley, Isham ⎫
⎪Crawford, John ⎪
⎨Moorman, Thos. ⎬ (see Francis Clark)
⎩Clark, Francis ⎭
*Haley, William #2912 - 22 Jany. 1773 - SW Peedee
Hall, Henry #4552 - 14 Oct. 1783 - Richardson's Cr.
*Hall, John #3624 - 25 July 1774 - Rocky River
Hall, John #3 - 4 Oct. 1751
*Hall, Joseph #0289 - 30 Mch. 1751 - NS Peedee
*Hall, Thomas #1213 - 24 Sept. 1754
Hellams [Helms], Tilman #4408 - 14 Nov. 1783 - Sw Peedee
Hellems, William #0536 - 31 Dec. 1779 - Cribs Cr.
Hallcome, Wm. #5066 - 9 July 1794
Halston, John #3046 - 24 May 1773 - west of Uwarry River
Haltom, Wm. #0514 - 26 Nov. 1757 - NE Peedee Bigg Cr.
Haltom, Wm. #3160 - 29 Apr. 1768 - Denson's Fk of Little Riv.
Ham, Elisha #4333 - 14 Oct. 1783 - SW Peedee
Hamblett, Peter #4563 - 14 Oct. 1783 - SW Peedee
*Hamer, John #1092 - 17 May 1754 - N of Peedee
Hamor, John Jr. #2638 - 9 Apr. 1770 - SW Peedee
Hamer, Wm. #4463 - 14 Oct. 1783

Hamilton, Wm. #3089 - 24 May 1773 - NE Peedee
Hammond, Geo. #4296 - 24 Oct. 1782
*Hammond, Wm. #4271 - 24 Oct. 1782
Hand, Isaac #5123 - 4 Dec. 1795
Hanagan, Derby #4191 - 29 Mar. 1780 - NE Peedee
Haney, Timothy #0539 - 3 Dec. 1781 - SW Lewis Branch
Harden, Benj. #1145 - 17 May 1754 (S.C.)
Hardy, John #4405 - 14 Oct. 1783 - Cribbs Cr.
Hargot, Henry #1601 - 20 Apr. 1763 - NE Peedee
Harly, Thos. #0538 - - Falling Cr.
*Harner, John #635 - 29 Sept. 1750 Hitchcock's Cr.
Harnett, Cornelius #0293 - 1 Sept. 1753 - Golden Grove
Harrell, James #4538 - 14 Oct. 1783
Harrell, Zachariah #4897 - 16 Nov. 1790
Harrill, Matthew #4562 - 14 Oct. 1783 - SW Peedee
*Harrington, Charles #3257 - 4 Mch. 1775 - adj. own land
*Harrington, Henry Wm. #3959 - 1 Mch. 1780 - NE Peedee
*Harrington, Thomas #491 - 1 July 1757 - NE Peedee
Harrington, Whitmell #3029 - 24 May 1773 - Rocky River
*Harrington, William #1822 - 27 Sept. 1756
Harris, Benj. #5080 - 8 Dec. 1794
*Harris, Charles #1305 - 13 Mch. 1756
Harris, Cunningham #0537 - 18 Apr. 1796 - Gould's Fk
Harris, Walter #3255 - 4 Mch. 1775 - Yadkin River
Harry, Jonathan #4146 - 3 Sept. 1779 - NE Peedee
Harry, Timothy #4365 - 24 Oct. 1782
Hart, Charles #0299 - 7 Apr. 1750 - Rocky River
Haymes, John #4109 - 3 Sept. 1779 - SW Peedee
Hays, John #0300 - 19 Apr. 1771 - Buffalow Cr.
Head, Sampson #4044 - 3 Sept. 1779 - Cribbs Cr.
Hearn, James #3738 - 3 Mch. 1775 - Mountain Cr.
Hern, Thomas #3238 - 4 Mch. 1775 - Mountain Cr.
Hearn, William #3578 - 25 July 1774 - Mountain Cr.
Heston, Leonard #644 - 11 Apr. 1752 - Leopard's Cr.
Heston, Robert #1048 - 25 Mch. 1752
*Hellbress, Robert #871 - - N of Peedee
Helms, George #722 - 11 Oct. 1749 - NS Peedee
Helms, John #5039 - 9 July 1794 - East of Pine Log Swamp
Helms, Tilman #2637 - 9 Apr. 1770 - Mill prong of Jones Cr.
Helms, Tilman #1514 - 27 Nov. 1762 - Little River
*Hemphill, James #361 - 28 Mch. 1755 - Catawba
Henderson, Rice #3897 - 6 Mch. 1775 - Beaver Dam Br.
Hendley, Wm. #4157 - 3 Sept. 1779 - NE Peedee
Hendon, Josiah #2768 - 18 Apr. 1771 - Black Jack Br.

LAND GRANTS

Hendon, Josiah Jr. #2660 - 11 Dec. 1770 - Richeson's Cr.
*Hendray, William #1285 - 5 Apr. 1753 - Rocky Creek
*Hendley, Peter #1372 - 26 May 1757 - SW Peedee
Henry, John #3027 - 24 May 1773 - SW Peedee
*Herld, Mathew #3377 - 11 Mch. 1775 - SW Peedee
*Herndon, Phillip #1323 - 27 Sept. 1756 - SW Peedee
Herrin, Benjamin #4220 - 20 Mch. 1780 - NE Peedee
Herrington, Phillip #0307 - 15 Mch. 1756 - S of Peedee
Hickman, Jesse #4301 - 24 Oct. 1782
*Hardick, William #1597 - 20 Apr. 1763 - NE Peedee
Hicks, Daniel #4752 - 7 Aug. 1787
*Hicks, William #2449 - 21 Oct. 1758 - NE Peedee
*Hide, Stephen #0534 - 16 June 1786 - adj. Hugh Ross
*Hide, Stephen #0535 - 13 Aug. 1787 - adj. John Cheek
*Higdon, Leonard #1564 - 24 Apr. 1762 - SW Peedee
*Higgins, Hallen #3210 - 4 Mch. 1775 - SW Yadkin
*Higgins, John #1592 - 22 Apr. 1763
Higgs, William #4366 - 14 Oct. 1783 - Flat Fk of Brown Cr.
*Hightower, Thomas #1540 - 24 Apr. 1762 - SW Peedee
*Hildreth, David #2842 - 19 May 1772 - Rocky River
*Hildreth, James #2843 - 19 May 1772 - adj. Jas, L. Polk
*Hill, Charles #1551 - 24 Apr. 1762 - NE Peedee
*Hill, James #1046 - 25 Mch. 1752
Hill, John #4790 - 16 Nov. 1790
Hill, Wm. #4638 - 23 Sept. 1785
Hillifield[1], William #4162 - 3 Sept. 1779 - SW Peedee
*Hinds, Charles #0309 - - Gould's Fk of Brown Cr.
*Hinds, Charles #2841 - 19 May 1772 - NE Peedee
Hinds, Joseph #246 [?] - 19 May 1772 - NE Peedee
Hines, Charles #3420 - 24 May 1773 - adj. Henry Falconberry
Hines, Thos. #2657 - 11 Dec. 1770 - Mill prong of Jones Cr.
Hinson, Daniel #5034 - 9 July 1794 - Richardson's Cr.
Hinson, John #3599 - 25 July 1774 - Old Mill Creek
Hodges, Moses #3357 - 11 Mch. 1775 - bet. Little PD and Shoeheel

Hogan, James #4298 - 24 Oct. 1782 - Rocky River
Hogan, Shadrack #2844 - 19 May 1772 - Rocky River
Hogan, Wm. G. #2618 - 9 Apr. 1770 - Rocky River
Holaday, Jno. #0310 - 20 Feb. 1754 - Reedy River
*Holly, Julius #2597 - 16 Dec. 1769 - Beaver Br of Lane's Cr.
*Holly, Nath'l. #3114 - 25 Apr. 1767 - Lane's Cr.
Holly, William #598 - 16 Dec. 1769 - Beaverdam Br.
Holmes [Helms], Geo. #2302 - 21 Oct. 1758 - NE Peedee
Holmes, John #332 - 25 Feb. 1754
Holmes, Tilman #2088 - 27 Nov. 1762 - Little River
Holton, John #2671 - 11 Dec. 1770 - Uwarry River
Home, William #596 - 11 Oct. 1749 - S of Peedee
Homer, John #2393 - 9 Nov. 1764 - NE Peedee
Honey, Elias #5020 - 27 June 1793
*Hood, John #768 - 6 Apr. 1752
*Hood, William #0137 - 7 Apr. 1752
Hoof, Amos #4835 - 16 Nov. 1790
*Hopkins, John #2586 - 11 Dec. 1766 - McLain's Cr.
*Hopkins, Lambert #2964 - 22 Jany. 1773 - SW Peedee
Hopper, Thos. #4911 - 16 Nov. 1790
Horne, William #538 - 11 Oct. 1749 - S of Peedee
*Hornback, John #2454 - 21 Oct. 1758 - S of Peedee
Hough, Hezekiah #4917 - 16 Nov. 1790
Hough, James #4925 - 16 Nov. 1790
Hough, Joseph #2507 - 22 Dec. 1778 - Brown Cr.
Hough, Joseph Jr. #0323 - 25 Sept. 1766 - Lane's Cr.
*Hough, Samuel #867 - 17 Nov. 1753 - S of Peedee
*Houston, Archibald #103 - 6 Apr. 1753
Houston, William #0532 -
Hover, Solomon #1348 - 13 Oct. 1756 - Adj. own improvement
Howard, Arkwell #1237 - 24 Sept. 1754 - Suggses line
Howard, Julius #3513 - 23 July 1774 - Rocky branch
Howbar [?], Solomon #0316 - 26 Sept. 1754 - Killian's Mill Cr.
Howell, Caleb #0315 - 2 Oct.
*Howell, Hopkin #0531 - 15 Dec. 1769 - NE Peedee
*Howell, Hopkin #654 - 11 Oct. 1749 - S of Peedee
Howell, James #4546 - 14 Oct. 1783 - SW Peedee
*Howell, John #376 - 26 Mch. 1755 - Black Walnut Cr.
*Howell, Joseph #3180 - 22 Dec. 1768 - SW Peedee Mill Cr.
Howlett, Thomas #4019 - 3 Sept. 1779 - Buffelow Cr.

---

1. This is William Hollifield in D.B. "H", pp. 77, 235.

Hucksby, Chas. #4235 - 30 Mch. 1780 - NE Peedee
Hudson, Joacim #4434 - - Rocky River
Huey, Henry #1045 - 25 Mch. 1752 - N bank of 4th Creek
Huggins, James #1044 - 25 Mch. 1752 - Buffalo Cr.
*Hughes, Edward #1047 - 27 Oct. 1752
Hull, Moses #3619 - 25 July 1774 - David's Cr.
Hunt, Christopher #1566 - 24 Apr. 1762 - NE Peedee
Hunt, John #3252 - 26 Oct. 1767 - Little River
Hunter, Samuel #4228 - - west of Bridge Cr.
*Hunter, William #2806 - 27 Nov. 1771 - Cartledge ledge's Cr.
*Huntley, Thomas #2619 - 9 Apr. 1770 - Jones Cr.
*Hurley, Edmund #3424 - 14 March 1775 - NE Yadkin
*Hurley, John #3228 - 4 Mch. 1775 - Jones Cr.
*Hurley, Thomas 2693 - 24 Dec. 1770 - East of Falling Cr.
*Husbands, John #1932 - 24 Dec. 1760 - SW Peedee
*Hutchins, Anthony #0322 - 15 May 1754
*Hutchins, Anthony #1512 - 27 Nov. 1762 - SW Peedee
*Hutchins, James #3154 - 26 Oct. 1767 - SW Peedee
Hutchins, Samuel #2945 - 22 Jany. 1773 - SW Peedee
*Hutton, James #1029 - 7 Aug. 1753 - Town Creek
*Hyatt, Mary #3270 - 4 Mch. 1775 - NE Peedee
Hycar, Lawrence #1983 - 10 Apr. 1761 - Beaver Dam Cr.
Hyde, Stephen #4945 - 16 Nov. 1790 - adj. John Cheek
*Inglas, Wm. #1542 - 24 Apr. 1762 - Drowning Cr.
Inglas, Wm. Jr. #0327
Ingram, Allen #4730 - 7 Aug. 1787
Ingram, Benj. #4498 - 14 Oct. 1783 - SW Peedee
Ingram, George #3489 - 23 July 1774 - SW Peedee
Ingram, Isham #3109 - 25 July 1774 - Palmetto Br.
Ingram, James #4907 - 16 Nov. 1790
Ingram, John #4792 - 16 Nov. 1790
Ingram, John Jr. #5075 - 9 July 1794
Ingram, Joseph #2867 - 20 May 1772 - SW Peedee
Ingram, Larkin #5374 - 7 June 1797
Ingram, Samuel #4424 - 14 Oct. 1783 - SW Peedee
Isenhart, Henry #0325 - - Beaver Dam Cr.
Isgate, Joseph #4468 - 14 Oct. 1783
Isler, Fred. #472 - 26 Nov. 1757 - SW Peedee

Isler, Wm. #472 - 26 Nov. 1757 - SW Peedee
Ivey, James #0324 - - NE Peedee
Ivey, Joseph #3016 - 22 Jany. 1758 - SW Peedee
Jackson, Benj. #486 - 1 July 1758 - SW Peedee
Jackson, Benj. #613 - 4 Apr. 1750
Jackson, Henry #4933 - 20 Dec. 1791
*Jackson, Isaac #2645 - 9 Apr. 1770 - NE Peedee
*Jackson, John #2732 - 18 Apr. 1771 - SW Peedee
*Jackson, John Jr. #0328 - 27 Sept. 1756 - SW Peedee
Jackson, Jonathan #0551 - 4 Dec. 1782 - Thompson's Cr.
Jackson, Peter #4114 - 3 Sept. 1779 - West of Peedee
*Jackson, Stephen #1388 - 6 Mch. 1759 - SW Peedee
Jakellar, John #0336 - 29 Sept. 1749
*James, John #1433 - 5 Dec. 1760 - NE Peedee
James, Richard #3163 - 29 Apr. 1768 - SW Peedee
*Jarman, John #2811 - 22 Nov. 1771
*Jarman, Robert #2952 - 22 Jany. 1773 - SW Peedee
*Jefferson, George #4133 - 3 Sept. 1779 - NE Peedee
Jeffrys, James #3465 - 23 July 1774 - Cabin Cr.
Jeffrys, John #3008 - 22 Jany. 1773 - Long Cr.
*Jenkins, John #437 - 26 May 1757 - SW Peedee
Jernagan, William #2519 - 16 Dec. 1769 - NE Peedee
Jetton, John #1694 - 21 May 1754
John, David #1633 - 17 May 1754
Johnston, Hugh #0331 - 14 Apr. 1762 - Little River
Johnston, John #2486 - 22 Dec. 1768 - Lane's Cr.
Johnston, Thos. #2552 - 4 Mch. 1769 - Shoe Heel Swamp
Johnston, William #3606 - 25 July 1774 - Brown Cr.
Johnston, Zachariah #4163 - 3 Sept. 1779 - Little River
Jones, Abraham #4043 - 3 Sept. 1779 - SW Peedee
*Jones, David #3787 - 29 Feb. 1775 - SW Peedee
*Jones, Edmund #3802 - - on Patt's Branch
Jones, Harrison #0332 - 26 Apr. 1768
*Jones, Jacob #3568 - 25 July 1774 - Jones Cr.
Jones, Jesse #4234 - Mar. 30, 1780 - Little River
Jones, John #2697 - 24 Dec. 1770 - Little River
*Jones, Joseph #1134 - 17 May 1754 - Little River
*Jones, Thomas #0529 - 17 Dec. 1784
Jones, Walter #2678 - 11 Dec. 1770 - Mill Cr.
*Jones, William #921 - 23 Feb. 1753
Jordan, Francis #3003 - 22 Jany. 1773 - Dick's Cr.
Jordan, River[a] #4025 - 3 Sept. 1779 - East of Peedee

2. Northampton Co. (N.C.) Probate of Wills and Admns. 1753-1790. Feb. Inf. Ct. [bef. 1763], #4 Over Jordan, admr. on Est. of River Jordan and Priscilla Jordan, decd.; Edward Pennington and Henry Howell, sec. for £1500. Sec'y. of State Papers; Returns of Probates, 1753-1790. SS884. Dept. of Arch. and Hist., Raleigh, N. C.

12 LAND GRANTS

Jordan, William #2987 - 22 Jany. 1773 - Little River
Jornigan, Sam'l. #5079 - 8 Dec. 1794 - James Lisles corner
Jowers, John #4577 - 14 Oct. 1783 - SW Peedee
Jowers, Jonathan #0528 - 13 Jany. 1773 - NE Peedee
Jowers, Thomas #3081 - 24 May 1773 - Buffalo Cr.
Kackey, Wm. #3006 - 22 Jany. 1773 - Hitchcock's Cr.
Keston, Leonard #23 - 11 Apr. 1752 - Leopard's Cr.
Kee, Henry #4430 - 14 Oct. 1783 - NE Peedee
Kellam, Elijah #2208 - 26 May 1757 - NE Peedee
*Kelley, Nelson #2578 - 16 Dec. 1769 - NE Peedee
*Kelly, William #3403 - 11 March 1775 - Brown Cr. Horsepen Br.
*Kemp, Joseph #2682 - 11 Dec. 1770 - Dry Fk of Mountain Cr.
Kemp, William #509 - 14 Apr. 1749
Kendall, William #4697 - 27 Nov. 1793 - Rocky River
Kenner, Casper #0341 - 7 Apr. 1752 - Leaper's Cr.
*Kershaw, Ely #3815 - 3 March 1775
Key, Robert #4970 - 27 Nov. 1792
Kildreth, William #4010 - 3 Sept. 1779 - Rocky River
Killeress, Robert #0345 - 13 Apr. 1749 - Cheek's Cr.
Killins, John #0344 - 13 Apr. 1749 - Killins Cr.
Kimbrough, John #3984 - 3 Sept. 1779.- SW Dison's Cr.
*Kimbrough, Nath'l #6352 -   1819 - adj. his own land
King, Sarah #4462 - 14 Oct. 1783
*Kirby, William #4499 - 14 Oct. 1783 - adj. own line
Kiser, Lawrence, #0352 -   - Beaver Dam Cr.
*Kitchen, Charles #737 - 6 Apr. 1753 - Rocky River
*Knotts, James #3446 - 23 July 1774 - SW Peedee
*Knotts, John #3045 - 24 May 1773
*Knowland, Dennis #2236 - 26 Nov. 1757 - NE Peedee
Kysar, Lawrence #1474 - 10 Apr. 1761 - Beaver Dam Cr.
Lacey, Thomas #0357 - 18 Apr. 1767 - Brown Cr. near Jos. White
Land, James #426 - 10 Oct. 1755
Land, Thomas #424 - 10 Oct. 1755
Land, Thomas #1298 - 17 Mch. 1756
*Landin [Lambden], Bexley John #2756 - 18 Apr. 1771 - N of Peedee
*Laniar, Burrel #4014 - 3 Sept. 1779 - SW Peedee, Gould's Fk

Lanier, Lewis #4862 - 16 Nov. 1790
*Lanier, Sampson #4690 - 5 Nov. 1787 - Lawyers Road
Lankford, John #1921 - 5 Dec. 1760 - NE Peedee
Lankford, William #1412 - 5 Dec. 1760 - NE Peedee
Larimore, James #1687 - 17 May 1754 - Camp Cr.
Lasider [Lassiter], Robert #3113 - 25 Apr. 1767 - Lane's Cr.
Lawrence, Peter #3253 - 4 Mch. 1775 - Cedar Cr.
Lawrence, William #3621 - 25 July 1774 - Cedar Cr.
*Lawson, Hugh #0358 -   - Davidson Cr. [S.C.]
*Leak, Richard #0361 - 26 Apr. 1768
Leak, Richard #2770 - 18 Apr. 1771 - NE Peedee
*Leak, William #3491 - 23 July 1774 - Walnut Br.
Leath, John #0378 -   - N of Peedee
Lee, Bryan #5002 - 27 Nov. 1792
Lee, George #3626 - 25 July 1774 - Yadkin
*Lee, James #4317 - 14 Oct. 1783 - S of Peedee
*Lee, John #1577 - 22 Oct. 1762 - S of Peedee
Lee, Richard #5045 - 9 July 1794
*Lee, Robt. #4416 - 14 Nov. 1783 - Lane's Cr.
Lee, Thos. #760 - 6 Apr. 1753
Leonard, John #744 - 6 Apr. 1753
Leonard, Thos. [S.C.]
Leonard, Robt. [S.C.]
Lesever [Lefever], Abraham #4431 - 14 Oct. 1783 - NW Savannah Cr.
*Leverett, John #2320 - 21 Dec. 1763 - Brown's Cr.
*Leveret, Robt. #3802 - 3 Mch. 1775 - Cheek's Cr.
*Leveritt, William #1431 - 5 Dec. 1760 - SW Peedee
*Leviner, John #3308 - 4 Mch. 1775
Lewellen, Jonathan #1411 - 5 Dec. 1760
*Lewis, Alexander #753 - 9 Apr. 1753
*Lewis, Benjamin #678 - 31 Mch. 1753
Lewis, David #4826 - 16 Nov. 1790
*Lewis, David #1164 - 17 May 1754
*Lewis, Elisha #3901 - 11 March 1775 - Little Shoe Heel
Lewis, Evan #652 - 10 Apr. 1752 - Indian Cr. [S.C]
*Lewis, Jonathan #677
Lewis, Samuel #2942 - 22 Jany. 1768
*Liggett, John #2890 - 22 May 1772 - Hitchcock's Cr.
Liggett, Elias #0366 - 26 Apr. 1768
*Liggett, William #2608 - 16 Dec. 1769 - Hitchcock's Cr.
*Liles, James #2738 - 18 Apr. 1771 - Island Cr.
*Liles, John #2740 - 18 Apr. 1771 - SW Peedee
Liles, William #4993 - 27 Nov. 1792
*Lilly, Edmond #150 - 10 Apr. 1753
Linch, Phillip #4022 - 3 Sept. 1779 - SW Peedee
Linn, Andrew #0379 - 20 Feb. 1754
Lindsey, Geo. #2834 - 23 Nov. 1772 - SW Peedee

Lindsey, Mary #4829 - 16 Nov. 1790
*Lindsey, William #3698 - 24 Feb. 1775 - SW Peedee
*Lipham, Jacob #1895 - 6 Mch. 1759 - NE Peedee
*Lisonby, Chas. #4646 - 23 Sept. 1785
*Lisonby, John #4889 - 16 Nov. 1790
Little, James #2916 - 22 Jany. 1773 - SW Peedee
Little, John #80 - 3 Apr. 1753 - Catawba River
*Little, William #1330 - 29 Sept. 1756 - SW Peedee
Lock, Mathew #1055 - 25 March 1752 - adj. John Brandon
Lockhart, Alexander #903 - 23 Feb. 1754 [S.C.]
Lockhart, Adam #6584 - Dec. 1825 - adj. John Kimbrough
Logan, David #2213 - 26 May 1757 - NE Peedee
London, John #2522 - 4 May 1769 - SW Peedee
Long, James #2529 - 23 July 1774 - Buffelow Cr
*Long, John #1937 - 5 Dec. 1760 - N of Peedee
Love, David #3537 - 23 July 1774 - NE Peedee
Love, William #774 - 11 May 1753 - Broad River [S.C.]
Low, Daniel #2343 - 16 Nov. 1764 - SW Peedee
Lowell, John #3796 - 3 Mch. 1775
*Lowry, James #2796 - 18 Nov. 1771 - SW Peedee
*Lowry, John #4640 - 23 Sept. 1785
*Lowry, Lewis #3775 - 29 Feb. 1775 - S prong of Jones Cr.
Lowery, Peter #4625 - 23 Sept. 1775
*Lowry, Robert #2719 - 18 Apr. 1771 - Jones Cr.
*Lowry, William #4965 - 27 Nov. 1792
*Lucas, John #1416 - 5 Dec. 1760 - NE Peedee
*Lucas, William #1545 - 24 Apr. 1762 - NE Peedee
Lundy, Abraham #0377 - 27 Sept. 1756 - SW Peedee
*Lyles, Ephraim #579 - 28 Mch. 1751 - N of Peedee
{Lyon, John   } #0380 - 23 Sept. 1766 - Brown
{Brownlow, James}   Cr.
Lyon, Richard #874 -   - Branch of Beaver Dam Cr.
Maberry, Francis #3981 - 3 Sept. 1779 - SW Peedee
Mackby [McBee], Samuel #1808 - 17 Mch. 1756 - N of Peedee
*Medcalf, John #4954 - 20 Dec. 1791 - N of Peedee
Medcalf, William #5086 - 8 Dec. 1794 - Richardson's Cr.
*Manus, Richard #4282 - 24 Oct. 1782 - Lacey's Cr.
Manor, Benjamin #2451 - 21 Oct. 1758 - NE Peedee
Manuel, David #681 - 31 Mch. 1753
*Marchbanks, George #2574 - 16 Dec. 1769 - Bailey's prong of Jones
Mark, William #3930 - 11 Mch. 1775
*Marshall, James #4728 - 7 Aug. 1787
Marsh, John #4820 - 16 Nov. 1790 - adj. Daniel Low

LAND GRANTS 13

Martin, Alexander #3674 - 16 Jany. 1773 - Naked Cr.
Martin, George #2227 - 26 Nov. 1757 - NE Peedee
*Martin, John #2901 - 23 Jany. 1773 - Mountain Cr.
Martin, John Hall #4909 - 16 Nov. 1790
Martin, Joseph #3030 - 24 May 1773 - Shoals of Peedee
Martin, Josiah #3533 - 23 July 1774 - SW Peedee
Martin, Kinchen #5011 - 27 Nov. 1792
Martin, William #4155 - 3 Sept. 1779 - SW Peedee
Martin, Zachariah #1057 - 24 June 1751
*Mask, John #3536 - 23 July 1774 - NE Peedee
*Mask, John Sr. #2856 - 20 May 1772 - N of Peedee
*Mask, William #2710 - 18 Apr. 1771 - SW Peedee
*Mason, John #3671 - 25 July 1774 - Adams Cr.
*Mason, Thomas #1917 - 5 Dec. 1760 - NE Peedee
*Mathew, John #731 - 6 Apr. 1753 - Rocky Cr.
Mattux, Robert #4454 - 14 Oct. 1783 - Brown Cr.
*May, John #2661 - 11 Dec. 1770 - N prong of Jones Cr.
*May, Phill #2726 - 28 Apr. 1771 - S prong of Jones Cr.
*May, Pleasant #4960 - 27 Nov. 1792
May, William #2797 - 18 Nov. 1777 - Mill Cr. of Jones Cr.
{McArthur, Neil   } #2895 - 22 May 1772
{Campbell, Archibald}
*McBride, John #2211 - 26 May 1757 - N of Peedee
*McCalman, John #3273 - 4 Mch. 1775 - Hedgecock's Cr.
*McCorcale, Robert #1740 - 24 Sept. 1754
McCarty, Charles #4352 - 14 Oct. 1783 - S of Peedee
McCaskill, James #107 - 6 Apr. 1753
McCleland, Robt. #2123 - 28 Mch. 1755
McCleary, Samuel #2020 - 24 Apr. 1762 - Sugar Cr.
McClenachan, Robt. #1261 - 28 Sept. 1754 - Catawba
McClenachan, Robt. #1733 - 24 Sept. 1754
*McClendon, Dennis #3436 - 16 Mch. 1775 - SW Peedee Brown Cr.
*McClendon, Ezekiel #0557 - 6 Sept. 1779 - Brown Cr.
*McClendon, Frederick #4736 - 7 Aug. 1787
*McClendon, Jesse #3663 - 25 July 1774 - SW Peedee
*McClendon, John #3260 - 4 Mch. 1775 - SW Peedee
*McClendon, Joel #3815 - 3 Mch. 1775 - Lane's Cr.
*McClure, James #1131 - 17 May 1754 - Beaver Dam
McCorkill, Robt. #736 - 6 Apr. 1753
*McCoy, Daniel #3317 - 4 Mch. 1775 - Hitchcock's Cr.
*McCoy, John #593 - 11 Oct. 1749 - N of Peedee
McCoy, Spruce #4576 - 5 June 1784
McCracken, Hugh #446 - 26 Nov. 1757 - Long Cr.
*McCulloch, Alex. #2273 - 1 July 1758 - SW Peedee

14   LAND GRANTS

*McCulloch, Henry E. #0409-16 Jan. 1773-Island Cr.
McDaniel, John #3463 - 23 July 1774 - Townsend's Fk of Cheek Cr
McDaniel, William #2821-22 Nov. 1771-Mountain Cr.
McDonald, Hugh #0413 - - Gill's Cr.
McDonald, John #3472 - 23 July 1774 - Silver Run
*McDonald, Soirle #3202 - 4 Mch. 1775 - Cheek's Cr.
McDowell, Charles #622 - 3 Apr. 1750
*McDuffie, Archibald #3095 - 24 May 1773 - Drowning Cr.
*McDuffie, Daniel #3508 - 23 July 1774 - Nell's Branch
McDuffie, Donald #3251 - 4 Mch. 1775
McDuffie, Malcolm #3421 - 23 July 1774
*McDugald, Archibald #7447
McEnvail, James #5122 - 30 Nov. 1795
McFarlan, David #1301 - 13° Mch. 1756 - Horsepen Branch
McGuire, Michael #4185 - 30 Mch. 1780 - SW Peedee
*McHenry, Jesse #4991 - 27 Nov. 1792
*McHenry, William #4367 - 14 Oct. 1783 - Brook's Br.
*McIlvale, John #4473 - 14 Oct. 1783 - Rocky River
*McIntire, John #2550 - 4 May 1769 - Drowning Cr.
McKay, Alexander #3498 - 23 July 1774
*McKee, John #1604 - 17 May 1754 - Shuger Cr.
McKey, Alexander #0436 - 20 Apr. 1762 - Sugar Cr.
McKenzie, Donald #3766 - 29 Feb. 1775 - Cheek's Cr.
{Mackelwean, Francis } #0233 - 5 Apr. 1749 - S
{White, Joseph } of Peedee
*MackIlwean, Francis #508 - 11 Apr. 1749 - S of Peedee
Mackilwean, James #0383 - - Yadkin and Rocky Rivers
McKimmon, Murdock #3111 - 22 July 1774 - NE Peedee
McKinne, Matthew #0439 - 16 Apr. 1767 - Brown Cr.
*McKelveney, Samuel #1161 - 18 May 1754
*McLeister, Joseph #3284 - 4 Mch. 1775 - SW Peedee
McLeod, Alex. #3197 - 4 Mch. 1775 - Dry Cr. of Mt. Cr.
McLeod, John #3581 - 25 July 1774
McLeod, Neill #3574 - 25 July 1774 - Buffelow Cr.
McLeod, Norman #3722 - March 1775 - Mountain Cr.
*McManus, James #1337 - 13 Oct. 1756 - Thompson's Cr.
*McManus, Thomas #1868 - 27 Sept. 1756 - Lane's Cr.

McMillan, Amos #5021 - 27 June 1793 - Richardson
*McMullen, Daniel #3481 - 23 July 1774 - Thorn's Br. Mt. Cr.
McMullen, Mary #3538 - 23 July 1774 - Beaver Dam Cr.
McNabb, James #748 - 5 Apr. 1753
McNabb, Andrew #126 - 6 Apr. 1753
McNatt, James #3133 - 24 Oct. 1767 - Brown Cr.
McNatt, James Jr. #0542 - 25 Sept. 1766 - Brown Cr.
McNatt, John #2767 - 18 Apr. 1771 - McNatt's Branch
*McNeill, Daniel #3778 - 29 Feb. 1775 - SE Hedgecock's Cr.
*McNatt, Wm. #0455 - 23 Sept. 1766 - Lane's Cr.
*McNeill, John #3550 - 23 July 1774 - Drowning Cr.
McNeill, Malcom #2556 - 6 May 1768 - Drowning Cr.
*McNish, Henry #0451 - 25 Oct. 1765 - SW Peedee
*McNish, James #1442 - 5 Dec. 1760 - SW Peedee
McPeters, Daniel #819 - 30 Apr. 1753
*McFerson, Alex. #2772 - 18 Apr. 1771 - Little Buffalo Cr.
*McPike, Sarah #2378 - 25 Apr. 1767 - SW Peedee Cedar Cr.
McQueen, Neil #4249 - 29 Mch. 1780 - Dees Cr.
McQueens, Thos. #1060 - 25 Mch. 1752 - Rocky River
McRay, Duncan #3497 - 23 July 1774 - NE Peedee
McRay, James #4873 - 16 Nov. 1790
*McShane, John #1973 - 10 Apr. 1761 - [S.C.]
McSwain, Allen #3478 - 23 July 1774 - Townsend Fk Cheek's Cr.
McSwain, James #0458 - - Davidson Cr.
*McVenny, Sam'l. #1156 - 18 May 1754
*McWharton, Jane #754 - 9 Apr. 1753 - adj. Alex. Osborn
*McWherter, John #2465 - 21 Oct. 1758 - adj. own land
Meacham, Henry #5116 - 27 Nov. 1795
Meador, Lewis #4763 - 16 Nov. 1790 - adj. Jesse Ballard
Meador, Job #4801 - 16 Nov. 1790
Meadows, Lewis #2530 - 4 May 1769 - Thompson's Cr.
Meadows, Job #2620 - 9 Apr. 1770 - Thompson's Cr.
Meadows, Jason Jr. #2663 - 11 Dec. 1770 - Jones Cr.
Meadows, Jason Sr. #2685 - 24 Dec. 1770 - Jones Cr.
*Meadows, Thomas #4726 - 7 Aug. 1787
Meanly, Richard #4760 - 16 Nov. 1790
Medlock, Charles #2428 - 25 Sept. 1766 - NE Peedee
Meek, Adam #1654 - 16 May 1754 - [S.C.]

LAND GRANTS

*Megginson, Thos. #3201 - 4 Mch. 1775 - NE
*Meguire, Wm. #3476 - 23 July 1774 - NE Peedee
Melton, Jesse #4914 - 16 Nov. 1790
Melton, Michael #4834 - 16 Nov. 1790
*Melton, Nathan #4603 - 23 Sept. 1785
Meredith, James #4384 - 14 Oct. 1783
Messer, Jeremiah #4789 - 16 Nov. 1790
Miers, Michael #1063 - 25 Mch. 1752
Miller, Abraham #4953 - 20 Dec. 1791 - adj. Kelleys
Miller, Chas. #2520 - 4 Mch. 1769 - Lane's Cr.
*Miller, James #1059 - 25 May 1752 - N fork of 5th Creek.
*Miller, Jerom #4376 - 14 Oct. 1783 - Lane's Cr.
*Miller, Jesse #4602 - 23 Sept. 1785
Miller, Richard #1650 - 17 May 1754 - Thickety Cr.
*Miller, Robert #421 - 3 Oct. 1755 - fork of Little River
*Miller, Stephen #2720 - 18 Apr. 1771 - SW Peedee
*Mills, Hugh #1963 - 10 Apr. 1761 - Clark's Cr.
*Mills, John #2014 - 23 Apr. 1762 - Clark's Cr.
Mims, Benjamin #4172 - 30 Mch. 1780 - NE Peedee
Mims, Samuel #3149 - 26 Oct. 1767 - Marks Cr.
Mims, William #4206 - 30 Mch. 1780 - NE Peedee
*Minasco, James #2339 - 16 Nov. 1763 - Townsend's Fork
*Minasco, Jeremiah #2338 - 16 Nov. 1780 - Townsend's Fork
Mires, Michael #4320 - 14 Oct. 1783
Mires, Thomas #4455 - 14 Oct. 1783
Mires, Thompson #4318 - 14 Oct. 1783
*Mitchell, Thomas #3002 - 22 Jany. 1773 - Jones Cr.
Mode, James #3501 - 23 July 1774 - Little River of Peedee
Monday, Arthur #3500 - 23 July 1774 - NE Peedee
Monday, Christopher #0541 - 22 July 1774
Monday, William #3514 - 23 July 1774 - Gun Smith's Road
Moore, Edward #2983 - 22 Jany. 1773 - NE Yadkin
Moore, John #2135 - 26 Mch. 1755 - N of Turkey Cr.
*Mooreman, Andrew Jr. #592 - 4 Apr. 1750 - N of Peedee
Mooreman, John #261 - 25 Feb. 1754
Mooreman, Andrew #547 - 4 Apr. 1750 - N of Peedee
Mooreman, Archelus #3181 - 22 Dec. 1768 - SW Peedee
Mooreman, Benjamin #2641 - 9 Apr. 1770 - NE Peedee
Mooreman, Benjamin #2456 - 21 Oct. 1758 - SW Peedee
Mooreman, John #893 - 26 Feb. 1754

*Mooreman, Thos. #1436 - 5 Dec. 1760 - NE Peedee
*Morgan, Going #3649 - 25 July 1774 - Clark's Cr.
*Morgan, John #3773 - 29 Feb. 1775 - SW Peedee
*Morgan, Joshua #3908 - 11 Mch. 1775 - Grindstone Cr.
Morgan, Nathaniel #3482 - 23 July 1783 - Jones Cr.
Morgan, William #2565 - 16 Dec. 1769 - Clark's Cr.
Morris, Edward #2489 - 22 Dec. 1768 - Little River
*Morris, Jacob #4893 - 16 Nov. 1790
Morris, Jeptha #5073 - 9 July 1794
*Morris, John #3842 - 4 Mch. 1775
Morris, William #0396 - - Little River of Peedee
*Morris, William #4074 - 3 Sept. 1779 - Lane's Cr.
Morrison, James #0540 - 14 Dec. 1769 - SW Peedee, Savannah Cr.
Moses, Samuel #4414 - 14 Oct. 1783 - SW Peedee
Moultery, James #5060 - 9 July 1794
Mayer, Michael #1842 - 26 Sept. 1756 - SW Peedee
*Muckilroy, James #2209 - 26 May 1756 - NE Peedee
Mundine, Kittrell #3170 - 29 Apr. 1768 - SW Peedee
*Mumfort, Joseph #1805 - 17 Mch. 1756
Munrow, Archibald #3411 - 11 Mch. 1775 - Nell's Branch
Munrow, Daniel #
Munroe, Malcom #2523 - 3 May 1769 - Drowning Cr.
Murfy, Joseph #2626 - 9 Apr. 1770 - Jones Cr.
Naron, Thomas #4336 - 14 Oct. 1783 - Rocky River
Nash, William #4438 - 14 Oct. 1783
*Neale, Christopher #2971 - 22 Jany. 1773 - NE Peedee
*Nelson, William #3936 - 11 Mch. 1775 - Lane's Cr.
{Nelson, Wm. } #0442 - 16 Jany. 1773 - Richard-
{Norton, David} son's Cr.
Newberry, Wm. #868 - 17 Nov. 1753 - Cartledge's Cr.
Newberry, Wm. 2803 - 22 Nov. 1771 - NE Peedee
Newman, George #4508 - 14 Oct. 1783 - SW Peedee
*Newman, Mary #3926 - 11 Mch. 1775 - Smith's Cr.
*Newman, Thomas #4353 - 14 Oct. 1783 - SW Peedee
Newton, John #3558 - 25 July 1774 - SW Peedee
Nicholas, George #546 - 30 Mch. 1751 - S of Peedee
Nicholas, Isaac #2931 - 22 Jany. 1773 - SW Peedee
*Nichols, Edmund #3142 - 26 Oct. 1767 - Goldsby Fk Little River
Nichols, Isaac #4756 - 7 Aug. 1787
Nickson, Robt. #0443 - 16 Apr. 1767 - adj. own land

LAND GRANTS

Nisbet, Alex. #2148 - - adj. Alex. McMahain
Noble, Thomas #4513 - 14 Oct. 1783 - SW Peedee
*Nobles, Gustavus⎫
  Peter   ⎬ #515 - 30 Mch. 1750 - S Peedee
  Joseph   ⎭
*Nobles, William #4034 - 3 Sept. 1779 - SW Peedee
Nollyboy [?], Hardiman #4680 - 25 Aug. 1786 - NW of Peedee
Nowland, John #0434 - 26 Apr. 1768 - adj. Jno. Cannon, Caleb Touchstone
Oberry, Henry #0420 - 28 Sept. 1750 - West of Little River
Obryan, Lawrence #3617 - 25 July 1774 - Beaverdam Cr.
*Odom, Isaac #0424 - 27 Sept. 1751 - Hogg Swamp
Odom, Isaac #499 - 1 July 1758 - Shoeheel Cr.
Odom, Richard #4903 - 16 Nov. 1790 - NE Peedee
Odum, Dion #4183 - 30 Mch. 1780 - Joe's Cr.
Oliver, James #3542 - 23 July 1774 - Cedar Cr.
Oliver, John #3364 - 11 Mch. 1775 - NE Peedee
O'Neal, Cornelius #3126 - 3 Sept. 1753 - Thickety Cr.
*O'neal, Henry #1158 - 17 May 1754
O'neal, Isham #4830 - 16 Nov. 1790
O'Neal, Sampson #4065 - 3 Sept. 1779 - Lane's Cr.
*Osborn, Alexander #0421 - 3 Apr. 1752 - Crowder's Cr. [S.C.]
Outlaw, Lodwick #2503 - 16 Dec. 1769 - Falling Cr.
Pace, Stephen #4593 - 23 Sept. 1785
*Palmer, Robert #423 - 10 Oct. 1755 - Thompson's Cr.
*Palmer, William #2809 - 22 Nov. 1771 - NE Peedee
*Park, David #283 - 23 Feb. 1754 - Little River
*Park, Hugh #1723 - 24 Sept. 1754 - Caudell's Cr.
*Parker, Elisha #2538 - 4 May 1769 - NE Peedee Mark's Cr.
Parker, Stephen #4706 - 7 Aug. 1787
Parkington, James #2245 - 5 Dec. 1757 - SW Peedee
*Parkinson, James #2244 - 5 Dec. 1757 - SW Peedee
Parnell, John #4050 - 3 Sept. 1779 - NE Peedee
*Parratt, James #3494 - 23 July 1774 - Black Jack Fork
*Parson, Francis #4610 - 23 Sept. 1785
Parson, Francis #3207 - 4 May 1775 - SW Peedee
*Parson, John #2785 - 18 Nov. 1771 - SW Peedee
Parsons, Joseph #4102 - 3 Sept. 1779 - Peedee
*Parsons, Samuel #2551 - 4 May 1769 - SE Yadkin
Parsons, Thomas #3639 - 25 July 1774 - SW Peedee
*Partin, Robert #1591 - 22 Apr. 1763 - Thompson's Cr.

Paslor [Preslar?], Peter #5072 - 9 July 1794 - NE Peedee
Paston [Poston], John #495 - 1 July 1758 - NE Peedee
Pates, Thoroughgood #2580 - 16 Dec. 1769 - Joe's Creek
Pate, William #2939 - 22 Jany. 1773 - SW Peedee
Pattishall, Richard C. 22 Aug. 1809 - adj. Faulkner's
Pattishall, Richard Coleman #6067 - 3 May 1811 - Jones Cr.
Pattison, Robt. #291 - 23 Feb. 1754 - (S.C.)
*Paul, Abraham #612 - 4 Apr. 1750 - S of Peedee
*Paul, Jacob #1479 - 10 Apr. 1761 - SW Peedee
*Pellum [Pelham], John #3147 - 26 Oct. 1761 - Richardson's Cr.
*Pellum, Thos. #3140 - 26 Oct. 1761 - Richardson's Cr.
Phelen, John #3529 - 23 July 1774 - Richardson's Cr.
Penick, George #0418 - 29 Sept. 1750
Perkins, John #0478 - 21 Dec. 1763 - Browns Cr.
Philemon, Thos. #4057 - 3 Sept. 1779 - NE Peedee
Phillips, James #1316 - 27 Sept. 1756 - SW Peedee
*Phillips, Joel #1439 - 5 Dec. 1750 - SW Peedee
*Phillips, John #964 - 20 Feb. 1754
*Phillips, Reuben #3392 - 11 Mch. 1775 - Little Brown Cr.
Phillips, Robert #4883 - 16 Nov. 1790
Phillips, Samuel #3477 - 23 July 1774 - SW Peedee
*Phillips, William #0417 - 27 Nov. 1762 - Lane's Creek.
*Phillips, Zachariah #2340 - 23 Nov. 1764 - Gould Br. of Brown Cr.
Phillips, Zachry #2266 - 1 July 1758 - SW Peedee
⎰Pickel, James⎱
⎨Ross, Andrew⎬ #5105 - 8 Dec. 1794
⎱Ross, Walter ⎰
Pickens, John #0493 - 14 Oct. 1752
*Pickens, Andrew #649 - 13 Apr. 1751
Pickens, Martha #1692 - 20 May 1754
⎰Pickens, William   ⎱ #2180 - 20 May 1754 - West of
⎱Rutherford, Griffith⎰ Rocky River
*Pickett, James #2372 - 26 Sept. 1766 - SW Peedee
*Pickett, James #4937 - 20 Dec. 1791 - adj. his old 300 ac survey
⎰Pickett, James ⎱ #5128 - 17 Oct. 1796 -
⎱Leak, Walter Jr.⎰
*Pickett, James   ⎱ #2825 - 22 Nov. 1771 - NE
*Coleman, William ⎰ Peedee (7 grants)
Pickett, William #3145 - 26 Oct. 1767 - SW Peedee
Pidingfield Bedinfield, Henry #875 - 23 Feb. 1754 - S of Peedee

LAND GRANTS   17

Pearce, Wright #4436 - 14 Oct. 1783 - Beaver-
Pike, John #1069 - 24 June 1751 - Cane Cr.
*Pilcher, James #3979 - 3 Sept. 1779 - SW Peedee
Pilcock, Stephen #0492 - 27 Sept. 1756 - NE Peedee
Pilman, William #477 - 1 July 1758 - NE Peedee
Pistole, Charles #4930 - 20 Dec. 1791
Pitman, Wm. #2247 - 1 July 1758 - NE Peedee
Player, Henry #4566 - 14 Oct. 1783 - Cedar Creek
Pledger, Joseph #4059 - 3 Sept. 1779 - Little River
*Plunkett, James #2735 - 18 Apr. 1776 - SW Peedee
*Plunkett, William #1361 - 25 May 1757 - S of Peedee
Polk, Charles #4823 - 16 Nov. 1790
Pollard, Thos. #4051 - 3 Sept. 1779 - SW Peedee
Pool, Arthur #5016 - 27 June 1793
Pool, John #5108 - 8 Dec. 1794
Pool, Mary #4377 - 14 Oct. 1783 - Rocky River
*Pool, Middleton #4474 - 14 Oct. 1783 - Rocky River
Pool, William #4512 - 14 Oct. 1783 - Rocky River
Poor, David #2590 - 16 Dec. 1769 - Little River
Porter, John #1921 - 5 Dec. 1760 - N of Peedee
*Poston, James #4302 - 24 Oct. 1782
Poston, James #2108 - 20 Apr. 1763 - NE Peedee
*Poston, John #1420 - 5 Dec. 1760 - NE Peedee
Poston, Robert #2848 - 19 May - 1772 NE Peedee
Powell, Benj. #2778 - 18 Nov. 1777 - Collins Cr.
Powell, Charles #0491 - 22 Sept. 1766 - Hitchcock's Cr.
*Powell, William #1844 - 29 Sept. 1756 - SW Peedee
Powers, John #3393 - 11 March 1775
Preslar, John #3336 - 4 Mch. 1775 - Lane's Cr.
Preslar, Levi #4122 - 3 Sept. 1779 - Lane's Cr.
Preslar, Peter #1492 - 2 Dec. 1761 - Mountain Cr.
Pressbey, John #0488 - 20 Oct. 1767 - adj. James Hutchins
Pressley, Andrew #898 - 25 Feb. 1754 - S of Yadkin
*Pressly, John #507 - 11 Apr. 1749 - N of Rocky River
Primrose, Violet #0486 -   - NE Peedee
Purviance, William #1490 - 10 Apr. 1761 - Thompson's Cr.
Quick, Solomon #4108 - 3 Sept. 1779 - NE Peedee
Raiford, James #4160 - 3 Sept. 1779 - NE Peedee
Raiford, Matthew #2753 - 18 Apr. 1771 - NE Peedee
*Raiford, Robert 1325 - 27 Sept. 1756 - NE Peedee
Rainer, Robert #2089 - 22 Apr. 1763 - S of Peedee
*Rainey, Robert #2094 - 22 Apr. 1763 - S of Peedee
Ramsey, John #3633 - 25 July 1774 - Lane's Cr.
Ramsey, Robert
Randall, Benajah #3073 - 24 May 1773 - NE Peedee

Randall, Ozburn #5052 - 9 July 1794
Randall, Thomas #1590 - 22 Apr. 1763
Randolph, John #4294 - 24 Oct. 1782 - SW Peedee
*Ratcliff, Richard #4332 - 14 Oct. 1783 - SW Peedee
Ratcliff, Thomas,#4283 - 14 Oct. 1783 - SW Peedee
Ratcliff, Wm. #2703 - 18 Apr. 1771 - SW Peedee
*Reaney, David #3320 - 4 Mch. 1775 - Old Mill Cr.
*Readfern, John #4482 - 14 Oct. 1783
Redish, Willy #4715 - 7 Aug. 1787
Reed [Rudd], Burlingham #563 - 11 Apr. 1749 - S of Peedee
Reed, Robert #1071 - 25 May 1751
Reed, William #953 - 25 Feb. 1754
Rees, Daniel #3900 -   - Drowning Cr.
Reilly, David #0462 - 21 Oct. 1767 - Long Cr.
Renfrow, Enoch #4530 - 14 Oct. 1783 - SE Peedee
Renfrow, Joel #4995 - 27 Nov. 1792
Renfrow, Nath'l #4525 - 14 Oct. 1783 - Lick Branch
Rentfrow, Stephen #4624 - 23 Sept. 1785
Reynolds, James #3047 - 24 May 1773 - NE Peedee
*Reynolds, Thomas #801 - 30 Aug. 1753 - Buffalow Cr.
Rice, John #0465 - 7 Apr. 1752 - Buffalo Cr.
Rice, William #4364 - 14 Oct. 1783 - SW Yadkin
Ricketts, Wm. #5077 - 8 Dec. 1794 - at Jarman's
Ridge, Thomas #1070 - 25 Mch. 1752
Right, Thos. #4193 - 29 Mch. 1780 - SW Peedee
Rion, Michael #5087 - 8 Dec. 1794 - Big Brown Cr.
Rivers, John #2780 - 18 Nov. 1771 - Shoe Heel Cr.
Robeson, Cornelius #3945 - 11 Mch. 1775 - Town Cr.
*Robeson, Luke #2509 - 22 Dec. 1768 - Cheek's Cr.
Robeson, Thomas #3177 - 29 Apr. 1768 - Drowning Cr.
Robeson, Charles #1589 - 22 Apr. 1763 - N of Peedee
Robeson, Townsend #1810 - 17 Mch. 1756
*Robertson, James #663 - 27 Sept. 1751 - Catawba
Robertson, Tyre #4515 - 14 Oct. 1783 - SW Peedee
Robinson, Benj. #1179 - 20 May 1754
*Robinson, Charles #2448 - 21 Oct. 1758 - N of Peedee
*Robinson, Charles #524 - 10 July 1760
Robinson, Drury, #4710 - 7 Aug. 1787
*Robinson, Luke [many]
*Robinson, Townsend #406 - 3 Oct. 1755 - Rocky Cr. [S.C.]
*Robinson, William #0512 - 4 Sept. 1753 - John Wilson, Catawba
Rod, George Lansdell, #3950 - 15 Mch. 1775 - Jones Cr.
Roe, John #3784 - 29 Feb. 1775 - Cheek's Cr.
Rogers, Mark #5101 - 8 Dec. 1794
Roland, John #4550 - 14 Oct. 1783 - Brown's Cr.
Rolander, Nicholas #4766 - 16 Nov. 1790
Rollin, Austin #4348 - 14 Oct. 1783 - SW Peedee
Rollin, Shearwood #4347 - 14 Oct. 1783 - SW Peedee

LAND GRANTS

Romage, George #4564 - 14 Oct. 1782 - SW Peedee
*Roper, James #4269 - 24 Oct. 1782 - SW Peedee
Rorie, James #4950 - 20 Dec. 1791
Rorie, Wm. #4291 - 24 Oct. 1782
Ross, Andrew #4886 - 16 Nov. 1790
{Ross, Coleman} #3479 - 23 July 1774 - SW
{Ross, Andrew} Peedee
Ross, Donald #5043 - 7 Jany. 1795 - Buffalo Cr.
Ross, Hugh #3315 - 4 Mch. 1775 - Buffalo Cr.
Roan, Adam #3245 - 4 Mch. 1775 - Mountain Cr.
Roan, Henry #4008 - 3 Sept. 1779 - SW Peedee
Roan, James #3582 - 25 July 1774 - SW Yadkin
Roan, Tunstall #3650 - 25 July 1774 - SW Yadkin
Rowland, John #3614 - 25 July 1774 - adj. John White
Rowlings, Samuel #4833 - 15 Nov. 1790
Royal, John #0500 - 13 Jany. 1773 - Rocky River
Rudd, George Lansdell #4501 - 14 Oct. 1783
*Rudesall, Philip #1610 - 20 May 1754
*Rudesal, Michael #1609 - 17 May 1754
*Rudesal, Yerrick #1614 - 20 May 1754
Rush, John #3598 - 25 July 1774 - Old Mill Cr.
Rusher, Robert #4664 - 25 Aug. 1786
*Rushing, Abraham #4878 - 16 Nov. 1790
Rushing, Abraham #3664 - 25 July 1774 - Thompson's Cr.
Rushing, John #3089 - 24 May 1773 - Brown Cr.
Rushing, Mark #4379 - 14 Oct. 1783
Rushing, Mathew #4634 - 23 Sept. 1785
Rushing, Noah #4777 - 16 Nov. 1790
Rushing, Philip #4951 - 20 Dec. 1791 - adj. own land
Rushing, Richard #2882 - 22 May 1772 - Brown Cr.
*Rushing, Robert #4381 - 14 Oct. 1783
*Rushing, William #0496 - 20 Apr. 1763 - Brown Cr.
Ruskin, William #0495 - 13 Oct. 1756 - Thompson's Cr.
Russell, Robert #1359 - 23 Oct. 1756
*Rutherford, Griffith #0498 - 7 Apr. 1752 - Clark's Cr.
Rutherford, John #2698 - 24 Dec. 1770 - Drowning Cr.
Rutledge, George #1608 - 20 May 1754 - Catawba
Rushing, Rowland #4622 - 23 Sept. 1785
Rye, Dunn #4177 - 30 Mch. 1780 - Solomon's Cr.
Rye, John #4171 - 30 Mch. 1780 - Gum Swamp
*Rye, Joseph #2924 - 22 Jany. 1773 - Little River
Rye, Solomon #4210 - 30 Mch. 1780 - NE Peedee
Ryle, James #2695 - 24 Dec. 1770 - SW Yadkin
Ryle, John #2656 - 25 July 1774 - Rocky River
*Saffert, Leonard #969 - 10 Apr. 1761 - adj. Sam'l. Bickerstaff
Samerlin, Henry #1224 - 24 Sept. 1754 - Little Peedee
*Sanders, Aaron #3080 - 24 May 1773 - Yadkin

Sanders, Nathaniel #2512 - 23 Dec. 1768 - Shoe Heel Cr.
*Sanders, Patrick #3379 - 11 Mch. 1775 - Mountain Cr.
Sanford, James #2537 - 4 May 1769 - Jones Cr.
Sapp, Thos. #4824 - 16 Nov. 1790
Sargent, James #3084 - 24 May 1773 - Yadkin
Scarbrough, Ephraim #4421 - 14 Oct. 1783 - Brown Cr.
Schrimsheer, John #3430 - 14 Mch. 1775 - Yadkin
Scott, Nath'l. #2963 - 22 Jany. 1773 - SW Peedee
Scott, William #2978 - 22 Jany. 1773 - NE Peedee
{Scotten, John} #3880 - 4 Mch. 1775 - Lick Cr.
{Bostick, James}
*Seago, John #2604 - 24 Dec. 1770 - Reedy prong of Jones Cr.
Seago, William #2528 - 4 May 1769 - Jones Cr.
Self, Vincent #4949 - 2 Dec. 1791
Settlington, Andrew #0170 - 14 Oct. 1752 - Cain's Cr. [S.C.]
*Shankle, George #2528 - 15 Dec. 1769 - Jacob's Cr.
Shankle, Jacob #4518 - 14 Oct. 1783 - Swift Island Br.
Shankle, John #4288 - 24 Oct. 1782 - SW Peedee
Sharpe, Anthony #4691 - 5 Nov. 1787 - Gould's Fork
*{Shaw, Robert} #0503 - 20 Feb. 1754 - Rocky
{Robinson, John} Cr.
Shaw, Thomas #5037 - 9 July 1794 - Thompson's Cr.
Shearley, William S. #1561 - 24 Apr. 1762 - NE Peedee
Shepard, James #2417 - 30 Oct. 1766 - NE Peedee
Shepard, Jasper #2097 - 22 Apr. 1763 - Brown Cr.
Shepard, John #2433 - 26 Sept. 1766 - SW Peedee
Shepard, William #4666 - 26 Aug. 1785 - Lane's Cr.
Shevers, William #4487 - 14 Oct. 1783
*Shirley, Wm. S. #2252 - 1 July 1758 - NE Peedee
Short, Daniel #650 - 4 Oct. 1752 - S of Peedee
Sidwell, John #1075 - 25 March 1752 - adj. John Pike
Sigrell, John #0163 - 28 Mch. 1753
Simkins, Joseph #4130 - 3 Sept. 1779 - Buffalo
Simmons, John #3412 - 11 Mch. 1775 - SW Peedee
Simonton, Robt. #959 - 20 Feb. 1754
Simpson, Thomas #2548 - 4 May 1769 - Mountain Cr.
Sims, Drury #3297 - 4 Mch. 1775 - SW Peedee
Sims, William #2409 - 30 Oct. 1765 - Little River
Singleton, Wm. #2553 - 4 May 1769 - Hitchcock's Cr.
Skipper, Barnaby #4056 - 3 Sept. 1779 - NE Peedee
Skipper, Benjamin #1938 - 5 Dec. 1760 - NE Peedee
Skipper, Samuel #4088 - 3 Sept. 1779 - E of Peedee
Skipper, Thomas #1818 - 27 Sept. 1756 - N of Peedee

*Slaughter, Owen #1565 - 24 Apr. 1762 - NE of Peedee
{Slaughter, Owen} #3541 - 23 July 1774 - Mill
{Bolton, William} Branch
Slay, Thomas #2622 - 9 Apr. 1770 - SW Peedee
Sloan, Joseph #0172 - 6 Mch. 1754 - Long Br. of Jones Cr.
Smith, Aaron #1441 - 5 Dec. 1760 - adj. Henry Walker
*Smith, Benjamin #1430 - 5 Dec. 1760 - SW Peedee
Smith, Charles #2566 - 16 Dec. 1769 - Cedar Cr.
Smith, Daniel #4200 - 30 March 1790 - Juniper Cr.
Smith, David #2888 - 22 May 1772 - main prong of Rocky Cr.
{Smith, David Baird, Benj. Smith, John [S.H.]} #3386 - 11 March 1775 - West of Little R.
*Smith, Edward #1417 - 5 Dec. 1760 - NE Peedee
*Smith, Francis #0173 - 25 Sept. 1766 - SW Peedee
Smith, George #0174 - 8 Apr. 1752
Smith, Henry #3511 - 23 July 1774 - Williams Cr.
Smith, James #0175 - 13 Jany. 1773 - east of Rocky River
Smith, Jasper #3510 - 23 July 1774 - Dison's Cr.
*Smith, John³ [S.H.] #1578 - 22 Oct. 1762 - Brown's Cr.
*Smith, John³ [L.R] #1443 - 5 Dec. 1760 - NE Peedee Thicketty Cr.
*Smith, John³ [Carp.] #3515 - 23 July 1774 - Smith's Branch
Smith, Joseph #5124 - 4 Dec. 1795
Smith, Michael #0176 - 23 Sept. 1766 - Drowning Cr.
Smith, Peter #3747 - 6 Apr. 1753
Smith, Richard #4812 - 16 Nov. 1790
Smith, Thomas #3120 - 27 Apr. 1767 - Bear Branch
Smith, William #2527 - 4 May 1769 - Hitchcock's
Smith, Willis #2427 - 25 Sept. 1766
Smith, Zachariah #2554 - 4 May 1769 - Mountain Cr.

*Snead, Henly #2669 - 11 Dec. 1770 - Hitchcock's
Snead, Israel #2965 - 22 Jany. 1773 - NE Peedee
*Snead, Samuel #3122 - 27 Apr. 1767 - Little River
*snead, William #3725 - Mch. 1775 - Cedar Cr.
Snider, Hance Adam #1862 - 13 Oct. 1756 - adj. his old place.
Snuggs, Robert #0537 - 13 Jany. 1773 - SW Peedee
Soward, Absolem #4500 - 14 Oct. 1783
Soward, Daniel #0179 - 20 Oct. 1767 - Cartledge Cr.
Spaight, Richard #0183 - 17 Mch. 1756 - S of Peedee
{Spaight, Richard Waddell, Hugh} #2478 - 1 July 1758 - S of Peedee
Spencer, John #3838 - 4 Mch. 1775 - Rocky River
Spencer, Joseph #3175 - 29 Apr. 1768 - Denson's Fk.
Spencer, Samuel #3035 - 24 May 1773 - SW Peedee
Spencer, William #3786 - 29 Feb. 1775 - West of Little River
Spier, Henry #2777 - 14 Nov. 1771 - SW Yadkin
Spier, John #0184 - 28 Sept. 1750
Spratt, James #0185 - 17 Apr. 1754
Stanfield, John #3556 - 25 July 1774 - Jones Cr.
Steed, Moses #3437 - 23 July 1774
Steed, Nathaniel #3468 - 23 July 1774 - NE Peedee
Steel, David #0186 - 1 Apr. 1751
Steele, Ambrose #2238 - 26 Nov. 1757 - SW Peedee
Steel, Thos. #1160 - 18 May 1754
Stephens, Francis #3135 - 24 Oct. 1767 - SW Peedee
Stephens, James #3131 - 24 Oct. 1767 - Flat Fork
*Stephens, John #2437 - 26 Sept. 1766 - SW Peedee
Stewart, William #4877 - 16 Nov. 1790
Stokes, David #4561 - 14 Oct. 1783
*Stokes, John #4770 - 16 Nov. 1790
Stokes, Micajah #3634 - 25 July 1774 - Rocky River
Stoke, Young #4248 - 30 Mch. 1780 - SW Peedee
Stone, John #862 - 30 Aug. 1753
*Stone, Wm. #2172 - 3 Oct. 1755
Strickland, Abraham #4563 - 14 Oct. 1793
Strickland, Joseph #3903 - 11 Mch. 1775 - Drowning Cr.
Strickland, Lott #4218 - 30 Mch. 1780 - Gum Swamp

3. There were three John Smiths in the early records of Anson County. The first, on Oct. 17, 1750, bought, for £35 Va. Cur., 200 acres east of Little River, below the mouth of Thicketty Creek, to which he added acreage from time to time.

The second was John Smith, a Scotch Highlander, who lived on Mill Cr. and the Yadkin Road at the edge of the Sandhills in Cumberland County, now Moore, and called himself "John Smith, Sandhill." Before 1753 he had a survey in Anson at the mouth of what became Smith's Creek, which he allowed, however, to lapse, settling south of Deep River in Cumberland County. In 1765 he sold his holdings in Cumberland and moved to Anson where he had procured a 200-acre grant on Brown's Cr. adj. his brother, Benj. Smith. It was when he came to Anson that the first John Smith began to be called "John Smith, Little River."

About 1770, another John Smith became prominent in Anson Co. records. He signed "John Smith, Carpenter." His first grants were on Cedar Cr. but later he settled permanently on Smith's Creek. Though not related, these three men appear often on each other's deeds as witnesses.

LAND GRANTS

Strother, Jeremiah #3570 - 25 July 1774
*Strudwick, Samuel #2905 - NE Yadkin
Stubbs, William #0526 - 20 Oct. 1767 - Mountain Cr.
Suggs, George #3032 - 24 May 1773 - NE Peedee
Suggs, John H. #2664 - 11 Dec. 1770 - David's Cr.
*Suggs, Rasha #3646 - 25 July 1774 - Suggs Cr.
Suggs, Richard #4745 - 7 Aug. 1787
Suggs, Robert #3660 - 25 July 1774 - SW Peedee
*Suggs, Thomas #2098 - 22 Apr. 1763 - Little River
Sullivent, Caleb #4941 - 20 Dec. 1781
*Summeral, Thos. #4082 - 3 Sept. 1779 - NE Peedee
Sumner, Benj. #3590 - 25 July 1774 - NE Peedee
Swore, John #2228 - 26 Nov. 1757 - NE Peedee
Swaringam [Swearingen] John #4365 - 14 Oct. 1783 - SW Peedee
Swaringam, Van #4850 - 16 Nov. 1790
Swaringam Van #2913 - 22 Jany. 1773 - Cheek's Cr.
Sweet, Robert #1271 - 23 Dec. 1754 - Little River
Sweet, William #3892 - 4 Mch. 1775 - Leeth's Cr.
Sweeting, Elisha #2692 - 24 Dec. 1770 - Shoe Heel Br.
Tabor, John #2260 - 1 July 1758 - NE Peedee
Tallant, Aaron #4939 - 20 Dec. 1791
Tallant, Moses #2933 - 22 Jany. 1773 - SW Peedee
Tallant, Thomas #
Talton, John #4938 - 20 Dec. 1791
Talton, Thos. #4635 - 23 Sept. 1785
Tanner, Thos. #0525
Taylor, George #1562 - 24 April 1762
Taylor, Isaac #738 - 1 Apr. 1753
Taylor, John #4426 - 17 Mch. 1780
Taylor, Michael #0193
Taylor, Timothy #3651 - 25 July 1774 - Lane's Cr.
Test, William #5107 - 8 Dec. 1794 - Buffalo Cr.
Temples, Frederick #4137 - 3 Sept. 1779
Templeton, David #848 - 30 Aug. 1753 [S.C.]
Terry, James #2231 - 26 Nov. 1757 - NE Peedee
Terry, James [Sav. Cr.] #4863 - 16 Nov. 1790
Terry, Matthew #2866 - 20 May 1772 - Drowning Cr.
Terry, William[4] [Sav. Cr.] #1309 - 27 Sept. 1756 - N Peedee
*Terry, William[4] [H. Cr.] #1798 - 15 March 1756 - Hitchcock's Cr.
Thirman, John #1435 - 5 Dec. 1760 - SW Peedee

Thomas, Benjamin #4075 - 3 Sept. 1779 - Gum Swamp
Thomas, Daniel #2773 - 28 Apr. 1758 - NE Peedee
Thomas, Enos #2253 - 1 July 1758 - NE Peedee
Thomas, Jacob #4451 - 14 Oct. 1783 - Rocky River
Thomas, James #4170 - 30 Mch. 1780 - Gum Swamp
*Thomas, John # - 22 Sept. 1766 - Peedee
Thomas, Leonard #3942 - 11 Mch. 1775
*Thomas, Lewis #3625 - 25 July 1774 - SW Peedee
Thomas, Philemon #3069 - 24 Mch. 1773 - Cartledge Cr.
Thomas, Rees #1118 - 17 May 1754
*Thomas, Robert #2810 - 22 Nov. 1771 - Pollock Fk.
Thomas, Samuel #4493 - 14 Oct. 1782
*Thomas, Stephen #0567 - 16 Dec. 1778 - Panther Cr.
*Thomas, Thomas #2526 - 4 May 1769 - NE Peedee
*Thomas, William #3485 - 23 July 1774 - Jones Cr.
Thomson, Benj. #1669 - 16 May 1754
Thomson, Charles #3447 - 23 July 1774 - Yadkin
Thomson, Elisha #3065 - 24 May 1773 - NE Peedee
*Thomson, George #1081 - 25 Mch. 1752 - S Fk of 5th Cr.
*Thomson, John #1078 - 25 Mch. 1752 - S fk of 5th Cr.
*Thomson, Joseph #4026 - 3 Sept. 1779 - SW Peedee
*Thomson, Shem #4314 - 14 Oct. 1783 - Richardson's Cr.
Thornton, Daniel #4839 - 16 Nov. 1790
Threadgill, John #4981 - 27 Nov. 1792
Threadgill, Thos. #5003 - 27 Nov. 1792
*Threadgill, William #4848 - 16 Nov. 1790
Tims, Joseph #1774 - 28 Sept. 1754 - N of Peedee
Tindle, James #6078 - 24 Nov. 1813
*Tippens, Henry #2421 - 30 Oct. 1765 - Big Cr.
Tisdall, Lidia #4305 - 24 Oct. 1782
Tomlison, Moses #4828 - 16 Nov. 1790
Tomkins, Thomas #115 - 27 Apr. 1767 - Mill Cr.
*Tomkins, Stephen #3375 - 11 Mch. 1775 - Old Mill Cr.
Tony, John #4207 - 30 Mch. 1780 - Hitchcock's Cr.
Tool, Mathew #1684 - 20 May 1754
Touchstone, Caleb #2506 - 22 Dec. 1768 - Little River
*Touchstone, Henry #2446 - 10 May 1760 - NE Peedee

---

4. To distinguish the two William Terrys who came to Anson County abt. the same time, one may be called "Wm. Terry, of Savannah Creek" or "William, west of the Peedee," and the other "William Terry of Hitchcock's Cr." or "William east of the Peedee." The latter, however, began to be called "William Terry, Jr." in the latter half of the 1750's to distinguish him from William Terry, of Savannah Creek, who was occasionally called Wm. Terry, Sr. If the two families were related there is no record of it.

*Touchstone, Stephen #3834 - 4 March 1775 - NE Peedee
*Towers, Jonathan #3462 - 23 July 1774 - NE Peedee
Townsend, Solomon #519 - 26 Apr. 1768 - Jones Cr.
Tradway, Daniel #4719 - 7 Aug. 1787
Traps, Joseph #0204 - 14 Oct. 1752
Travis, Edward #4002 - 30 Sept. 1779 - Cribbs Cr.
*Travis, William #4852 - 16 Nov. 1790
Trull, Stephen #5063 - 9 July 1794
*Trull, Thomas #4670 - 25 Aug. 1786
Tucker, George #4287 - 24 Oct. 1782 - SW Peedee
Turnage, John #4054 - 3 Sept. 1779 - Gum Swamp
Turner, John #3018 - 22 Jany. 1773 - Leith's Cr.
Turner, Jonathan #3218 - 16 Jany. 1775 - Mountain Cr.
Turner, Matthew #4785 - 16 Nov. 1790
Turner, Moses #4121 - 3 Sept. 1779 - Gum Swamp
Turner, Thomas #3351 - 6 Mch. 1775 - Bull Br.
*Underwood, Thomas #1186 - 24 Sept. 1754 - SW Peedee
Underwood, Benjamin #0210 - 24 May 1773
*Ussery, John #0209 - 23 Sept. 1766 - Peedee and Little River
*Ussery, William #2576 - 16 Dec. 1769 - Buffelow Cr. Cheek's Cr.
*Vanderford, James #4510 - 14 Oct. 1783 - SW Peedee
*Vanhoser, Jacob #3307 - 22 July 1774
Vanhoser, John #493 - 1 July 1758 - SW Peedee
Vanhoser, Valentine #3659 - 25 July 1774 - SW Peedee
Vanlandingham, Francis #4708 - 7 Aug. 1787
Vaughan, William #4275 - 24 Oct. 1782 - adj. Jas. Brooks
Vick, Jacob #4264 - 24 Oct. 1782
Vickers, Ralph #4617 - 23 Sept. 1785
Vickory, Joseph #4066 - 3 Sept. 1779 - S of Peedee
Vickory, Hezekiah #4556 - 14 Oct. 1783 - Rocky River
*Vines, Benj. #2239 - 26 Nov. 1757 - NE Peedee
Vining, Thomas #4733 - 7 Aug. 1787
*Waddell, Hugh #1089 - 10 Aug. 1761 - Dutch Buffelow
*Wade, John #2349 - 30 Oct. 1765 - Brown Cr.
*Wade, Thomas, #2672 - 11 Dec. 1770 - Davis Br.
Walker, Henry, Sr. #0212 - 17 Nov. 1752 - S of Peedee
Walker, James #2891 - 22 May 1773 - Clark's Cr.
Walker, John #2878 - 22 May 1772 - Yadkin
Wall, Arthur #0215 - 18 Apr. 1767 - Brown Cr.
Wall, Benj. #0216 - 27 Sept. 1756
Wall, John #2595 - 16 Dec. 1769 - Cartledge's Cr.
Wall, John Jr. #0217 - 27 Sept. 1756
Wall, Nathan'l #0218 - 27 Sept. 1756
Wallock, Martin #1085 - 25 Mch. 1752

Walsh, Nicholas #2082 - 15 Nov. 1762 - Clark's Cr.
Walsh, William #1510 - 15 Nov. 1762 - Clark's Cr.
Ward, Thomas #1448 - 5 Dec. 1760 - NE Peedee
Warren, Hosenton [?] #2953 - 22 Jany. 1773 - SW Peedee
Warthen, Richard #4182 - 30 Mch. 1780 - NW Peedee
Watkins, Christopher #2701 - 18 Apr. 1771 - SW Peedee
Watson, Mathew #3862 - 4 Mch. 1775 - Bear Cr.
Watson, Peter #4616 - 23 Sept. 1785
Watson, William #213 - 30 Aug. 1753 - Catawba
Watson, William #4435 - 14 Oct. 1783 - SW Peedee
Watson, Benj. #2826 - 22 Nov. 1771 - Young's Br.
Watson, Garrett #5125 - 4 Dec. 1795
Watson, Malachi #5065 - 9 July 1794
Waughope, James #1455 - 10 Apr. 1761 - adj. Robt. Caldwell
Weakley, James #2179 - 3 Oct. 1755
Weatherford, Charles #2717 - 18 Apr. 1771 - SW Peedee
Wever, Jethro #4400 - 14 Oct. 1783 - SW Peedee
Weaver, John #4441-- 11 Oct. 1783 - SW Peedee
Weaver, Joshua #476 - 1 July 1758 - NE Peedee
Weaver, Stephen #4671 - 25 Aug. 1786 - Lane's Cr.
Weaver, William #4363 - 14 Oct. 1783 - SW Peedee
*Webb, John #428 - 25 May 1757 - N of Peedee
*Webb, George #2659 - Dec. 11, 1770 - NE Peedee
*Webb, James #2676 - 11 Dec. 1770 - Williams Cr.
*Webb, Robert #2741 - 18 Apr. 1771 - NE Peedee
*Webb, Theoderick #0219 - 16 Apr. 1767 - Brown Cr.
*Webb, William #4209 - 30 March 1780 - Gum Swamp
Wells, George #4165 - 3 Sept. 1779 - SW Peedee
Wells, Joseph #1084 - 24 June 1751 - Cane Cr.
Welsh, John #1457 - 10 Apr. 1761 - Clark's Cr.
West, John #5074 - 9 July 1794
Westfield, David #433 - 25 May 1757 - SW Peedee
White, Damiel #4168 - 30 Mch. 1780 - NW Peedee
White, David #755 - 9 Apr. 1753
*White, George #4971 - 16 Nov. 1790
*White, Henry #27 - 13 Apr. 1752
*White, James #2264 - 1 July 1758 - SW Peedee
White, Jamima #2534 - 4 May 1769 - Savannah Cr.
*White, John #1223 - 24 Sept. 1754 - Catawba Cr.
White, John #3139 - 26 Oct. 1767 - Richardson's Cr.
White, Joseph #16 - 3 Apr. 1752 - N of Peedee
White, Joseph #1268 - 28 Sept. 1754 - SW Peedee Brown Cr.
White, Joseph Jr. #0232 - 5 Apr. 1749 - Brown Cr.
White, Josiah #0229 - 20 Oct. 1767 - Lane's Cr.
White, Moses #1087 - 25 Mch. 1753
White, Nicholas #1422 - 5 Dec. 1760 - SW Peedee
White, Robert #2502 - 22 Dec. 1768 - Brown Cr.
White, Stephen #1335 - 24 Sept. 1754

White, Zachariah #2359 - 30 Oct. 1765 - Brown Cr.
White, Zedekiah #0235 - 20 Oct. 1767 - Brown Cr.
Whiteside, Hugh #1450 - 10 Apr. 1761 - Fishing Cr. [S.C.]
Whitley, George #4361 - 14 Oct. 1783 - SW Peedee
*Whitner, Henry #576 - 28 Mch. 1751 - Catawba
Wicker, Robt. #2419 - 30 Oct. 1765 - Lane's Cr.
Wilkeson, Wm. #775 - 11 May 1753 - Gr. Swamp
*Wilkins, John #0236 - 24 Sept. 1754 - Catawba Cr.
*Wilkins, John #2617 - 7 Apr. 1770 - Clark's Cr.
Wilkins, Samuel #0237 - Aug. 1753 - Jones Cr.
Williams, Boling #4073 - 3 Sept. 1779 - Lane's Cr.
Williams, Christopher #4149 - 3 Sept. 1779 - Cribbs Cr.
Williams, Edward #4599 - 23 Sept. 1785
Williams, Holton #2254 - 1 July 1758 - NE Peedee
*Williams, Henry #2508 - 22 Dec. 1768 - Mountain Cr.
Williams, John #2793 - 18 Nov. 1771 - Hitchcock's Cr.
Williams, Joshua #4308 - 24 Oct. 1782 - Rocky River
*Williams, Rowland #2389 - 9 Nov. 1764 - Lane's Cr.
*Williams, Sampson #3020 - 22 Jany. 1773 - Dry Branch
*Williams, Samuel #1445 - 5 Dec. 1760 - NE Peedee
Williams, Solomon #0238 - 18 Apr. 1767 - N of Peedee
Williams, Thomas #0239 - 14 Oct. 1752
Williamson, John #4539 - 14 Oct. 1783 - SW Peedee
Williamson, Sterling #4115 - 3 Sept. 1783 - SW Peedee
Wilsher, Williams #459 - 26 Nov. 1757 - NE Peedee
Wilson, Francis #1137 - 16 May 1754 - Little River
Wilson, James #0240 - 26 Sept. 1751 - Catawba
*Wilson, John #75 - 31 Mch. 1753 - Broad River
Willson, John #3417 - 11 Mch. 1775 - adj. Underwood Clark's Cr.
Wilson, John #0243 -   - Big Cr. of Little River
Wilson, Matthew #1279 - 3 Oct. 1755
*Wilson, Samuel #1259 - 29 Sept. 1754 - Clark's Cr.
Whitehead, Richard #5057 - 9 July 1794

*Wilson, Thomas #3033 - 25 May 1773
*Wilson, William #1264 - 18 Nov. 1752 - Broad
Wilson, Zacheus #1194 - 24 Sept. 1754 - Catawba
Winfield, Peter #4846 - 16 Nov. 1790
Winnehan, Francis #2336 - 16 Nov. 1764 - SW Peedee
Winsley, Benj. #1086 - 25 Mch. 1752
Wisdow, Wm. #4731 - 7 Aug. 1787
Wise, Frederick #1722 - 24 Sept. 1754 - Howard's Cr.
Wise, Jane Ann #3247 - 3 Mch. 1775 - Mark's Cr.
Wise, Samuel #3199 - 4 Mch. 1775 - Mark's Cr.
Woods, Andrew #666 - 3 Mch. 1753 - Catawba
Woods, Bartholomew #846 - 30 Aug. 1753 - Duncan's Cr.
Wood, Cartus #239 - 30 Aug. 1753 - Tiger River
*Woods, James #0251 - 17 May 1754 - Reedy River
*Woods, John #0252 - 7 Apr. 1752
Woods, Joseph #4998 - 27 Nov. 1792
Woods, Robert #0254 - 14 Oct. 1752 - Broad River
*Woods, William #4689 - 5 Nov. 1787 - Brown Cr.
Woods, William } #4866 - 16 Nov. 1790
Brown, Morgan }
Woodle, Wm. #4052 - 3 Sept. 1779 - NE Peedee
Worrell, Nathan #3036 - 24 May 1773 - NE Yadkin
Worthen, Richard #4517 - 14 Oct. 1783 - SW Peedee
Wright, Carna #2594 - 16 Dec. 1769 - SW Peedee
*Wright, John #3179 - 22 Dec. 1768 - SW Peedee
Wright, Josiah #5084 - 8 Dec. 1794
Wright, Kency #4166 - 3 Sept. 1779 - SW Peedee
*Wright, Thomas #3569 - 25 July 1774 - Long Br.
Wrisley, Benj. #1086 - 25 Mch. 1752 - adj. John McCamel
Wyatt, William #2356 - 30 Oct. 1765 - SW Peedee
Yarborough, Humphrey #3525 - 23 July 1774 Lane's Cr.
Yarborough, Jonathan #3627 - 25 July 1774 - Lane's Cr.
Yates, James #3512 - 23 July 1774 - Drowning Cr.
Yates, William #4663 - 25 Aug. 1786 - Flat Fk Brown Cr.
Yerkes, Sam'l #4243 - 30 Mch. 1780 - SW of Peedee
Yoe, James #4615 - 23 Sept. 1785
Yerby [Irby], William #3988 - 3 Sept. 1779 - bet. Rocky R. & Long Cr.
*Young, Samuel #1088 - 25 Mch. 1752 - 3rd Creek
Youngblood,   #445 - 26 Nov. 1757 - NE Peedee

ABSTRACTS OF LAND GRANT SURVEYS

Anson County

#3567. Benjamin Baird; 400 acres sw of Peedee; ent. 16 May 1772; issued 25 July 1774; on Jones Creek, adj. Christopher Clark's lower line. . . Robt. Thomas' corner. . . Diggs corner; surveyed June 29, 1773 by Walter Cunningham, surveyor; chainers: William Thomas, Benj. Baird.

#3563. Benjamin Baird; 100 acres on Dison's Creek, joining Fanning's line and John Smith's and Benj. Baird's line; ent. 21 May 1773; issued 25 July 1774; surveyed June 17, 1773 by Walter Cunningham, Surveyor; ch: Jacob Williams and John Graham.

#3554. Benjamin Baird and John Smith (Sandhill); 400 acres adj. land formerly pat. to Robt. Mills on west side of Little River; ent. 16 Jany. 1773; iss. 23 July 1774; surv. 17 June 1773 by Walter Cunningham, Surveyor; ch: David Smith, Jacob Williams.

#3510. Jasper Smith; 150 acres on Dyson's Creek about a mile below Charles Smith's land; ent. 16 May 1772; iss. 23 July 1774; Surv. 24 June 1773 by Walter Cunningham; ch: David Smith, Jasper Smith.

#3465. James Jeffreys; 150 acres in Anson and Cumberland Cos.; sw of Cabbin Cr. inc. own improvement; ent. 13 Jany. 1773; iss. 23 July 1774; ch: Jas. Saunders, John Jeffreys.

#3473. James Bounds; 100 acres on Cow Br. of Hedgecock's Cr. at Wm. Terry's corner; ent. 13 Jany. 1773; iss. 23 July 1774; no plat.

#3483. Smith Fields; 200 acres sw Peedee in forks of McCay's Cr. near other survey; ent. Dec. 2, 1770; iss.   ; Surv. 20 Sept. 1771, adj. wid. Franklin's line. . . John Jarman's line. . . on Buffalo and Mt. Creeks. . . ch: John Smith, John Jarman.

#3487. Caleb Touchstone, on Dry fork of Mt. Cr.; ent. 18 May 1772; iss. 23 July 1774; ch: Josiah Swearingen, Caleb Touchstone

#3515. John Smith; 100 a on Smith Br. of Peedee. John Smith's cor; 19 May 1772; 23 July 1774; ch: Wm. Lyndsey, John Smith

#3523. John Stouchbery; Feb. 9, 1774; on Tuckahoe Br. east of Gum Swamp; ch: John Smith, Thos. Durham.

#3558. James Pickett and William Coleman; 21 May 1773; 25 July 1774; 200 acres sw of Yadkin; ch: Walton Harris, James Fry.

#3570. Jeremiah Strother; June 1774; ch: self and Aaron Vick.

#3619. Moses Hull; issued 25 July 1774, David's Cr; surv. 6 Aug. 1773 by James Cotton; ch. John Smith, Moses Hull.

#3620. Moses Hull; Aug. 6, 1773; ch: Joseph Smith, Joseph Hull.

#3637. Henry Adcock; 25 July 1774; Nov. 18, 1779; surv. 21 Mch. 1772 [?] by Ro. Edwards, surveyor; John Poston's corner; John Tabor's and William Terry's lines; ch: Geo. Webb, William Terry, Jr.

#3647. Walter Ashmore; 14 Nov. 1771; 25 July 1774; 100 a upper side of Uwary River, at mouth; surv. 12 Mch. 1772 by Ro. Edwards, Surv. ch: Walter Ashmore, Joseph McLester.

#1952. John Smith (Little River); issued 5 Dec. 1760; 100 a s side of Little River; Thos. Jones' upper corner; surveyed 1758; ch: Phillip Sutton, John Cockeral.

#2322. William Terry; issued Feb. 22, 1764; 200 acres sw of Peedee, beg at mouth of Savannah Cr. at own land, formerly Joseph White's land; surv. 10 July 1763 by Wm. Dickson, Dep. Surv.; ch: William Coleman and William Terry.

#1915. William Terry; issued 13 Dec. 1760; 50 acres ne of Peedee. . . James Denson's lower corner, to

---

1. From Secretary of State's Office, Raleigh, N. C.

24   ABSTRACTS OF LAND GRANT SURVEYS

include ferry landing. surv. by M. Brown, dep. surv.

#1309. William Terry [Esq.]; 27 Sept. 1756; 300 acres no. of Peedee, on so. fork of Mountain Cr.; surv. Feb. 23, 1756 [plat illegible]

#3101. John Smith; Nov. 25 1771; 100 a sw Peedee, east of Cedar Cr. 3rd line of his other survey, sold to John Henry; adj. Joseph Dunham, Geo. Lindsey. No plat.

#3309. James Pickett; May 1773; Mch. 1775; 100 a adj. own land where he now lives sw of Peedee; ch: James Terry, James Pickett.

#3386. Benj. Baird, John Smith and David Smith: 22 July 1774 - 11 Mch. 1775; 200 acres west of Little River joining 4th line of their surveyor. ch: Thos. Parker, Benj. Baird.

#2874. Edward Smith; 300 acres sw of Peedee, Island Creek. ch: Darious Burns, Smith Field.

#2833. Benj. Smith; 300 acres sw of Peedee, beg east side of Gould's Fork of Brown's Cr. at Robt. Rainey's lower corner; surv. 18 Jany. 1771; ch: Joshua Morgan, Benj. Smith. Iss: 22 Nov. 1771

#3136. Benj. Smith; issued 24 Oct. 1767; 150 acres beg John Smith's lower corner on s bank of Brown's Cr. . . . both sides of Brown's Cr. surv. by Ro. Edwards, [date torn off]; ch: James Stewart and John Pressley [Preslar].

#1430. Benj. Smith; iss. 5 Dec. 1760; surv. Mch. 18, 1758; no chainers; 75 acres sw of Peedee, beg. on Young's Island, adj. Robt. Parker. . . Thos. George's upper back corner.

#3505. William Terry [William Terry, Sr. in the warrant]; 21 May 1773, 23 July 1774; surv. 11 Feb. 1774 by James Cotton, surveyor; 300 acres on Savannah Creek adjoining old survey; ch: James Terry, James Pickett.

#2884. John Smith (Sandhill); Issued 22 May 1772; no warrant; surv. 17 July 1770, by Ro. Edwards: ch: David Smith, John Graham.

#1888. David Smith; iss. 22 May 1772; 200 acres on the main prong of Rocky Creek west of Little River, upper side about 3/4 mi. above the fork; surv. 17 July 1770 by Ro. Edwards: ch: Walter Ashmore, Joseph Cunningham.

#1885. John Smith (Sandhill); 100 acres sw of Little River joining two surveys pat by David Miles near bluff; surv. for Sandhill John Smith by Ro. Edwards 14 July 1770; ch: Saml. Parsons, David Smith.

#4101. John Smith (Sandhill); iss. Sept. 3 1779; 100 acres on Dison's Creek, John Mitchell's corner; surv. 27 January 1779; ch: David Smith, Nicholas Christian.

#4115. John Smith (Sandhill): Iss: 3 Sept. 1779; warrant 28 Jany. 1779, Clark's Cr. inc. imp. of Saml. Swearingen, Jr.; ch: John Kimbrough and Nicholas Christian.

#3984. John Kimbrough; 3 Sept. 1779 - 10 Dec. 1779; surv. by Wm. Love, dep. surv. Jany. 27, 1779; ch: David Smith, John Kimbrough. 150 acres on Dison's Cr. John Mitchell's corner, inc. Ruth Smith's improvement.

#3676. Solomon Dearman; 14 Nov. 1771 - July 25, 1774 on the Dismal s of Gum Swamp, including imp. of Josiah Smith; surv. 3 Dec. 1772 by Ro. Edwards, surveyor. ch: Wm. Levina, Thos. Dearman.

#3771. Wm. Smith; 16 Jany. 1773 - 29 Feb. 1775; west side of Hedgecock Cr, near Gibson's old fork, near his own land; ch: Allen Martin, Ranatus Downing.

#3945. Cornelius Robeson; May 1773 - Mch. 11, 1775; 200 a on fork of Town Creek near his own land, west of Little River; surv. 24 June 1773; by Walter Cunningham, Surveyor; ch: Wm. Almond, Cornelius Robinson.

#4138. William Pickett; 28 Jany. 1779 - 3 Sept. 1779; 100 a nw of Cheek's Cr. John Ussery's 3rd corner. . . Robert Edwards line, including the imp. made by Wm. Ussery; surv. 26 June 1779; by Wm. Love, D. S.; ch: Wm. Ussery and Welcom Ussery.

#4160. James Rayford; 10 Dec. 1778 - 3 Sept. 1779; 200 acres ne Peedee and west of Little River at Wm. McGuire's corner. . . Mathew Raiford's line, Thos. Chiles' corner; surv. 30 Jany. 1779 by Wm. Love, Dep. Sur.; ch: Mathew Rayford Jr. and James Rayford.

#4098. Christopher Christian: 10 July 1778 - 3 Sept. 1779; 300 a ne Peedee on Rocky Creek and Monger's Road, including Phillips Cabbins and Samuel Swearingen's imp.; surv. 15 July 1778 by Wm. Love, Dep. Surv.; ch: Jesse Christian, Samuel Swearingen.

#2572. John Smith, Jr.; 7 Oct. 1768 - 16 Dec. 1769;

ne [?] of Peedee on Smith's Cr. adj. Saml. Flake; ch: John Flake and John Smith.

#1578. John Smith (Sandhill); issued 22 Oct. 1762; 300 a s side of Browns Cr nigh Gould's lines; surveyed for Mr. John Smith by John Shepard 15 Jany. 1762; ch: Benj. Smith, William Yurby [Irby].

#2753. Mathew Raiford; issued 11 April 1771; 150 a ne of Peedee, adj. Andrew Moorman, said Rayford and Jacob Sheppard; surv. by Robert Jarman; ch: Mathew Rayford Jr. and Mathew Rayford Sr.

#2921. John Smith; surveyed 27 Aug. 1771 for John Smith of Little River, 100 acres in forks of Dison's Cr. of Little River, abt. a mile below other survey: ch: Saml. Swearingen, Richard Downs.

#2172. William Stone; surveyed 24 July 1754 by Chas. Robinson; 200 a near a Long Br. of a fork of Little River; ch: John Smith and Queen.

#2231. James Terry; surveyed 2 Mch. 1757; issued 26 Nov. 1757; ne of Peedee, at John Webb's upper cor. north side of Hitchcock's Cr.; ch: John Webb, Francis Davenport.

#2662. Wm. Terry, Jr.; 200 a on Hitchcock's Cr.; surveyed 9 Oct. 1769; ch: James Bounds and Mathew Terry.

#2650. James Pickett; issued 11 Dec. 1770; 150 acres sw of Peedee on River bank at end of William Terry's 3rd line; surveyed 1 March 1770 by Robert Jarman, surveyor; ch: William Pickett and James Pickett.

#2431. James Pickett; surveyed 2 June 1766, 300 a sw of Peedee, near Terry's line; by Robt. Edwards, surveyor; ch: James Stevens and Cornelius Robeson.

#3064. Richard Leak; 24 May 1773; ch: Mathew Terry, Robt. Webb.

#3366. William Pickett; 24 May 1773 - 11 Mch. 1775; sw of Peedee on Cedar Cr. his own corner, joining Wm. Mask's lower line, chainers Walter Cunningham and Wm. Pickett.

#4253. Nicholas Christian; 10 April 1779 - March 1780; 50 acres west of Little River and sw of a branch called Little Rockey, beg. near John Kimbrough's line; Wm. Love, dep. surveyor; ch: John Kimbrough and David Smith.

#3270. Mary Hiatt; issued 4 Mch. 1775; 100 a w of Little River on west side of Rocky Creek; ch: John Morris and Edward Corwell. Surveyed 4 Dec. 1774.

ABSTRACTS OF DEEDS*

DEED BOOK 1

Page 20--March 3, 1749. Nicholas Smith, of Bladen, to Nath'l Hillen, of Anson, 200 a north of Peedee, half of 400 a gr Nicholas Smith Oct. 5, 1748.
Wit: C. Robinson, Chas. Robinson, Jr.

Page 33--April 17, 1751. John Fitzgarrald and Hugh Willson, both of Anson to Isaac Falkenbourgh, of same, for 40 pounds, 200 a in Anson, on the south of the Peedee, called Pleasant Hill, a grant to said Fitzgarrald, Sept. 30, 1748, 100 acres then sold by him to the said Hugh Willson for 8 pounds Va. Cur., June 1750.
Wit: Caleb Howell, John Berryman, Andrew Falkenbourgh

Page 40--June 11, 1750. Nicholas Smith, of Bladen, to Townsend Robinson, of Anson, for 20 pounds, land on Peedee gr to Nicholas Smith Oct. 13, 1749.
Wit: Chas. Robinson, Sr., Chas. Robinson, Jr.

Page 59--May 23, 1750. Thos. Hopper, of Anson, to John Smith, [L.R.], of same, for 10 pounds, tract of 5 a. on lower side of Little River of Peedee near the mouth of Thicketty Creek, part of a tract gr Thos. Holmes and conveyed to Hopper.
Wit: Jonathan Holmes (Helms), Benj. Horne

Page 61--March 3, 1748. Nicholas Smith,[1] of Bladen, to Wm. Phillips, of Anson, for 20 pounds, 200 acres in Anson north of the Peedee, beginning at the lower end of tract where Lee's cabin was, and granted to Nicholas Smith in 1748.
Wit: C. Robinson, Nath'l Hillis. (Hillen)

Page 63--June 22, 1750. James Denson, senr. to Wm. Downs, both of Anson, 10 pounds, Virginia currency, tract [100 acres] on north side of the Peedee, on the river bank, pat.sd Denson Nov. 22, 1746.
Wit: Thos. Ridge, Luke Blakely, Samuel Armstrong

Page 64--June 21, 1750. James Denson, Sr. to James Denson, Jr., of Anson, for 5 sh. Va. currency, tract granted to James Denson, Sr. 22 Nov. 1746.
Wit: Wm. Downs, Luke Blakely

Page 105--June 26, 1750. John Fitzgerald, of Anson, to Hugh Willson, of same, for 8 pounds Va. currency, land in Anson, formerly Bladen, on south side of the great Peedee River, 100 acres a part of a grant to said John Fitzgerald, Sept. 13, 1748.
Wit: John Dunn, Thos. Jones

Page 123--Nov. 10, 1754. John Willson, of Rowan County, to Rev. Mr. Joseph Tate, of Lancaster, Pa. for 20 pounds Va. currency, land in Anson County, above James Mitchell and above the fall of Big Creek of Little River, 432 acres.
Wit: Jno Braley, Robt. McPherson

Page 137--6 Jany. 1756. John Hornbeck to Marshall Diggs, both of Anson, for 10 pounds, 100 acres on Island Creek.
Wit: James Mackelbray, Francis Parker

Page 139--March 12, 1756. Townsend Robinson, Esq. to William Terry, Esq., of Anson County, for 50 pounds, 300 acres in Anson County, on south bank of the Peedee, begin. above the mouth of Little River, opposite the bluff in Denson's land, granted to Townsend Robinson by Samuel Martin; to Martin

---

*The Chronological order of the deed books seems to be as follows: Bk"A", bound in Bk 1, the first 120 pages; Bk"B"#1; Bk"C#1"; Bk 1; Bk 5; Bk 6: Bk 3; Bk "H#1"; Bk 7; Bk"K"; Bk 4; Bk"H", Bk"B#2"; Bk"C#2"; Bk "H#2"; Bk"D & E"; Bk"F & G"; Bk"L & M"; Bk"N & O"; Bk"S"; Bk"T"; Bk"V"; Bk"W"; Bk"Y"; Bk"Z". This information may be helpful in using the microfilms at the Dept. of Arch. and Hist.

The deed books in use now and from which the microfilms were made are transcriptions and naturally the paging is different but the paging of the original records is given, too, beside the caption of the deed. It was difficult to always remember to turn the reel back for the new page number, so some of the paging may be that of the original. If requesting a copy of a deed, or looking it up, it might be well to remember that if it is not on the page indicated look for it in the old paging which is also on every deed.

ABSTRACTS OF DEEDS

by Hugh Lorrimer, first patentee.
Wit: John Collson, Wm. Downs,
Thos. Prestwood

Page 141--April 19, 1756. Richard Bradford to William Terry, Esq., both of Anson County; for 25 pounds 300 acres on the north side of the Great Peedee, beg at a white oak, to Thos. Stafford Williams on east bank of Hitchcocks Creek, granted to Bradford, 15 March, 1756.
Wit: E. Cartledge, Jas Gordon,
Thos. Stafford Williams

Page 144--Apr. 27, 1756. Wm. Stone, of Anson Co., to Samuel Parsons, of same, for 20 pounds, 100 acres in Anson, part of a tract granted to Wm. Stone 3 Oct. 1755, on Long Branch on north side of Little River.
Wit: Wm. Downs, John Smith [L.R.]

Page 148--April 26, 1756. William Terry, [E-PD] of Anson, to John James, for 20 pounds, 100 acres on branch of Hitchcocks Creek.
Charles Robinson
E. Cartledge   July 8 [sic]

Page 150--Nov. 5, 1755. Leonard Dyson, of Edgcomb County, N.C., to Thos. Armstrong of Cumberland, for 40 pounds 300 acres northeast side of Great Peedee, begin. at the great bluff on the Southwest side of Little River... to bank of sd Little River. By deed to Leonard Dyson from Nicholas Dyson, 6 Feb. 1747.
Wit: John Verrell
   William Lane.   Ack. Nov. 6, 1755.

Page 153--Benj. and Martha Dumas, of Anson County, to John Collson, of same, for 50 pounds, 151 acres on south side of the Peedee, adj. John Hall and sd Collson, granted 23 Feb. 1756.
Wit: Jeremias Dumas, Zechariah Smith,
   Edmund Lily

Page 216--April 24, 1756. William Beard, of Anson County, Province of N.C. to Robt. Davis, of same, for 30 pounds Virginia currency, 300 acres, on Waxhaw Creek.   [S.C.]
Wit: Jno. Crockett, Robt. Ramsey,
   Repentance Townsend

Page 244--26 Jany. 1757. Burlingham Rudd, Senr. to Burlingham Rudd, Jr., both of Anson Co. 20 pounds sterling 200 a on Jones Creek part of grant to Burlingham Rudd April 11, 1749.
Wit: Henr. Downs, John Frolock,
   John Smith [Little River]

Page 247--28 Oct. 1756. Thos. Prestwood to Zechariah Smith both of Anson, for 25 pounds 200 a north side of Great Peedee, James Denson's line, gr to Joseph White.
Tow Robinson, Alex Lewis

Page 248--8 May, 1756. Sam'l Coburn and Margaret, his wife, of Anson County, to Mathias Claus, of same, for 10 pounds, 200 acres south of the Catawba River on Chigles Creek about 1/2 mile above the fall, surveyed for Peter Ereack [Erick] for 400 acres.
Andrew Barry, Hugh Barry,
Jeanet Barry

Page 253--24 Sept. 1757. Andrew Barry, Esq. to Richard Barry, 540 acres where Andrew Barry now lives gr sd Barry, 23 Feb. 1754, north side of Tanyard Branch, adj. Samuel Wilson.
Alex Osburn, Matthew Poole

Page 163--18 Feb. 1756. Townsend Robinson and his wife, of Anson to John Leonard and his wife, of same, for £ 40, 227 acres on south side of Fishing Creek, adj. Thos. Steel, and Kilpatrick's line, pat Townsend Robinson and his wife, 3 Oct. 1755.
[S.C.]
Wit: John Betty, Patrick Ker

Page 269--Jany. 24, 1758. Capt. William Terry, of Anson Co., to Samuel Wilkins of same, for 50 pounds 100 acres, part of a tract gr James Denson, Nov. 22, 1746, for 500 acres, by James Denson to Wm. Downs, June 22, 1750; by Downs to said Terry Oct. 1757; also 100 acres conveyed by said James Denson to James Denson, Jr. June 21, 1750, and by said James Denson, Jr. to said Wm. Terry Oct. 1757... including land sold by Jas. Denson to son James.
Wit: M. Brown, Daniel Holladay,
   Ambrose Steele

Page 271--29 Oct. 1757. James Denson, Jr. to William Terry, [Capt.] both of Anson County, for 20 pounds sterling money of Great Britain, 100 acres on northeast side of the Great Peedee, deeded to James Denson June 21, 1750.
Wit: John Frolock, James Robinson

Page 278--25 Jany. 1757. Richard Yarbrough to Joel Yarbrough, for 30 pounds; 100 acres.
Wm. Downs, Jonathan Downs,
William Stone

Page 280--28 March 1757. John Pickens of Craven Co. to Robt. McClenachan, Esq.; 55 pounds

Va. cur. 500 acres.
Andrew Pickens, Arch Crockett,
Wm. Davis

Page 282--Aug. 7, 1756. Ambrose Joshua Smith, of Rowan Co., N.C. to Benj. Dumas, of Anson, for 150 pounds Va. currency, two tracts, 900 acres, south of the Peedee in Anson County. First, 400 acres at mouth of Rockey River, granted Robt. Parks, Sept. 1745. Second, 500 acres granted sd Parks March 14, 1745, in Bladen; from said Parks to John Spann, Oct. 14, 1747; from Spann to Ambrose J. Smith, June 22, 1756.
Wit: Jeremiah Dumas, Francis Smith,
James Powers

Page 286--29 Oct. 1756. John Severight to Richard Yarbrough, both of Anson, for 30 pounds, 100 acres east of Little River of Peedee, adj. Chas. Robinson, surveyed for John McCoy.
John Leeth, Wm. Downs,
James Pickett

Page 291--16 Nov. 1756. Gasper Sliger and wife, Elizabeth, to Archibald Elliott, for 10 pounds, 348 acres west of the Catawba, being one-half of land (768 acres) belonging to Gasper Sliger and wife, whereon George Neals now lives.
Archibald Cairns, John Stone

Page 294--Dec. 29, 1755. John and Judith Clement, of Halifax County Ga. [Va.?], to Sam'l Coburn, of Anson County, N.C., for 5 shillings, land on south side of the Catawba above Sam'l Coburn's corner on Tuckaseged path, granted Judith Coburn, now wife of John Clement, 29 Aug. 1753.   [S.C.]
Wit: Alexr. Lewis
     Jacob Coburn
     Wm. Card

Page 298--7 March 1757. John Beaty, of Anson Co., schoolmaster, and Mary, his wife, to Edward Hogan, for 40 pounds, 200 acres on Doctor's Cr., west of Catawba, joining two tracts of Coburn's land, by Schoolhouse Branch.
Andrew Barry, Hugh Barry,
Janet Barry   [S.C.]

Page 301--July 3, 1758. Sam'l McCleery, of Anson, to John Frolock, of same, for 20 pounds, lawful money of Great Britain, land on 12 Mile Creek, granted McClerry 31 March 1753.
Jas. Cumming   [S.C.]
Chas. Alexander.

Page 303--July 2, 1758. Wm. Barnet to John Frolock, for 40 pounds sterling, 400 acres on south side of Catawba on 12 mile creek.
Jas. Cumming   [S.C.]
Chas. Alexander

Page 309--26 July, 1758. Archibald Grimes to Alexander Gordon, both of Anson, for 20 pounds Va. Money, 200 acres north of the Peedee.
Wit: Nicholas Bond, Bentley Franklyn

Page 311--Nov. 28, 1757. James Terry, of Anson, to James Downing, of same, for 20 pounds of the province, 200 acres granted to James Terry Nov. 26, 1757, at John Webb's upper corner on the north side of Hitchcocks Creek.
M. Brown, Isaac Davenport

Page 314--Oct. 29, 1757. William Downs, now of Anson Co., Prov. of N.C., to William Terry, [Capt.], of same, for 20 pounds sterling money of Great Britain, 100 acres north side of Peedee, to Downs by deed 22 June 1750.
John Frolock, James Robinson

Page 320--26 July, 1757. Marmaduke Kimbrough to Wm. Little, both of Anson, for 100 pounds, 200 acres.
George Little, Robert Abrams

Page 326--July 25, 1757. Ambrose Joshua Smith, of Orange County, N.C. to William Little, of Anson, for 20 pounds Va. currency, 300 acres on lower side of Little River of Peedee, on both sides of Dry Creek in Anson, adjoining land granted to Robt. Parks 28 Sept. 1745 and made over with other lands in Johnson (Johnston) and Anson to John Spann and registered in Bladen.
George Little, Robert Abrams

Page 330--25 March 1758. Charles Burnet and wife, Anne, to James Gamble; 36 pounds; 300 acres, land he purchased of Thos. McElhony, on north side of Catawba River.   [S.C.]
John Crockett, Robt McClenachan

Page 361--Oct. 24, 1758. Thomas Land, of Anson, to Robert McClenachan, of same, for 30 pounds, 427 acres on south side of the north branch of Rockey Creek, adj. Thos. Burns.
James Robinson, Repentance Townsend

Page 366--Oct. 6, 1758. Thos. Land and wife, Elinor, of Anson, to George Sliger, of same, for 50 pounds, part of 193 acres conveyed from Robert McClenachan to Thomas Land by virtue of a patent, dated Feb. 25, 1754, on west side of Catawba River at Caspar Culp's corner, and thence down the river.
Robt. McClenachan, Wm. Taylor

ABSTRACTS OF DEEDS

Page 368--Feb. 3, 1759. William Terry,[Sav. Cr.] of Anson, to Cornelius Robinson, of same, for 50 pounds Va. currency, 300 acres on south side of Peedee, begin. at river opposite land of James Denson, granted Hugh Larrimor March 14, 1745 and by him conveyed to Sam'l Martin June 10, 1750; from him to Townsend Robinson; from Townsend Robinson to William Terry.
James Alley, Shadrach Denson,
Chas. Robinson

---

1. Cumberland Co. (N.C.) D.B. 2-16. 10 May 1752, Nicholas Smith, of Bladen, for £ 30 Va. money, to Thos. Collins, of same, 450 acres south of Deep River on Buck Creek, whole of pat., it being the land and plantation where the sd Nicholas Smith settled and cleared on. Wit: Thos. Richardson, Robt. Love. Prov. 12 Oct.-1754:

2. Dyson and Denson seem interchangeable. The Dyson Creek of the records, on current maps, is Denson's Creek.

3. The natural conclusion that Capt. William Terry was William Terry, of Savannah Creek, is upheld by the following facts: William Terry, of Savannah Creek on the Peedee, was a neighbor and associate of Samuel Wilkins, from whom he bought in 1750 his homeplace of 300 a and to whom "Capt. William Terry" sold the two tracts of land, and of the Densons from whom he bought one of the tracts and to whom the other was originally granted; for these tracts he paid "£ 40 sterling money of Great Britain" 29 Oct. 1757, and on 27 Oct. 1756 he had received from Thos. Cockran £ 30 sterling money of Gr. Britain, for a 300-acre grant on Mountain Cr. (In those days a man could be spotted by the sterling he possessed. Most land sales were made for proclamation (N.C.) or Va. money); on June 18, 1759, William Terry and Mary Terry witnessed a deed from Mathew Raiford, of Anson, to Robt. Raiford, of Cumberland, for land in Cumberland, proved Oct. Court in Cumberland by William Terry, (who was there probably to leave his wife and children with her mother, Mourning Raiford, while he and his company were ranging against the Cherokees); in 1759, William Terry also made a deed gift of his plantation on Savannah Creek to his only son, James, then a boy 13 years old. In 1760, Capt. William Terry and company were paid £ 36 for ranging in the Cherokee expedition. (N.C. State Rec. Vol. 22-822). On the other hand, there is nothing in the records to connect William Terry, who lived east of the Peedee, with the deed from "Capt. William Terry" to Samuel Wilkins. (Ref. for Cumb. deed; Bk1-326). Besides, William Terry, of Hitchcock's Creek, was generally called William Terry, Jr. about this time.

4. Spanish Census, 1792, Natchez District, West Fla. (Miss.) On Bayou Pierre (now Claiborne Co.) Jacabo Cobbun (Cobun), Samuel Cobbun, Juan Burnet, Daniel Burnet. Hist. of Miss., the Heart of the South, by Dunbar Rowland, Vol. 1-326. Samuel Cobun married Margaret Burnett, sister of John and Daniel Burnett (Will of Daniel Burnett, Claiborne Co. Miss. Dec. 28, 1826-May 15, 1827; grandchildren; Geo. W. Humphreys, stepson; sister Jane Bonner; bro-in-law, Dr. Thos. Anderson; nephews Samuel and John B. Cobun, niece Kitty Cobun; brothers, David and John.)

DEED BOOK B #1

Page 164--June 2, 1750. Sam'l Arnold, of Anson, to John McDonald, of same, on north side of the Peedee, beg. at mouth of Little River, the upper side thereof.
Absolem Macdaniel, Wm Hallam

Page 181--Dec. 8, 1751. Thos. Reed [Redd], of Bladen Co. to William Terrey, [E-Pd], for 20 pounds Va. money, 100 acres on north side of Peedee, at Thos. Jones's lower corner, granted to Thos. Reed Nov. 1746.
John Scoff, John McCoy,
Joseph White

Page 198--17 Oct. 1751. Thos. Hopper, of Anson, to John Smith, [Little River], of same, for 35 pounds Va. currency, 200 acres on east side of Little River begin. below mouth of Thicketty Creek, granted Oct. 6, 1751.
Henry Downes, Gilbert Hayes,
Wm. Downes

Page 223--21 April 1752. William Smith, of Anson County, St. George's parish, planter, to Benjamin Smith, of same, for 35 pounds proc. 380 acres, south side of the Peedee ... Thos. George's line, granted Wm. Smith 28 Sept. 1750.

ABSTRACTS OF DEEDS

Wit: John Leath,
M. Brown

Page 226--20 Jany. 1751. Jacob Paul to James Terry, for 30 pounds 300 acres on north side of Peedee above mouth of Hitchcocks Creek, gr 7 Oct. 1748.
Wm. Terrey, Henry Bedinfield

Page 240--23 April 1748. Joseph White and Margaret, his wife, to Sam'l Wilkins, all of Anson, for 20 pounds Va. money, 300 acres in the Parish of St. George, Anson Co., on south side of Great Peedee, beg. at mouth of Savannah Creek... to river and down same to beginning.
John Dunn, Saml. Davis

Page 292--15 Jany. 1753. Benjamin Dumas to Edmond and Sarah Lilly, for 5 sh. and fatherly love for his child, 350 acres north of the Peedee, beg. in Buffelow Island.
Thomas George, Jeremiah Dumas, David Dumas, Benj. Dumas

Page 294--15 July, 1753. Isaac Norman to James Pickett, both of Anson Co. for 30 pounds Virginia money, plantation on south side of the Peedee where Isaac Norman lived about three years, conveyed to him by Joseph White by deed, in Bladen Office.
Antho. Hutchins, M. Brown

Page 295--20 July, 1753. John Clark to Chas. Robertson, Caleb Howell and Andrew Pickens, Justices for Anson County, 5 acres, for use of Anson County, a site for courthouse, etc.
Wit: A.F. Smith, Joseph White

Page 295--23 Oct. 1752. Thos. Redd, of Augusta in ye Province of Georgia, appoints trusty friend, Joseph White, lawful attorney, to keep, get possession of, etc. of any or all of my lands in Anson County, more especially that tract at Mount Pleasant where Caleb Howell now resides unlawfully, etc.
Sam'l Davis, Henry Hendry,
Anthy. Hutchins

Page 296--Jany. 16, 1753. Edmund Cartledge to William Terry, [E-PD], for 2 pounds 10 shillings, 12-1/2 acres, part of a tract patented to Thos. Jones 10 April, 1745.
Alex. Osburn, James Carter

Page 306--June 22, 1753. George Ronicks [Renick] and Mary, his wife, of Anson Co. to John Wilson, of same, land in Anson south side of south fork of Catawba River, 300 acres, granted to sd. Ronicks April 2, 1753. S.C.
Jno. Thomas, William Watson

Page 340--17 Jany. 1754. Daniel Touchstone, to Benj. Smith, both of Anson, for 20 pounds sterling 100 acres in Anson on the south side of the Peedee.
Chas. Betty, Jno. Dunn

Page 342--17 Jany 1754. Benj. Smith, to William and Zacheriah Phillips, all of Anson, for 25 pounds sterling, 260 acres, on Brown's Cr. below Thos. George.
John Dunn, James McDugal

Page 352--5 Sept. 1759. Francis McIllwean to John Leeth, both of Anson, for 30 pounds Va. money, 200 acres gr. to Francis McIlwean 11 Apr. 1749; from sd McIlwean to Samuel French; fr. him to Francis by deed, Jany. 17, 1750/1; on south side of Peedee, both sides of Cedar Creek.
Anthony Hutchins, M. Brown

Page 353--8 Aug. 1753. Henery Downs, of Anson, to Richard Downs, for 20 pounds Va. money, 100 acres, part of 500 acres granted Robert Mills, west side of Little River.
John Stone, Benj. Vines

Page 384--17 Jany. 1755. John White* to Robt. McCorkel, both of Anson, for 15 pounds Va. money, 300 acres in the Par. of St. George, Anson Co. on north side of the Catawba River, adj. William White and Joseph White.
David White, Stephen White,
Benj. Jokoy (?)   *Indexed as Joseph White

Page 431--July 4, 1754. Robert McClenachan,[1] of Anson, to Thos. Land,[1] of same, for 10 pounds lawful money of Great Britain, 213 acres west of the Catawba River, patented to McClenachan Feb. 7, 1754.
Chas. Robinson,[1] William Fleming,
James Patton

Page 510--15 Oct. 1754. Torrance Carrel to John Leeth, both of Anson, ____ Va. money, ____ acres gr. Henry Falkenburg 6 April, 1750; by him conveyed (to Carrel).
Morgan Brown, William Downs

Page 512--Jany. 10, 1754. John Kimbrough, of Anson, to William Little for 150 Va. money, 640 acres on Pedee purchased of John Westerfield.
Nath'l Kimbrough, Edmond Irby, Jeremiah Atwood

ABSTRACTS OF DEEDS

Page 515--8 March 1754. Henry Bedinfield to Wm. Little, for 10 pounds Va money, 200 acres, north of Peedee, on Solomon Hues line, gr. sd Bedinfield 25 Feb. 1754.
Wit: Edmond Irby, Goldman Kimbrough, William Bedinfield

Page 520--4 July, 1751. Sam'l Martin to Townsend Robinson,[1] 300 acres on south bank of Peedee, beg. above mouth of Little River.
Patrick Ker, Lawrence Bryan, James Pickett[2]

---

[1]. The Robinsons, (Charles and Townsend), Robert McClenachan, Repentance Townsend, Andrew and John Pickens, Thomas and John Land were all from Augusta Co. Va. as were many other early settlers whose Anson Co. land grants fell in S. C. (See: The Expansion of Upper South Carolina by Robt. L. Meriwether.)

[2]. Apparently the first record of James Pickett in Anson County. His first purchase was 100 acres fr. Isaac Norman July 15, 1753.

DEED BOOK C#1

Page 71--March 16, 1754. Peter Smith, of Anson, to James Land, of same, for 20 pounds, sterling, 340 acres on both sides of Rocky Creek in said county, patented to said Smith April 6, 1753.
Wm. Pickens, Patrick Ker, [S.C.] John Kenedy

Page 209--28 Oct. 1755. Henry Falkenbourg, of Anson, to James Pickett, for 27 pounds Virginia money, 200 acres, part of 500 acres in Anson formerly Bladen granted to Joseph White, Sept. 26, 1746, on the south side of the Peedee, John Leeth's corner; from White to Falkenborg 2 April 1748.
Morgan Brown, Antho. Hutchins

Page 245--20 July 1755. Tilman Helms, of Anson, to William Terry Esq., of same, for 25 pounds proc., 150 acres on the north side of Little River opposite an Island called Cheeks, granted to John McCoy 11 Oct. 1749.
Morgan Brown, Elizabeth Brown

Page 251--30 July 1755. Townsend Robinson to James Pickett, both of Anson, for 34 pounds Virginia money, 200 acres on south side of Peedee above ye mouth of Little River about a half-mile above the wagon ford, being the tract conveyed by Nicholas Smith to said Townsend Robinson.
William Harrison, John Dunn

Page 325--29 July 1758. Anthony Hutchins, of Anson, to James Pickett, Jr. of same, for 100 pounds province money, 200 acres, part of 500 acres patented to Joseph White 26 Sept. 1746, corner of Leeth's land, being part of same tract, conveyed by deed from Joseph White unto Henry Falkenburg Apr. 2, 1740; unto James Pickett 20 Oct. 1755; by James Pickett to Anthony Hutchins 20 May 1757; also 100 acres on south side of Peedee whereon said James Pickett now lives, conveyed by Isaac Norman to James Pickett 15 July 1753; to Anthony Hutchins 20 Jany 1757; also a tract patented to Nicholas Smith on the south side of the Peedee above the mouth of Little River beginning above the Waggon Ford, conveyed by deed to Townsend Robinson to James Pickett; by Pickett to A. Hutchins 20 Jany. 1757.
Jno Hamer, Violet Primrose, Thos. Primrose

Page 328--10 July 1758. Edmund Cartledge to William Blewett for 100 pounds... on Cartledge's Creek.
M. Brown, James Downing, William Terry

Page 332--24 Aug. 1750. Samuel Wilkins to William Terry, both of Anson, for 20 pounds Va. money, 300 acres on the south side of the Peedee River at the mouth of Savannah Creek, gr. to Joseph White Nov. 22, 1746.
Richard Downs, Richard Yarbrough, John Freman

Page 430--John and Mary Withrow to Robt. Pritchet, for 10 pounds, 300 acres north of the Broad River, pat. to John Withrow 4 Sept. 1753.
Saml. Young, Luke Dean

ABSTRACTS OF DEEDS

Page 435--13 Nov. 1758. William Terry and Mary Terry, his wife, to Matthew Reford, all of Anson, for 60 pounds, 150 acres north of the Peedee, opposite an island formerly called Cheek's, granted to John McCoy 11 Oct. 1749.
Richard Yarbrough, Chas. Cox

On the last page of Bk. C#1

"So ends Book C; N 3 [No 3]

by me Robt. Harris Jun

Oct. 10, 1759"

****

---

1. Tilman Helms (D.B. "C#1"-245) sold this land to William Terry, Esq. hence it was William Terry, of Savannah Creek (wife Mary) who was Justice of Peace (Esquire) 1755-1756.

DEED BOOK 5

Page 29--8 Aug. 1758. William Terry, [E-PD], of Anson, to James Terry, for 40 pounds current money, tract granted Thos. Redd.
Henry Downs, Benj. Martin, Sam'l O. Bryan

Page 33--26 Oct. 1756. William Terry, Esq. to Wm. Byrd, both of Anson, for 30 pounds 300 acres beg. at Thos. Stafford Williams on the south bank of Hitchcock's Creek.
Tow Robinson, Matthew Raiford

Page 102--21 Jany. 1758. Thomas Land and Eleanor, his wife, of Anson County, S.C. [sic] to Alex. Rattery of Craven Co., S.C. for 7 pounds 100 acres west side of Catawba River, purchased from John Linard, adj. James Rattery, Robt. McClenachan.
James Patton, Robt. McClenachan

Page 105--2 April 1758. Wm. Stone to Sam'l Parsons, both of Anson, 20 pounds 100 acres on both sides of Little River of Great Peedee, in Anson County, joining tract Parsons bought of Stone, pat. 20 March 1757.
John Cockeral, Wm. Crittenden, Eleanor Crittenden

Page 111--22 Nov. 1757. Wm. Byrd to Jonathan Llewellyn, both of Anson, for 30 pounds 300 acres, northeast of Peedee, Thos. Stafford Williams corner, east br. of Hitchcock's Cr., gr. Richd. Bradford 15 Mch. 1756; by him to Wm. Terry; from Wm. Terry to Byrd.
Wit: Will Terry, Will Blewett,
    E. Cartledge

Page 112--28 Oct. 1758. Anthony Hutchins, of Anson, executor of will of John Leeth, to James Pickett, Jr. land sold at sale to discharge debts, 200 acres on south side of the Peedee, both sides of Cedar Creek, pat. 11 Apr. 1749; to Francis Macklewean; to Samuel French; reconveyed to Mackelwean; to John Leeth, dec'd.
John Collson, Benj. Rennolds

Page 122--22 June 1756. John Span of Anson Co. to Ambrose Joshua Smith, of Rowan Co. N.C. three tracts, 1200 acres on Peedee River and Little River, for 150 pounds Va. Currency.
John Culpepper, Abraham Hay

Page 267--8 Aug. 1759. Samuel Macby, of Anson, to Thos. Harrington, of same, 100 acres north side of Peedee, granted to him 17 March 1756, on north side of Cheek's Creek.
Jacob Cockerham, Chas. Robinson

Page 147--21 July 1758. Thos. Leonard to Davis Leonard, both of Anson, for 15 pounds 220 acres on west side of Catawba, part of tract on which the said Thos. Leonard lives.
James Patton, Robt. McClenachan

Page 318-- [No date] Wm. Terry, of Anson Co., for love to my well-beloved and dutiful son, James Terry, 300 acres on south side of Great Peedee in St. George's Parish, at mouth of Savannah Creek
                                    signed Will. Terry
Nicholas Bond, James Alley,
James Culcaster

ABSTRACTS OF DEEDS

Page 153--26 Aug. 1760. Thos. McKelhenny and wife, Jean, to Wm. Richardson, for 30 pounds 150 acres on north side of Catawba, part of a patent 3 April 1752.
Robt. McClenachan, S.C.
Samuel Dunlap, Sam'l Thompson

Page 154--19 July 1760. James Robinson and wife, Hannah to Robert Gant Tyler, all of Anson.
Robt. McClenachan, Eliz. Sellers, Richard Hughs

Page 157--28 Oct. 1760. Robert McClenachan and wife, Elizabeth, to John Castolo, for 20 pounds, 100 acres west of Catawba, adj. Thomas Williams, part of 939 acres. S.C.
Wit: Samuel Thompson, Wm. Kennedy, Jacob Taylor

Page 164--20 Sept. 1759. John Brown, of Anson, to Jordan Gibson, of same, for 50 pounds, 300 acres on north side of Hitchcock's Cr. adj. John Crawford, James Halls, inc. Abraham Sellers improvement, gr. 6 Mch. 1759.
M. Brown, James Brown

Page 165--10 Dec. 1760. Thos. Conally, of Anson, to John James, for 30 pounds 300 acres northeast of Peedee, on Long Br. of Hitchcock's Cr. gr. sd Conally 5 Dec. 1760
Wit: M. Brown, Eliz. Brown

Page 169--20 May, 1760. George Renick and Mary, his wife, to Abraham Scott, all of Anson, 400 acres on south side of Catawba on north fork of Fishing Creek, called Wild Cat Branch, granted Geo. Renick 28 Mch. 1753.

Page 170--4 July 1759. James Pickett, Jr. to James Pickett, Sr. both of Anson, for 90 pounds, 200 acres, part of 500 acres granted to Joseph White, Sept. 1746. [Same lands described in deed from Anthony Hutchins to James Pickett, Jr. Bk. C#1, page 325.]
Wit: Jesse Sumerall, Anthony Hutchins

Page 171--10 June, 1759. James Pickett, Jr., of Anson Co., to Joel Phillips, of same, for 35 pistoles 200 acres on south side of Peedee, on both sides of Cedar Cr., gr. Francis McElwean 11 Apr. 1749; by him to Saml. French; and back to McElwean 17 Jany. 1750; and by him to John Leeth, dec'd., and sold by Anthony Hutchins, exor. of John Leeth.
John Collson, Benj. Rennolds, Anth. Hutchins

Page 357--14 Apr.1759. John Poston, Sr. to John Cole, Jr., for 15 pounds, 100 acres on N.E. side of Peedee near Wm. Terry, Jr., on lower cr. on south side of Hitchcocks Creek.
Benj. Martin, Stephen Cole.

Page 176--7 Nov. 1759. Joseph White, Sr. to James Denson, Jr. for 20 pounds, 100 acres on south side of Peedee beg. below the Waggon Ford, pat. dated 1749 and conveyed by sd Gregs (sic) to Joseph White.
Sha Denson, Zach Phillips

Page 197--10 July, 1757. Thos. Land and Eleanor, his wife, of Anson, to John Lee, for 16 pounds, 546 acres on south side of the Catawba, north side of north fork of Rockey Creek, pat. to Townsend Robinson 3 Oct. 1755, transferred to Land 20 Oct. 1756.
Jno. Sallis, Robt. McClenachan

Page 209--9 Apr. 1755. Samuel Wilson, of Anson, to John Parker, of Rowan Co., for 100 pounds, land in Anson on Clark's River, at the mouth of Fisher's Creek.
Pierce Costillo, Pershanna Sherrill

Page 211--25 Sept. 1758. Thos. Land, of Anson, to Thos. Addison, of same, for 20 pounds, 100 acres, part of tract conveyed to Land by John Leonard 6 April 1753, on which Sam'l. Waggoner hath made some improvement, west side of the Catawba.
R. Downs, Robt. McClenachan

Page 216--10 April, 1758. Henry Walker to Aaron Smith, for 30 pounds, 75 acres on south side of the Peedee, upper side of Robt. Park's land on Walker Island, to land Walker sold James Adams, dec'd., part of 300 acres gr. to John Giles, Nov. 26, 1746.
John Hall, Wm. Gamble, Robt. Lee

Page 225--27 Sept. 1758. Thos. Land, of Anson, to Repentance Townsend, for 5 pounds and other good causes and considerations, land 20 x 24 poles on west side of Catawba, part of a tract conveyed by Robt. McClenachan to said Thos. Land.
Robt. McClenachan, R. Downs

Page 240--10 July, 1755. James Willson to James Patton, for 25 pounds, 424 acres in Anson Co. on south side of the Catawba, on Allison's Creek, pat. 31 Aug. 1753.
Charles Cogdell, Sam'l. Young

34 ABSTRACTS OF DEEDS

Page 255--31 July, 1759. George Helliams [Helms] to John Parnold, for 10 pounds, 25 acres east of Little River of Peedee.
Dennis Nowland, Richard Yarbrough, Mary Ann Francis

Page 296--5 Jany. 1759. James Armstrong and Jean, his wife, to Wm. Smith for 15 pounds, 229 acres, adj. Beaver Dam Creek that runs into the south fork of the Catawba, granted to James Armstrong 30 Aug. 1753.
Martin Armstrong, John Thomas

Page 310--15 Jany. 1760. Repentance Townsend[2] and wife, Mary, to John Lants [Land], for 5 pounds, part of land, 20 x 24 poles, conveyed from Robt. McClenachan to Thos. Land, bearing patent date 25 Feb. 1754, and also by deed conveyed by said Land unto Repentance Townsend.
Robt. McClenachan, Joseph Steel

Page 367--6 Feb. 1761. Henry Downs, of Anson Co., N.C. to James Shepperd, of Halifax Co., Va., for 10 pounds Va. money, 100 acres southwest of the Peedee on River bank, beg. tree of tract surveyed for Wm. Phillips.
Bentley Franklyn, James Parsons, James Gouldsbury

Page 109--27 Oct. 1756. Wm. Terry, [Esq.] to Thomas Cockroon, both of Anson, for £ 30 sterling of Gr. Britain; 300 acres, north of Peedee, north side of South Fork of Mt. Cr. pat. to Wm. Terry 27 Sept. 1756. Wit: Matthew Raiford, Tillotston Kebelson (?). (No probate)

1. Will of William Magbee, of Halifax Co., Antrim Parish, Virginia. 20 Aug. 1758. Exrs: wife Susannah, sons James and Matthias Magbee. To son Vadry 200 acres; son James 200 acres; son Matthias 200 acres; son Samuel 1 sh; dau. Elizabeth Howard 1 sh; dau. Johannah Walters 1 sh; dau. Mary Austin 1 sh. Wit: Richard Davis, Henry Farmer, Christopher Snead. Proved 10 March 1759 by Susannah Magbee, relict, and James Magbee; the other exr. not of age of twenty-one. Christopher Snead and Richard Davis, subscribing wit. proved same. Robert Walters and Abraham Little securities for the exrs. Test. John Currie, clk of Hal. Co. Will Bk "O"-55, Halifax County, Va.
Of the above: Vadry Magby (McBee) settled in Spartanburg County, S. C. (Spartanburg Co. Rec. passim); James McBee a signer of pet. from Anson Co. to Assembly, on land grants wh. fell within S. C. No date. Between articles dated 1775. N. C. Col. Rec. Vol. 9-1260-62; Samuel Mackby, land gr. Anson Co. 17 Mch. 1756 (Rachel Magby and Vardry Magby in 1790 Census of Anson Co. prob. widow and son of Samuel); the Walters and Austins of Anson prob. gr-sons of Wm; will of Matthew McBee, Spartanburg Co. S.C., Jan. 9, 1818-Oct. 23, 1818 prob. the same as Mathias, as identical l.g. made to Mathias and to Mathew McBee indicate they were.
2. Jany. 6, 1773. Repentance Townsend witness to a deed by Henry and Elizabeth Neely to James Young. Laurens Co. S. C. Deeds. Bk "A"-7, (1767-1789)

DEED BOOK 6

Page 1--1 Jany. 1761. Benj. Smith to William Crittenden, for 25 pounds, 100 acres south west of Great Peedee...Young's land...Robt. Park's... to Thos. George's upper back corner...to Wm. Yearby (Irby)'s corner.
Robt. Lea,   [No probate]
Wm. Yearby [Irby], Zach. Phillips

Page 15--May 1761. John Smith [L.R.] to William Smith, both of Anson, for 25 pounds, 100 acres northeast side of Peedee, south side of Little River. .. Thos. Holmes... Thicketty Creek.
Wm. Queen, Margaret Queen, Richard Downs

Page 10--4 May 1761. Wm. Pellam [Pelham] to John Helms, for 32 pounds, tract granted to William Holton, 200 acres, north side of Great Buffalo Creek of Little River.
Chas. Robinson, George Helms

Page 176--4 Jany. 1762. Wm. Crittenden to Benj. Smith, for 25 pounds, 100 acres on southwest side of Peedee... Young's Island.
Marget Irby, Peter Presler[1], Shadrack Hogan

ABSTRACTS OF DEEDS 35

Page 91--4 May 1761. James Goldsby, of Anson Co., to James Shepherd of Co. Allifax (Halifax, Va.), for 20 pounds, 200 acres northeast of Peedee, or Rumpas Fork of Little River.
Jacob Shepherd, James Pickett, Jr.
Wm. Pickett

Page 139--2 March 1761. Jacob Coburn and wife, Mary, to Bostin Best, all of Anson, tract north of south fork of Catawba.
Wit: James Moore, Jean Thomas,
John Thomas

Page 78--July 17, 1760. John Wilson, of Anson, to Robt. Adams, of Rowan, for 26 pounds 10 sh., land in Anson on the south side of the Catawba River below George Cathey's claim, 350 acres, on a branch of Allison's Creek, adj. Joseph Clark's land and Joseph Davis's, being a grant to Renick and released unto Wilson.
John Thomson   [S.C.]
Alex. Lewis

Page 154--3 Oct. 1761. Joel Phillips, of Anson, to Nicholas Smith, of Cumberland Co., for 10 pounds, 200 acres on the southwest side of Peedee...Wm. Powell...Gould's fork...granted Dec. 5, 1760.
Wm. Reed, Chas. Robinson

Page 86--10 Jany. 1760. Jacob Lipham, of Anson Co., to William Black, Jr., son to William and Helen, daughter of George Metland, merchant of Aberdeen, for 30 pounds, 240 a. granted Jacob Lipham 6 March 1759.
John Crawford, Chas. Thompson,
Andrew Preslar

Page 41--10 Jany. 1761, William Terry, [Savannah Cr.], of Anson, to Sam'l Wilkins, of same, for £6, 50 acres, begin. at James Denson's corner near the ferry landing, pat. to William Terry 5 Dec. 1760.
Jer. Terry   John Grinnan,
Lauréance Franklin

Page 4--May 1, 1760. James McClellan of Anson and wife, Jennet, to John Burnet, of Rowan, for £10; 300 acres north of Catawba, adj. John Bravard.
Wit: Robt. Tinnes, John Brandon,
John Patterson, John Nesbit

Page 9--2 March 1761. William Holton to Charles Smith for 11 pounds, 100 acres on northeast side of Peedee on Big Creek.
Wit: Thos. Harrington, Sam'l. Parsons

Page 73--July 1, 1761. Alexr. Gordon, Esq., of Anson to Stephen Cole, of Bladen Co. for £ 5; one-half acre in Prince George Town in Anson; Cole to put building on lot and pay rent 4 sh.6d per year.
Wit: John Culcaster, Wm. Temple Cole[3]

Page 98--31 Jany. 1761. John Crouch to Nath'l Dennis, of Anson, on west side of Thicketty Creek, 100 acres.
John Smith, L.R., Archibald Black,
F. C. Downer

Page 108--30 Jan. 1761. Thos. Sugg and wife, Mary, to Thomas Randolph, for 11 pounds proc., patent to Sugg July 1, 1758, on Little River, 100 acres.
Thos. Sugg, Joseph Attaway,
Thos. Franklin

Page 132--May 1, 1761. Nath'l Hillen to Nath'l Hillen, Jr. for 70 pounds Proc. northeast of Peedee beg. above the mouth of Little River at Nicholas Smith's upper corner...to Jacob Collson's line. granted John Collson, 400 acres.
Zacheriah Smith, Francis Cooper

Page 166--20 July 1761. John Lants [Land] and Catherine, his wife, of Anson, to Jacob Culp, tract 20 x 24 poles on Mill Creek, conveyed to Robert McClenachan by Thos. Lands and also from him to the said John Lants 15 Jany. 1760.
Wm. Temple Coles,   [Chester Co., S.C.]
Robt. McClenachan, John Smith

Page 232--15 Sept. 1758. Samuel Coburn and Margaret, his wife, to John Richman, for 12 pounds, 200 acres south of Catawba, adj. lower end of where Sam'l. Coburn lives; gr. to him Aug. 30, 1753.
Andrew Barry, Richard Barry,
Jennet Barry

Page 206--11 Feby. 1761. Benj. Roberts, of Anson Co., to William Queen, of same, 100 acres, 30 pounds; part of a tract of 200 acres gr to Robert Mills 24 Mch. 1747.
Sam'l Ratcliff, Wm. Jones

Page 278--John Harvey and Mary, his wife, to Wm. Cleghorn, for 30 pounds land on the south side of the Catawba River and on Cain Creek, 280 (acres)
                                        Chester Co. S.C.
John Arnolpender [John Arnold Pender]
Wm. Baird
Andrew Pickens

Page 302--22 Nov. 1758. Sam'l Cobren [Coburn] and wife, Margaret, to William Cleghorn, for 25 pounds, 378 acres on south side of the Catawba above Sam'l Cobren'l land on Tuckasegee path, being granted to Judith Cobren 30 Aug. 1753 and conveyed by her and her husband John Clemmons to Sam'l Cobren 28 Dec. 1755.
Wm. Haecker, John Thomas

Page 210--4 Aug. 1761. John Smith [L.R.], of Anson, to Jasper Smith, of same, for 35 pounds Virginia money, 200 acres on east side of Little River of Peedee below mouth of Thickety Creek, conveyed to John Smith by Thos. Hopper 6 Oct. 1748.
Sam'l Parsons, R. Downs

Page 174--26 Jany. 1762. Shadrack Jacobs to Zacheriah Smith, both of Anson; for 40 pounds; 200 acres northeast of Little River, on Townsend Fork of Cheek Cr. gr Jno. Butler 5 Dec. 1760; to Low; to Richard Yarbrough; to Jacobs.
Wit: Shadrach Denson, Joseph Jones

Page 221 (115)--26 Sept. 1761. John Cartwright to John McDaniel, both of Anson; £12; 100 acres north of Peedee; Francis' corner.
Wm. Terry, Mary Terry

Page 248--30 March, 1758. Edward Givens and wife, Agnes, to Matthew McCorcle: 100 pounds; two surveys, south of Beaver Dam Cr., north of Catawba River, where Mathew McCorcle now lives.
Wit: Andrew Barry

Page 392--17 June, 1762. Aaron Smith to Wm. Crittenden, both of Anson; 51 pounds; 75 acres south of Peedee, pat. to John Giles, and 50 acres adj. same, patented to Aaron Smith 5 Dec. 1760.
W. Terry, Andrew Preslar, Francis Smith

Page 432--20 Oct. 1756. Townsend Robinson, of Anson, to Thomas Land,⁴ of same, 546 acres on south side of Catawba on north side of south fork of Rockey Creek, granted 3 Oct. 1755. [Top part is missing.].
Thos. Prestwood, Robert Kerr

Page 380--March 5, 1762. Thos. Davis, of Anson, to John Wilson, of same, for 21 pounds, 200 acres in Anson on Clark's Creek, north side of Peedee.
Edmund Lilly, David Snead

Page 385--May 10, 1762. John Parker, of Rowan Co. to Sam'l Wilson, of Anson for 100 pounds, 400 acres on south side of Clerk's Creek, at mouth of Fisher's Creek.
Robt. Harris, Sr., Stephen Jones, Robt. Harris, Jr.

Page 434--14 May 1762. Sam'l Parsons to Henry Tippins, both of Anson, for £10, one... acres, on both sides of north fork of Little River, part of grant to Wm. Stone, Oct. 3, 1755.
J. Pickett, Jr., Nicholas Bond, Samuel Parson

Page 425--8 Jany. 1760. John Elkins to Wm. Watkins, both of Anson, for £10 Va. money, 100 acres on Hitchcocks Creek.
Wit: Benj. Mims, Marshall Diggs, Israel Snead

Page 290--8 May 1762. Chas. Beaty, of Anson, to James Young, of Augusta Co., Va., for £20, 795 acres on north side of Catawba.
Matthew Young, S.C.
Francis Beaty, James Watson

Page 40--27 Feb. 1758. Sam'l Beason to James McAfee,ᶜ of the Province of N.C., for £13/13, 230 acres in Anson County, on north side of Catawba River, on south side of Clark's Cr., adj. Preston Goforth.
Wit: John Patton, Alex. Lewis

Page 114--14 Dec. 1761. Nicholas White, to James Short, both of Anson, for £10, 100 acres in Anson, sw of Peedee, on north side of Jones Creek, crossing McDaniel's branch, gr. 5 Dec. 1760.
Wit: James Pickett, John Pickett

Page 113--6 Aug. 1761. Shadrach Jacobs to Eliee Yarbrough, both of Anson, for £20, 100 acres in Anson west of Little River of Peedee, adj. Chas. Robinson, gr. Shadrach Jacobs by George Clemons, by his pat. 4 Apr. 1750. Signed by Shadrach Jacobs and Patty Brian Jacobs.
Wit: Henry Touchstone, Zacheriah Smith

Page 117--26 July 1759. Patrick Saunders to Little Bird Shepherd, both of Anson, 100 acres gr. William Terry, Esq. 27 Sept. 1756, containing 300 acres; fr. Terry to Cochran; fr. Cochran to Saunders; 100 acres fr. Saunders to Shepherd, beg. on Mt. Creek.
Wit: M. Brown, Paul Barringer, George Pennington

Page 203--5 Aug. 1761. Jonathan Helms to Ailee Yarbrough, both of Anson; £5; 50 acres, west

ABSTRACTS OF DEEDS 37

side of Little River. Wit: John Wilkins, Will Reed Page 205--5 June, 1761. Richard Yarbrough to	Shadrach Jacobs, £20, 100 acres west of Little River. Signed also by Ealie Yarbrough. Wit: John Crawford Wm. Welchear.

---

1. Peter Presley (Presler) in 1792 Spanish Census of the Natchez District, West Fla. (Mississippi) Hist. of Miss., the Heart of the South, by Dunbar Rowland Vol. 1, page 326.
2. Jeremiah Terry was the only Terry to appear in any record of William Terry, of Savannah Cr. and this is the only record of him in Anson County. Was he the Jeremiah Terry who had an English land grant in the Natchez Dist. dated 23 June 1769? John Terry and James Terry who were in the 1792 Spanish Census of the District were probably his sons.
3. William Temple Coles, Sheriff of Rowan, County, allowed his claim, £ 52. 11 Dec. 1770. N. C. State Records Vol. 22, page 861.
4. Chalkley's Chronicles of Augusta County, Va. give Thomas Land and his oldest son, James, in a 1752-3 list to work a new road from Walter Cunningham's to the County line. However the Land family was established by June 1753 on Rocky Cr. a west branch of the Catawba River (now Chester County, S. C.) which Land had purchased as of Anson County. Although the tract was surveyed by N. C. he was uneasy about the title and entered a petition at Charles Town, asking for a S. C. grant of 400 acres for the tract. He declared that he had a wife and six children and had come from the northward to settle in the Province. His petition was granted. (Proceedings of His Majesty's Honourable Council of the Province of S. C., page 461 - 5 June 1753, Charles Town.)
Thomas Land's family consisted of his wife, Eleanor, sons, James, John, William and Benjamin, and two daus. who prob. married Andrew Hemphill and George Morris. (Chester Co. Court Records.)
5. Administration granted on the estate of James McAfee, executors: Robt. McAfee and Joseph Hardin. Inf. Ct. of Tryon County (N. C.) Probate Returns, July 1771, Secy. of State Papers (SS 884) Dept. of Arch. and Hist. Raleigh, N. C.

DEED BOOK 3

Page 1--9 April 1762. Nicholas Smith, of Cumberland County, to Benj. Thompson, for 24 pounds proc., tract on south side of Peedee, begin. on Wm. Powell's line on Gould's Fork, 200 acres granted to said Nicholas Smith 5 Dec. 1760.
John Thompson, John Leverett

Page 2--28 Sept. 1761. William Craig and Sarah Thompson, for natural love and affection, to William Thompson, Elisha Thompson, Mary Thompson, Elizabeth Thompson, and John Thompson, the three sons and two daughters of John Thompson, decd., five young breeding mares and increase to remain in our care until Mary comes to the age of eighteen years which will be Sept. 15, 1769.
John Colson, Sam'l Ratcliff

Page 13--25 Oct. 1763. Jonathan Helms, of Anson Co., to Edward Smith, of same, for 20 pounds, 100 acres on north side of Peedee, the south side of Little Buffalo Creek of Little River.
William Terry, Cons. Robinson,
John Poster

Page 15--3 May 1762. Aaron Smith to William Irby, both of Anson Co. for 40 pounds, 180 acres on south side of Great Peedee above the mouth of Brown's Creek.
John Smith, Anthony Hutchins

Page 22--15 Jany. 1763. Henry Touchstone to Frederick Touchstone, for 20 pounds, 250 acres on east side of Little River, at Lake Island, granted John Francis; from him to Richard Touchstone; from Richard descended to Henry Touchstone, heir-at-law; adj. Christopher Touchstone; part of grant was conveyed to Stephen Touchstone by Richard.
Wit: Matthew Raeford, Chas Robinson

Page 45--27 Sept. 1763. Joseph Oats to William Pickett, both of Anson, for 40 pounds two tracts, 260 acres on south side of Peedee below Brown's Creek...Thos. George's land...the river bank, also 25 acres on south side of the Peedee below the mouth of Brown's Creek on land run out for William Smith,* being all that part belonging to said Joseph Oats below the mouth of Brown's Creek.

ABSTRACTS OF DEEDS

Jas. Pickett
James Terry
*(granted to William Smith 22 Sept. 1750.)

Page 69--21 Nov. 1763. William Irby to Randolph Creek, both of Anson Co., for 50 pounds 180 acres, on south side of Peedee down river to mouth of Brown's creek, confirmed to said Irby by deed.
David Dumas, Benj. Smith,
Macajah Pickett

Page 118 (94)--14 Oct. 1763. Jacob Underwood to Morgan Brown, Jr., 100 acres northeast side of the Peedee River, for 50 pounds.
John Webb, Nicholas White,
George Terry

Page 83--14 May 1763. John Donohoe to John Carpenter, for 10 pounds proc., 100 acres in St. George's Parish, Anson Co., granted to John Donohoe 22 Apr. 1763, on Cabin Creek.
John Jeffrey, John Smith

Page 106--10 Dec. 1763. Thos. Bingham to John Purkins, both of Anson County, for 100 pounds, 200 acres on Brown's Creek on the southwest side of Peedee by the side of old Catawba path.
William Terry, Benj. Jackson

Page 88--8 Dec. 1763. James Denson to James Shepard, for 20 pounds proc., 150 acres, part of a tract granted to James Denson July 26, 1756, on northeast side of the Peedee...at the red bluff.
Dorsey Pentecost, Charles Robinson

Page 111--10 May 1761. James Pickett to William Pickett, both of Anson Co., for 100 pounds proc., 300 acres on south side of the Peedee, one tract on Turkey Cock Creek where Isaac Norman formerly lived, 100 acres; other tract where Henry Falkenburg formerly lived, 200 acres.
Charity Regny, Thos. Dixon

Page 119--9 Feby. 1764. William Crittenden to Joseph Wilkie, both of Anson Co., for 30 pounds, 100 acres on Little River, part of tract granted Robt. Mills 2 Aug. 1758.
John Smith S.H., Sam'l Ratcliff Downs

Page 64--22 Jany. 1763. Sam'l. Davis to George Terry, for 5 pounds Virginia money, 200 acres on north side of Peedee at mouth of Lake Creek* patented to said Davis 24 Dec. 1754.
John Terry, James Terry   *Thicketty Creek
Eliz. Terry

Page 129--3 March 1764. George Terry to William Cole, for 30 pounds proc., 200 acres on north side of the Peedee, granted to Sam'l. Davis 24 Dec. 1754.
John Cole, John Terry,
Joseph Brent

Page 154--11 July 1764. James Terry to Francis Clark, both of Anson, for 10 sh. proc., an acre on north bank of Hitchcock's Creek, condemned by order of court on petition of Thos. Moorman[1] and Francis Clark,[1] for use of their mill, part of 300 acres granted to Jacob Paul (7 Oct. 1748) and conveyed to James Terry (20 Jany. 1751).
Wm. Mask, Edward Smith,
Thos. Moorman

Page 160--4 Aug. 1764. Benjamin Smith, of Anson, to Joseph Murphey, of same, for £40, 100 acres on southwest side of Peedee begin. in Young's Island on river bank...to Robt. Parke's...Thos. George's line, which Thos. George sold to said Smith, up the river to beginning, patented to said Smith Dec. 5, 1760; Smith to retain one-half of gold and silver mines.
Walter Gibson, William Irby

Page 133--11 April 1764. Wm. Crittenden and wife, Sarah, to Francis Smith, for 51 pounds, 75 acres, on south side of Peedee, Robt Parke's upper corner, Walker's Island.
Tirey Robinson, Rich. Dixon

Page 136--19 Feb. 1761. Thos. Armstrong[3] to John Smith, S.H. both of Cumberland County, for £30 proc.; 300 acres on northeast side of Peedee begin. at Great Bluff on southwest side of Little River.
Wm. Ainsworth, David Gordony (Gordon?)

Page 137--26 July 1764. John Check and wife, Jane, of Anson to John Stevens of Cumberland 200 acres beg. above mouth of Browns Creek at John Clark's lower corner, granted to John Collson 26 Nov. 1746; conveyed to John Cheek 12 June 1750.

Page 131--18 June 1765. Joseph Murphey to John Cheek, both of Anson, for 40 pounds, 100 acres, cutting off 25 acres of Thos. George's land which he sold to Benj. Smith, then up the river.
Walter Gibson   signed by Joseph Murphey
Shadrach Hogan*   Valentine Murphey

Page 148--3 July 1764. John Edwards to John Ashley, 100 acres on north side of the Peedee, on

ABSTRACTS OF DEEDS

Cheek's Creek, for £ 30.
J. Pickett, Sam'l. Ray

Page 191--Oct. 23, 1764. Chas. Higdon' to Elizabeth Tallant, £4; 100 acres, part of a grant to Leonard Higdon 1762.
John Pickett, Marshall Digge

Page 200--20 April, 1765. Richard Downs, of Anson Co., N.C., to John Smith, [S.H.], of same, planter, for 20 pounds proc. money, 100 acres part of 500 acres granted Robt. Mills 22 Nov. 1746; from Robt. Mills to Nathan Mills; from Nathan Mills to Henry Downs and by him acknowledged to Richard Downs; west side of Little River, crossing river to Parker's line and to Buffalo Lick.
John Smith [Little River], Joseph Wilkins

Page 266--1 Nov. 1763. William and Mourning Pickett to Cornelius Robinson, for 50 pounds, 300 acres granted to Wm. Phillips on south bank of the Peedee at mouth of Hamer's gut.
J. Pickett, Chas. Robinson

Page 272--20 Sept. 1764. Tilman Helms to Chas. Robinson, both of Anson, for 10 pounds, 50 acres granted Tilman Helms 27 Nov. 1762.
Cornelius Robinson, Thos. Boldin, Zacheriah Smith

Page 205--22 April 1765. Anson Co. N.C. Charles Smith to Henry Williams, for 20 pounds current lawful money, 100 acres on northeast side of the Peedee, pat. to Wm. Walton [Holton] 1 July, 1758, conveyed by Walton [Holton] to Charles Smith by deed Mar. 2, 1761*
Wm. Burt, Roland Williams

Page 331--5 Oct. 1765. Jerome Miller of Anson Co. N.C. to William Raiford, of same, for 40 pounds proc. money, 200 acres on south side of Peedee beg at Wm. Powell's upper line on Gould's Fork.
Pickett[4]
Martha Pickett   Prov. July term 1766.

Page 333--16 Oct. 1765. John Sheppard, of Anson Co. to Matthew McKinne, of Anson, for 20 pounds proc., 200 acres in Anson on Brown's Creek below Matthew McKinnie's improvement... McManness line, granted John Sheppard Apr. 22, 1765.

Page 270--30 Oct. 1764. Wm. Downs, of Berkeley County, S.C. to Henry Downs, of Mecklenburg County, N.C., for 100 pounds proc., 300 acres on west side of Little River near Dyson's line, granted Robt. Mills 22 Nov. 1746.
Thos. Huston, _____ Johns

Page 274--21 July 1764. Elisha Parker Sr. to Elisha Parker Jr., his son, for love and affection, 300 acres northeast of Peedee, begin. at Goodman's upper line...Mark's Creek, granted to Samuel Goodman 17 June 1746.
Morgan Brown, John Thomas

Page 113--21 July 1764. John Ekins, of Craven Co., S.C., to Zachariah Moorman, of Anson, land southwest of Peedee on Rocky River, adj. Wm. Dry.
Joseph Kemp, Thos. Moorman,
Benj. Moorman

Page 291--9 May 1765. William Crittenden, of the Province of S.C. to Joseph Wilkins of Anson County, N.C. for 30 pounds proc., 35 acres on the northeast side of Little River, begin at David Miles upper survey, granted Wm. Crittenden 25 May 1757.
Sam'l Ratcliff, John Smith [Sandhill],
Christopher Christian

Page 293--9 May 1765. Joseph Wilkins, of Anson, to Christopher Christian, of same, for 50 pounds, 100 acres on north side of Peedee on Little River, lower part of tract granted Robert Mills 2 Aug. 1748.
H. Downs, John Pool,
Jacob Sheppard

Page 312--9 May 1765. Joseph Wilkins to Christopher Christian, for 30 pounds, 35 acres on northeast side of Little River, beginning at David Miles upper survey, granted Wm. Crittenden, from him to Joseph Wilkins.
Wm. Young, Joseph Fincher,
J. Downs

Page 337--22 Feby. 1765. Walter Gibson to Shadrach Hogan; both of Anson, for 10 pounds, 100 acres southwest of Peedee and southwest of Rockey River.
Joseph Culpepper   July Term 1765
Elijah Clark[6]

Page 274--21 July, 1764. Elisha Parker for natural love to beloved son, Stephen Parker, my manor plantation 300 acres on north side of Peedee on Mark's Creek, granted William Colson 13 March 1758.
Morgan Brown
John Thomas

ABSTRACTS OF DEEDS

Page 283--29 Jany. 1765. William Pickett, of Anson Co. to John Stevens, of Cumberland, for 80 pounds paid by John Stevens, Jr. son of said John Stevens, 260 acres on south side of the Peedee below mouth of Browns Creek as per deed from Zachary Phillips to Joseph Oats Sept. 5, 1761 and by said Oats to Wm. Pickett 20 Sept. 1763.
Morgan Brown, Wm. Temple Cole

Page 276--20 July, 1764. Sam'l. Parsons and Rachel, his wife, to Haden Morris, for 30 pounds, 100 acres north side of Little River.
Matthew Raiford, Wm. Queen

Page 289 (283)--21 April 1765. David Bruton to Wm. Page, both of Anson, for 12 pounds proc., 100 acres on north side of Denson's fork of Little River above the mill... Sam'l Parson's land, pat. to George Fields 1 Dec. 1760.
Wm. Queen, Wm. Holton,
Mathew Raiford

Page 307--23 July 1765. Tilman Helms, of Anson, to Wm. Burt, of Cumberland County, tract on northeast side of Peedee, south fork of Buffalo Creek, £20; 100 acres.
Thomas Frolock
Henry Williams   July Term 1765.

Page 68 (82)--21 Nov. 1763. Elizabeth Gould, of Bertie County, N.C., sole extrix and heir to the estate of George Gould, dec'd, her late husband, by his last will and testament, to John Campbell, for 20 pounds proc., 640 acres on 3rd northern fork of Jones Creek, east [West] of Peedee, patented to said Gould March 1748.
Robt. Raney, Alex. Ford

Page 24--29 April 1762. Rowland Williams to Jonathan Helms, both of Anson, for 16 pounds proc., 100 acres, northeast of the Peedee, patented to George Helms Oct. 21, 1758 and by Geo. Helms conveyed to Rowland Williams.
Thos. Boldin, Chas Robinson

Page 29--5 Feb. 1762. Sam'l. Wilkins, of Anson to James Sheppard, of Halifax County, Va., 50 acres northeast of Peedee in James Denson's lower corner... down river, including the Ferry landing, as per grant to William Terry Dec. 13, 1760, and conveyed by sd Terry to Samuel Wilkins.
W. Brown, Crto. Cewin [Owen?],
Wm. Wilkins

Page 195--20 March 1765. Tilman Helms, of Anson, to Dennis Nollen [Noland?] of Georgia, for 15 pounds, 150 acres granted Helms 27 Nov. 1762, east of Little River... Chas. Robinson's corner.
Daniel McDaniel, Chas. Robinson

---

1. The Moormans, Clarks and other Quakers settled on Hitchcock and Solomon Creeks and their Meeting House and cemetery was near Hayley's Ferry on the Peedee (The Rockingham Post-Dispatch. The Everett Sketches, July - Oct. 1927.)

2. Bladen County Land Grants, Secy. of State's Office, Raleigh, N. C. #421 Thomas Armstrong 100 acres on the south side of the Adkin (Yadkin) Road where John Nicholas settled; issued 10 April 1753.

3. Natchez Dist. (Miss.) Spanish Records, Bk. "A", p. 245. March 1, 1785. Mary Higdon to son, Jeptha Higdon, gift deed of slaves, cattle, etc., with restrictions. Wit: Stephen Minor, D. Smith (David Smith, son of John Smith, Sandhill, of Anson and Montgomery Cos. The Spanish Records at Natchez are made up of the original papers and the identity of D. Smith is proved by his signature. That of his wife, Margaret Smith, is also recorded there.)

4. James Pickett, son of James Pickett, Sr., signed occasionally simply "Pickett". See Deed Bk. 7, p. 214 when he signed as witness thusly and the deed was proved by "James Pickett".

5. Petition to Assembly of Shadrack Hogan, of Rutherford County, presenting his resignation as Justice of the Peace, signed. July.17, 1789. Test: W. Avery, Clk. R. C., James Gray, J. Willison, Sheriff.

6. Moved to S. C. and then to Wilkes County, Ga. where he became famous as General Elijah Clark.

ABSTRACTS OF DEEDS

DEED BOOK H#1

Page 1--12 July 1766. Philemon Terrill, of South Carolina, to Vann Swearingen, of Anson, for 5 pounds, tract in Anson on Check's Creek, 100 acres granted to John Cannon, Dec. 5, 1760.
Thos. Swearingen   Prov. Jany. Term 1767
Samuel Davis   by Thos. Swearingen
           Sam'l. Spencer C.C.

Page 7--26 Jany. 1767. John Smith, Sandhill, of Anson, to Benjamin Smith, of same, for 10 pounds proc. money, 100 acres on the south side of Brown's Creek, being a part of a tract granted to John Smith Oct. 22, 1762.
Wm. Raford   Ack. by grantor Jany. Term 1767
Sam'l. Parsons   Sam'l Spencer C.C.
J. Pickett

Page 10--26 Jany. 1767. Thos. Swearingen to Vann Swearingen, both of Anson, for 21 pounds, 200 acres in Anson on the Peedee River, adjoining land Thos. Swearingen bought of Richard Caswell, ... Vann Swearingen's Spring branch... across Cheek's Creek.
Samuel Swearingen   Ack. Jany. Term 1767
Sam'l. Swearingen Jr.   Sam'l Spencer C.C.

Page 11--26 Jany. 1767. James Terry to James Sheppard, both of Anson Co. for 100 pounds Va. money, 200 acres on north side of Peedee above mouth of Hitchcock's Creek.
Geo. Wilson   Prov. Jany. Term 1767
John Pickett   by Geo. Wilson.
           Sam'l Spencer C.C.

Page 21--24 Feb. 1767 William Yearby [Irby] and wife, Margaret, to John Stevens, all of Anson County, for 80 pounds, 75 acres on south side of Peedee, beginning at Young's Island on the River bank... Aaron Smith's corner.
         Proven in open court April term 1767.
Abraham Belyeu, Robert Snuggs,
John Cheek

Page 26--7 April 1767. Thos. Randel [Randolph] to Wm. Ussery, both of Anson, for £ 20, 100 acres part of 763 acres at cross roads of Peedee and Cape Fear.
Wm. Mask,   Ack. April Term 1767
Soll. Gross, William Shephard

Page 26--28 April 1767. John Ussery and Elizabeth, his wife, of Anson, to Wm. Leake, of Buckingham Co., Va.; 230 pounds; 300 acres northeast of Peedee, gr. to John Francis 21 June 1746; to Richard Touchstone by him bequeathed to Frederick, Christopher and Steven Touchstone and Haner (Hannah) Steven Touchstone.
Wm. Ussery   Ack. April Term 1767
S. Gross, Rebeckah Mask

Page 30--1767. Wm. Raiford to Rolling (Roland) Williams, both of Anson, for £40, 200 acres south of Peedee on Wm. Powell's line of Gold's fork.
Wit: Stephen Miller   Ack. July Term 1767
Jerome Miller

Page 44--9 Feb. 1767. Wm. Sanders to Jaret (Jared) Elison Gross, both of Anson, for £ 30, 200 acres granted Morgan Brown 26 Nov. 1767,... division line bet. Jaret Elison Gross and John Pellam; signed also by Susan Saunders.
Jas. Shepherd,   Ack. July Term 1767
Solomon Gross, John Ussery

Page 35--27 Oct. 1767. Edward Smith to Dennis Nowlin, both of Anson Co., 25 pounds, 100 acres on the northeast side of Peedee on south side of Little Buffalo that runs into Little River.
Wit: Sam'l Spencer   July Term 1767
Isham Haley

Page 47--28 April 1767. Samuel and Mary Ratcliff to John Smith, [S.H.], all of Anson, for 60 pounds proc. money, 100 acres, part of 300 acres Sam'l Ratcliff bought of Leonard Dison and all that part of said tract below Creek (Cheek?) Creek beginning at the mouth of said creek... to a hickory on west bank of Little River of the Peedee, then up the river to include 100 acres.
Christopher Christian, William Ratcliff

Page 71--20 May 1767. John Almond to Samuel Davis, Jr., both of Anson, for 15 pounds, 100 acres north east of Peedee on Mill Creek. pat. to Sam'l Davis, Sr. in 1760.
John Terry   July Term 1767
Dan'l. Davis, Sam'l. Davis

Page 78--13 July 1767. Wm. Queen, of Anson, to Wm. Mears, of Cumberland Co., for 30 pounds, 100 aeres on southwest side of Peedee, dividing line of Wm. Stone and Wm. Crittenden, part of 200 acres granted to Robt. Mills 24 Mch. 1747 and conveyed by Robt. Mills to Wm. Stone; from Stone to Richard Downs; from Downs to Benj. Roberts; from Roberts to Wm. Queen, which the record will show.
John Smith, Sandhill   Proved July Term 1767
Mary Hount   Reg. Oct. 10, 1767

ABSTRACTS OF DEEDS

Page 42--1 Jany. 1767. Jesse and Anne Bound to James Bound, Jr., all of Anson, for £ 20, land northeast of Falling Creek, adj. Richard Dearman, gr. Jesse Bounds 5 Dec. 1760.
Wit: John Crawford   Ack. July Term 1767
John Coley

Page 53--1 May 1767. John and Jane Cheek to John Stevens, all of Anson, 200 acres on Brown Creek, John Clark's lower corner, gr. to John Collson 1746, for 5 shillings.
Sam'l Spencer   Receipt for 5 sh.
James Spencer   wit. Saml. Spencer.
Ack. July Term 1767.

[See page 137 Bk. 5. Is this to complete that deed?]

Page 80--3 March 1767. George Augustus Selwyn, of Gloucester Co., Great Britain, Esq. son and heir of John Selwyn, Esq., dec'd. to Wm. Phillips, of Anson Co. for £ 6, 65 acres, part of tract of 8 grants, of 100,000 acres form His Majesty King George II to John Selwyn, Esq. on Rockey River, commonly known as Tract Number One. Phillips to pay rents annually. Signed by Henry Eustace McCulloch.
Wit: Thos. Froloch, Wm. Froloch

Plat and survey: Surveyed by Thos Froloch 17 Feb. 1767; on Richardson's Creek near head of Savannah near his house, crossing Creek to contain 65 acres.
Wit: Nathan Erwyn, Ruben Duland

Page 102--2 March 1767. Same as the above for Elijah Clarke, £12, 100 acres on south side of Rockey River, above John Clarke's. Survey and plat, Feb. 15, 1767.
Wit: Thos. Froloch, Wm. Froloch

Page 192--8 April 1768. Thomas Smith and Deborah, his wife, to Nelson Gibson, 10 pounds, 200 acres on north side of Hitchcock's Creek, northeast of Peedee, patented April 1767 to said Smith.
Lawrence Obryen   Prov. by Lawrence Obryen
Wm. Smith   April Term 1768
Sam'l Spencer Clk.

Page 205--13 Jany. 1768. Wm. Stoutly Shirley, of St. Paul's Parish, Province of Georgia, to Micajah Pickett Jr., of the waters of Craven Co. [S.C.] for 20 pounds, tract on northeast side of Peedee River to west side of Cartledge's Creek, granted him 24 Apr. 1762. [no acreage given.]
Isom Hanson   April Term 1768

Eliz. Pickett   Prov. by Eliz. Pickett
John Sutton   Sam'l Spencer Clk.

Page 210--12 Jany. 1768. Wm. Stoutly Shirley, of St. Paul's Parish, Ga. to Micajah Pickett Jr., for 12 pounds, 125 acres granted to Wm. Blewett 6 March 1750, on north bank of Cartledge Creek... to Dry Fork, northeast of Peedee.
Same wit. as above.   April Term 1768
[Two other deeds from same to same on pages 212 & 216.]

Page 235--30 July 1768. Wm. Cole, of Rowan County, to Richard Leak, of Anson, for 50 pounds, 200 acres on Thicketty Creek, each side, patented to Sam'l. Davis 24 Sept. 1754; from Davis to Geo. Terry; from Terry to Wm. Cole Mch. 3, 1764.
Wm. Pickett   Ack. July Term 1768
Chas. Medlock   by Wm. Cole
Marshall Diggs

Page 237--8 Apr. 1767. James and William Pickett to Benj. Ingram, all of Anson, for 160 pounds proc. money, 200 acres on Turkey Cock Creek, part of two tracts on the south side of the Great Peedee, beginning at the mouth of the said creek on the upper side of Nicholas Smith's line.
Wm Dammont, Wm. Mask
Prov. by Wm. Mask July Term 1768
Saml. Spencer Clk.

Page 238--South Carolina, 16 July 1768. John Wright, of Anson to Claddius Pegues, for 334 pounds a negro named Jack.
Wit: John Smith, N.C.
Anson Co.
Ack. in open Court by vendor, Anson Co. July Term 1768.

Memo of estate of John Wright. Public auction, 29 July 1767, for use of James Gordon, merchant, Georgetown [S.C.]
Wit: John Smith. 16 July 1768. Ack. by James Gordon and John Wright in court July 1768.

Page 253--17 Feb. 1768, James Sheppard to Solomon Gross, all of Anson, for 20 pounds, 100 acres on west side of Little River of the Peedee... line of Chas. Robinson, being a grant to George Cleamons, 4 Apr. 1750.
J. Shepherd   Prov. July Term 1768
Jno. Bound   by Jacob Shepherd, witness.
Saml. Spencer, Clk.

ABSTRACTS OF DEEDS 43

Page 261--25 Feb. 1746. John Clark of Bladen County, to Chas. Harrington for 500 pounds, land in Bladen north of great Peedee. [He is also called Chas. Arrington.]
Chas. Robinson   Ack. July Term 1768
Joseph White   Saml. Spencer, Clk.

Page 305--19 May 1767. James Terry, of Anson, to Thos. Wade, merchant, of South Carolina, for £300, 300 acres below mouth of Hitchcock's Creek, pat to Jacob Paul 11 Oct. 1748.
Wit: Geo. Wilson   Prov. Anson Oct. Term 1768
Thos. Moorman   by Geo. Wilson
    S. Spencer, Clk.

Page 275--10 May 1768. Wm. Holloway, of Anson, to Robert Jarman, of Queen Anne's Co., Maryland, for £25, 100 acres south of Peedee, adj. John McCoy, pat. to John Hamer 27 Sept. 1756; from him to Wm. Holloway.
Wit: Sam'l Spencer   Prov. July Term 1768 by
Chas Medlock   Samuel Spencer.

Page 314--19 Oct. 1768. James Shepperd, of Rowan Co., to Thos. Rundel (Randolph in heading), for £30; 200 acres northeast of Peedee.
Wit: Wm. Shepperd   Prov. Oct. Term 1768 by
Thos. Burgess   Wm. Shepperd
    S. Spencer, Clk.

Page 315--5 Sept. 1767. James Sheppard and wife, Lucy, to John Crawford, all of Anson, for £400, 249 acres north of Peedee, at mouth of Hitchcock's Creek, pat. to Jacob Paul 11 Oct. 1749; thence conveyed to James Terry; to Sheppard 26 Jany. 1767.
Wit: Jarrut [Jared] Gross   Prov. Oct. Court 1768
Wm. Sheppard   by Wm. Sheppard
    Saml. Spencer, Clk.

Page 316--10 Oct. 1768. John Webb to Stephen Cole, for £50, 170 acres on north side of Peedee on upper side of Hitchcock's Creek. Both of Anson County.
Wit: Sam'l Snead,   Ack. October Term 1768.
Matthew Raeford, Samuel Davis

Page 330--20 Oct. 1768. John Lee to Henry Stokes, for 5 pounds, 50 acres begin. at mouth of Lee Spring Branch, thence up River to Thoroughfare Branch, part of 180 acres granted to John Lee 27 Oct. 1762.
John Hall   Ack. Oct. Term 1768
John Smith

Page 337--7 Sept. 1768. James Terry to Augustine Prestwood, both of Anson, for 100 pounds, 200 acres on the north side of the Peedee... Thos. Jones' corner, down river to low ground of John Redd's lower line 100 acres conveyed by said Redd to Wm. Terry, [E-PD] Dec. 23, 1751, also part of a grant to Thomas Jones Apr. 10, 1747, by him to Edmund Cartledge Apr. 12, 1749; to Wm. Terry Jany. 16, 1753 and by said Wm. to James Terry as per deed.
John Terry   Jany. Term 1769.
James Terry   prov. by John Terry
Fany Terry

Page 358--26 Jany. 1769. John Condall to Edward Smith, for 10 pounds, 100 acres south side of Mountain Creek, adj. Jonathan Evans.
Sam'l Snead,   April Term 1769
Henley Snead, John Smith

Page 329--20 Oct. 1768. Henry Stokes to John Lee, both of Anson, for 5 pounds, 5 acres containint a mill seat lying on the Thoroughfare Creek, at the mouth of Duck Branch.
John Smith   Oct. Term 1768
John Hall   ack by Henry Stokes

Page 37--6 Oct. 1766, John Thomson to Joshua Morgan, both of Anson, for 25 pounds, 200 acres in Anson on the Peedee River on the east side of Grindstone Fork of Gould's Creek, adj. Zachary Phillips, granted to said Thomson Nov. 26, 1757, assigned to Joshua Morgan.
Julius Holley   July Term 1767
William Nelson.   Reg. Aug. 24, 1767

Page 23--16 March 1767. Timothy Taylor to John Hagler, both of Anson, for 5 pounds on south side of the Peedee, gr. Joshua Weaver 1754.
Wit: Edmond Lilly,   Ack. Apr. Term 1767
Josan? Jacob, Nathaniel Lilly

Page 25--8 Apr. 1767. Marshall Diggs and wife, Ann, to Philip Paul, all of Anson, for £10; 100 acres south of Peedee, gr. John Newberry.
Wit: Jacob Paul   Apr. Term 1767
John Coleman

Page 28--John Brown to John Grimes, both of Anson, for £27, 150 acres on north side of Peedee, south side of Hitchcock's Cr., adj. John Crawford.
Wit: Nicholas Smith,   Ack. Apr. Term 1767
Solomon Gross, John Ussery

Page 40--30 July, 1767. John Ashley, of Craven Co., S.C. to John Robertson, of Anson, for £40, 100 acres on north side of Cheek's Cr. of Great Peedee.
Wit: Thos Ussery   Ack. July Term 1767

ABSTRACTS OF DEEDS

Luke Robinson
Wm. Ussery

Page 188--23 Oct. 1767. Wm. Ashley, of S.C. to Cornelius Robinson, of Anson, for £33, 100 acres northeast of Peedee, east of Little River, part of a grant to John Ashley in 1746 and devised to William Ashley by said John.
Wit: Solomon Gross   Jany. Term 1768.
John Smith, Little River

Page 157--20 Aug. 1766. Benj. Vines and Elizabeth Vines to Joseph Spencer, for £40, 100 acres on the west side of Little River on a branch a mile from the mouth, gr. James Denson 15 Nov. 1753.
Wit: John Jeffery, John Spencer

Page 190--21 March 1768. Jacob and Hannah Underwood, of Edgecombe County, N.C. to John Wilson, of Anson, for £25, land in Anson on Clark's Creek, a branch of Peedee.
Wit: Harbert Haynes   Ack. April Term 1768
William Bennett   Saml. Spencer, Clk.
Shadrach Underwood

Page 154--24 Oct. 1767. Mathew Bailey and wife, Rachel, to Anthony Cook, all of Anson, for £35, 200 acres southwest of Peedee, granted to Jacob Paul; to Hugh McBride; to Matthew Bailey.
Wit: J. Shepperd   Ack. Oct. Term 1767
Marshall Diggs, Sheriff

Page 168--15 Oct. 1767. John Blalock and Lydia, his wife, to James Fry, all of Anson, for £75, 100 acres on Beaver Dam Creek.
Wit: David Dumas, Benj. Dumas, Wm. Thompson

Page 171--12 Dec. 1767. Jonathan Llewellyn and wife, Ruth, to George Webb, all of Anson, for £80, 300 acres northeast of Peedee, adj. Thos. Stafford Williams, on east br. of Hitchcock's Creek.
Wit: John Gold   Prov. Jany. Term 1768
Samuel Bryen   by Joseph Harrison
Joseph Harrison

Page 173--12 Dec. 1767. George Martin and Susannah, his wife, to Sabey Stone, all of Anson, for £85, 200 acres northeast of Peedee, on south fork of Cartledge's Cr., crossing Peter's Branch.
Wit: John Crawford, Mary Selvey

Page 176--18 Dec. 1767. Laurence Obryen and Frances, his wife, to Henry Covington, all of Anson, for £40, 100 acres on Cartledge Cr.
Wit: John Crawford   Ack. April Term 1768
Nelson Kelly

Page 194--4 Apr. 1768. Samuel Snead, Sr. to David Snead, his son, both of Anson, for £30, 300 acres on north of Hitchcock's Cr., adj. Thos. Connelly, pat. to Israel Snead 27 Apr. 1767.
Wit: Samuel Snead   Prov. April Term 1768
Solomon Snead   by Samuel Snead
Israel Snead

Page 201--4 March 1768. Anthony Acock and Charity, his wife, for love and affection, to son, Odom Acock, 200 acres granted to Charity, for natural life and then to son Odom.
Wit: Daniel Murpe [Murphy]
Bartholomew Murpe   Prov. April Term 1768
Wm. Fieldin   by Wm. Fielding
Saml. Spencer, Clk.

Page 211--1 Jany. 1765. John and William Mask to Short Long, for £110, paid by James Long, we deliver to Short Long, son of James Long, negro woman, Nan.
Wit: Dennis Nollen [Nowland]   Ack. by Wm Mask
Chas. Robinson   July Term 1768
Sam'l. Spencer, Clk.

Page 249--14 May 1768. James Bounds and Elizabeth, his wife, to Timothy Hurley, all of Anson, for £23, 125 acres northeast of Peedee, part of 200 acres.
Wit: Joseph Harrison   Prov. July Term 1768
Timmey James   by Jos. Harrison

Page 255--23 July, 1767. John Pelham and wife, Dorcas, to Penelope Shepherd, for £16, 100 acres on Mountain Creek, part of tract granted to Morgan Brown Nov. 26, 1757.
Wit: George Thomas   Prov. July Term 1768
Chas. Robinson   by Chas. Robinson.
John Jenkins   Samuel Spencer, Clk.

Page 327--2 Aug. 1768. Nath'l Hillen and Mary, his wife, to John Mask, Sr., for £89, 400 acres on north side of Peedee.   Prov. Oct. Term 1768
Wit: Wm. Mask, Edward Burk,   by Wm. Mask.
Shadrach Denson

Page 345--18 Jany. 1769. Isham Haley and Eliz., his wife, to Joseph Hinds, for £30, 100 acres, northeast of Peedee on north fork of Mountain Cr., adj. Wm. Coleman, granted Wm. Ferrill 1756; to Isham Haley 1768.
Wit: Chas. Medford,   Ack. Jany. Term 1769
Wm. Raiford, Shadrach Denson

ABSTRACTS OF DEEDS 45

1. From fam. records, the Gross fam. were div dur. the Rev. and Jared Elison Gross, a patriot, mov. to Lincoln Co. Ga.; changed his name to Groce. His son, Jared Ellison Groce III was one of "the 300" of Stephen F. Austin's colony in Texas, 1821; 1st planter of cotton in Brazos Riv.; wealthy and influential. (Hist. of Grimes Co. Tex. by Blair, 76-80; SW Quart. XX, 356-368. "Jared Ellison Groce" by Rosa Groce Berleth. In Anson, Solomon Gross was a Loyalist. Sheppard Groce, a bro. of Jared III, m. Susan Steele in Ga.

DEED BOOK 7

Page 1--1 April 1757. Sam'l. Coburn, of Anson County, and wife, Margaret Coburn, to Patrick McKindrick, of same, 302 acres granted to Samuel Coburn 24 Sept. 1754, including an Indian path below Dutchman's Creek, south side of the Catawba.
Chrs. Beaty, John Kendall,
John Thomas

Page 9--5 Feby. 1760. James Armstrong, of Anson, to George Rutledge, of same; 14 pounds, 62 acres on Dutchman's Creek, granted to Robt. Leeper 31 March 1750. [S.C.]
John Armstrong, Francis Beaty

Page 3--30 Aug. 1757. Benj. Thomason and Margaret, his wife, to Alexander Thomason, for 20 pounds, 200 acres in Waxhaw on Run Creek, north side of Catawba on Baird's line, adj. Thos. Simmons.
Thos. McElhany, Chas. Burnett,
Sam'l. Burnett

Page 17--6 Jany. 1776. John Mitchell, of St. David's Parish, S.C., merchant, to Solomon Gross, of Anson, for 50 pounds proc. money, 100 acres on southwest side of Little River, joining two surveys said to be patented by David Miles, 8 miles above mouth of Little River, conveyed by deed from John Smith, Sandhill, and Sarah, his wife, to said Mitchell, Nov. 1774.
John Smith   Prov. Oct. Court 1778.
James Cotton   by John Smith
                                  John Auld, Clk.

Page 18--6 Jany. 1776. John Mitchell, of St. David's Parish, S.C., to Solomon Gross, of Anson, for 250 pounds, 100 acres, part of 300 acres that Sam'l Ratcliff bought of Leonard Davidson [Dyson], all that lies below Dyson's Creek on west bank of Little River of Peedee which was conveyed by John Smith, Sandhill, and Sarah, his wife, to John Mitchell Nov. 15, 1774.   Oct Court 1778.
Wit: John Smith, James Cotton

Page 13--1 Jany. 1775. Christopher Christian to James McDonald, both of Anson, for £150 acres, 100 acres and 75 acres, lower part of tract granted to Robert Mills.
Wit: Soule McDonald,   Ack. Oct. Ct. 1778
John McDonald, Roderick McKinnon

Page 13--13 Nov. 1756. Thos. Gordon and wife, Elizabeth, to John Gordon, brother of sd. Thos. Gordon, for £20, 300 acres in Anson County, N.C. pat. 23 Feb. 1754, on north side of the Enoree River and joining the place whereon Ruth Gordon, widow, now lives, above the only sons and heirs-at-law of Mr. John Gordon, dec'd.
Wit: Jacob Brown, Benj. Gordon,
     Adam McCoole

Page 25--16 July 1774. Lewis Lowry and wife, Susannah, to John Street, all of Anson, for £25, 96 acres on north of Mill Prong of Jones Creek, part of a survey granted Lewis Lowry 18 Apr. 1771.
Wit: John May,   Ack. Jany. Court 1775.
Nath'l. Melton, Judy Lowry[1]

Page 27--20 Sept. 1776. Abraham Strickland to John Dunkin, both of Anson, for _____, 200 acres southwest of Peedee, west of Williams Cr. part of grant to Wm. Leverett 17 Nov. 1775.
Wit: Mallachi Watts   Prov. Jany. Ct. 1779
     William Gulledge   by Malachi Watts

Page 38--18 Dec. 1778. Jeremiah Terrell and Louisa, his wife, and Wm. Terrell, to James Auld, all of Anson, for £150, 150 acre-tract where Jeremiah Terrel now lives, west of Peedee, as specified in deed Gordon and wife to Terrel.
Wit: John Auld,   Ack. Jany. Ct. 1779
     Geo. Wilson, Ann Auld

Page 19--6 Jany. 1776. John Mitchell, of St. David's Parish, S.C., merchant, to Solomon Gross, of Anson County, 99 acres on west side of Little River of Great Peedee, being the plantation whereon Sam'l Swearingen formerly lived...

ABSTRACTS OF DEEDS

between Wm. Stone and Wm. Crittenden who holdeth the other hundred acres, granted Robt. Mills 24 March 1747 and conveyed from sd Robert Mills to Wm. Stone, then conveyed from him to Wm. Mares [Mears] and from him to Samuel Swearingen and from Swearingen to said David Smith,* reference being had to the records of the inferior court (minutes) and the registers office of Anson County.
James Cotton   Prov. Oct. Court 1778.
Wm. Mask   by Wm. Mask.
Walter Cunningham   John Auld, Clk.
*(Anson Co. Court Minutes, p. 89. 16 July 1772. Samuel Swearingen and Mary, his wife, to David Smith, 100 acres, proven by John Smith and ordered recorded)

Page 24 (15)--7 May 1778. John Batt Baird, to Wm. Mask, both of Anson, for 252 pounds proc. money, 200 acres, part of 600 acres granted to Richard Caswell 7 July 1750; to Thos. Swearingen 14 Feb. 1765. Begin at dividing line between said Baird and John Mitchell... to Jerry Menasco's old line... Townsend's Fork, including the plantation he owns whereon Solomon Gross now lives.
Sol Gross, Geo. Watkins

Page 53--_____ William May to James Gordon, both of Anson, for £17/10, 123 1/2 acres, patented 25 July, 1775.
Wit: Jeremiah Gulledge   Prov. Jany. Ct. 1779
     Mallachi Watts   by Malachi Watts

Page 31--27 July 1778. Wm. May, Sr., late of Anson to Gideon Brown, of same, for _____, 640 acres south of Peedee on fork of Jones Creek, being the place where Gideon Brown now lives, granted to Wm. May and Robert Edwards; Edwards sold to James Brooks, north of Wilkey's Mill Cr., adj. Drury Sims.
John Hurley   Ack. Oct. Ct. 1778.
Nathan Melton

Page 22--4 March 1776. George Mathews, of Anson, to Henry Wm. Harrington, for £640 (?) S.C. money, 107 acres, part of 640 acres granted to Solomon Hews 2 May 1741; to John Lee 27 Aug. 1746; to John Hornbeck_____; to Andrew Moorman, east of Peedee.
Wit: Isham Haley   Prov. Jany. Ct. 1779
     John Flowers   by John Thomas
     John Thomas
     Zachariah Moorman

Page 32--5 Oct. 1778. Wm. May and Lucy, his wife, to Sarah Flandegin, for £40, 200 acres, part of 640 acres gr. Wm. May July 25,____.
No witnesses.   Ack. in Court Oct. 1778.

Page 58--3 Oct. 1776. Thos. Meggison to Joseph Ingram, both of Anson, for £250, 300 acres south of Peedee, gr. Wm. Phillips, at mouth of Hamer's Gut.
Wit: Thos. Pickett   Prov. Jany. Ct. 1777
     John Watson   by Humphrey Rogers
     Humphrey Rogers

Page 61--4 Oct. 1778. Walter Ashmore, of Guilford County, N.C., to John Harris, of Anson, for £50, 100 acres in Anson, on Dutchman's Cr., lower side of Wherry [Uwharry] below Great Falls, gr. Walter Ashmore 24 May 1778.
Wit: Chas. Traves   Prov. Jany. Ct. 1779
     Eliz. Chappell   by Henry Mounger
     Henry Mounger

Page 67--27 Jany. 1778. Samuel Howell and Elizabeth, his wife, of Cheraws Dist., S.C. to Robert Gray, of same, for £80, 100 acres gr. Hopkins Howell, 16 Dec. 1769, by him for £50 to Sam'l Howell, northeast of Peedee, Mumford's line, below mouth of Jones Creek.
Wit: Walter Jones   Prov. Oct. Ct. 1778
     Frances Howell   by Walter Jones

Page 71--7 Sept. 1778. Wm. Mask and Rebecca, his wife, of Anson, to Capt. Wm. Hoy, [Hay] for £2000, three tracts in Anson; (1) land adj. tract Wm. Mask deeded to Frances Morly and now the property of Walter Leak, (2) tract gr. to James Denson, Sr. 5 Dec. 1760, and descended to his son James Denson, who deeded it to Shadrach Denson; by him to Wm. Mask Aug. 23, 1771, (3) 200 acres pat. to Joseph White and by several conveyances to Wm. Mask from Richard Pemberton and wife, 11 Nov. 1771; on Hamer's Creek and Great Peedee.
Wit: Geo Davidson, John Dejarnett,
     Benj. Baird
                     Prov. in court by John Dejarnett.

Page 44--26 March 1778. James Pickett and William Coleman, of Anson, to Wm. Taller, of same, for £65, 300 acres southwest of Peedee, one-half mile below Green's improvement.
John Coleman, Owen Slaughter

Page 46--11 April 1776. Henry Williams to Wm McCurry, for £20, 100 acres northeast of Peedee, north side of Big Cr., granted to Wm. Holton 1 July, 1758; by Holten to Chas. Smith [L.R.], 2 March 1761.
Wit: John Richardson, Joseph Hines

ABSTRACTS OF DEEDS 47

Page 79-- _____ 1779. Morgan Brown to John Donaldson, both of Anson, for £25, 200 acres northeast of Peedee on Mark's Br., granted Morgan Brown 1 July, 1758.
Wit: John Hamer, Ack. Apr. Ct. 1779
Nath'l Curtis, William Haley

Page 107--10 March 1779. Benj. Covington and wife, Fanny, to Thos. Everett, all of Anson, for £13/16/8., 325 acres south of Peedee on Jones Creek, pat. 22 Nov. 1771.
Wit: Wm. Hunter   Prov. Apr. Ct. 1779
Henry Covington   by Wm. Hunter

Page 110--23 Nov. 1778. Chas. Clark and Eliz., his wife, of Anson, to David Jemison, of Prince Frederick Parish, S.C., for £400, 700 acres west side of Lick Br. of Gould's Fork of Brown Creek.
Wit: Burwell Lanier   Prov. April Ct. 1779
Cornelius Clark   by Burwell Lanier
David Watts

Page 116--10 Jany. 1777. Joseph Stette, son and heir of Ambrose Stette, dec'd., to Edward Chambers, both of Anson, for £85, 200 acres on Little River, northeast of Peedee, being lower part of tract formerly belonging to Abraham Boyd and adj. John McKay's lower tract; from Boyd to Ephraim Liles; to Ambrose Stette; also signed by Ann Stette.
Wit: Hopkin Howell   Prov. Jany. Ct. 1778
John Hamer   by Wm. Hendley
Wm. Hendley

Page 123--8 Sept. 1778. Townsend Robinson and wife. Sophia, to Edward Chambers, all of Anson, for £90, 200 acres east of Little River of Peedee, being tract which Chas. Robinson, father of sd. Townsend Robinson, by last will, dated 29 Dec. 1754, gave to his two daughters, Sarah and Eliz., and further sayeth not, and the sd Sarah and Eliz. being now dead, he, the sd Townsend, being the proper heir at law to aforesaid Charles Robinson, now claims the land.
Wit: John Roe   Prov. Oct. Ct. 1778
John Ussery   by Wm. Chambers
Wm. Chambers

Page 314--25 Feb. 1769. Jacob Shepherd to Richard Downs, both of Anson, for £35, 100 acres northeast of Peedee, west side of Thicketty Creek, gr to John Crouch Dec. 1760.
John Smith, Benj. Bunts (?)

Page 224--15 Nov. 1768. Jordan Gibson, of Craven Co., S.C., to Benj. Dees, of Anson, for £100, 200 acres northeast of Little River, gr. to Jordan Gibson 1 July 1758.
Wit: Gideon Gibson   Ack. July Court 1769
Benj. Terry

Page 298--17 April 1770. John Cook to Rowland Williams, both of Anson, for £30, 200 acres on Williams Cr. gr. Thos. Highlowerby, 24 Apr. 1762.
John Collson, James Terry

Page 347--9 Jany. 1769. Wm. Lucas to Richard Downs, both of Anson, for £15, 100 acres northeast of Peedee, on Hickory Cr.
John Smith, Wm. Lucas, Jr.,
Sam'l. Parsons

Page 353--17 Oct. 1768. Augustine Prestwood and Elizabeth, his wife, to John Crawford, all of Anson, for £50, 100 acres northeast of Peedee, gr. Thos. Jones Nov. 22, 1746; to Wm. Terry 1751.
Sam'l Snead, Zacheriah Smith

Page 126--23 Feb. 1779. Benj. Beard (Baird) and John Smith, Sandhill, of Anson, for £100, to George Jefferson, of same, 340 acres southwest of Little River, part of 400 acres granted to said Benj. Beard and John Smith, adj. John Kimbrough.
Anson Co. July Ct. 1779. This deed prov. by John Kimbrough as to Benj. Baird, one of the parties, and duly ack. by John Smith, the other party. Test: Mich. Auld.
Wit: Drury Mays, Bennet Graham,
Peter Lewis, John Kimbrough

Page 256--11 Aug. 1769. Robt. and Susannah Rayford to William Rayford, for £150, 100 acres on west side of Drowning Creek, gr. to Robt. Rayford 26 Sept. 1760.
Wit: James Terry   Prov. Jany. 1770 by
Ezekiel McClendon   James Terry.

Page 249--11 Jany. 1770. Thos. Coleman to Simon Hooker, both of Anson, for £200, one-third part of tract my father devised to my brothers, William, John and myself in common. My father, Wm. Coleman's will May 1, 1750.
Wit: Shadrach Denson, William Coleman,
John Coleman

Page 242--22 Aug. 1768. Haten (Haden) Morris and wife, Elizabeth, to Thos. Deeton, all of Anson, for £30, 30 acres on Little River, gr. to Wm. Stevens 1760 and by conveyance to Samuel Parsons; to Haten Morris.
Wit: Sam'l. Parsons, Rachel Parsons

ABSTRACTS OF DEEDS

Page 111--6 Feby. 1779, John Smith [Sandhill] to George Jefferson, for 150 pounds, 200 acres, on both sides of Little River, patented to Edmund Fanning, from Richard Fanning to said Smith 25 Aug. 1770, including Fannings old mills.
Benj. Baird   Prov. April Ct. 1779
John Kimbrough   by Benj. Baird.

Page 127--6 Feby. 1779. John Kimbrough to Geo. Jefferson, for £50, 4 acres on Little River adj. mill acre, being part of tract purchased by sd Kimbrough of Solomon Gross, begin. at river bank on lower corner of the acre bought by John Smith of Samuel Swearingen.
John Smith, Sandhill   Ack. April Ct. 1779
Benjamin Baird   by John Kimbrough

Page 135--11 March 1778. William Coleman and wife, Patience, to John Coleman, all of Anson, 200 acres on north side of Peedee, begin. at Bear Island near upper end thereof, granted to John Clark 20 June, 1740, deeded to Coleman May 30, 1771.
James Terry, Savannah Cr.   Ack. July 1779
Hardy Hook, Hooker, Mary Vick

Page 153--9 May 1774. William and Thos. Pickett to James Allen, all of Anson, for £100, two tracts: 100 acres on Turkey Cock Creek, upper side, including plantation and house whereon Benj. Ingram, dec'd., formerly lived; and 50 acres gr. Wm. Pickett, near Nicholas Smith's line and near the springs of Benj. Ingram, dec'd.
Wit: Moody Ingram   Prov. July Ct. 1774
     Barnett Randel   by Moody Ingram

Page 163--12 May 1779. Thos. Polk, atty. for David Oliphant of Mecklenburg County, to Going Morgan, for 80 pounds, land in Anson including mill.
John Wallis, John Reay,
Goen Morgan

Page 205--10 Oct. 1775. John Jarman, of Anson, to Geo. Wilson of same, for 20 pounds, 150 acres in Anson, southwest of Peedee.
John Wright   ack. Oct. Ct. 1775
John Smith, Carpenter   John Auld, Clk.

Page 327--11 Apr. 1770. Zacheriah Smith and Frances, his wife, to Richard Pemberton, for 200 pounds, 200 acres north side of Peedee on Denson's line, granted to Joseph White and sold by Joseph White to Zacheriah Smith 23 July 1766.
Chas. Robinson, Wm. Mask,
Benj. Baird, S. Gross

Page 245--15 Feb. 1770. John Smith [Sandhill] to John Jones, for 25 pounds, pat. granted to Robt. Mills 22 Nov. 1746; to son Nathan, by him to Henry Downs, on west side of Little River, corner's on Parker's land.
Mathew Raiford   Prov. July Ct. 1770
Stephen Cole   by Mathew Raiford

Page 234--19 Sept. 1769. Wm. McDaniel, of Anson, to Zacheriah Smith, for 30 pounds proc., part of 400 acres granted to James Jowers on east side of Little River on a branch called Buffalo.
Wm. Pickett, Chas. Robinson

Page 207--26 Aug. 1776. Joseph Ingram to James Pickett, for 50 pounds proc., 80 acres on southwest side of Peedee...Wm. Mask's lower line, to James Pickett's upper line.
James Terry (Savannah Cr.)   Prov. Apr. Ct. 1777
Hun Rogers   by James Terry.

Page 209--26 Feby. 1768. Wm. Queen to Sam'l Parsons, for 100 pounds proc., 100 acres granted to Wm. Stone; 33 Dec. 1750, from Stone to Wm. Queen, on bank of Little River below Ridge's Creek, where said Wm. Queen now lives. Margaret, wife of Wm. Queen relinquishes rights.
John Curlo Smith
John Smith, Sandhill   Aprl Term 1769 proved
                               in court by oath of John
                               Smith Sandhill.

Page 213--16 Jany. 1769. John Bounds and Mary, his wife, to John Cole, for 50 pounds, 200 acres gr. David Clark 1757 in Bladen Co. on Indian Swamp.
James Bounds Sr., James Bound, Jr.,
James Williams, James Terry

Page 152--6 July 1779. James Arrington to Richard Odam, both of Anson, for _____, 50 acres southwest of Peedee, part of a tract of 250 acres surveyed for Wm. Fielding and conveyed to Henry Bailey; to Solomon Townsend; to sd James Arrington, beg. below John Evans.
Wit: Robt. Hall   Prov. Oct. Ct. 1779
     Nevell Bennett   by Robt. Hall.

Page 173--5 Oct. 1779. George Jefferson, of Anson, to David Garland, of Lunenburg County, Va., for £500, Va. money, 275 acres southwest of Peedee below mouth of Brown Creek, part of a tract conveyed from John Stevens, Jr. 4 March 1779.
No witnesses.   Ack. Oct. Ct. 1779

ABSTRACTS OF DEEDS 49

Page 174--4 March 1779, John Stevens, Jr., of Cumberland Co., N.C., to George Jefferson, of Anson, for £600, 285 acres southwest of Peedee below mouth of Brown Cr.... Thos. George's... gr. Wm. Smith 22 Sept. 1750; also 25 acres below mouth of Browns Cr. adj. the above, being part of Thos. George's land as by deed to Zachariah Philips; to Joseph Oats, Sept 5, 1751, to Wm. Pickett 20 Sept. 1763; to John Stevens, Jr. 29 Jan. 1763.
Wit: Mary Nichols   Prov. Oct. Ct. 1779
      Wm. Nichols   by Benjamin Smith.
      Benj. Smith

Page 175--10 Nov. 1775. Thos. Bailey to John Seago, both of Anson, for £80, 150 acres east side of Rock br. of Jones Cr., adj Joseph Murphey, gr. Tilman Helms 18 Apr. 1771; to Thos. Bailey 5 Oct. 1772.
Wit: Nevel Bennett   Ack. Oct. Ct. 1779.
      David Hildreth

Page 177--6 Oct. 1779. Wm. Boggan to Patrick Boggan, both of Anson, for £100, 200 acres south of Peedee, on Gould's Fork of Brown Creek. Jemima Boggan also signs.
Wit: Wm. Morgan   Prov. in Oct. Ct. 1779
      Patrick Boggan   by Wm. Morgan

Page 180--2 Nov. 1778. Thos. Wade, for nat. love to my granddaughter, Margaret Vining, of Anson Co., a negro girl named Milly, about 7 yrs. old and a negro boy, Ben, aged 4, bought by me at the Vendue of est. of my deceased daughter, Margaret Mosely.
Wit: Holden Wade   Prov. Oct. Ct. 1779
      Edwin Ingram   by Holden Wade.

Page 200--5 Oct. 1779. William Hunter, for love, etc. to my dau., Dianah Lefeavor, lawful wife of Abraham Lefeavor, 50 acres, part of tract gr. sd Wm. Hunter, 22 Jany. 1773, on Savannah Cr., west side of Peedee.
Wit: George Wilson, John Thomas

Page 202--2 Aug. 1778. Thos. Wright and wife, Martha, to Thos. Wade, all of Anson, for £100, 150 acres, being lower part of 200 acres gr. John Husbands; by him to Nicholas Brodway; to Chas. Spradling; to Thos. Wright, beg. Howells upper corner, adj. Anthony Hutchins' 1st line of survey, called Mount Pleasant Lands.
John Wright   Prov. Jany. Ct. 1780
Wm. Wright   by Jno. Wright.

Page 208--3 March 1780. Peter Lawrence to Benj. Ingram, both of Anson, for £13/10, 100 acres on Cedar Creek.
Wit: James Moody Ingram, Wm. Lawrence

Page 140--6 July, 1779. Solomon Townsend to James Arrington, both of Anson, for "the sum of N.C. currency to him in hand paid", 100 acres southwest of Peedee on a br. of Lick Cr., part of 250 acres surveyed to William Fielding and conveyed to Henry Bailey, which is the division of a part of sd tract conveyed to Thos. Bailey, Jr. and on the line of a 50 acre tract given off to Mathew Bailey, Sr. from sd Fielding's survey.
Wit: John Hornbeck,   Prov. July Ct. 1779
      Wm. Bennett,   by Wm. Pratt.
      Joseph Pretnett, William Pratt

Page 141--10 Oct. 1778. Stephen Miller, of Anson, to John Hill, of Halifax Co., N.C., for £100, 200 acres, upper one-half of 400 acres gr. Theodorock Miller 21 Dec. 1770, southwest of Peedee on Lick Cr. lower side of Brown Creek.
Wit: Abram Hill,   Ack. July Ct. 1779
      Sam'l. Hill, Nath'l. Dobbs

Page 143--5 July 1779. Thos. Wade, Esq. to Christopher Davis, both of Anson, for £400, 200 acres on east side of Brown Creek.
Wit: Wm. Boggan   Ack. July Ct. 1779
      James Bruton

Page 148--27 Aug. 1778. Henry Bailey to Richard Odom, both of Anson, for £50, 50 acres southwest of Peedee on south side of Lick Br. of Jones Cr., it being part of a tract taken up by Wm. Fielding and conveyed to Henry Bailey.
Wit: Thos. Conner   Prov. Oct. St. 1778
      Joseph Engoss   by Thos. Conner.

Page 149--3 Aug. 1778. Mathew and Rachel Bailey, of Anson, to Richard Odom, of Duplin Co., N.C., for £200, 100 acres southwest of Peedee on Jones Cr., adj. Bailey's lower corner.
Wit: Solomon Townsend   Prov. in Oct. Ct. 1778
      Wm. Bennett   by Solomon Townsend.
      Odam Cock

Page 211--16 Jany. 1769. Stephen Cole, of Mecklenburg Co. to John Bounds, of Anson, for £50, 200 acres in Bladen Co., on Ash Pole Swamp and Indian Swamp, gr. David Clark in 1757. Elinor Cole also signs.
Wit: James Bounds, Sr.   Prov. Apr. Ct. 1769
      John Cole   by James Bounds, Sr.

Page 219--17 June 1769. Samuel Snead to Solomon Snead, for £12, 100 acres on Solomon's Cr., gr Samuel Snead 29 Apr. 1769.

ABSTRACTS OF DEEDS

Wit: John Snead Ack. July Term 1769.
Israel Snead

Page 221--3 June, 1769, John and Susanna Spencer, of Anson to Wm. Harvey, of Rowan Co., for £ 100, land on Little River, granted Wm. Stone in 1757.
Wit: William Ward, James Resnall

Page 226--8 July 1769. Israel Snead to David Snead, both of Anson, for £ 30, 200 acres on Hitchcock's Creek. Ack. July Term 1769
Wit: Samuel Spencer, Jacob Paul

Page 252--9 Nov. 1769. Archelas Mooreman to Wm. Pratt, both of Anson, for £ 50, 300 acres patented 22 Dec. 1768, beg. near place where Jones and Hopkins Howell's lines interfere one with the other.
Wit: Stephen Thomas Prov. Jany. Term 1770
Stephen Thomas, Jr. by Stephen Thomas, Jr.
Thos. Moorman

Page 195--Lately settled in Anson County, connected with or depending on Thos. Dockery, about 50 years old, to wit: Ann, his wife, aged about 32, Michael, his son, about 18 1/2, John Covington, his son-in-law, aged 35, Mathew Covington, his grandson, aged abt. 10, Hannah Covington, his granddau. aged abt. 7 1/2 yrs; Mary Covington, his Grdau. aged abt. 3 1/2, Sarah Covington, his gr. dau. aged abt. 3 1/2, and Joseph Hull, his cousin, aged abt. 16.
Anson County Inf. Ct. Jany. Term, 1770.
Test. Sam'l. Spencer, Clk.

Page 193--"Whereas Thomas Dockery, of Queen Ann's County, Maryland, aged about 55 years, having an inclination to remove himself and family out of this province and settle elsewhere" obtained certificates of character, etc. from both the Justices of said county and from a number of other citizens (29 March 1769) and from the ruling elders of the Presbyterian Church in said county. (4 April 1769).

Page 278--16 Nov. 1769. Randolph Creek, of Rowan Co. to Joel McClendon, for £ 60, 76 acres adj. Thos. Underwood, Thos. George, gr. sd Cheek 27 Apr. 1767.
Wit: John Collson, Wm. Collson,
Jesse McClendon.

Page 280--The beginning of deed missing. Zacheriah Moorman and wife, Mary, to Archelus Moorman, 300 acres.

Wit: Benj. Moorman Prov. Apr. Term 1770
Israel Snead, Jr. by Israel Snead, Jr.

Page 282--Joseph Hinds and Easter, his wife, to Isham Hailey, all of Anson, for £ 30, 100 acres northeast of Peedee, on Mountain Cr., adj. Wm. Coleman, pat. to Wm. Terrell, 27 Sept. 1756, to Isham Hailey 8 Sept. 1768; by Isham and Eliz. Hailey to Joseph Hinds, Jany. 1769, said conveyance disapproved of and now deeded back to Isham Hailey.
Wit: Thos. Dockery, Sam'l Swearingen, Sela Hailey

Page 343--21 June, 1770. Solomon Gross and Mary, his wife, to Wm. Muguaire (McGuire), for £ 20, 100 acres northeast of Peedee, gr. to George Cummons 4 April, 1750.
Wit: Matthew Raiford Prov. July Ct. 1770
_____ Raiford by Matthew Raiford.

Page 240--9 Oct. 1769. Cornelius Robinson and Elizabeth, his wife, to Sam'l Yerkes, £ 22, 200 acres south side of the Peedee, Thos. Jones' corner.
Wit: John Mims Ack. Oct. Term 1769
Mary Mims Sam'l. Spencer, Clk.

Page 262--1 Feb. 1769. John Ussery and Eliz., his wife, of Anson, to William Leak, of Buckingham Co., Va., for £170 Va currency, two tracts north of the Peedee, (1) gr. to Thos. Holmes 7 Apr. 1749; by sd Holmes to Thos. Coleman; by sd Coleman bequeathed to son, John Coleman, and by him to Peter Brister, and by Brister to John Ussery 22 Jany. 1762, 100 acres; (2) second tract granted Saml. Parsons, from Parsons to Haten [Haden] Morris.
Wit: John Skinner Prov. Jany. 1770
Solomon Gross by Wm. Mask.
Wm. Mask

Page 470--20 Aug. 1774. William Coleman and James Pickett, of Anson, to George Jefferson, of Lunenburg County, Colony of Virginia, for 60 pounds, 200 acres on northeast side of the Peedee, lower side of Mountain Creek on north side of small branch that enters the Grassy Islands.
John Chiles, John Cartright

Page 92--27 May 1778. Joshua Morgan, of Anson, to Wm. Threadgill, of same, for 150 pounds, 300 acres in Anson, line between Morgan and Burwell Lanier.
George Davidson, Johnsend (Johnson)

ABSTRACTS OF DEEDS

Page 310--9 Apr. 1770. Joshua Morgan, of Anson, to Sam'l. Bloodworth, for 20 pounds, tract on south side of Peedee River, on Grindstone Fork of Gold's Fork, 100 acres.
John Leverett, John Bloodworth

Page 106--12 June 1776. John Polk and Ellender, his wife, of Anson to Goin Morgan, for 5 pounds, 26 acres on north side of Rockey River.
John Morgan, Benj. Bolling

Page 509--14 June 1777. William Hay to George Jefferson, for 43 pounds, on both sides of Brown Creek... Thos. George's line.
Thos. Chiles, Mary Nichools, Susannah Nickools, John White

Page 511--27 Jany. 1778. Hopkin Howell to Robt. Gray, of Cheraws District (S.C.), land on north side of the Peedee.
Duke Glen, Sam'l Howell, Ack. Apr. Court 1778
William Magby (McBee)

Page 515--Henry Harris to Arthur Harris, his son, a negro boy.
Hen. Mounger

Page 516--7 April 1778. William Coleman to Jesse Harris.
Henry Mounger, Jas. Terry

Page 519--18 Feby. 1775. Thos. Wilson to Henry Mounger tract on northeast side of the Peedee on both sides of Island Creek.
John Harris, Job Wilson, Martha Wilson

Page 474--22 Sept. 1774. Benjamin Smith to John McClendon for 60 pounds proc. tract on southwest side of Peedee, east side of Gold's fork of Brown's Creek, at Robt. Rainey's lower corner.
Thos. Leverett, John Leverett

Page 259--24 Oct. 1768. Edmund Fanning, of Orange County, N.C. to Richard Fanning of the county aforesaid, for 400 pounds proc., 200 acres in Anson County, Province of N.C., on both side of Little River, granted to Edmund Fanning April 6, 1765. Ack. in Anson Court June 1770
Ransom Sutherland, by Ransom Sutherland.
Benja. Wynns Jr., Jas. Howard

Page 214 (164)--3 Nov. 1768. John Stevens and wife, Sarah, of Cumberland Co. to Robert Raiford, of Anson, for £200; 200 acres at mouth of Brown's Creek on Peedee, at John Clark's lower corner.

Pickett Ack. by oath of James Pickett
Wm. Pickett July Term 1769.

Page 233--16 Feb. 1769. Townsend Robinson, of Ga., and wife, Sophia, to Cornelius Robinson, of Anson, for £40, 200 acres pat. to Townsend Robinson 7 March 1756.
Wit: Thos. George Prov. Oct. Term 1769
John Menes by Thos. George.

Page 267--29 Aug. 1769. William and Mary Raiford to John Cole, all of Anson County, for 150 pounds proc., 100 acres on Drowning Creek, granted Robt. Raiford 26 Sept. 1760.
(end of deed missing.)

Page 547--24 March 1777. Wm. and Mourning Pickett, for 100 pounds N.C. currency, to Cornelius Robinson, acres on Hurricane Branch of Brown's Creek, granted to Hannah Cheek 13 Oct. 1765.
Philip Raiford, Ack. July Court 1778.
John Kimbrough, Wm. Chaplin

Page 501--2 Dec. 1776. John Walters to George Walters, for 400 pounds, tract purchased of Dennis Nowlin that said Nowlin purchased of Edward Smith on north east side of the Peedee on south side of Little Buffelow Creek that runs into Little River.
Wm. Mask, West Harris, Nancy Walters

Page 494--Jany. 1777. James Hogan to James Roper and Wm. Collson for 10 pounds on southwest side of Rockey River.
John Hogan

Page 490--Nov. 1, 1777. Thos. G. Megginson to John Walter on northeast side of Little River. Rachel Marby (Macby or McBee. See 1790 census.)
Walter Leak Ack. Jany. 1778

Page 485--10 July 1776. Sampson Culpeper to Patrick Boggan.
John Coleman, James Ray, James Boggan

Page 476--4 Nov. 1777. William Johnson to William Love on Smith's Branch of Brown's Creek.
Richard Rushing, William Smith

Page 552--7 Sept. 1778. Isaac Vick, of Northhampton County, N.C. makes well-beloved and trusty friend, James Terry, son of William Terry, his attorney in Anson and any county in the U.S. to

ABSTRACTS OF DEEDS

demand and receive for me anything justly belonging to me, in particular six negroes in Anson County.
John Wade, Martha Wade,
William Coleman

Page 549--1 July 1778. Henry Mounger, Esq. of Anson County to Wm. McGrigger, of same.

Page 542--21 April 1778. Thos. Wade, of Anson, to James Meredith, of same, for 1100 pounds of proc. of N.C., three tracts of 360 acres north side of the Peedee.
W. Terry, Mary Terry,   Ack. July Court 1778
Joseph Bretwell

Page 521--20 June 1778. Renatus Downing, of Cumberland County to John Bound, land on Rocky fork of Hedgecock [Hitchcocks Creek,] beginning at corner of William Smith 100 acre-tract.

Page 506--3 April 1778. This is to certify that I, Sarah Hay, wife of said Capt. Wm. Hay, did receive one bay geldin of him that the said Capt. Wm. Hay bought of Mr. Wm. Threadgill and all other dower and all claim or claims against the estate of Capt. Wm. Hay.
Wm. Mask, Wm. Threadgill,
John De Jarnett

Page 505--25 July 1774. Jesse McClendon, of Anson, to George Davidson, of same, for 250 pounds money, tract on the south side of the Peedee, northeast side of the main road, deemed near the said McClendon's old back line, being a tract granted to Jesse McClendon 25 July 1774, 250 acres.
D. Smith   Anson Co. Court 1778.
Salathiel Clifton.   Proved by David Smith
                         and ordered registered.
                                    John Auld, Clk.

Page 503--7 April 1777. Henry Mounter to Ethelred Harris..........Island Creek.
James Terry, Shd. Hogan,
West Harris

Page 503--Sias Billings [Billingsley] to Ethelred Harris, for 40 pounds, tract on northeast or lower side of Uharrey River.
Henry Mounger, West Harris, Lewis Caudell

---

1. Did this Lowry family move to Wilkes County, Georgia? A Judye Lowry was witness to a will there in 1786, with Benj. Baird and his wife, formerly of Anson and Montgomery Cos.
2. Spartanburg District, S. C. Deed Bk. "B", p. 114. 19 Mch. 1788. Vardry and Hannah McBee to David Állen, 250 a on Thicketty Cr. wit: Joseph Morris (son-in-law of Vardry McBee) and Jordan Gibson. D. B. "B" p. 260. Jany. 29, 1787. John Sanders, of Louisa Co. (Va.) for £ 19-17, Va. money, to Jordan Gibson, one wagon and harness for four horses. D.B. "B", page 325.___1789. Nathan Gibson to Henry Gibson. Wit: John Sanders, Lewis Sanders and George Gibson. D.B. "D", p. 74. Gideon Gibson wit. to deed, 14 Sept. 1795.
List of tithes in Fredrickville Parish, Louisa County, 1777: Gideon, George and Nathan Gibson. Hist. of Louisa, Co. Va. (p. 162,) by Malcolm Harris.
3. Benjamin Baird, or his wife, Micha (Miche, Mickey), was apparently related to or connected with John Smith, Sandhill, in some way. They had two land grants together and one with David Smith, son of John Smith, Sandhill. These three also jointly owned a saw mill and grist mill in 1773 on Little River, in the corner of a tract bought by David Smith from Saml. Swearingen. Was Benj. Baird son-in-law, or brother-in-law of John Smith, Sandhill? Although entry-taker in Montgomery County from its organization, he also served in the Revolution. Auld and Chiles, commissioners for Anson, Montgomery and Richmond Cos. in the Salisbury Dist. paid his certificate for $139.10 over to the entry-taker of lands for him in July 1782. N. C. Rev. Acc'ts, Vol. XII, p. 27-4. Dept. of Arch. and Hist., Raleigh. After the Rev. he moved to Wilkes Co., Ga. where he died before Feb. 1794 when his inventory was returned to the County Ct. His wife, Micha, was one of the purchasers at the sale of the perishable estate in Sept. 1794. He was taxed in 1785 with 2 polls, 2 slaves and 500 acres in Wilkes County, and, with wife, Mickey, and Judye Lowry, witnessed the will of William Rasbury, Apr. 7, 1786. Early Records of Georgia- Wilkes County by Grace Gillam Davidson, Vol. I-49, 109; Vol. II-27.
4. Henry Mounger moved to Wilkes County, Georgia, where his son Edwin married Fanny, the dau. of Gen. Elijah Clark. Hero of Hornet's Nest, a Biography of Elijah Clark, by Louise Frederick Hays, pp. 295-360.

ABSTRACTS OF DEEDS 53

DEED BOOK K

Page 19--26 Apr. 1772. Wm. May, of Anson, to Chas. Booth, 150 acres granted 18 May 1771; £7, land southwest of Peedee.
Wit: John Jackson
Stephen Miller
Prov. by John Jackson
Jany. Ct. 1773.
J. Auld, Clk.

Page 32--2 Oct. 1772. William Coleman to Drury Ledbetter, both of Anson, for £30, 200 acres southwest of Yadkin River.
Wit: Mary Munday
Walter Harris
Robertah Harris
Ack. Jany. Ct. 1773
J. Auld Clk.

Page 43--12 July 1773. William and Rebecca Mask, of Anson, to Wm. Leake, for 10 pounds proc,, a tract granted to said Mask 18 Apr. 1771, below mouth of Little River, 390 acres.
Wit: Wm. Mask
Wm. Symon
Geo. Eastes
John Turnage.
Prov. Apr. 1774.
by John Turnage
J. Auld, Clk.

Page 40--14 Apr. 1773. Wm. Linsey to James Vanderford, for 50 pounds proc. 200 acres on southwest side of the Peedee on the south side of Camp Branch of Savannah Creek, about one-mile from Lawyer's Road, granted to Lindsey Nov. 22, 1771.
Wit: J. Pickett
Benj. Baird
Morgan Brown
Prov. Apr. Ct. 1774 by
James Pickett

Page 47--1 Jany. 1773. James Olliver to John Smith, both of Anson County, for 50 pounds proc., 200 acres, on southwest side of Peedee, begin. at James Vanderford's line on south side of small branch of Savanna Creek, including the plantation whereon Samuel Phillips now dwells, lying between the head branches of Savannah Creek and Cedar Creek, part of 400 acres granted to John Smith, 16 Dec. 1769, and since conveyed to Timothy Montseer by his death to his brother, Thos. Montseer, and from him to James Olliver. Mary Olliver also relinquishes rights.
Mark Allen
Wm. Bond
Prov. Apr. Court 1774.
by Mark Allen

Page 54--13 Apr. 1774. James Vanderford and wife, Sarah, of Anson, to Wm. Lindsey, of same, for 80 pounds proc., 200 acres on Southwest side of the Peedee on head branches of Savannah Creek, begin at lower side of John Smith's survey, being a part of 400 acres granted to sd. John Smith Dec.

1769 and conveyed by him to said James Vanderford.
Ack. April Court 1774
J. Pickett, John Smith,
Sol. Gross

Page 57-8--11 Apr. 1774. John Smith [Little River][1] of Anson, to Charles Smith, of same, for 12 pounds proc., acres on north side of the Peedee beg. on forks of Dixon's [Dison's] Creek of Little River about a mile below his other survey, granted to Jno. Smith 22 Jany. 1773.
Richard Downs, Jasper Smith,
Wm. Smith
Ack. Apr. 1774.

Page 80--18 Apr. 1773. Hannah Check, of Anson, to William Pickett, of same, for 30 pounds, 300 acres southwest of Peedee on Hamer's Creek of Browns Creek... Elizabeth Cheek's line..., granted 18 Oct. 1765.
Joel McClendon,
Wm. Ware, Jno. Cheek
Ack. Apr. Court 1774.

Page 82--15 Feby. 1772. John Sheppard, of Chester County, S.C., to William Pickett, of Anson County, N.C., for 60 pounds, 350 acres on southwest side of the Peedee, beginning on river bank at Jno. Pickett's upper corner... Colson's lower corner... granted Sheppard 26 Dec. 1766.
Sol. Gross
J. Pickett
Prov. Apr. Court 1774.
by James Pickett

Page 86--18 Oct. 1772. Anthony Hutchins[2] of the Province of West Florida, Esq. for good causes and consideration, appoints his friend Samuel Spencer, of St. David's Parish, in the Province of S.C. to transact and settle my quarrels, controvernssuits, judgments, execution seizure bonds, etc., within the provinces of North or South Carolina.
David Wade, David Jernigan
Ack. Jany. Court 1773.

Page 87--7 March 1773. John Smith, Sandhill, of Anson County, Province of North Carolina, planter, sendeth greetings. Whereas a tract of land in Anson County on the southwest side of the Peedee including the mouth of Smith's Creek and comprehending the low grounds of the River and of both sides of this creek from the lower line of James Inkgralds [Ingram?] survey as far as the highly land on the river nearly against the falls; was heretofore, to wit above twenty years ago entered, surveyed, and granted to the said Smith and the said Smith, Sandhill, did not enter upon, settle, cultivate the same in pursuance of the said grant

to him made, whereby, in consequence thereof part of the same tract of land hath been lately granted to Samuel Spencer, lately of said Anson County, Atty. at Law, and as the other part and remainder thereof hath likewise been granted to Robt. Jerman and the same being lately purchased of him by the said Samuel Spencer, whereby the said Spencer is now in full and legal possession of all of the said premises thereof, and the said John Smith, Sandhill, for 5 shillings hath assigned all rights, etc. to said Samuel Spencer.
Jno Grimes   Prov. April Ct. 1774 by
Benj. Beard   Benj. Beard
    J. Auld, Clk.

Page 95--7 Oct. 1773. John Flower and Obedience, his wife, to the Duke of Glen..........the said Duke Glen; for 220 pounds, 200 acres southwest of the Peedee, part of 585 acres gr. to John Flowers.
Wit: Joseph Howell   Prov. in open court by
    Joseph Rye   Joseph Howell (no date)
    Dan Rye   J. Auld, Clk.

Page 147--1 July 1774, John Smith to Wm. Seward, for 25 proc., 100 acres on southwest side of Peedee on east side of Cedar Creek on 3rd line of his other survey on west side of small drain sold to John Henry...Joseph Durham's line...pat. to John Smith Dec. 1771.
Wm. Bennett, Jr.   Prov. July Court 1774
Thomas Bailey   by William Bennett.

Page 148--July 15, 1774. Thomas Wade to Francis Smith, both of Anson, for £ 50; 100 acres southwest of Peedee, on fork of Brown Creek.
Wit: Jacob McClendon   Prov. July Ct. 1774
    Zacheriah McDaniel   by Zach. McDaniel.

Page 204--May 3, 1774. Zachariah Smith and Fanny, his wife, of South Carolina, to Wm. Newberry, 20 pounds, 50 acres on north side of the Peedee near Mountain Creek.
Joseph Hines   Prov. by Joseph Hinds
Esther Hines   July Ct. 1774

Page 94--1 June 1773. John Smith, Sandhill, and Sarah, his wife, of Anson, to Benj. Beard, of same, for 100 pounds proc. money, a certain piece or parcel of land, that is to say, one just full and equal third part of that acre of land which the said John Smith, Sandhill, bought of Samuel Swearingen, lying on Little River where the said John Smith, the said Benj. Beard and David Smith hath now a saw mill in joint partnership together, with one full third of all buildings and improvements, etc.

which is to remain entirely without any division and to be held in partnership by the said John Smith and Benjamin Beard and David Smith.
David Smith   Prov. Apr. Ct. 1774 by
Zachariah Hogan   Zachariah Hogan.
    J. Auld, Clk.

Page 13--Oct. 10, 1772. John[3] Coleman and Morning, his wife, of Anson County to Jeremiah Strother, for 80 pounds proc., 150 acres on the northeast side of the Peedee, north side of Mountain Creek, being the lower corner of the tract that William Coleman, dec'd., bought of John Clark... to John Newberry's, which land was granted to William Thomas and John Coleman 27 Sept. 1756.
Wm. Coleman   Prov. Jany. Ct. 1774 by
Wm. McDonald   William Coleman
Simon Shocker [Hooker]   J. Auld, Clk.

Page 120--23 Dec. 1772. Chas. Harrington to Wm. Pickett, both of Anson, for 60 pounds, 200 acres formerly in Bladen, granted John Harrington 25 March 1748, on the south side of the Peedee... Colson's line...
Absolum Tatum,   Prov. Apr. Ct. 1774 by
Ann Oliver,   J. Pickett.
J. Pickett, Jno. Colson

Page 247--3 Apr. 1773. James Terry[4] of Anson County, in consideration of a judgment recovered at Salisbury for 97 pounds and the cost and for Chas. Medlock for 2 pounds 7 shillings, paid by Richard Leak, I do hereby sell, deliver, etc. to Richard Leak five negroes, Ralph, Esther, Rodge, Ben, Jude.
Robert Webb   Ack. Oct. Term 1774
John Cole

Page 230--1 Dec. 1772. Francis Mosley, of Anson, to Wm. Leak, of same, for 50 pounds Va. money, 100 acres on southeast side of the Peedee, land Francis Mosley bought of Wm. Mask 15 Apr. 1771, granted to Henry Downs 26 May, 1757.
Moody Ingram   Prov. July Ct. 1774 by
Sam'l Ingram   Joseph Hindes
Joseph Hindes   J. Auld, Clk.

Page 278--8 May 1773. Chas. Medlock and wife, Agatha, to Sam'l. Spencer, of St. David's Parish, S.C., for 40 pounds proc., 100 acres in Anson formerly Bladen on south side of the Peedee, begin. in the fork of Smith's Creek at Sam'l Flake's lower corner, being part of a tract originally granted to Joseph White and Francis Mackle-'wain 13 Apr. 1749; to Thos. Berry 18 July 1752; to Nicholas Broadway 20 Jany. 1768; to Medlock

ABSTRACTS OF DEEDS

5 Oct. 1768. Prov. Apr. 1774
Wm. Pickett by Wm. Pickett. .
　　　　　　　J. Auld, Clk.

Page 303--23 Dec. 1773. Mark Allen to Solomon Gross, both of Anson, for 200 pounds, 400 acres on both sides of Yellow Lick Branch of Cheek's Creek ...John Batt Baird's line.
James Allen　　　Prov. Jany. Ct. 1775 by
Luke Robinson　　　Luke Robinson.
　　　　　　　　　　J. Auld, Clk.

Page 324--6 March 1772. John Lucas and wife, Mary, to Alexander Baird, 6 March, 1772, all of Anson, for 40 pounds, 100 acres on Cedar Creek part of a 200 acre grant to John Lucas, 1760.
John Jennings　　Prov. Jany. Ct. 1775 by
Jno. Batt Baird　　　　　　John Jennings.
Edward Morris

Page 325--21 May, 1773. Sam'l. Spencer and his wife, Sibyl, of St. David's Parish, S.C. to Samuel Flake, of Anson, land bought of Charles and Agatha Medlock May 8, 1773, southwest side of Peedee on Smith's Creek, 500 acres granted to Joseph White and McIlwaine.
Wit: Jerusha Tisdale　　Ack. October Ct. 1775.
　　　Enoch Tisdale

Page 331--15 Nov. 1774. Jasper Smith to John Mitchel and Benja. Baird, for 20 pounds proc., one acre on east side of Little River beg. one rod above the Main Saw Mill Dam on the water edge ... for their use except Fishery.
Sol Gross　　　　　Prov. Jany. Term 1775 by
John Smith, Carpenter　　　　John Smith

Page 333--15 Nov. 1774. John Smith, Sandhill and Sarah Smith, his wife, to John Mitchel, for 50 pounds, 100 acres, part of 300 acres that Samuel Ratcliff bought of Leonard Denson, all below Denson's Creek on west bank of Little River of Peedee.
Sol Gross　　　　　　Prov. Jany. Ct. 1775
John Smith, Carp.　　　　by John Smith.

Page 333--15 Nov. 1774. John Smith, Sandhill, and Sarah Smith, his wife, to John Mitchel, for 50 pounds, 100 acres, joining two surveys said to be patents to David Miles...near the bluff of the river (Little).
Sol Gross　　　　　　Prov. Jany. Ct. 1775
John Smith, Carp.　　　　by John Smith.

Page 346--8 May 1772. Jeremiah Menasco to John Batt Baird, for 15 pounds proc. 50 acres beginning at Zacheriah Smith's corner a new line to Gravelly Lick Branch.
Thos. Jennings　　Prov. April Ct. 1774
Solomon Williams　　by Thos. Jennings.
　　　　　　　　　　J. Auld, Clk.

Page 374--13 July, 1775. Joseph Dunham and Mary, his wife, to Allan MacCaskill, all of Anson, for_____,150 acres on Peedee.
Margt. MacCaskill　　　Ack. July Ct. 1775.
　　　　　　　　　　　　J. Auld, Clk.

Page 442--2 Oct. 1777. Henry Tippins to Alexander Baird, both of Anson, for 100 pounds proc. money, 200 acres on Big Creek of Little River.
Wit: Jno Jennings　　Prov. Oct. Ct. 1777
　　Thos. Stanback　　by Thos. Jennings.
　　Thos. Jennings

Page 360--15 April 1775. Benjamin Baird, of Anson, to Wm. Thomas, of same, for 30 pounds Proc. money, 400 acres on Jones's Creek, Robt. Thomas's corner, gr. to Benj. Baird 25 July 1774.
Wit: Thos. Wade　　　Prov. July Ct. 1775
　　Stephen Jackson　　by Thos. Wade.
　　　　　　　　　　　J. Auld, Clk.

Page 126--(upper part missing) Israel? Elison Gross to Nancy Shepherd, for_____ proc. money, 100 acres, part of a tract granted to Morgan Brown Nov. 26, 1757, on south side of Mountain Creek.
Sol Gross, Marke Allen,　　　　(no probate)
Gd. C_____

Page 304--18 May 1774. Solomon Gross to Malcom Martin, for 50 pounds proc. money, 200 acres northeast of Peedee beginning at Luke Robinson's on Cheek's Creek of Little River, between Rich Mt. and Stony Mt. granted to Robert Jarman. Mary Gross also relinquishes.
Soirle McDonald　　Ack. July Court, 1774.
John Powell　　　　　　J. Auld, Clk.

Page 392--20 Jany. 1775. Micajah Pickett, of Craven County, S.C. to Philemon Thomas, for 60 pounds, on the northeast side of the Peedee on main fork of Cartledge's Creek, granted to Wm. Stutely Shirley, July 1, 1775; from him to Micajah Pickett.
James Terry　　　Proved by James Terry
Joseph Hall　　　　　　July Ct. 1777.

Page 452--12 Nov. 1774. John Long to Simon Thomas, Wm. Covington & Thos. Dockery for 5 sh; 3 acres, part of 400 acres granted to Wm. Blewett, on Cartledge's Creek, for a Baptist Meeting House.
Wit: Daniel Smith　　Prov. Apr. Ct. 1775 by
　　Joseph Hull　　　Daniel Smith. J. Auld, Clk.

Page 305--7 March 1775. James Allen to his daughter-in-law, Elizabeth Ingram,* a negro girl named Jane, four years old.
Wit: Philip Raiford Ack. Apr. Ct. 1775
*step-daughter J. Auld, Clk.

Page 262--11 Feb. 1774. Simon Hooker and wife, Elizabeth Hooker, to Wm. Coleman, for 100 pounds proc. money, 206 acres.
Wit: Jeremiah Strother, Ack. Oct. Ct. 1774
Catharine Strother, Solomon Strother

Page 190--12 July 1774. Wm. Terry, Jr.^{s} to Matthew Terry, for divers good causes, etc. 275 acres on north side of Peedee.
Geo. Wilson Ack. July Ct. 1774
Joseph Hind (Hines) by Wm. Terry, Jr. Auld, Clk.

Page 138--10 Feb. 1774. John Stevens and wife, Sarah, of Cumberland County, N.C. to Joel McClendon, of Anson, for 20 pounds, land southwest of Peedee, on Dumas' line.
Jesse McClendon Prov. April Ct. 1774 by
Philip Raiford Jesse McClendon J. Auld, Clk.

Page 137--A Register of Births and Marriages. Hannah Fanning, daughter of Richard and Susanna Fanning was born Friday 21 Jany. 1774.
William Collson and Jane Cooper were married July 6, 1773.
Jane Collson, daughter of Wm. and Jane Collson was born Monday, 11 July 1774.

Page 540--6 Feb. 1778. William and Mourning Pickett to John Dejarnett, all of Anson, for 200 pounds N.C. money, 148 acres granted to William Pickett 22 May 1772.
Thos. Megginson Ack. July Court 1778.
Wm. Threadgill John Auld, Clk.
Thos. Pickett

Page 539--6 Feb. 1778. William and Mourning Pickett to John'Dejarnett, all of Anson County, for 315 pounds, 325 acres on southwest side of Peedee, granted to John Sheppard and conveyed to said Pickett by deed.
Thos. Megginson Ack. July Ct. 1778
Wm. Threadgill John Auld, Clk.
Thos. Pickett

Page 382--17 Nov. 1772. Anthony Hutchins, of Anson County, N.C. to Joseph Brown, of Georgetown, S.C. tract granted to Anthony Hutchins Feb. 22, 1764, on Little Fork of Richardson's Creek.
Wit: John Wright Prov. July Ct. 1774 by
Carney Wright Daniel Spencer
Daniel Spencer J. Auld, Clk.

Page 325--29 Sept. 1774. Stephen Cole to Wm. Coleman, both of Anson. Whereas Stephen Cole and Wm. Coleman had a patent for 200 acres May 24, 1773, at the only costs to said William Coleman, Cole conveys same to him, the tract on the west side of the Huwarry on south side of Mockason Branch near Poplar Shoals.
Wm. Mask Ack. Jany. Ct. 1775
Wm. Leak J. Auld, Clk.
Mathew Raiford

Page 113--17 Jany 1772. John Cartright to Wm. Coleman and James Pickett, all of Anson, for 82 pounds, tract on north side of Peedee on northeast side of Mountain Creek.
Wit: Joseph Hinds, Jno. Almond,
J. Duncan
(proven in open court by Joseph Hinds.)

Page 340--25 Jany. 1772. Richard Brasswell to Christopher Christian, both of Anson, for 35 pounds, 200 acres on Little River in Anson County, granted Richard Brasswell Nov. 25, 1771, on east bank of said Little River...Wm. Stone's lower corner...river bank in David Poor's land.
Goen Morgan Ack. Jany. Ct. 1775.
Geo. Brasswell J. Auld, Clk.

Page 348--29 June 1775. Christopher Christian to Henry Burcham, both of Anson, for 50 pounds, 200 acres on Little River bought from Richard Brasswell. Prov. by James Cotton, Esq.
Wit: James Cotton Oct. Ct. 1775.
Walter Cunningham

Page 24--1 Jany. 1771. Isaac and Elizabeth Jackson to Wm. Moody; £30; 200 acres, northeast of Peedee at a pine deemed near John Land's corner, east of Cartledge's Creek, pat. 9 Apr. 1770.
Wit: Chas. Hines Ack. Oct. Ct. 1775
Annah Thomas J. Auld, Clk.
Mary Smith

Page 309--15 Sept. 1772. Fred. Gibble, of Dobbs County, N.C. to Nathaniel Holton, of Cumberland County, N.C.; £10; 100 acres north of Peedee.
Wit: Robt. Campbell Prov. Jany. Ct. 1775.
Archibald Homes by Archd. Homes. J. Auld, Clk.

Page 408--10 July 1774. Josiah Swearingen, of Anson, to John Jennings, of same, for 40 pounds,

ABSTRACTS OF DEEDS

300 acres on east side of Cheek's Creek.
Wit: John Batts Baird   Ack. Jany. Ct. 1775
Jennie Baird   J. Auld, Clk.
Alex. Baird

Page 255--12 Oct. 1774. Joshua Morgan to John Morgan, both of Anson, for 25 pounds, 180 acres granted Wm. Phillips Nov. 26, 1757, on south side of Peedee River, west side of Grindstone Branch above Morgan's mill.
Wit: John Leverett   Prov. Oct. Ct. by
Wm. Leverett   John Leverett,
    J. Auld, Clk.

Page 285--27 May, 1774. Van Swearingen, of the Province of S.C. to Josiah Swearingen, of Anson, planter, of Province of N.C. for 15 pounds proc., 468 acres on both sides of a branch of Check's Creek in Anson... to Smith's line, with said line to Baird's line, north to Allen's line thence with Touchstone's line.
John Jennings   Prov. Oct. Ct. 1774 by
Eliz. Woodard   John Jennings,
Mary Swearingen   J. Auld, Clk.

Page 285--8 Sept. 1774. John Batt Baird to Thos. Jennings, both of Anson County, for 50 pounds proc., 100 acres... Zachariah Smith's corner... to Gravelly Lick Branch... path to Caleb Touchstone's... Woodward's branch near the Mill place.
John Jennings   Prov. Oct. Ct. 1774 by
Alexander Baird   John Jennings,
    J. Auld, Clk.

Page 300--27 Oct. 1774. Josiah Swearingen to Duncan McNabb, both of Anson, for 40 pounds proc, on Cheeks Creek east of Little River... Baird's line... Allen's... Touchstone's... Woodward's Branch on Jenning's line, 300 acres. Mary Swearingen also relinquishes.
Sol Gross   Prov. Jany. Ct. 1775 by
Mary Anderson   Solomon Gross,
Sam'l Swearingen, Sr.   J. Auld, Clk.

Page 301--6 Sept. 1773. James Allen to Solomon Gross, both of Anson, for 100 pounds, tract on both side of Cheek's Creek, part of tract Thos. Swearingen bought of Richard Caswell, west side of Cheek's Creek below mouth of small creek that runs between Bat Baird's plantation and where Josiah Swearingen did live, to a place called Woodward's. Mary Allen also relinquishes.
George Hodge   Ack. Apr. 1774,
Isaa Jones   J. Auld, Clk.
Bettey Allen

Page 487--29 March 1776. Solomon Gross and Mary, his wife, to Thos. Gowers, all of Anson, land on Cheek's Creek.
Dun McNabb   Ack. Jany. Term 1778
Sarah Gross   J. Auld, Clk.

Page 534--6 Feb. 1778. William and Mourning Pickett to John DeJarnett, all of Anson, for 500 pounds, 200 acres, gr. to John Harrington, 25 Mch. 1748; conveyed or willed to son Chas. Harrington, by deed from Chas. to William Pickett.
Thos. Megginson   Ack. Anson Co.
Wm. Threadgill   July Court 1778.
Thos. Pickett   J. Auld, Clk.

Page 372--20 Jany. 1775. Micajah Pickett of Craven County, S.C., to Daniel Smith, of Anson, for 70 pounds, tract in Anson granted Christopher Hunt by patent 1762, on Cartledge's Creek, 100 acres, granted Wm. Blewett Mch. 6, 1759 and sold to George Carter; then by deed to Wm. Stutely Shirley. It is said to have been granted in 1750 by mistake and is now in possession of Micajah Pickett.   Prov. July Ct. 1775
James Terry   by Chas. Hines.
Char. Hines   J. Auld, Clk.

Page 310--24 Jany. 1774. Going Morgan to Sias Billinsley, both of Anson, for 40 pounds, land on Clark's Creek, adjoining Thomas Underwood, to Harrington's corner.
Thomas Wilson   Prov. Apr. Ct. 1775 by
John Wilson   Thos. Wilson.
Job Wilson   J. Auld, Clk.

Page 486--26 April 1777. Joshua Morgan to Burwell Lanier, both of Anson, for 40 pounds, 150 acres on Grindstone Fork of Gold's Fork, part of a larger tract of 300 acres.
Micajah Stinson   Prov. July Ct. 1777 by
John Everett   John McClendon,
John McClendon   J. Auld, Clk.

Page 496--4 Nov. 1775. Joshua Morgan and Ann, his wife, to Burwell Lanier, both of Anson, for 80 pounds, 200 acres part of a tract of 500 acres granted Joshua Morgan Apr. 18, 1771. Grindstone Fork of Brown's Creek, adj. Wm. Phillips.
Betty Gresham   Prov. Jany. 1776 by
Micajah Stinson   Micajah Stinson,
William Morgan   J. Auld, Clk.

Page 341--12 Apr. 1775. George Wilson to John Jarman, both of Anson, for 20 shillings, tract on south side of the Peedee granted John McCoy, 300

ABSTRACTS OF DEEDS

acres, Mch. 15, 1756, adj. John McCoy and Cartledge.
William Leak   Ack. April Ct. 1775,
Morgan Brown   J. Auld, Clk.

Page 519--11 Feb. 1775. Thos. Wilson to Henry Mounger, both of Anson, 150 acres on northeast side of Great Peedee, on both sides of Island Creek, granted to Thos. Wilson 4 May 1773.
John Harris   Ack. April Ct. 1775,
Job Wilson   J. Auld, Clk.
Martha Wilson

Page 528--27 Apr. 1778. John Wilson to John James, Sr., both of Anson, for 200 pounds, two tracts: one, pat. to James Bowns (Bounds), deeded to John Bowns, and by him deeded to John Wilson, on south side of Hitchcock's Creek on Falling Creek; the 2nd: tract gr. to Henry Snead and deeded to John Bowns, on Falling Creek, lower side of Hitchcock's, adj. James Bown's home and Wm Husbands.
Robt. Webb   Prov. July Ct. 1777 by
John James, Jr.   John James, Jr.

Page 34--26 Feb. 1774. Wm Fielding to George Wilson, both of Anson, for 25 pounds, 132 acres in Anson on south side of Peedee River.
John Jarman   Prov. April Ct. 1774
Daniel Morris   by John Jarman,
    J. Auld, Clk.

Page 35--30 Nov. 1773. Robert Jarman to George Wilson, both of Anson, part of 185 acres granted to Robt. Jarman Jany. 22, 1773, adjoining Edmond Cartledge's grant dated Apr. 7, 1745, adj. John McCoy's grant dated 15 Mch. 1756.
Joseph Martin   Prov. April Ct. 1774
Wm.? Jackson   by Joseph Martin,
    J. Auld, Clk.

Page 329--12 April 1775. John Jarman and Jane, his wife, to George Wilson, all of Anson, for 20 pounds, on south side of the Peedee, being a part of 250 acres granted to John Jarman Jan. 27, 1771, adjoining John McCoy and Robt. Jarman.
Wit: William Leak   Ack. April Ct. 1775
Morgan Brown   J. Auld, Clk.

Page 366--11 July 1775. John Bound to John Wilson, both of Anson, for 160 pounds, three tracts; first, 100 acres granted James Bound, Sr. in Anson on south side of Hitchcock's Creek on Falling Creek, adjoining John Crawford...Richard Deerman; 2nd, 100 acres patented by Henly Snead Dec. 22, 1770, on Falling Creek on lower side of Hitchcock's Creek, adj. Stafford Williams; 3rd, 8 acres pat. Jno. Bownd May 19, 1772, north side of Peedee, adj James Bounds home line. Mary Bounds relinquishes rights.
Wit: John Cole   Prov. July Ct. 1775
William Briley   by Wm. Briley,
    J. Auld, Clk.

Page 523--25 Feb. 1777. John Oliver to Matthew Terry, both of Anson, for 20 pounds, 100 acres in Anson, adj. Solomon Deerman, granted said Oliver Mch. 11, 1775.   July Ct. 1778,
Wit: John Bound,   J. Auld, Clk.
Dunn Grant, Thomas Freeman

Page 500--6 Jany. 1777. Ezra Bostick to James Smith, both of Anson, for 50 pounds, land on Cedar Creek of Peedee, 150 acres.
Jno. Skinner   Prov. Jany. Ct. 1777
Wm. Thomas   by John Skinner,
    J. Auld, Clk.

Page 282--16 Dec. 1772. Wm. McDonald to Malcolm Munroe, both of Anson, for 35 pounds, land on Mountain Creek granted to William McDonald 20 Nov. 1772.
Arch. Munroe, Catron Munroe

Page 352--8 Apr. 1775. Soirle McDonald to Norman McLeod, both of Anson, land in Anson on Mountain Creek, adj. Wm. McDonald and Stephen Touchstone. Flora McDonald also relinquishes.
Duncan McNabb, Roderick Mackinnon

Page 373--8 July, 1775. Soirle and Florrie McDonald to Donald McDonald, all of Anson, for 20 pounds, 100 acres in Anson on Cheek's Creek, patented 23 July, 1774.
Roderick Mc_____,
Thos. Jennings, John Jennings

Page 376--16 Feb. 1775. Alex. McDonald, of Mount Pleasant, to Norman McLeod, of Anson, for 112 pounds, land in Anson on Mountain Cr. granted to Luke Robinson Dec. 16, 1769 and deeded by him to Alex. McDonald, Oct. 26, 1772. Anabella MacDonald also relinquishes.
Murdo MacCaskill, Kenneth MacDonald

Page 223--8 Oct. 1774. Wm. McDonald to Daniel McDaniel, both of Anson, for 50 pounds, land on Buffalo Creek, part of 150 acres granted to said William McDonald, May 19, 1772.
Josiah Swearingen, Chas. Robinson, Jacob Cockerham

Page 42--8 Jany. 1774. Solomon Gross to Isaac Armstrong, both of Anson, for 40 pounds, 100 acres on Great Buffalo Creek, east of Little River. Mary Gross also relinquishes.
John Skinner   Ack. April Ct. 1774,
Jeremiah Marasked (Maresco)   J. Auld, Clk.
John Swor

Page 559--15 May 1775. Jasper Smith, of Anson, to John Kimbrough, of Gilford (Guilford) County, N.C., for 8 pounds 4 shillings proc. money, 150 acres on Dison's Creek, granted to Jasper Smith 23 July 1774.   Prov. Oct. Court 1778.
R. Downs   by Benj. Baird,
Benj. Baird   J. Auld, Clk.

Page 569--30 March 1776. Solomon Gross and wife, Mary, of Anson County, for 100 pounds, to John Kimbrough, of Anson, the plantation whereon Samuel Swearingen formerly lived, containing 99 acres..... to patent lines between Wm. Stone and Wm. Crittenden who holdeth the other 100 acres of 200 acres granted to Robert Mills 24 March 1747.
Benj. Baird   Ack. Oct. Court 1778.
Wm. McNabb, James Almond,
Cornelius Robison (Robinson)

Page 468--_____1778. John Walters to George Walters, both of Anson, for £200, land northeast of Little River, adj. Dennis Nowland.
Wit: Walter Leak   Prov. Jany. Term 1778,
     James Burns   by Walter Leak

Page 501--2 Dec. 1776. John Walters to George Walters, both of Anson, for £400, 300 acres.
Wit: Wm. Mask   Prov. April Ct. 1777
     James Burns   by Wm. Mask.
     Nancy Walters

Page 519--1 Nov. 1777. John Walters to Thos. Meggison, both of Anson.
Wit: Rachel Maoby, Walter Leak

Page 328-11 Dec. 1774. Rebecca Lisles, widow, relict, and extrix. of will of John Lisles, late of Anson, to James Auld, of same, for £30, 200 acres on Island Creek.   Prov. Jany. 1775
Wit: Christopher Clark   by Morgan Brown,
     Morgan Brown   J. Auld, Clk.

Page 249--3 Oct. 1776. John Walters to Thos. Megginson, both of Anson, for £225, 300 acres.
Wit: Thos. Pickett   Ack. Oct. Ct. 1777.
     Jos. Ingram   J. Auld, Clk.
     Humphrey Rogers

Page 46--23 Oct. 1773. Matthew Raiford, senr., and Judah, his wife, to Matthew Raiford, Jun., all of Anson, for ₤10, 100 acres, at the foot of Cheek Mountain on Little River, adj Matthew Raiford, senr. and James Sheppard.
Wit: Js. Pickett   Ack. April Court 1774.
     James Raiford   J. Auld, Clk.

---

1. John Smith, Little River (and Thicketty Cr.) had the following sons: Jasper, Charles, William, Joseph and probably James. (Anson Co. Deeds passim).

2. Anthony Hutchins, born in New Jersey, a staunch Loyalist, seeing that war was inevitable, about 1770, went to the Natchez Dist. (Miss.) then British territory, where his brother, Thomas, was a successful surveyor, and obtained large land grants there. (Hist. of Miss. by Dunbar Rowland, Vol. 1 - 266)

3. As James Coleman, bro. of John, married Mourning Terry, the original deed book was checked to be sure that it is John and not James in this record. Both seem to have married a Mourning.

4. James Terry married Elizabeth, dau. of Richard Leak. Their sons, John and Richard Leak, who were named in Richard Leak's will (Orange Co. N.C.), died in Chester Co. S. C. in 1804 and 1801. (Chester Co. S. C. Probate Rec. File 66-1038, 1030)

5. The first mention yet discovered of "William Terry, Jr." is in a deed dated 14 Apr. 1759 (Bk 5-357), and there is nothing to contradict his being the William Terry, east of the Peedee, who was in Anson as early as Jany. 1751, and came to be called William Terry Jr. to be distinguished from William Terry of Savannah Cr. He was certainly married by 1751 for his oldest son, Mathew, was a "chain-carrier" in 1769 and had a grant issued to him in 1772. Besides, the will of his father-in-law, Mathew Raiford, Sr. of Cumberland Co, written 21 July 1752, says: "to my dau. Anne one shilling sterling to be paid within one year, together with what she has heretofore received "which shows that before that date she was married at which time she received her portion. Only the unmarried daus. of Mathew Raiford received anything more than one shilling in his will, and none of the sons-in-law were named. William Terry Jr's son, Champness, suggests that he was probably of the Southside Virginia Terrys and connected with those of Louisa Co. James Terry who apparently came to Anson with him may have been a brother. William Terry, of Savannah Cr., was the son of James and Margaret Terry, of Edge-

60   ABSTRACTS OF DEEDS

combe Co. where James bought land in what is now Halifax Co. in 1739, and in 1741 received a land grant which he deeded to his son, William, in 1746. (Halifax Co. Deed Books 5-209,483:4-38)
   6. While this gift deed apparently has no connection with the above Robt. Jarman, it is given for what help it may be to the other line. Deed of Gift from Joseph Elkins of Cumberland Co. for love and aff. to Eliz. Jarman, wife of Robert Jarman, late of S. C., and her children, Viz: Priscilla, Nancy, Alice, Ullis (?) and Molly, slaves, furniture, horses, cattle, hogs, etc. After the death of Elizabeth Jarman, George Bletcherton, of Granville Co. N. C., to be trustee for children until each is married. 15 Jany. 1760. Wit: Wm. Ainsworth, Michael Dickerson. (Cumb. Co. D. B. 1 -345)

DEED BOOK 4

Page 33--10 Apr. 1778. Nathan Falkner to Henry Wilson, of same, for 100 pounds, 200 acres in Anson, on south fork of Jones Creek, granted to Thos. Mitchell Jan. 22, 1773.
Robt. Jarman, Elisha Brelar

Page 359--24 Nov. 1780. Jonathan Wise, of Craven County, S.C. to George Wilson, of Anson, whereas Edmund Cartledge had granted to him land on the south side of the Peedee Apr. 17, 1745, transferred same to John McCoy, Jan. 15, 1750, and whereas John McCoy had granted to him south side of the Peedee contiguous to Edmund Cartledge, adjoining a certain Wm. McCay's, containing 300 acres. After the death of the said McCoy the two tracts did descend to the seven daughters and co-heirs of sd John McCoy, namely Ann, Alecy, Mildred, Elizabeth, Frances, Molly and Sarah and whereas Ann intermarried with a certain John Red, Alcey with Zacheriah Fenn, Mildred with Philip Alston, who together with the said Elizabeth did make over 4/7th of above two tracts to Jonathan Wise, for a valuable consideration as per deeds, witnesseth that Jonathan Wise, for 650 Spanish milled dollars paid to him by George Wilson deeds to him 4/7th part of the above, 100 acres, patented to Edmund Cartledge and 300 acres of McCoy.
Susanna Wise, Henry William Harrington

Page 142--9 Aug. 1780. Henry Wilson to Richard Odom, of same, for 1500 pounds, 100 acres in Anson, adj. Thos. Mitchell, granted to Thos. Mitchell 22 January 1773 and sold to John Mitchell 18 March 1774; by him to Nathan Falkner 21 Nov. 1777, by him to Henry Wilson, 10 Apr. 1778, it being the lower part of a 200 acre tract.
William Gulledge, Elisha Brular, Sukey Granade

Page 159--19 Aug. 1777. John Smith to John K. Hutcheson, for £24, 100 acres on Savannah Creek.
Wit: Abraham Belyeu   Alex. McCaskill

Page 171--8 Aug. 1782. John May to Pleasant May, both of Anson, for 200 pounds, 200 acres southwest of Peedee, on north prong of Jones's Creek.   Jany. Term 1784.
Written Bennett, George Hammond

Page 181--9 Oct. 1783. Joseph Curbo to Thos. Jones, of Craven County, S.C., for £50, 70 acres southwest of Peedee.

Page 320--14 May 1782. Mourning Coleman to Mary Terry, both of Anson County, for 50 pounds, in hand paid by Mary Terry, widow, negro boy named Sharper, aged 13 years, "which negro was given to by my father, William Terry, dec'd. and all the rest of my part of goods and chattels in hand of my father's executors."
John Everett, Benjamin Ingram

Page 328--22 Apr. 1778. Wm. Yoe to John Smith, land on southwest side of Peedee, on Savannah Creek.
Comfort Baluck [?]   Anson Court 1783
Thos Tallant, James Terry

Page 348--17 Apr. 1784. John Roland to John Baker, for 100 pounds, 200 acres in Anson on south side of Brown Creek, including Roland's improvement, John Roland's patent 25 July, 1774.
Ezekial Roland, James Baker

Page 217--20 Feb. 1785. Mesaniah Wilson, of Anson, for love and affection, to my son, David Wilson, one full half part of all my part of estate of George Wilson, dec'd., as his widow, to be laid off at the division of the estate.
Wit: John Auld, John Jarman

Page 217--29 May 1784. Benjamin Smith, of Brunswick County, N.C., Esq. and Sarah, his wife, late Sarah Dry, spinster, only child and heir-at-law of William Dry, late of Brunswick County, Esq., dec'd., to James Williams, of Hillsborough,

ABSTRACTS OF DEEDS 61

Orange County, N.C., for £500, 300 acres on the east side of Richardson's Cr., below mouth of Owens Br.; also 300 acres on south side of Peedee on north branch of Jones Cr; also 250 acres on Gould's Fork of Brown Cr, pat. to Wm. Powell 29 Sept. 1756; also land in Bladen Co.
Wit: John Auld
John Speed

---

1. Benjamin Smith, Jr. was married to Sarah Dry, 20 Nov. 1777 in Charleston, S. C. (S. C. Marriages by Clemens).
Will of Sarah Dry Smith, of Orton, Brunswick, N. C. July 18, 1818. Husband all estate except $485 to Miss Mary Rowan and $300 to Mrs. Rebecca Ann Sullivan; to my husband all title to rich lands on New River which, though contested, I swear before God to be my right. (signed) Sarah Dry Smith. wit: Mary Rowan, R. Harvey, Angus McClellan. Prob. Brunswick Co. April 1822. Recorded Bk 1E, p. 312, Knox County, Tennessee. From the description of the lands in above deed Benjamin Smith was the son of Benjamin and Ruth Smith of Anson Co. William Dry, of Brunswick County, was a large land-holder. Among his holdings was a tract in Anson south of the Peedee.

DEED BOOK H

Page 77--26 April 1787, James Terry [Savannah Cr.] to John Phillips [no residence given], for 50 pounds, 130 acres on southwest side of the Peedee River on Jones Creek, being a part of a tract of land granted to William Hollifield 3 Sept. 1779.
Jos. Ingram   Ack. by James Terry
Andw. Ross   in July Court 1787

Page 235--20 April 1786. Avington Cox to James Terry, [Savannah Cr.] both of Anson County, for 50 pounds, 130 acres southwest of Peedee on Jones Creek, granted to William Hollifield 3 Sept. 1779.
John Smith   Ack. Anson County
Hugh Ross   July Court 1786

Page 236--4 March 1786. William Hunter, of Richmond County, to Hardy Hooker, of Anson County, land southwest wide of Peedee adj. James Morgan, above James White's survey.
Wit: James Terry (Savannah Cr.)
Wm. Williams   Prov. July Ct. 1786
                      by James Terry
                      Mich. Auld Clk.

Page 319--2 Apr. 1785. John Smith to Samuel Flake, both of Anson, for £100, 100 acres southwest of Peedee, on Smith's Cr.
Wit: James Terry   Prov. July Ct. 1786
     Thos. Smith   by Jas. Terry.

Page 316--23 Dec. 1785. John Smith, and Mary, his wife, to Wm. Henry, all of Anson, for £50, 200 acres, southwest of Peedee on west side of Cedar Creek, in Samuel French's 3rd line.
Wit: Thos. Bailey, Thos. Smith

Page 44--31 May 1786. John Lee and Elizabeth, his wife, of Montgomery Co., to Richard Manly, of Anson, for £200, 100 acres gr. John Lee 14 Oct. 1783, on north side of Lane's Creek.
Wit: Thos Threadgill   Prov. Apr. Ct. 1787
     Wm. Davenport   by Thos. Threadgill.
     Nat Chambers   Mich. Auld, clk

Page 132--8 July, 1784. John Collson, of Montgomery Co., to Stephen Hyde, of Anson, for £200, 3 tracts of land in Anson, on both sides of Brown Cr., beg. at John Smith's lower corner on south bank of Brown Cr. ... Shadrach Denson's ...
Wit: Geo. Davidson,   [no probate]
     Hugh Ross, John Smith

Page 135--8 July 1784. John Collson, Sr. of Montgomery County, to John C. Hyde, beloved grandson, son of Stephen Hyde, four negroes.
Wit: Geo. Davidson   Prov. July Ct. 1785 by
     Hugh Ross   Geo. Davidson.
     John Smith

Page 138--3 Jany. 1786. Wm. Strickland to James Little, both of Anson, for £40, 160 acres adj. Lewis Lowry, James Smith, Thompson's Cr.
Wit: Peter Lowry, John Talton

Page 142--7 Apr. 1785. Thomas Wade to Wm. Boggan, Jr., both of Anson, for nat. love and affection, 200 acres.

Page 144--7 Apr. 1785. Thomas Wade to John Boggan, Jr. for £3, one-half acre in town of Newton.

Page 139--Burwell Lanier to William Lanier, both of Anson, for 5 sh., 200 acres adj. Joel Phillips on Brown Cr.
Wit: Morgan Brown   Ack. April Ct. 1786.
Lewis Lanier

Page 183--28 Dec. 1782. Robt. Broadway to Christopher Williams, both of Anson, for £12, 150 acres on Cribbs Creek.
Wit: Wm. Yarbrough,   Ack. Anson Ct. 1785.
Frankey Yarbrough, Wm. Remey

Page 191--3 June 1786. Thos. Wade, Sr., Esq. to George Wade, his son, for love and affection, seven tracts in Anson where Thos. Wade now lives called Mt. Pleasant, 400 acres, orig. gr. Caleb Howell, 300 acres gr. Anthony Hutchins, 150 acres gr. sd Wade, 75 acres gr. Leonard Higdon and conveyed to sd Wade by John and Mary Higdon, heir and widow of Leonard Higdon, adj. above, etc., also slaves.   Prov. Oct. Ct. 1786 by
Wit: T. Wade, Jr.   Eliz. Brown and
Eliz. Brown   Grizzel Boggan
Grizzel Boggan   Mich. Auld, clk.

Page 196--1 June, 1785. Thos. Wade, Sr. Esq. to Sarah Wade, his dau., 6 negroes. Same wit. as above and same probate.

Page 233--18 Sept. 1786. Michael Auld to Thos. Ellis, both of Anson, for £45, 100 acres on Island Cr. gr. James Lyles, 14 Oct. 1783, adj. John Knotts.   Oct. Ct. 1786
Wit: James Jerry, Joseph Martin

Page 230--11 Jany. 1785. Thos. Jones, of Craven Co., S.C. to James Farr, for £40, 150 acres pat. to sd Jones 1774.

Page 310--11 Jany. 1787. Jonathan Jackson, former Sheriff of Anson Co., to George Davidson, of Montgomery, for £72/10, recovered in court by sd Davidson agst. Peter Lewis and Nath'l. Lewis, late of this bailiwick, 300 acres, sold at auction, on Buck Cr. of Brown Cr. ... Cheek's line.
Wit: John Pemberton   Ack. Anson Ct. 1787.
Daniel Gould

Page 165--24 Oct. 1782. Thomas Bailey's grant, #464, 100 acres in Anson on Gould's upper corner east side of Lick Creek and sd Bailey's old line.

Page 200--10 March 1785. William Smith and Mary, his wife, to Henry Jackson, all of Anson, for £60, 150 acres, gr. to Wm. Smith Oct. 8, 1783, adj. William Rushing, Wm. Love.
[end of deed missing.]

DEED BOOK B#2

Page 65--Sept. 4, 1779. Joshua Morgan's grant. In consideration of 50 shillings for every hundred acres paid by Joshua Morgan, 150 acres in Anson County southwest of the Peedee River on the Flat Fork of Brown's Creek, adj. George Belew... to Burwell Lanier's corner.

Page 81--23 Jany. 1787. James Fanning, of Suffolk County, N.Y. to Stephen Hyde, of Anson County, N.C. for 20 pounds, tract of land in Anson on the south side of Brown's Creek below Gould's Fork... to John Colson's line... Smith's line [S.H.] ... Phillips line, 140 acres, a quit claim deed.
Wm. Threadgill   Proved by Thos. Threadgill
Thos. Threadgill   July Court 1788
       Reg. 10 Oct. 1788.

Page 103--10 March 1787. Peter Smith and wife, Susanna, to Chas. Sparks, for £80, one-half of 200 acres, to Peter Smith from Simon Churchill and wife, Sarah, 9 Sept. 1756.
Isaac Jackson   Ack._____Ct. 1788
Samuel Blythe Dickson

Page 341--3 Jany. 1791. Edward Smith and wife, Easter Smith, to James Liles, for £100, 155 acres as per patent to Thomas Thomas, 18 Apr. 1771, except graveyard, on east side of Jones Cr.
Wit: Lewis Lanier   Jany. Ct. 1791
Christopher Watkins

Page 125--9 Sept. 1786. Francis Woods to John Ball, Daniel Jennings, John Woodrow, George Smith, Josiah Smith, David Desaussure, and Edward Darrell, of Charleston, S.C. merchants, £760, mortage.
Duncan McRae, Thos. Ellerby

Page 386--16 Nov. 1790. Van Swearingen Grant. For 10 pounds, 100 acres in Anson County, adjoining George Linsey... Robt. Seago.

Page 405--21 July 1791. Van Swearingen, to Stephen Hyde, both of Anson, for 40 pounds, tract in Anson, adj. George Linsey, Robt. Sego, 100 acres.
Richard Smith, Zedekiah Ledbetter

ABSTRACTS OF DEEDS 63

Page 114--4 Jany. 1783. David Dumas, of Montgomery Co., to John DeJarnett, of Anson, for £40, 200 acres southwest of Peedee, adj. Charles Harrington.
Wit: Ford DeJarnett
Richard DeJarnett
January Court 1783

DEED BOOK C#2

Page 30--14 Sept. 1790. John Smith to William Smith, [Little River,] both of Anson County, for 25 pounds, 100 acres on Little River of Peedee, granted to said John Smith Dec. 5, 1760.
Richard Downs, Wm. Queen,
Margaret Queen

Page 444--April 1790. Jacob Tison, of Anson, to Arthur Smith, of same, 200 acres on Peedee, for $200, northwest of Brown Creek, adj. Dennis McClendon.
Wit: Hugh Ross, A.Wade

Page 445--25 _____ 1795. William Woods, of Anson, to Arthur Smith, of same, southwest of Peedee, adj. Ezekiel McClendon's former line.
Wit: A. Wade

Page 275--3 Aug. 1792. John McDaniel and wife, Ann, of county of Pring [?] State of South Carolina, to Jacob Tison, of Anson, land in Anson southwest of the Peedee on Brown's Creek, 150 acres, granted to John McClendon 3 Sept. 1779.
Nathan Morris, Jeremiah Mercer

Page 182--Apr. 1, 1793. Liday Bailey to Mathew Bailey, both of Anson, for £20, 100 acres southwest of Peedee, adj. Thos. Bailey, granted Liday Bailey 16 Nov. 1790.
Wit: Mathew Bailey   Prov. July Ct. 1793 by
    Thomas Bailey   Thos. Bailey

Page 207--15 Sept. 1793. Mathew Bailey to Thomas Bailey, for £20, 100 acres southwest of Peedee, gr. Thos. Bailey 1784, adj. Phillips old fields.
Wit: James Lee   Ack. Oct. Ct. 1793.
    John Bloodworth   Wm. Johnson, clk.

Page 211--31 Aug. 1793. Burwell Lanier and Wm. Lanier to Thos. Bailey, all of Anson, for £30, paid to Sampson Lanier by bond bearing date, June 7, 1786, 150 acres on both sides of Lawyers Road on Cowpen Br. of Cedar Creek, pat. to Sampson Lanier Dec. 1787.
Wit: Wm. Wood   Ack. Oct. Ct. 1793.
    Matthew Bailey

DEED BOOK H#2

Page 4--3 Oct. 1800. Francis Baker, of Anson Co. to Reese Shelby, Jr., of Chesterfield Co. S.C., for $100, 250 acres on Lane's Creek, Wm. Shepherd's corner.   Prov. Jany Ct. 1801
Wit: Jacob Phillips   by Jacob Phillips,
    Evan Shelby   Tod Robinson, clk.

Page 6--27 May 1795. Francis Baker, of Anson Co., to Reese Shelby, Jr. for $20, 90 acres on Lane's Creek.   Jany. Term 1797
Wit: Rees Shelby, Sen., Evan Shelby, Jr.

Page 12--31 March 1801. Jane Wade, of Anson, for nat. aff. to my grandchildren, Janes Wade Prout, Jane Vining, Joshua Prout, Jr., and Holden Wade Prout, 4 lots in Wadesboro, whereon I now live, on Green Street, Nos. 30, 39, 68, 69, which I purchased of John Hallaway, and two other lots. Nos. 62 and 63, wh. I pur. of Joshua Prout, to remain in my possession and under my control during my life.
Wit: James Boggan, Sr.   Ack. in April Ct. 1801
    Eliz. Wade   Tod Robinson, clk.

Page 13-17--Other gift deeds acknowledged in April Court 1801, by Jane Wade: 31 March 1801, to 4 gr.ch.: Wm Hambleton Wade, and Judith Wade, ch. of my son, Thomas, and Mary and Sarah Wade, ch. of my son, Holden; 30 March 1801, to Lydia Prout, silver buckles, sugar tongs, etc. my dau. Sarah Prout to keep same in her possession; 15 Sept. 1800, to Polly Wade, lot in Wadesboro; to Jane W. Prout, a negro girl; to Holden Wade Prout and Joshua Prout negroes; to Sarah Wade, dau. of

ABSTRACTS OF DEEDS

Holden Wade, lot #25 in Wadesboro; and 28 Apr. 1795, to Judith Wade 100 acres.

Page 224--24 Apr. 1801. David Dumas, of Montgomery Co., to Edward Avery Luch [Lucy], for £185, 200 acres pat. to John Collson, 5 Dec. 1760, on east side of Brown Creek.
Wit: Obadiah Dumas   Prov. Oct. Ct. 1801 by
     Azariah Dumas   Obadiah Dumas,
                          Tod Robinson, clk.

Page 188--15 July 1801. James Hough to Isham Ingram, both of Anson, for £250, land on Brown Creek on north bank of Lick Branch, Threadgill's corner, adj. Stephen Hyde.
Wit: Kinchen Martin   Ack. Oct. Ct. 1801.
     Kinchen Wall   Tod Robinson, clk.

Page 297--12 April 1802. Wm. Johnson to Wm. Terry, of Anson, for $200, all that tract in Anson and the town of Sneydesboro (Sneedboro), 16 lots: Nos. 151, 152, 153, 154, 155, 156, 167, 168, 203, 204, 205, 206, 219, 220, 221, and 222.
Wit: Jas. Johnson   Ack. April Court 1802.

Page 491--19 June 1800. Toddy Robinson and Eli Terry to Robt. Webb, all of Richmond Co., N.C. for £300, 212 acres sw of Peedee.
Wit: R. Poe
     Hester Hinson

Page 257--4 Apr. 1799. Samuel Wilson to Henry Adcock, both of Anson, for £200, 115 acres, west of Peedee, Solomon Wilson's corner.
Wit: Jesse Pitman   Ack. Jany. Ct. 1802.
     Chas Hamer

Page 437--2 Feb. 1802. Samuel, Solomon, John and David Wilson, of Anson Co., to John Haley, of Richmond Co., for £200, 125 acres in Anson southwest of Peedee River.
Wit: Robert Clark   Prov. by Robt. Clark
     Buck Nance   (no date)
                      Tod Robinson, clk.

Page 496--January Term, 1803. Surveyor and Jurors dividing lands belonging to the heirs of John Smith, dec'd. (of Smith's Cr.)
#1 John Smith .... 99 1/2 acres
#2 George Lindsey............ 99 1/2 acres
#3 Eli Smith................ 99 1/2 acres
#4 James Smith .... 99 1/2 acres
#5 Jesse Smith.............. 99 1/2 acres
#6 Samuel Smith .... 99 1/2 acres
The widow, Mary Smith, to get part of Lots 4 and 5 which, at her death, go to James and Jesse.
              Certified 22 Jany. 1803.
              Tod Robinson, Clerk.
List of jurors: Ezra Bostick, Daniel Murphey, Chas. Campbell, George Briley, John Knotts, Samuel Moses.

DEED BOOK D & E

Page 87--12 March 1796. Zedekiah White to Wm. Morgan, both of Anson, for 80 pounds, 150 acres granted to Aleck Beacham July 9, 1794, on a branch of Brown's Creek near Wm. Beacham's line.
Josiah White, William White

Page 226--30 Aug. 1791. Jonathan Morgan, of Montgomery County, to Gideon Green, of Anson, land including his mill.
Jacob Green, Richard Austin

Page 434--4 March 1797. Jonathan Morgan, of Montgomery County, to William Henson, of Anson, for £100, 100 acres on south side of Rockey River.
William Megbe [McBee], Richard Austin

Page 71--11 June, 1795. Sam'l Wilson of Anson, to Henry Adcock, for 200 pounds, land in Anson on southwest side of Peedee, adjoining David Love,

115 acres, being part of tract bequeathed by George Wilson to his four sons, Samuel, Solomon, Andrew and John.
Leonard Webb, Robert Webb

Page 171--13 Oct. 1795. John Bloodworth to William Hare, [no residence given] for 25 pounds, 200 acres in Anson County, adjoining Davd Love and Thos. Bailey, part of tract granted John Bloodworth, Aug. 7, 1767.
John Speed   Proven in Court April 1796.
Micajah Ganey

Page 220--20 March 1796. Arthur Smith to Barnaby Porter, both of Anson, for 100 pounds, land in Anson, southwest of the Peedee, on Brown's Creek and both sides of Jack's Branch.
John Tison, Chas. Porter

ABSTRACTS OF DEEDS

Page 106--15 Apr. 1797. Cornelius Robinson, of Montgomery County, for love and good will to my loving friend, James Kimbrough, son of John Kimbrough, a negro boy.
Jam. Pickett[1]   Prov. July Ct. 1797 by
Solomon Boggan   Solomon Boggan

Page 107--7 April 1796. James Pickett, of Anson, for love and good will to my loving friend Ann Kimbrough, a negro girl named Jane, daughter of Eady.   (no probate)
Chrislars (?) Jameson, Elizabeth Allen

Page 261--10 Mch. 1795. James Pickett, of Anson, for love, good will and affection to my loving son, Joseph Pickett, of same county, three negroes, Suckey and her two children Sam and Lum.
Josiah Williams   Deed of gift ack.
Wm. Williams   Jany. Court 1797.

Page 262--10 March 1795. James Pickett, of Anson, for love, good will and affection to my loving son Martin Pickett, of same county, three tracts: 300 acres on southwest side of the Peedee, 100 acres on south side of Peedee, and 150 acres joining on the upper line of the Terry old tract, 550 acres in all.
Josiah Williams, Wm. Williams

Page 263--10 March 1795. James Pickett, of Anson, to Frankie Hannah Pickett, my loving daughter, for love, good will and affection, three negroes, Amy, Peter and Ernest.
Josiah Williams, Wm. Williams

Page 263--10 March 1795. James Pickett, of Anson, to my loving son William Raiford Pickett, for love, good will and affection, three negroes, Kissy and her two children, Jabeter [Jupiter?] and Frank and her increase.
Josiah Williams, Wm. Williams

Page 62--28 January 1797. James Terry* of Richmond County, N.C. to Joseph and William Raiford Pickett, of Anson County, for 1000 pounds 890 acres in Anson County, in the following tracts: 300 acres at or near the mouth of the Savannah Creek, except one-half acre including the graveyard; 200 acres also southwest of the Peedee at the mouth of the Savannah Creek,... the beginning tree of the above tract, formerly Joseph White's land... up the River to the beginning; also 300 acres on Savannah Creek adj. the above tracts; also 40 acres on Savannah Creek; and another tract of 50 acres in Anson County on Horse Pen Glade.
Wit: William Robinson   Ack. by Walter Leak in Walter Leak   Anson County April Court 1797

---

1. This is the usual signature of James Pickett, of Richmond County, son of William and Mourning Pickett.

DEED BOOK F & G

Page 31--31 Jany. 1800. Robt. Liles to Samuel Wilson, both of Anson, for £15, a tract in Anson on the southwest of the Peedee River, belonging to the estate of Andrew Wilson, dec'd. where the said Samuel Wilson now lives, adj. Robert Webb, Esq. and Henry Adcock, being a part of land bequeathed by George Wilson to his four sons, Sam'l., Solomon, Andrew, and John Wilson.
B. Nance, John Wilson

Page 71--15 Feby. 1799. John Wilson, of Bullock County, Ga., to Andrew Wilson, of Anson County, N.C. for 150 pounds, 115 acres on west side of the Peedee River, adj. Robert Webb and David Love.
Wit: Solomon Wilson.

Page 187--25 Jany. 1800. Solomon Wilson, of Anson County, to William Wall, Jr., of Richmond County, N.C. for 213 pounds, two tracts in Anson on the southwest side of the Peedee, adjoining Henry Adcocks, Blewett, Robt. Webb, 111 acres, being 1/4 part of all land bequeathed by George Wilson to his four sons: Samuel, Andrew, Solomon and John.
John Wall, Jr., David Miller

Page 33--14 Jany. 1800. Robert Wilson, of Richmond County, N.C. to Solomon Wilson, of Anson County, John Wilson, of Bullock County, Ga. to Samuel Wilson, of Anson County, for 50 pounds, rights, title, etc. in estate of George Wilson, dec'd.
Thos. Adcock, Francis Clark

Page 54--3 Nov. 1795. William May, Sheriff, of Anson County, to Stephen Hyde, planter, whereas May, in official capacity did adv. to sell six tracts

ABSTRACTS OF DEEDS

to raise and levy taxes due thereon for year 1794, there being no personal property in said county, the six tracts being the property of Richard Fanning and Hannah Fanning, lying and being in Anson County on Brown's Creek, one tract granted to Richard Fanning... Randolph Cheek's line; second tract on upper side of Brown's Creek; 3rd granted to Hannah Fanning, beginning at Benj. Smith's 2nd corner... to Denson's line; 4th tract beg. due west from Benj. Smith 73 1/2 poles, crossing Brown's Creek and Palmetto Branch, 100 acres, being part of the tract which has been conveyed by John Smith, [Sandhill] the first purchaser (?) (grantee), to Benjamin Smith thence with his division line; 5th, granted to Hannah Fanning on south side of Branch Creek, 200 acres; 6th, land adj. Elisha Kindred and Isham Ingram. Land offered in 50 acre tracts. No bidder. Then all at one time. Stephen Hyde, the highest bidder, for 14 pounds, 14 shillings 6 pence.
Dan'l. Ross, Buck Nance

Page 151--19 Aug. 1798. Smith Fields and Elizabeth, his wife, to Joseph Clark, who is to maintain Fields and wife, Elizabeth, during their natural lives.
Ezra Bostick, Sarah Hull

Page 134--11 March, 1800. William Raiford Pickett, for love and natural affection which I bear to my mother, Martha Pickett, during her natural life and no longer, lot in Anson beginning in the 4th line of the town of Wadesborough, 6 acres.
Wm. Robards   Ack. April Session 1800.
A. Wade

Page 2--1 Sept. 1794. Jonathan Morgan, of Montgomery County, to William Brooks, of same, for 20 pounds, 50 acres in Anson County on both sides of Taylor's branch of Richardson's Creek.
John Brooks
Wm. Brooks

DEED BOOK N & O

Page 387--13 July 1813. John and James Kimbrough to Sampson Jones, all of Anson County, for $255, 63 acres [part of the tracts bought from Ezekiel McLendon, p. 407.]
George Bryant   Ack. Oct. Ct. 1813
Artemus Watson   Tod Robinson, clk.

Page 182--4 Jany. 1812. James Terry, Sr. [Savannah Cr.] of Richmond County, N.C. to James Carter, of Anson, for $500, 250 acres on Jones Creek, part of two tracts gr. Henry Covington and Benj. Covington.
Wit: Tod Robinson, J. H. Tindall[1]

Page 116--27 Dec. 1811. Benj. Smith, Jr. and John Cochran, for real love and natural affection that we have for the Baptist Society, to Elder Daniel Gould and his society and their Baptist successors, forever, to the only use of the Baptist paternity for the express purpose of building a meeting house and performing the worship of God, one acre of land on both sides of the public road from Spere's Mill to Wadesborough.
Wm. A. Caraway, Malachi Gould

Page 163--5 Jany. 1807. George Wilson, of Anson County, N.C. to John Lambden, for $600, 200 acres in Anson on Jones's Creek, adj. Cock's Mill Pond, surveyed for Wm. Fielding 14 Oct. 1765.
Daniel May, Jno King

Page 406--20 Nov. 1812. Mary Coatney, Courtney, and John Coatney to John Kimbrough, for $500, 235 acres on east side of Flat Fork, beginning on at Gould's line.
Samuel Kindred, Richard Allen

Page 407--   1796. Ezekiel McClendon to John Kimbrough, Jr. and his brother, James Kimbrough, sons of John Kimbrough, all of Anson County, for 182 pounds, two tracts of land in Anson, on Gold's Fork of Brown's Creek. First, beginning at Robt. Raney's corner, granted to John Leverett 25 April 1778; second, 69 acres, beg. at Abraham Williams' corner to Boggan's line, part of a tract of 1000 acres granted to George Gold in 1747.
Gabriel Allen,   Prov. Oct. Term 1813
Benjamin McLendon,   Tod Robinson, clk.
Randle Threadgill, Jesse Tison,
John _____

Page 21--8 Oct. 1810. William Legrand, of Richmond County, to Nathaniel Kimbrough, of Anson, for $100, 200 acres on Gould's Fork... John Leverett's line, granted to Robt. Raney in 1763, a quit claim deed.
A. Belyeu   Proved in Oct. Session, 1810 by
Elisha Kindred   Abraham Belyeu

Page 347--2 March 1813. Jonathan Morgan, of Montgomery County, to Elizabeth Green, of Anson

ABSTRACTS OF DEEDS 67

County, for 50 pounds, 100 acres in Anson on Rocky River.

Wit: James Little
George Wagner

---
1. As Mary Robards married a Tindall, this J. H. Tindall is probably the brother-in-law of James Terry, who married Ann Robards.

DEED BOOK S

Page 39--25 Nov. 1817. William Terry, of Cumberland County, N.C. to Martin Pickett, of Anson, for $125, interest in a certain lot in Wadesboro, Anson Co, #1, conveyed by Nelson P. Jones to Leak, Pickett and Co.
Tod Robinson, John W. Lynch

Page 40--16 Jany. 1818. Andrew Polk, Sheriff, to Martin Pickett, highest bidder, for $1000, 463 acres, [result of suit of some bank versus] Wm. Hammond, Wm. Dusmukes, James Buchanan, John May, Fred. Staton and Patrick Boggan.
Wit: Chas. Stinson, Benj. T. Douglas

Page 27--2 Jany. 1817. Angus McRae, of Anson, to William Terry, of Cumberland, for £90, 57 acres.
Wit: Tod Robinson, ____Wood

Page 29--22 Oct. 1805. William Terry, of Anson, to Toddy Robinson of same, land on Jones Creek, 325 acres, part of a tract granted Benj. Covington, 400 acres, by various deeds to Toddy Robinson who conveyed one-half interest to William Terry.
Robt. Troy,   Anson Term 1818, Joseph Troyd?
Jas. Terry¹   also identified the handwriting of James Terry subscribing witness to said deed.

Page 224--Richard Pattishall, of Dist. of Chesterfield, S.C. to Alex. McRae, 10 Oct. 1817, for $3.00, ten acres in Anson.

Page 320--3 Dec. 1818. Wm. T. Caraway to James Coleman for $2500, all my title and interest to within described lots.   Ack. April Ct. 1819.
Wit: Joseph Pickett   Tod Robinson, clk.

---
1. James Terry, who was father of above William Terry and father-in-law to Toddy Robinson, died May 27, 1816.)

DEED BOOK T

Page 95--James Coleman, Sr. to Thomas Coleman, power of attorney, both of Richmond Co., to do things as shall become necessary in settling my business, to collect debts, etc. as consistent with the funds in his hands for that purpose, to sell such property, furniture, etc. in Richmond as well as in Anson, to take possession of the books at Wadesboro heretofore conducted by James Coleman, Jr.
Wit: Dan Phelan.   Prov. July Ct. 1820 by
Dan'l Phelan.
Tod Robinson, clk.

DEED BOOK L & M

Page 277--5 Dec. 1804. George Lawrence to William Morgan, both of Anson, for 40 pounds 10 shillings, 60 acres in Anson on the north side of Brown's Creek...Delilah Johnson's Branch.
David Rushing
Michal Ryans

ABSTRACTS OF DEEDS

DEED BOOK X

Page 384--14 Oct. 1830. Martha Clark relinquishes right in estate of Joseph Clark.

DEED BOOK V

Page 431--4 Feb. 1825. James Kimbrough to John Kimbrough, both of Anson, for $850, his part of 210 acres on Gould's Fork of Brown's Creek, beginning at Nathaniel Kimbrough's corner. Joseph C. Russell Ack. Jany. Term 1827
John C. Threadgill

DEED BOOK W

Page 449--29 Dec. 1830. Nelly Allen, widow of Drury Allen, decd., Julius Allen, Thomas Allen and Jeremiah Smith and Susannah Smith, his wife, David Allen, Benj. Allen, Philip Kiker and Nancy Kiker, his wife, John Edwards and Sarah Edwards, his wife, and William Allen...

Page 225--18 Feby. 1828. John A. Smith and wife, Lucy Smith, to Michael McKay, on Cedar Creek...

DEED BOOK Z

Page 124--23 Jany. 1835. Nath'l Smith and Lydia, his wife, to   , tract deeded to Elizabeth Webb and her heirs by Robert Huntley, Senr., on both sides of Jones Creek.
Thos. H. Gulledge, William Webb

Page 125--13 Mch. 1834. Joseph Pickett, of Anson County, N.C. to Thos. Robinson, of Marlborough Dist., S.C. for $100...
Wit: W. Little

ABSTRACTS OF COUNTY COURT MINUTES, 1771-1777

p. 51--At an Inferior Court of Pleas and Quarter Sessions begun and held for the County of Anson on 2nd Tuesday in July, to wit, the 9th, 1771. Present: William Mask and James Pickett, Esquires Justices.

July 10th 1771

Present: Samuel Snead, James Picket, William Blewett, Chas. Medlock, John Collson, John Crawford, Justices.

Ordered recorded:
Isaac Clark to Frances Clark.......... [missing]
Nathan Thompson

John Smith and
proved by Shad[rack Hogan]

John Smith
proved

Stephen Jackson to Thomas Curtas, deed, proved by Wm. Hamer. William Dry to Jason Meadow, deed, proved by James Fee. Thomas Fee to William Cox, deed, proved by James Fee. Robert Thorn to Daniel McMillan, deed, proved by Wm. Hamer. John Hamer, Sr. to Sam'l Williams, deed, proved by Wm. Hamer. John Leverett to Joseph Moody Ingram, deed, proved by John Ingram (p. 52) Carney Wright to Robert Gordon deed, acknowledged.
Philip Alston and wife to Zachariah Fenn and wife and Elizabeth McCoy to Robert Gordon, deed, proved by Carney Wright.
.... and wife, Zachariah Fenn and wife, to .... Wise, deed, proved by ....
John Mims and wife to William Meguire, deed proved by Wm. Mask, Esq. Chas. Miller to John Praton, Jr., deed, pr. by Joel McClendon.
Ordered that John Hornbeck, aged and infirm, be recommended to next Assembly to be exempted from any future tax.

John Preto to Jesse McClendon, deed, acknowledged.

Thomas Gibson and wife to Valentine Morris, deed, proved by Nelson Gibson.

July 10th 1771 (cont.)

John McClevael to John Spencer, deed, pr. by Wm. Culpeper.

Thos. Presley to John Spencer, deed, pr. by John McClevael.

John Dawson   pr. by Jonathan.......
                          deed, pr. by Wm. Wall.

William Pickett, Esq. produced commission from Governor appointing him Sheriff for 1771; bondsmen: Thos. Wade, Joel McClendon, Sam. Flake, John Smith (Carp.), James Pickett and Charles Hines.

Ord. that Brumfield Redley, Esq. be appointed to prosecute on behalf of the Crown until the (p. 53) King's Atty come to this court.

Grand jury; Thos. Dockery, foreman, John Bostwick, Joel McClendon, George Ingram, Shadrack Denson, William Coleman, Francis Smith, William Hogan, William Culpepper, Henry......., John Covington, Joseph Dunham, ...,....
.... Isaac Falconberry.

John Bennett and wife to Jesse Wallace, deed, proved by James Saunders.

Shadrack Denson to Wm. Jowers, deed, prov. by Joseph Ingram.

George Marchbanks and wife to Wm. Bennet, deed, pr. by Patrick Boggan.

Geo. Marchbanks and wife to John Seago, deed, pr. by Patrick Boggan.

Joel Phillips to Isham Ingram, deed, pr. by Joel McClendon.

Wm. Pickett, Esq., Sheriff, protested agst the public goal as being insufficient.

July 11, 1771

Present: John Crawford, James Picket, Matthew Raiford, Wm. Blewett, Chas. Medlock, Sam'l. Snead, Justices.

July 11, 1771 (cont.)

John Johnson and w. to Julius Holly, deed, pr. by William Holly.

Robert Thorn and w. to John Bostwick, deed, pr. by Wm. Bert.

Ord. the following persons to lay out a road the nearest and best way to John Smith's (Sandhill) (p. 54), on Little River, crossing at Hullins ford near the mouth of Turkey Cock Cr., to wit: William Coleman, John Coleman, James Pickett, Richard James, James Turkey[?], Benj. Ingram, James Hutchins, George_____, Cornelius Robertson, Richard Downs, John Smith,_____, Joseph Ingram,_____ _____, _____ Meguire and Matthew Raiford._____ _____ (and)_____ Ingram be overseers thereof.

Joseph Murphey to Wm. Bennet, Sr. deed, pr. by Wm. Seago.

Ord. that Philemon Thomas be overseer of road from Chalkfork to ford over Hitchcock's Creek near mouth of Falling Cr. with Wm. Watkins overseer..... to Stephen Cole's. All hands in same district to work under him.

Ord. that Wm. Morris a poor, aged and infirm man be rec. to Assembly to be exempt from future tax.

Ord. that Nancy Maner be bound to John Webb til 21, being now about 11 years.

On motion of Ann Stitt, (p. 55) ord. that Sheriff or Constable bring before this court immediately Joseph Stitt and Samuel Stitt, orphans, apprentices to Wm. [Mr.] Anthony Hutchins and Anthony Hutchins be given notice to appear to answer her complaint.

Admr. on est. of Julius Holly gr. to Sarah Holly; bondsmen, William Holly and John Jackson for £1200.

Grand jurors to serve next Superior Ct. in Sept. Charles Medlock,_____ _____, James Picket; Petit jurors, Shadrack_____,_____ _____, Charles Hines.

Ord. that John Seago a poor, aged and infirm man be rec. to Assembly for exemption of future tax.

Ord. the same for Burlingham Rudd.

July 11, 1771 (cont.)

Ordinary license gr. to James Cotten; bondsmen, Samuel Snead and Henley Snead.

July 12, 1771

Present: John Collson, John Crawford, and Samuel Snead, Justices.

(p. 56)--Ordinary license gr. John Coleson; bondsmen, John Crawford, and Samuel Snead.

William Haley appointed overseer of road from Charles Medlock's to Pedler's Cabbins, crossing Hitchcock's at Wm. Wade's Mill and that the hands be, to wit: John Wall, Thos. Moorman, Archibald [Archelaus] Moorman, Benj. Moorman, William Haley, Isham Haley, and George Mathews.

Ord. that fol; Israel Snead and John Coles be added and work the road under John James from Stephen Cole's to Main Road by Samuel Snead's.

Wm. [Mr.] Anthony Hutchins having been served with order of court on complaint of Ann Stitt, informing the court of his intention to leave this province, that he give security for his not carrying out of this province two orphan apprentices, sd Hutchins did not appear and it is ordered that the sd [Joseph] Stitt and Samuel Stitt be placed _____ _____ Lyles until next court and that the sd James Lyles have orphans before Ct. Whereupon George Willison gave bond for not carrying out of the Province the orphans, on the behalf of sd Anthony Hutchins.

William Coleman appt. overseer of road from Little River to Mountain Cr. all hands subject to work.

Ord. that Robert Jarman be overseer of road in room of Samuel Flake from Blewett ferry to Courthouse and that his own hands and those of Joseph Martin work and keep same.

William Mask to Francis Moseley, deed, acknowledged.

(p. 57)--Ord. that George Webb be Constable for the district of Rocky fork of Hitchcock's Cr where he was formerly Constable.

Samuel Snead Esq. appt to get tax list of taxables from _____ line, all below Hitchcock's Cr._____ Thoroughgood Pate are Constables.

ABSTRACTS OF COUNTY COURT MINUTES, 1771-1777

12 July 1771 (cont.)

Wm. Blewett, Esq. to take taxables from Hitchcock's to Mt. Cr. Edward Almond and John Webb to warn in the people within the same.

Ord. Chas. Medlock, William Coleman, John Crawford, Charles Robertson, Cornelius Robertson apptd to view and build a bridge in the most convenient place on Hitchcock's Cr. near Wm. Wade's Mill, bet. mouth of sd Creek and the ford at Wm. [Mr.] Philemon Thomas, and make report.

Ord. that Wm. Mask, Edmund Lyles, Francis Smith, James Picket, and John Colson be appt. Com. to choose place and build bridge over Brown Creek.

____ ____ ____ appt. to take the list ___ Mt. Cr to Hughwarry [Huwharry] and up Little River as high as John Smith (Sandhill).

James Sanders and Luke Robertson, Constables, are appt. to warn people ____ and up Little River as high as Smith's (Sandhill) and give list of taxables to Matthew Raiford's, Esq.

Samuel Parsons is appointed to take list of taxables from John Smith (Sandhill) up to Co. line. John Wilson and William Page Constables and to give their lists of taxables to Sam'l Parsons.

James Picket and Charles Medlock, Esquires, appt. to take lists of taxables on Southwest of Peedee below Brown Creek to Province line. John Leverett, Bartholomew Murphey, and Samuel Blackford appt. Constables to warn.

John Collson, Esq. appt. to take list of taxables from Brown Cr. upward to the county line. Jacob Vanhoose and John ____ Constables.

Ordinary license gr. to Geo. Wilson; bond with Wm. Picket.

(p. 59)--Thos. Fanning to Samuel Snead, deed, pr by John Wright.

Court adjourned.
****

9th [October] 1771

Present: Matthew Raiford, Samuel Parsons, Samuel Snead, James Picket, Esquires.

9th [October 1771](cont.)

Edward Morris and w. to Frances Jurden, deed, pr by Saml. Parsons, Esq.

David Dumas to John Spencer, deed, ...

Wm. Phillips to Henry Talley, deed, pr by John Culpeper.

John Clark to Wm. Coleman, deed, pr by Anthony Hutchins.

Claudius Pegues to Stephen Wright, Jonathan Wright, Elizabeth Wright, and Catherine Wright, pr by John Wright.

Joseph Howell to Richard Farr, deed, pr by Wm. Pickett.

Nicholas Green to Rice Henderson, Jr. by John Herren, deed of gift.

Nicholas Green (p. 60) to Rice Henderson, by John Herren, deed of gift.

Ord. that John Alston, Maj. David Poor, Albright Bright, James Sargent, Wm. Alton, Edwd. Morris, Haten Morris, Danl. Hicks, James Fry, Edward Nicholas, Saml. Parsons, Thomas Parker, and Wm. Wyvell layout road fr. Yadkin Riv. wh. Anson line crosses the most convenient way to Cross ..... Cr.

John Ussery to James Cotton by Sam'l. Parsons.

Ordinary license gr. Samuel Snead; bond: James Pickett and John Auld.

10 [October] 1771

Present: Matthew Raeford, James Pickett, Samuel Parsons, Esquires.

Ordinary license gr. Carney Wright; bondsmen, John Parsons and Benj. Hinson.

John Wilson to Joseph Downing, deed, by James Downing.

Chas. Hill to William Mackahey pr by John Cole.

Josiah Downing to David Dumas, deed, pr by Thos. Wilson.

William Griffin Hogan to ____ Hogan, deed, ack by Wm. Hogan.

ABSTRACTS OF COUNTY COURT MINUTES, 1771-1777

10 [October] 1771 (cont.)

Grand jury: _____ _____, _____ _____,
Wm. Coleman, Stephen Thomas, Wm. Ratliff, John Hamer, Jr., Wm. Moody, Besley John Lambden, Stephen Cole, Wm. Bennett, Henry Stokes, Wm. Leverett, Christopher Watkins, Wm. Thomas, Wm. Pratt and Robert Thomas.

Ord. (p.61) Stephen Miller be overseer of road in room of Wm. Leverett from Love's Cr. to province line, by Thos. Wade's store.

Ord. Chas. Smith a poor, aged and infirm man be rec. exempt from future tax.

Ord. that Wm Allton be app. Constable in the room of William Page.

Ord. Abraham Rushing, Thomas Creet[?], Job Meadows, Lewis Meadows, Joel Chivers, Wm. Johnson, Wm. Rushing, James_____, Charles Booth, Thomas Huntley, John Jackson, _____ Bales lay out road from Province line at the end of Cheraw road.

John Newberry and w. to Wm. Newberry, deed, by William Newberry, Jr.

Ordinary license to John Cole; bond: Saml. Snead and James Auld.

[11 October 1771]

Present: John Colson, John Crawford, Matthew Raiford, William Blewett, James Pickett, Chas. Medlock, Saml. Parsons, Saml. Snead, Esquires.

(p.62) George Wilson and [wife] [Messaniah] [to] Thos. Wade. deed, pr by John Spencer. Wife relinq. bef. James Pickett, Esq.

Geo. Wilson and w. Messaniah to Thos. Wade, [300 ac.] pr as above.

Edward Almond and Samuel Davis to Thomas Mims, pr by John Wall

John Creek[Cheek?] to Wm. White, pr by Reuben Phillips.

John Crawford and Ann Crawford to John Wall, pr by Archilus Moorman.

Inv. of est. of Julius Holley by Sarah Holley, admx.
Ord. that perishable estate be sold by Sheriff.

[11 October 1771] (cont.)

Benj. Covington to Joseph Dunham, deed, pr by Joshua Collins.

James Sheppard and Lucy, his w. to John Mask, Sr. by Jacob Sheppard.

James Almond and w. to Thos. Wade, deed, by Wm. Mask, Esq.

Ord: _____ _____, Thomas Tomkins, John Parsons, John Hinson, Burlingham Rudd, Jason Meadows, John May, James Langford, Lewis Lowry, Robert Lowry, William Fielding, Stephen Tompkins (p. 63) John Wright and Thomas Dickson lay out road from Mecklenburg to Cheraws bet. branches of Westfield Cr and those of Huckleberry Cr into new road from Cheraws to Anson C. H., Lawrence Franklin to be overseer, and to lay out road from the above new road from Cheraws to continue same, leading by or near Dr. Thomas Dickson to Anson C. H. and Nicholas White be overseer.

Samuel Bloodworth to Ezekiel McClendon, deed, pr by John Leverett.

Ord. John Skinner be appt.............in room of Luke Robert[son].

Philip Herndon to Samuel Blackford, deed, by Elizabeth Brown.

Ann Hutchins, wife of Anthony Hutchins, to Thomas Wade, relinq. of dower before James Pickett, Esq, pr. by same.

John Smith, Sandhill, to Richard Fanning, pr. by Wm. Mask, Esq.

Thos. Meadows to Lewis Lowry, pr by John May.

****

[12 October 1771]

Present: John Crawford, Matthew Raiford, William Blewett, Esq.

The King vs William Doster. Jury: Cornelius Robertson, Thos. Slay, Sam'l. Davis, Joseph White, John Jenkins, John Hornbeck, Benj. Hinson (p. 68) Thos. Curtis, Nicholas White, Joshua Collins, Stephen Jackson, John Bostick. Verdict: Not Guilty.

ABSTRACTS OF COUNTY COURT MINUTES, 1771-1777

[12 October 1771] (cont.)

Thos. Wade vs Thos. Horn. Same jury as above. Verdict: Damage Ł 7/16/0.

Ale[x] Jordan vs Thos. Sheppard. Same jury. Verdict: one penny.

John Coleman vs Wm. Rogers. Same jury; Verdict: one penny.

Ord. Francis Clark, John Jones, James Williams, John Lee, and Wm. Strickling's hands to be added to and work road from Chas. Medlock's to Pedler's Cabbin under William Haley, the present overseer.

George Wilson vs John Webb. Same jury Damage Ł 6/17/10

James Cotten vs Augustine Prestwood. Same jury. Dam: Ł 3/0/0.

Francis Stevens vs James Terry. Same jury. Verdict; for defendant.

Morgan Brown vs Bexley John Lambden. Same jury. Verd: Ł 1 & cost.

Robert Jarman to James Auld, deed, pr by Wm. Pickett, Esq.

Ord. Jacob Calloway, Job Calloway, Robert Carr, Jacob Bankson, William Hendley, Edward Moore, Joshua Carter, Daniel Bankson, Jacob Carter, Drury Ledbetter, Junstal[?] Crane and George Lee to lay out road from Edward Moore's store on the Yadkin River leading to _____ the lower Lawyer's Springs, the above with John Blalock, Geo. Bagley, James Ryle, Robt. Walker, John Gose, John Barnett. to work same.

Inv. of est. of Timothy Monseer returned by oath of Thos. Monseer.

Isaac Jackson and w. to Wm. Moody deed pr by Chas. Hines.

(p.65) Joel McClendall vs Thos. Swearingen. Same jury. Damage Ł 8/11/3.

Mark Allen vs Thos. Swearingen. Same jury. Verdict: dam. Ł 16/6/9

Ord. Cornelius Robertson, James Wilson, John Jeffry, Goen Morgan, Wm. Morgan, Thomas

[12 October 1771] (cont.)

Simpson, Getbird? Simpson, John _____, Jacob Vanhover, William Thompson, _____ _____, Gabriel Davis, John Wilson, George Shankle, Wm. Yearby, Timothy Taylor, Nathl. Lilly, and Mathew Raiford to lay out road from Salisbury road near or about the Lawyers Springs to cross Peedee at the Swift Island or Davis ford, and from thence to John Wilson's ford on Clark's Cr. to Mathew Raiford's ford over Little River, where the Cross Creek road crosses the Little River.

13 October 1771

Present: John Colson, John Crawford, Wm. Blewett, Wm. Mask, Sam'l. Parsons, Esquires.

James Pickett, Esq. Sheriff of Anson Co. for year of 1768 came into court and produced acct in order to settle for year 1768, which was admitted, and signed by the Justices present.

(p.66) Marshall Diggs, Esq., Sheriff of Anson Co. for 1767 came into court and produces his acct. His settlement signed by John Colson, John Crawford, Wm. Blewett, James Pickett and Matthew Raiford.

(p.67) Ord. road from Mr. John Colson's ferry to Buffelow Head be divided into two districts and John Hagler be overseer from the Ferry to Jacob's Cr and George Shankle be overseer of upper part of said division.

Jeremiah Terrill to Wm. Terrill, deed of gift, ack. in Ct.

James Denson to Samuel Hutchins, deed, pr by James Pickett, Esq.

The King Vs John Smith, Carp. Jury sworn: Cornelius Robertson, Thos. Slay, Saml. Davis, Joseph White, John Hornbeck, Benj. Hinson, Thos. Curtis, Nicholas White, Joseph Martin, Thos. Tallant, Bexley John Lambden and John Jenkins. Verdict: Not guilty. Wit: (for defendant) Elizabeth White, Moses White, Isaac Belew, Abraham Belew, Jr., Shadrack Denson. For plaintiff, Daniel Murphy, Richard James, Ann James, Wm. Bennet, Eliz. Higdon, Joseph Martin, Saml. Flake.

Claims made on County; allowed. Chas. Medlock, Esq.; John Colson, Esq; Chas. Robertson, Esq.; Thomas Gibson, Shadrack Denson, Abraham

13 October 1771 (cont.)

Belew, John Crawford, Esq. Zacheriah Smith, James Auld, clk; Samuel Snead, for 5 wolf sclaps; Chas. Medlock for 1 wolf scalp;

(p.69) Wm. Pickett, Esq. Sheriff 1769 produced acct. 896 taxables, signed by John Colson, Sam'l Parson, William Blewett, Matthew Raiford, and Wm. Mask.

Chas. Medlock, Sheriff for 1765, produced acct, 715 taxables. Signed by John Colson, Saml. Parsons, Wm. Blewett, Wm. Mask and James Pickett.

(p.70) Chas. Medlock, Sheriff in 1766, produced acct, 785 taxables, signed by same as above.

(p.71) Ord. that a road be opened from the Cheraw Road at Naked Cr. to cross Little Mt. Cr. at or near Joseph Hines ford, thence to Solomon Gross's and another road in the fork of Mt. Creek to Cross Creek road with Zachariah Smith, Joshua Collins, Patrick Sanders, Wm. Burns, John Jenkins, James Sanders, James Addams, Jacob Cockeram, Bexley John Lambden, Stephen Touchstone, John Bostwick and Manly John Cockeram's hands from Stephen Touchstone's and low as Zachariah Smith's Mill and from sd road up Little Cr as far as Patrick Sanders and to keep same.

The following Justices returned their lists of taxables: John Colson, Saml. Snead, James Pickett, Wm. Blewett, Matthew Raiford, Samuel Parsons and Chas. Medlock for 1771.

The Court Adjourned.

(p.72)   13 January 1772

Present; John Crawford, Chas. Medlock, Matthew Raiford, Saml. Parsons, Esquires Justices.

Ordinary license gr Matthew Raiford. Bond: Cornelius Robertson and James Auld.

Ord. Francis Clark be appt. overseer to road from the Province line to Solomon's Creek and that his own hands and those of John Thomas, Benj. Skipper, James Bagget, Dunn Rice, John Mencer [Moonseer] and Barnaby Skipper work same and in connection with the company under Capt. Saml. Snead build a bridge over Solomon's Cr.

Saml. Snead overseer to road from Falling Cr to Solomon's Cr.

13 January 1772 (cont.)

James Adcock and wife to Philemon Thomas, deed, pr by Robt. Thomas.

John Bostwick and w. to James Bostwick, deed, pr by Chas. Robinson.

(p.73) John Ussery and w. to John Bostwick pr. by Mark Allen.

Ord. Joel McClendon be overseer of road in room of John Ryle from Colson's ford on Rocky River to Brown Cr.

John Davis to William Irby, deed, pr by Robt. Snuggs.

Jason Meadow, Jr. to Jason Meadow, Sr., deed, acknowledged.

Wm. Dry to Jason Meadow, deed, pr by Wm. Coleman.

Wm. Fielding and w. to Geo. Wilson, deed, acknowledged.

Grand jurors: Richard Farr, Shadrack Denson, Richard Downs, Wm. Newberry, Dennis McClendon, John May, Lawrence Franklin, John Henry, Abraham Belew, Thomas Jower, Joseph Mar......, Solomon Gross, Wm. Scott, James Hutchins and Wm. Bennet.

Vann Swarengen to James Allen, deed, pr. by Mark Allen.

Thos. Swearengen and w. to James Allen, deed, pr by Samuel Swearengen, Sr.

Ord. Goin Morgan, constable on Clark's Cr in room of John Wilson.

Thos. Dockery and w., Ann, to Joseph Hines, deed, ack. and femme relinq. before John Crawford.

John Cartwright and w. to John Almond, deed, pr by Joseph Hinds.

(p.74) Thos. Smith and Deborah, wife, to Nelson Gibson, deed, pr. by Thomas Gibson.

John Long and Mary, his wife, to Thos. Dockery, deed, pr by Wm. Blewett, Esq. Femme relinq. before same.

13 January 1772 (cont.)

Ord. John Cole, on Hitchcock's, constable in room of Edward Almond.

William Coleman to John Poston, deed, pr. by Joseph Hinds.

14 January 1772

Present: John Colson, Chas. Medlock, Saml. Parsons, Esquires.

Ord. Wm. Phillips, Wm. Nelson, Reuben Phillips, Wm. Holly, Jesse Pearse, Joseph White, Jr., Joseph White, Sr., Thos. Lacy, Wm. Rushing, Wm. Johnston, John Scisco and Wm. Brook, to lay out road from the pine tree where it crosses at the province line between head of Liles Cr. and Brown Cr. through Anson toward Salisbury till it shall intersect the line of Roan Co. Nathl. Holly overseer.

His Majesty's Commission of the Peace for Anson Co.: John Colson, John Crawford, Wm. Blewett, Chas. Medlock, Sam'l. Snead, Sam'l. Parsons, Mathew Raiford, James Pickett, Chas. Robinson, John Hamer, John Jackson, James Cotten, (p. 75) Stephen Miller, Wm. Hogan, Thos. Wade, and Drury Ledbetter; thereupon John Colson, Chas. Medlock, Saml. Parsons, Matthew Raiford, James Pickett, John Hamer and James Cotten Esq. qualified by taking oath.

Mr. Joseph Hinds produced a commission from Gov. appt. him Colonel[1] for the Court and took oath.

Ord. Wm. Carter be overseer of road in room of Wm. Newberry, Jr. from Mt. Cr. to Wm. Blewett's ferry road.

Acct of Gdn. of Joshua Weaver returned and recorded.

Robt. Jarman to Wm. Blewett, deed, pr. by Joseph Martin.

Francis Moseley, Esq. produced commision appt. him Sheriff of Anson and entered bond with Wm. Mask, John Mask, Jr. John Waters, Solomon Gross, James Hutchins and Mark Allen.

Mr. John Collson commission appt. him Register of Anson Co. Bond, John Colson and Chas. Medlock.

Ordinary license to Wm. Leak. Bond, Samuel Snead and Chas. Medlock.

14 January 1772 (cont.)

Ord. that the Clerk of Co. deliver up to Mr. Wm. Pickett, late Sheriff, the bond for the collection of taxes by him given for the year 1771.(p76). Mr. Francis Moseley, the present Sheriff qualified.

[15] January 1772

Present: John Colson, Chas. Medlock, James Cotten.

Ord. that John Crawford, Saml. Snead, Wm. Blewett, be appt. grand jurors to serve next Ct. for Dist. of Salisbury in March next. Petit jurors to serve same Wm. Holley, Thos. Nixon, & George Ingram.

Moses Saunders is appt. Constable in room of Ephraim Fonder in upper part of Uharie.

John Dewey to David Rich, deed, pr. by Jeremiah Terrill.

Robt. Webb and w. to John Wall, deed, pr. by David Jernigan.

Thos. Downer to Smith Fields, deed, acknowledged.

Wm. Temple Coles vs James Pickett. Jury: Sam'l Flake, Wm. Terry, Jr.; John Smith, John Mims, John Pelham, Sam'l Faulkenburg, James Moore, John Jarman, Wm. McFadding, Robt. Jarman, Wm. Watkins, Pate Saunders. Verdict for defendant.

Patrick McDaniel vs John Pelham. Same jury except, in room of Pelham, Carney Wright. Verdict for defendant.

Robt. Blacksher vs Jacob Whitehead. Same jury except Wm. Pratt in room of Coleman. Penny damage.

Samuel Swearingen to John Smith, Sandhill, 100 acres, pr. by Benj Bunts [Baird].

Robert Raiford and w. to Daniel Lipscomb, deed, pr. by Wm. Mask (p. 77) and feme relinq. before same.

Shadrack Denson and Mary, wife, to Wm. Mask, deed, pr by John Mask.

Richard Fanning to John Smith, Sandhill, 200 a, pr by Wm. Mask.

[15] January 1772 (cont.)

Richard Farr to James Farr, deed. Acknowledged.

Richard, Frances and Mary Ann Saralson(?) to Robert Leverett, prov. by Isham Haley.

Mark Allen vs Vann Swearingen. Jury: Saml. Flake, Wm. Terry, Jr., John Smith, John Mims, John Pelham, Saml. Touchberry, James Moore, John Douglass, Wm. Watkins, Wm. Pratt, Patrick Sanders and John Jarman. Verdict: £11/3/11.

Nicholas Broadaway vs Wm. Hamer. Same jury. Verd: £7/4/4.

Stephen Miller, Chas. Robertson and Thos. Wade, Esq. qualified as Justices.
    Adjourned until

January 18 [?][16] 1772 (Saturday)

Present: John Colson, Thos. Wade, James Pickett, Justices.

John Culpeper to David Dumas, acknowledged.

Ord. James Saunders constable in room of Bexley John Lambden in Mt. Creek Dist.

p. 78--The Sheriff, Francis Moseley, came into court and protested against the County gaol as being insufficient for security and safe-keeping of prisoners.

    The court adjourned   James Pickett, Thos. Wade, Chas. Robinson.

14 April 1772

Present: James Picket, Mathew Raiford, Thos. Wade, James Cotten, Esquires Justices.

Abraham Rushing to Thomas Skelton, deed, pr. by Saml. Shumak.

George Bagly,² Jr. to Edward Moore, Jr. deed, acknowledged.

John Jackson, Esq. named as a Commr. of Peace and qualified.

Ord. by court that Sam'l Swearingen, Sr. poor, infirm and aged, be recommended exempt from tax.

14 April 1772 (cont.)

Ord. John Mask, Jr. overseer of the road in room of Benj. Dumas from Colson Ferry to ford of Little River.

15 April 1772

p. 79--Present: John Colson, Mathew Raiford, Chas. Medlock, James Cotten, James Pickett, Thos. Wade, Chas. Robertson, John Jackson, Stephen Miller, John Hamer, Justices.

Ord. Aaron Miller constable in room of Thoroughgood Pate.

Christopher Clark to Darius Burns, 100 acres. Ack.

Wm. Blewett to Robt. Jarman, 30 acres, pr. by Nathl. Ashley.

Joshua Collins and w. to James Phillips 100 acres. Ack.

Grand jury: Francis Smith, foreman, Benj. Dumas, Robert Lee, Joel McClendell, Wm. Coleman, Charles Hines, Richard Farr, Stephen Cole, John Wall, Joshua Morgan, Joseph Martin, Saml. Swearingen, Wm. Rorie, Robt. Jarman.

Wm. Blewett to Saml. Williams, deed, pr by Thos. Wade.

Robert Thorn and w. to Ralph Mason, pr by Wm. McDaniel.

Ord. that Sampson Williams overseer of road in room of Wm. McDaniel from Stubbs ford to Mountain Cr. Hands bet. Mt. Cr and Drowning Cr. as high as Anson Co. line and as low as Patrick Sandersons work same.

John Thomas and Molly, his wife, to Thos. Morris (p. 80) deed, pr. by Saml. Snead.

Benj. Mims to Saml. Snead 82 ac. by John Cole.

John Thomas and w. to Saml. Snead, 45 ac. by Daniel Snead.

Thos. Hines to John Hurley 300 acres by Thos. Hurley.

Ordinary license to John Lee. Bond; Joseph Martin and Saml. Blackford.

ABSTRACTS OF COUNTY COURT MINUTES, 1771-1777

15 April 1772 (cont.)

William Legget and wife to Duncan McCurry 100 a, by Nathl. Williams.

Jonathan Llewelling and w. to John McKay, 100 a, by Mathew Watson.

Wm. Hunter and w. to John Covington, 12 a, by John Crawford.

Thomas Coleman to John Coleman, 50 a, pr. by Aaron Vick.

Nelson Gibson and w. to Neal McQueen, 100 a, by John Martin.

Ordinary license gr to John James. Bond: Chas. Medlock and John Wall.

Ord. that Wm. Pickett, Cornelius Robertson and James Pickett be rec. to serve as Sheriff. Wm. Pickett and Cornelius Robertson 9 votes each and James Pickett 7.

Cornelius Robinson vs Stephen Cole. Jury: Henry Stokes, Shadrack Denson, Wm. Moody, Richard Leek, Saml. Snead, Wm. Wilkins, John Presley, Robt. Webb, Nathl Ashley, Abraham Belew, James Denson, Peter Meselie. Verd: £ 8-15-8.

p. 81--Ord. Mary Owens, orphan of John Owens, be bound to Stephen Miller until of lawful age being now 14 years old.

Ord. that a subpoena issue agst Thos. Mitchell to appear at next ct. and that he bring to court Elizabeth Owen, orphan of John Owen.
  Adjourned.

Thursday   16 April 1772

Present: Saml. Parsons, Thos. Wade, Stephen Miller, Esq. Justices.

Wm. Scott to Richard Lyon, 300 acres, pr by John Bounds.

Nathaniel Dobbs constable in district of Little Brown Creek.

Ord. John Bounds overseer of road in room of Philemon Thomas, that leads from Hitchcock ford near the said Thomas to the Chalk fork and that the hands bet Falling Cr. and Hitchcock's work thereon and build a bridge over the ford at Hitchcock.

16 April 1772 (cont.)

Jacob Vanhooser constable in room of John McClevael.

Ord. Benj. Hinson overseer of road from Jones Cr to province line.

In suit Peter Meselee vs Joseph Martin, jury: John Presley, John Wall, Wm. Pratt, Joseph Howell, Job Jackson, Silvanus Gibson, Sam'l Flake, John Crowson, Shadrack Denson, James Webb, James Moss, John Duglass. Verdict: £ 12,7:10.

John Hayward vs John Hunt. Same jury. Verdict £20.

Wm. Harrington vs James Hutchins. Same jury. For defendant.

Ord: Thomas Wilson Constable (p. 82) in room of Goin Morgan.

Thomas Curtis in room of Stephen Jackson from John Hamer's ferry into the main road.

Henry McNish to George Loundell Rudd 150 a, by Burlingham Rudd.

Geo. Webb and w. to Thos. Dockery 200 a. Ack.; femme relinq. before James Pickett, Esq.

Daniel Thomas and Sarah, his wife, to Thos. Dockery, 200 a, proved by Chas. Medlock; femme relinq. before same.

Ord. that Bexley John Lambden be constable in room of James Sanders.

On petition of Francis Smith it is ord. John Colson and John Royal [Ryle] view the mill of Francis Smith and value one acre of land adjacent thereto for the use of sd mill and dam and make return to next court.

Samuel Wise, admr. of Ellerby vs John Touchberry. Jury: John Presley, John Wall, Wm. Pratt, Joseph Howell, Job Jackson, Samuel Flake, Shadrack Denson, James Webb, James Moss, James Dew, James Hutchins, Jesse Wallace. Verdict for defendant.

John Presley vs Benj. Dumas. Same jury only Wm. Woods and Jacob Vanhooser in room of John Presley and John Wall. Verdict £6.

16 April 1772 (cont.)

Ord. John Jeffery be Constable of the road from Buffelow head on Long Creek to county line on the road to Salisbury, in room of Wm. Noble.
Court adjourned.

Friday   17 April 1772

p. 83--Present: John Colson, Matthew Raiford, Chas. Roberson, James Cotton, John Hamer, Thos. Wade, Stephen Jackson, Justices.

Francis Lee to Arthur Taylor, 100 acres, by Solomon Gross.

Thos. Wade to Hopkins Howell, 300 a, acknowledged.

Ord: that Wm. Rorie be constable in Capt. Jackson's District.

Ord. that Saml. Blackford be constable from Island Creek to Brown Creek.

Ord: List of rates for inn-keepers . . . .

Ord. John Wallers [Walters?] be overseer of road in room of Wm. Coleman, from Little River to Mountain Cr.

Ord. that John Lambden be Constable in room of James Sanders be made null and void.

Richard Farr vs Joseph Martin. Jury: Wm. Pratt, Joseph Howell, Job Jackson, Samuel Flake, Shadrack Denson, James Webb, James Moss, James Dew, James Hutchins, Jesse Wallace, Wm. Moody, Jacob Vanhooser. Verdict £3.2.6.

Ord. that Subpoena issue agst Eliza McDowell, admr. of James Long, to appear to render an acct. of her administration.
Adjourned.

---

15 July 1772

p. 85--Present: Chas. Medlock, Mathew Raiford, James Cotten, John Hamer, Chas. Robertson, John Jackson, Esquires.

Thos. Ward and wife, to Wm. Bland, deed, acknowledged.

Ord. John Crowson overseer of road from Stephen Coles to Hitchcock's Cr. in room of Wm. Watkins

15 July 1772 (cont.)

and that the hands of Stephen Cole, Henry Covington, Wm. Hunter, John Covington, Jesse Bounds, John Davidson, Wm. Watkins and Nicholas Crowson work on sd road and build a bridge over Hitchcock Cr. in conjunction with John Bounds.

Richard Farr to Duke Glen, 200 a, acknowledged.

Ordinary license gr. to James Farr. Bond; Richard Farr and Wm. Mask.

Grand jury: Wm. Mask, foreman, Richard Downs, Luke Robertson, Christopher Christian, Richard Farr, John James Sr., Jasper Smith, John Poston, Marshall Diggs, John Bostick, George Ingram, Wm. Seago, John Bounds, Edmond Almond, Thos. Ussery, Wm. Hunter.

Affidavit of Nicholas Friday, Sr. to Nicholas Friday, Jr. with release from Thos. Hover, to John Thomas, Esq, of Tryon County, prov. by John Dunn, Esq.

Thos. Huntley to Wm. May, 100 a, pr. by Chas. Hinds.

p. 86--Wm. Pickett, with commission appt. him Sheriff, dated May 4, 1772, for the ensuing year. Bond: Chas. Medlock, George Wilson, Wm. Coleman, John James.

Samuel Williams and w. to John McDonald, 127 a, pr. by Soirle McDonald.

Ord. that John Poston, poor, aged and infirm, be rec. exempt from future tax.

Henry Williams and wife to Soirle McDonald, 200 a, prov. by John McDonald.

Admr. on est. John Hicks gr. Francis Hicks. Bond: Chas. Medlock and Samuel Snead for £1000.

Admr. est. Wm. Little gr Catherine Little   Bond: Chas. Medlock and Samuel Snead for £2000.

Wm. Barrentine to Henry Williams, 200 a, pr by James Sanders.

Henry Williams and w. to Hugh McDonald, 200 a, by Jno. McDonald.

Robt. Edwards to John Cole, 250a, acknowledged.

ABSTRACTS OF COUNTY COURT MINUTES, 1771-1777

15 July 1772 (cont.)

Ord. Charles Powell, poor, aged, infirm, rec. exempt from tax.

Order. Benj. Baird have leave to build a water grist mill on his own land on Jones Creek.

John Hopkins to Thos. Hearne, 200 a, pr. by John Smith, Sandhill.

Ord. that a road be laid out the nearest and best way from Dr. Dickson's to where Wm. Pegge left off clearing the road at the province line and that (p. 87) Tho. Tompkins, John Parsons, Nicholas White, Thomas Dickson, John Hinson, Benj. Hinson, Charles Hinson, Stephen Jackson, Saml. Blackford, Saml. Yerkes, John Wright, Richard Farr, James Farr, Stephen Tompkins, Joseph Howell, Wm. Hamer, Hopkins Howell lay out same.
Adjourned.

Thursday 16 July 1772

Present: Chas. Medlock, Chas. Robertson, John Jackson, Justices.

Ord. Mark Allen be overseer of road from Hamer's Cr. to Mt. Cr. in room of Robt. Leverett and that the hands work under him.

Ord. that Eliz. Owens, orphan of John Owens, decd., be bound to James Webb until she arrives to the age of 18, being now 11 yrs. and seven months old, to learn the art of a spinster.

William Watts vs. Richard Ingram. Jury: Lewis Lowry, Zachariah Hogan, Goin Morgan, Thomas Thomas, Andrew Griffin, James Hutchins, Stephen Cole, Joseph Martin, Thomas Wilson, Samuel Flake, Patrick Sanders, James Downing. Non-suit.

John Lee vs Rice Henderson. Same jury above except Jesse Wallace and Isham Ingram in place of James Hutchins and Stephen Cole.

Ord. John Wall overseer in room of Wm. Haley from Chas. Medlock's to Pedler's Cabbin crossing Hitchcock (p. 88) at Mr. Wade's Mill. Hands of Thos. Moorman, Arch. Moorman, Benj. Moorman, Wm. Haley, Isham Haley, George Mathis, Francis Clark, John Jones, James Williams, John Lee and Strickland's work on said road.

Wm. May to Malachi Watts, 100 a, pr. by Thomas Ford.

16 July 1772 (cont.)

John Husbands and wife, Tabitha, Wm. Blewett and Eliz., his wife, to Wm. Thomas, 65 a, prov. by Simon Thomas.

Wm. Pickett to Cornelius Robertson, 300 a, acknowledged.

John Husbands and wife to Wm. Blewett, 65 a, pr. by Wm. Thomas.

Thos. Wade vs Thomas Charlton and Hopkins Howell. Same jury. Verdict for £17.18.5.

Solomon Gross to Thos. Megginson, 100 a, pr by Francis Moseley.

John Dunn vs Stephen Cole. Same Jury. Verdict: £5.13.8.

Ord. James Denson overseer on road from Mask's Ferry to C.H. Road in room of Joseph Ingram.

Friday 18 July 1772

Present: John Colson, Thos. Wade, Chas. Medlock, Saml. Parsons, John Hamer, Esquires Justices.

Thos. Moorman and Zachariah Moorman to Isham Haley, 106 a, pr. by Archlaus Moorman.

Edward Moorman and w. to James Campbell, 120 a, by Samuel Parsons, Esq.

p. 89--Thos. Lacy to Wm. Benton, 150 a, pr by Stephen Miller, Esq.

Ord. that Goin Morgan have leave to record mill built over Clark's Creek as a Public Mill, etc.

Luke Robertson and wife to Stephen Touchstone, 100 a, ack.

John Frolock to Whitmell Harrington, 60 a, pr. by John Colson.

Alexander Gordon vs David Jarnigen. Jury: Saml. Williams, Wm. Leverett, James Farr, John Horner, Joseph Martin, Joseph Benton, Stephen Cole, Jesse Wallace, James Webb, Josiah Swearingen, Robert Webb, James Downing. Verdict: Damages £10.

Thos. Coneley and wife to Henry Adcock, 15 a, pr. by John Mitchell.

18 July 1772 (cont.)

Alexander Gordon vs Stephen Cole. Judgment confessed in person, £11.18.8.

Alexander Gordon vs Joseph Martin. Same as above. £6.3.0.

John James vs Joseph Martin. Confessed. £7.4.10.

Benj. Horn, assignee of M. Brown vs Stephen Cole. Confessed £4.

Samuel Swearingen³ and Mary, his wife to David Smith, 100 acres, prov. by John Smith, Sandhill.

Thos. Moonseer to James Oliver, 200 acres, pr. by Shadrack Denson.

p. 90--Return of John Colson and John Ryle to value one acre, adj. Francis Smith's Mill dam, valued 5 sh, province money.

Charles Medlock, Esq. vs. James Webb. Same jury only Thos. Wilson in room of James Webb. Verdict: £0.7.2. Appeal prayed and granted plaintiff. Bond: Benj. Ingram and James Farr, Sr.

John Mitchell vs Benj. Mims and Wm. Mims. Judgment Bond confessed.

Court appoints Wm. Terry guardian to Short Long, orphan of James Long. Bond: Cornelius Robertson and William Pickett for £200. Ord. that William Terry take the said orphan's estate immediately into his possession and care.

Ord. that Walter Long, orphan of James Long, dec'd., be bound to William Terry till of lawful age, being now 16 years old, to learn the trade of cordwainer. Indenture made out and delivered.

Ord. Thomas Slay be overseer of the road from Isham Haley's ferry to Jones Cr. with hands of Christopher Clark, Smith Fields, Darius Burns and Benj. Carter.

Ord. Wm. Ratcliff be overseer of road from Jones Cr. to Burns Path and following work under him: Stephen Thomas, Wm. Pratt, Thomas Dinkins, John Hilburn and James Farr.

p. 91--Grand jurors for Superior Ct. Salisbury Dist. in September: Chas. Medlock, Wm. Blewett, John Smith, Sandhill. Petit jurors: Cornelius Robinson, Robert Jarman, Richard Farr.

18 July 1772 (cont.)

Ord. that Subpoena agst James Farr be issued to summon him to bring Edward Daniel a pale born child to next court.

Stephen Cole to Wm. Coleman, 100 a, pr. by John Coleman.

James Downing vs Wm. Mask. Jury: Saml. Williams, Jesse Wallace, John Smith, Sandhill, John Horn, John Wilson, George Lindsey, Stephen Cole, Wm. Griffin Hogan, Robert Jarman. For defendant.

Adjourned.

Saturday   18 (19) July 1772

Present: John Colson, Saml. Parsons, James Cotton, Esquires Just.

Ord. Mr. Samuel Williams have leave to build a publick water grist mill on the northeast side of PeeDee on his own land at the place known as Blewett Falls.

Ord. George Carter, a witness in suit Polson vs Downs, be fined 50 sh in next court for non-attendance. The sd Carter came into court and on motion fine ordered remitted.

Henry Polson vs Richard Downs. Jury: Richd Farr, James Downing, Joseph Martin, Job Benton, _____, James Farr, John Smith, Carp. John Smith, Adjt (L.R.) Luke Robertson, Saml. Phillips, Solomon Gross, Thos. Usery, Saml. Williams. Then the above jury withdrawn by consent of the parties and following jury sworn: (same as above with Stephen Cole, James Hutchins and Wm. Sneed in place of John Smith Adjt., Luke Robertson, and Solomon Gross.) Verdict: Guilty £6.10

Ord. that John Hamer, Esq. be appted to take list of taxables from County line to Smith's Cr and that Saml. Blackford and Bartholomew Murphy summon masters, witnesses and overseers; to give in their lists to said John Hamer, Esq.

James Pickett, Esq likewise from Smith's Cr. to Brown Creek. John Douglas appointed to summons.

John Colson, Sr. from Brown Cr. to County line and John Lee and Jacob Vanhooser summon.

18 (19) July 1772 (cont.)

John Jackson Esq. to take list of taxables in his company and Nathl. Dobbs and Wm. Nelson constables summon.

Stephen Miller to take lists in his neighborhood and above constables to summon.

Mathew Raiford, Esq. to take lists of Taxables in his company militia. James Sanders, Constable, to summon.

Charles Robertson, Esq. to take lists of taxables in his neighborhood and to Mt. Creek. James Sanders, Constable, to summons.

Chas. Medlock, Esq. from Mt. Creek to County line and Joseph Hall, John Cole, Arson Minshew be constables to summon.

Ord. Isaac Falkenberry (bourg) and Nelson Kelley be added to work road, whereof Robt. Jarman is overseer.

John Mercer (Moore) vs Sam'l Swearingen. Same jury, only George Carter in room of Thos. Ussery. Non-suit.

Peter Mesles vs Chas. Medlock, Esq. Jury: James Farr, John Smith, Carp., Samuel Williams, Stephen Cole, Robert Jarman, George Wilson, Ralph Mason, Richard Downs, Solomon Gross, Henry Polson, Thomas Ussery, Luke Robertson. Verdict: Damage £5. Motion in arrest of judgment and reasons to be filed next court.

The King vs Chas. Hinds. Jury: James Farr, John Smith, Carp., Henry Polson, John Thomas, Lewis Thomas, _____ Fanning, James Hutchins, Robt. Jarman and Joseph Martin. Guilty. Fine 50 sh.

James Hutchins to John Frolock, 300 a, pr. by John Dunn, Esq. (Several deeds from Hutchins to Frolock).

Adjourned.

14 October [1772]

p. 94--Present: Charles Medlock, Thomas Wade, James Cotten, Justices.

Shadrack Denson and wife to Frederick Bass, 200 a, ack.

14 October [1772] (cont.)

John Jones to Thos. Murphey, deed, pr. by Saml. Snead.

Sam'l. Williams to Mathew Inglish, deed, ack.

Henry Williams and wife to Renny Clark, 100 a, pr by John Inglish.

George Bagley, Sr. to Wm. Ellis, 300 a.

Joseph Martin and wife to John Hale Martin, deed of gift, ack.

John Flowers to Wm. Hamer, 160 acres, pr. by Jos. Howell.

Thos. Dunchow to Chas. Dunchow, deed of gift, pr. by Wm. Dunchow.

Lodowick Outlaw to Cassandra Freeman, pr. by George Bounds. [Several from same to same].

Lodwick Outlaw to George Freeman, pr. by George Bounds.

Gordon vs Jarnegan..........

p. 95--Wm. Newberry, Sr. and wife to Joshua Collins, ack.

James Campbell to Jacob Humble, 120 a, pr. by Saml. Parsons.

Grand jury: John Hamer, Jr. foreman, Wm. Hamer, Josiah Downing, John Smith, Carp., Nathaniel Curtis, Wm. Lindsey, Wm. Holley, Wm. Johnson, Jonathan Llewellyn, Wm. Newberry, John Almond, John Cockran, Thomas Chevers, Joseph Howell, Thos. Tallant and Samuel Flake.

Robt. Webb to Daniel McNeal, 300 a, pr. by John McNair.

Barnaby Skipper to Wm. Speed, 150 a, pr. by Joseph Ryle.

Wm. Coleman to John Cole, 170 a, ack.

Ord. Jonathan Llewelling constable of the road in room of Wm. McKahey.

Thomas Deaton overseer of road from John Smith, Adjt., to Saml. Parsons.

14 October [1772] (cont.)

Wm. McKahey and wife to Isaac Copeland, 100 a. ack.

Ord. Joseph Buschan, poor, aged, infirm, be rec. exempt from tax.

Philip May and wife to Thos. Jones, 250 a, pr. by Thos. Conner.

John Lee vs Rice Henderson. Jury: Samuel Williams, Abram Bellieu, Wm. Bond, Joel McClendon, John Poston, Morgan Brown, Henry Williams, Wm. Burt, Wm. Ashley, Shadrack Denson, Stephen Touchstone, Wm. Thomas. Verdict. Non-suit.

James Hutchins to Christopher Christian (p.96) 30 acres by Mark Allen. Tilman Helms to Thos. Bailey, 150 a, pr. by William Seago.

William Newberry and wife to Owen Slaughter, 20 a, acknowledged.

Inv. est of John Hicks, decd. returned on oath.

Edward Smith to Thomas Bolton, pr by Wm. Bolton.

Adjourned to

Thursday   15 October [1772]

Present: James Pickett, Saml. Parsons, James Cotten, Esquires.

William Coleman to John Coleman, 200 a, pr. by Aaron Vick

Thomas English and wife to John Robins, pr. by John Medling [?]

Thomas Gibson and wife to Alex Martin, pr. by Alex. Martin, Jr.

Acct of sale of est of Wm. Robins, decd., returned on oath of widow and admx of Robert McClenachan, decd., who was admr. of sd Wm. Robins.

John Flowers to Joseph Howell, pr by Wm. Hamer.

p. 97--Joseph Dunham to Thomas Baley, 159 a, acknowledged.

John Cook to Benj. Sanders, 200 acres, pr. by Stephen Miller.

15 October [1772] (cont.)

John Bostick to Avis Thomas, wife of Thomas Thomas, 294 acres, pr. by Chas. Robinson, Esq.

Admr. on est. of John Henry, decd., to Catherine Henry. Bond: Shadrack Denson, Nathl. Ashley. £ 500. Inventory of above est. returned on oath. Ord. perishable est. be sold by sheriff.

Owen Slater [Slaughter] to Richard Pemberton, 50 a, by Wm. Coleman.

Will of John Jackson, decd. ex. and proved by Job Meadows and Charles Booth, sub. wit. An appeal prayed and granted John Jackson Esq. Bond: James Hutchins and Wm. Pickett.

adjourned to

Friday   (no date) (16 October 1772)

Present; Chas. Medlock, Chas. Robertson, James Cotten, John Jackson, Thos. Wade, Esquires Justices.

Ord. Joseph Martin be overseer of road in room of John Jarman, and that Mr. Auld's hands work on sd. road whereof Robert? Jarman is overseer.

Ord. Wm. Rushing, overseer of road from south line as far as Thos. Mitchels and that Insign Bettis and his hands work on same.

p. 98--Ord. road be laid out from Province line bet. head of Brown Cr. and Hills Cr. to the County line, directly towards Salisbury. Wm. Johnson, Wm. Rorey, Joseph White, Jr., Thomas Chivers, Nathl. Holly, Wm. Holley, Wm. Rushing, Wm. Wilson, Job Meadows, Lewis Meadows, James Lowery, Willis Smith, Stephen Jackson, Thos. Lacey, Jesse Ball, John Pelham, Chas. Booth, Abraham Rushing, Thos. Shelton, to lay out same.

Saturday   [17 October, 1772]

Present: John Hamer, Thos. Wade, Chas. Medlock, Jas. Cotten, John Jackson, James Pickett, Esquires Justices.

John Mitchell and wife to George Megoune, pr by John Dunn.

Jeremiah Menasco, constable in room of John Skinner.

17 October, 1772 (cont.)

Ordinary license gr. Thos. Wade. Bond: James Auld and Wm. Coleman.

Ordinary license gr. John Cole. Bond: James Auld and Robt. Jarman.

p. 99--1770. Francis Moseley (Sheriff) debtor to Anson County for 963 taxables............ 1771 Same to same for 1069 taxables.

p. 100--above allowed by court for Sheriff for aforesaid year.

Ord. Chas. Medlock and Saml. Snead, Esq. guardians to Francis Hicks and Martha Hicks, orphans of John Hicks, decd. Bond with James Pickett and John Jackson, £300 for each orphan.

Robert Jarman to Solomon Gross, 400 acres, acknowledged.

Ord. John Carpenter be overseer of road from Saml. Parsons, Esq, to Randall's cabbin in room of Christopher Butler.

Ord. Edmund Nichols be Constable in room of William Alton.

Ord. that Clerk be allowed £12.10 for ex-officio services for County.

Ord. that Wm. Pickett, Sheriff, be allowed £10 for same.

Ord. that James Pickett be allowed his claim (£7) agst Co.

Ord. that Thos. Wade and James Auld be apptd commrs. to repair gaol.

Ord. Geo. Wilson be allowed his account, 30 sh.

Ord. that James Auld be allowed £2.9.4 to procure Acts of Assembly for County.

p. 101--Ord. that Thos. Wade have leave to front the gaol to the road at his own expense.

Ord that Onesphorus West be overseer of road from Haley's ferry to Hamer's old place and Jeremiah Terrill, Thomas Smith, William Thomas and Benjamin Carter's hands work same.

Ord. Isaac Nichols overseer road in room of

17 October 1772 (cont.)

Stephen Miller.

Ord. that the recommendation of Joseph Burcham to General Assembly to be exempted from tax be expunged and be null and void and not sent to Gen'l. Assembly.

Court Adjourned.

Wednesday   13 January 1772

Present: Chas. Medlock, Thos. Wade, John Jackson.

Ord. Isaac Falconberry be overseer of road in room of Robt. Jarman from Blewett's Ferry to C.H. and his own hands and the hands of Joseph Martin, James Auld, Stephen Jackson and Nelson Kelley work thereon.

Anthony Hutchins to Samuel Spencer, Esq. Power of Atty. Prov. by Thos. Wade.

Ordinary License gr. John Hamer, Sr. Bond: Chas. Medlock, Thos. Wade.

William Harvey and wife to John Holdings, pr by Wm. Spencer.

William Spencer and wife to Richard Jackson, deed, acknowledged.

Giles Runnels to William Holley, pr by Robt. Lassiter.

John Thompson and wife, to Wm. Holley, pr. by Robt Lassiter.

William Burns and wife to Wm. Coleman, pr. by Joshua Collins.

Anthony Hutchins to Dennis McClendell [McClendon] pr by James Pickett.

Grand jury: Shadrack Denson, foreman, Thos. Wright, James Poston, John Thomas, Henry Adcock, James Denson, William Meguire, Joshua Collins, John Covington, Thomas Dockery, John Knotts, John Jarman, Thos. Curtis, Isaac Falconberry, John Walters and George Ingram.

Ord. that Adlai Osborn, Esq. be apptd King's Attorney.

14 January 1773

Present: Stpn. Miller, Thos. Wade, John Jackson, Esquires.

p. 103--George Freeman to Atten [?] Martin, pr. by Geo. Bounds.

Wm. Coleman to Drury Ledbetter, deed, acknowledged.

John Smith (Sandhill) and wife to Richard Fanning, pr by Benjamin Baird.

Lewis Lowry and wife to James Little, deed acknowledged.

Robert Jarman to Stephen Jackson, deed, pr. by Geo. Wilson.

Thomas Cannon to Moses White, deed, pr. by Abraham Belew.

Ordinary license gr. Joel McClendon. Bond: Wm. Pickett and Isham Ingram.

Ord. that John Smith, Sandhill, Benjmon Baird and David Smith have leave to build a water grist mill on Little River at a place where they now have a saw mill in joint partnership.

Cornelius Robertson and wife to Thomas Megginson, deed, pr. by John Walters.

Henry Talley to Thomas Inglish, deed, pr. by John Robbins.

Will of Philip May proved by James Langford and Lewis Lowry. James Lowry, the exor. qualified.

Stephen Thomas to Dunkin Smith, deed, pr. by Lewis Thomas.

William Seago to Stephen Thomas, deed, pr. by Lewis Thomas.

William Pratt to Stephen Thomas, deed, pr. by Lewis Thomas.

Edward Ford to Jacob Perkin, deed, pr. by John Cole.

William May to Charles Boothby, deed, pr. by John Jackson.

Jurors for Sup. Ct. at Salisbury in March (p.104)

14 January 1773 (cont.)

Wm. Blewett, Isaac Falconberry, Chas. Medlock, Morgan Brown, John Smith, Sandhill, and Cornelius Robertson.

Ord. that Samuel Blackford be Constable for ensuing year, William Rorie to continue DC and Nathaniel Dobbs Constable. John Knotts Constable in room of Bartholomew Murphy on Jones Cr. Ord. that several constables in this county be continued, Wm. Nelson only excepted.

Ord. perishable est. of Philip May be sold by Sheriff. Inventory of sd estate returned and recorded.

Friday   [no date][15 January 1773]

John Coleman and wife to Jeremiah Strother, deed, pr. by Wm. Coleman.

Valentine Morris and wife to Oston [?] Morris, pr. by David Love.

15 January 1773 (cont.)

Edward Ford to John Perkins, deed, pr. by Thos. Hurley.

Ord. Edmund Lily have leave to build a water grist mill on Rockey River on own land opposite Walter Gibson's land at the Great Shoals, and that the same be a public mill.

Ord. that Alexander McDonald be bound to Thos. Chiles till of lawfull age, now 15 years and 6 months; to learn trade of house carpenter and joiner.

Townsend Robinson to John Dickerson, deed, pr. by John Gwin.

p. 105--Susannah Bell to John Crowson, deed, pr. by John Bounds.

James Bounds Sr. to John Bounds, deed, pr. by John Crowson,

Thomas Stafford Williams to Luke Williams, deed, pr. by John Bounds.

Agnes Watts, wife and relict of William Watts, decd., relinq. admrn on decd's estate.

Saturday (16 January 1773)

Present: Chas. Medlock, James Pickett, Thomas Wade... Justices.

Ord. Peter Hubberd, John Hubberd and Manoah, orphans of Peter Hubberd, decd. be bound to John Chiles till of lawful age to learn the trade of a carpenter, joiner, or blacksmith. Peter now 17; John 10, and Manoah 7 years old.

Acct. of estate of John Henry, decd. ord. recorded.

Ord. John Ryal appted overseer of road in room of Joel McClendon.

Wm. Coleman to Thomas Gowers, deed, acknowledged.

Ordinary license gr, John Chiles. Bond: Wm. Pickett and Shadrack Denson.
Adjourned

Chas. Medlock, James Pickett, Thos. Wade.

N.B. The road leading from Blewett's ferry to Drowning Creek over Rocky Fork of Hitchcock's Cr. to have an overseer. Order therefore Thos. Dockery former overseer. Feb. 26, 1773.

Wednesday 13 April 1774

Present: Chas. Roberson, Thos. Wade, Joshua Collins and Mathew Raiford qualified as Justices.

James Williams, Esq. qualified as an attorney, with commission from the Governor.

George Bagley to Joseph Henderson, deed, pr. by Tunstall Rone.

George Bagley to Tunstall Rone, deed, pr by Joseph Henderson.

Robert Carr and wife to Buckley Kimball, deed, by Daniel Bankston.

George Bagley [or Bagby] to Wm. Graig [Gregg?], deed, pr. by Tunstall Rone.

Lambert Hopkins to Daniel Bankston, deed, pr. by Job Calloway.

Benjamin Griffith to Richard Snuggs, deed, pr. by Robert Snuggs.

13 April 1774 (cont.)

Jacob Bankston to Job Calloway, deed, pr. by Daniel Bankston.

Lambert Hopkins to John Calloway, deed, pr. by Daniel Bankston.

Edward Moore to Walter Ashmore, deed, acknowledged.

Samuel Yerkes and wife to Thos. Harris, deed, pr. by Richard Farr.

William Phillips, Jr. to Patrick Boggan Jr. deed, pr. by Wm. Boggan.

Richard Caswell to John Smith, deed, pr. by Chas. Smith.

p. 107--John Smith to Chas. Smith, deed, pr. by Jasper Smith.

Ordinary license gr. James Allen, he having entered bond.

Edward Chambers to John Jennings, deed, pr. by Thos. Stainback.

Jeremiah Mandles to John Batts Baird, deed, pr. by John Jennings.

Ordinary license gr. James Moore, he having entered bond.

Ord. Edward Moore to have leave to keep ferry over Peedee River below Bald Mountain, entering bond for same.

Richard Frances to Robt. Leverett, deed, pr. by John Auld.

Ord. Henry Mounger have leave to keep a ferry over Peedee River at his own plantation and that his rates be as follows: loaded wagon 6/1; loaded cart 4/; a light wagon 3/; man and horse 8d.

Ord. road be laid out the best way from Salisbury road above Andrew Banks [Bankston] to the mouth of Huwary River and the following: Daniel Bankston, Jacob Bankston, Job Calloway, Lambeth Hopkins, John Martin, Jacob Carter, Joshua Carter, Buckner Kimbell, Andrew Bankston, Dunkin Rone, William Hendley, Drury Ledbetter, John Walker and John Calloway lay out the same.

ABSTRACTS OF COUNTY COURT MINUTES, 1771-1777

12 April 1774 (cont.)

Ord. that a road be laid out the nearest and best way from the mouth of _____ to Mark Allen's store on the Cross Creek Road near the ford of Little River, and that the following: Wm. Coleman, James Allen, John Wilson, Elisha Thomson, Samuel Williams, Solomon Williams, Cornelius Robertson, Sias Billingsley, Mathew Raiford Sr., Mathew Raiford Jr., Edward Chambers and Wm. McGuire lay out same.

---

13 April 1774

The following: James Pickett, Samuel Parsons, Chas. Medlock, James Cotten, William Blewett and John Jackson qualified as Justices.

John Auld produced Commission and qualified as Clerk of Ct. Bond: James Auld and James _____

Walter Gibson to William Sanders, deed, pr. by Edmund Lilly.

John Liles and wife to Christopher Clarke, deed, pr. by Smith Fields.

William Griffin Hogan to James Roper, deed, acknowledged.

Robert Jarman to George Wilson, deed, pr. by Joseph Martin.

Charles Harrington and wife to William Pickett, deed, pr. by James Pickett.

John Shepard to William Pickett, deed, pr. by James Pickett.

Edward Smith and wife to Robt. Phillips, deed, acknowledged.

Samuel Wise and wife to John Crowson, pr. by Tristam Thomas.

Abraham Freeman to Dunkin Curry, deed, pr. by John Crowson.

p. 109 -- Luke Robertson and wife to _____ pr. by John McLeod.

Grand Jury: Samuel Williams, Solomon Gross, William Coleman, Owen Slaughter, Luke Robertson, Wm. Newbury, Wm. Mask, John Ro[we], Bexley John Lambden, Isaac Armstrong, Wm.

13 April 1774 (cont.)

Leake, John Bostick, James Philips, Walton Harris, Morgan Brown and Isaac Falconberry.

William Lucas and wife to Adrack Hix, deed, pr. by Saml. Parsons.

Samuel Parsons and wife to Reuben Holdings, deed, acknowledged.

Adrack Hix and wife to Joshua Butten, deed, pr. by Saml. Parsons.

Robert Poston and wife to James Downing, deed, pr. by Joshua Collins.

Bartho. Murphey and wife to Marcus Andrews, deed, pr. by Wm. Bennett Jr.

William Coleman and wife to Simon Hooker, deed, acknowledged.

Jarratt Gross to Nancy Shepperd, deed, pr. by Solomon Gross.

John Flowers and wife to Duke Glenn, deed, pr. by Joseph Howell.

William Hames and wife to Duke Glenn, deed, pr. by Joseph Howell.

John Cockerham to Mathew English, deed, pr. by James Sanders.

Thos. Dockery and wife to Jeremiah Strother, pr. by John Long, Jr.

William Pratt and wife to Lewis Thomas, deed, pr. by Wm. Thomas.

Luke Robertson to Joseph Tarbutton, deed, pr. by John Rox [Rowe].

Bexley John Lambden to John C _____ , deed, acknowledged.

Luke Robertson and wife to Wilson Williams, deed, pr. by Stephen Touchstone.

John Williams to Thomas Gibson, deed, pr. by Nelson Gibson.

Solomon Gross and wife to Isaac Armstrong, deed, acknowledged.

ABSTRACTS OF COUNTY COURT MINUTES, 1771-1777 87

13 April 1774 (cont.)

John Bostick to Anne Harrington, deed, pr. by Chas. Robertson.

Luke Robertson and wife to John _____, deed, pr. by John Skinner.

Luke Robertson and wife to Alexr. McCoy, deed, acknowledged.

Luke Robertson and wife to Isaac Armstrong, deed, pr. by Jno. Skinner.

Stephen Thomas and wife to Wm. Thomas, deed, pr. by Lewis Thomas.

William Thomas to Mark Rushing, deed, acknowledged.

William Thomas to Stephen Thomas, Jr. deed, acknowledged.

Will of Jennett McL[eod], proved by oath of John McL[eod].

Will of John Husbands by Blewett and Wm. Thomas. Tabitha Husbands, extrx. qualified.

Anthony Hutchins to John Chiles, pr. by James Pickett.

John Smith, Sandhill, and wife to Benj. Baird, pr. by [Shadrack] Hogan.

John Smith, Sandhill, to Samuel Spencer, pr. by Benj. Baird.

Ordinary license to John Hames, Jr. Bond: Saml. Spencer, James Auld.

Ordinary license gr. to John Cole. Bond: John James, James Auld.

Admn. on estate of Stephen Thomas. Bond: Chas. Medlock, Smith Fields, £150.

Ord. that John Smith, Sandhill, have leave to keep (p. 111) ferry across Peedee near mouth of Jacob's Creek.

Petition: Flora McDonald setting forth that she is detained unjustly as a servant by Roderick McKennon. Court ord. that she be discharged.

13 April 1774 (cont.)

Ord. road from Edward Moore's store to Williams old store on Cape Fear Road. West Harris, James Sargent, Moses Sanders, David Poor, Edward Moore, Richard Harrell, Walter Ashmore, Joseph Fry, Wm. Allton, Heaton Morris, Sam'l. Parsons, John Holton, Edw. Hurley, and Walter Harris.

Ord. Thos. Butler be Constable in room of Edmd. Nichols.

Will of Wm. Cox, decd. pr. by Joseph _____ and Chas. Burmingham, on oath of John Wade. Margaret Cox qualified as extrix.

John Poston and wife to Wm. Newberry, deed, pr. by Joseph Hinds.

Will of John Hamer, pr. by Saml. Spencer and John Knotts. John and William Hamer, exrs.

John Smith, Little River, to Joseph Smith, deed, by Chas. Smith.

Wm. Fielding to Geo. Wilson, 132 acres, pr. by John Jarman.

Theoderick Webb to John Richardson by John Wilson.

p. 112--Hopkins Howell to Wm. Pratt, deed, pr by William Hamer.

Ord. John Powell be Constable, Dist. _____ Cr., Nath'l. Dobbs in Dist. Brown's Cr., Thos. Gulledge in Thompson's Cr. Dist., John Knotts in Island Cr. Dist., John Cole in Hitchcock's Cr. Dist., Joseph Hall Sr in Falling Cr., Bexley John Lambden continue as Constable.

Thursday 15 April 1774

Present: Chas. Medlock, James Cotten, Saml. Parsons, ... Justices.

Henley _____ to Niell McNair, deed, pr by Chas. Medlock.

John Cheek to Joel McClendon, deed, pr. by Jesse McClendon.

Thos. Cockerham to Jonathan Turner, deed, pr. by Joshua Collins.

15 April 1774 (cont.)

John Stephens and wife to Joel McClendon, deed, by Jesse McClendon.

Francis Moseley, sheriff, to John Simmon, deed, by Saml. Parsons.

Ord. William Alton be Constable for ensuing year.

Ord. that Wm. Thomas have leave to build a grist mill on his land on Jones Creek.

Wm. Lindsey to James Vandeford, deed, pr. by James Pickett.

John _____ to John Patterson, deed, pr. by Allen Martin.

p. 113--James Saunders, Constable, in room of Jacob Cockeran.

Ord. Jeremiah Gulledge and Nicholas Green be Constables for ensuing year in lower part of county.

Ordinary license gr. Saml. Parsons. Bond: Chas. Medlock, John Jackson.

John Newberry to Richard Pemberton, deed, by Zacheriah Hogan.

Mr. Joseph Hinds came into court and protested agst the gaol as insufficient.

Ordinary license gr. John Wilson. Bond: John Bounds, Isham Haley.

John Colson, Esq. com. as Justice; qualified.

James Oliver to John Smith, deed, pr. by Mark Allen.

James Vanderford and wife to Wm. Lindsey, pr. by John Smith.

Mathew Raiford and wife to Mathew Raiford, Jr. deed, ack.

Admn. estate of Wm. McCahey gr. Margaret and Wm. McCahey. Bond; John Crawford and Wm. Blewett for £700. Admx. qualified.

Admn. est. Richard Fanning gr. Susannah Fanning. Bond: John Colson, £500. Admx. qualified.

Ord. that Robt. Webb have leave to build grist mill on own land on the Rocky Fork of Hitchcock's Creek.

15 April 1774 (cont.)

Ord. John Colson be guardian of Mary and Whitmell Harrington, orphans of Whitmell Harrington, decd., he having given bond with Francis Smith, £150 each.

Will of Timothy Taylor, decd. pr. by John Jeffery and rec. Eliz. Taylor extrx qualified.

Ord. that Samuel Blackford be Constable, continued.

Ord. Chas. Hinson be overseer of road in room of Benj. Hinson.

Admn. on estate of Jas. Wells, decd., gr. Theoderick Wells. Bond: Stephen Miller £150.

Ord. road laid out from John James's Jr. to Hall's Ferry on Drowning Creek. Jury: Jeremiah Gulledge, Moses Johnston, Samuel Touchstone, Thos. Johnston, John B _____, John James, John James Jr., Wm. Terry, Isaac Brigman, John Touchberry and Solomon Dearman.

Robt. Jarman to Thomas Downer by Joseph Martin.

Ord. John Douglas be continued Constable for ensuing year.

Ord. James Gray overseer of road from Buffalo head to County line.

Ord. John Jeffery be overseer of road from the Causeway agst Mt. Cr. to Buffalo head.

Ordinary license gr. Matthew Raiford. Bond: James Auld, Thos. Ussery.

16 April 1774

p. 115--Present: James Pickett, James Cotten, Wm. Blewett, Joshua Collins, John Jackson, Stephen Miller, Matthew Raiford, Charles Medlock, Chas. Robertson, John Colson, Thos. Wade, ... Justices.

Ord. that William Pickett, Cornelius Robinson, and Wm. Thomas be rec. for sheriff for ensuing year. Wm. Pickett and Cornelius Robinson ten votes each; Wm. Thomas seven.

Randolph Cheek and wife, to Hannah Fanning, deed, pr. by James Hogan, Jr.

Richard Adams and wife to Jesse Wallace, deed, pr. by Jacob Cockran.

ABSTRACTS OF COUNTY COURT MINUTES, 1771-1777 89

16 April 1774 (cont.)

Luke Robertson and wife to John Powell, deed, by Isaac Armstrong.

Inv. Wm. McKahey's estate ret. by Margaret McKahey. Ord. that personal estate of above be sold.

Friday [17 April 1774]

Present: James Pickett, James Cotten, Wm. Blewett, Joshua Collins, Justices.

Admn. on estate Benj. Gardner, decd., gr. Isaac Falconberry. Bond: William Terry and Stephen Jackson. £100.

Henry Williams to John Broff, deed, acknowledged.

Ord. Jasper Smith be Constable on lower part of Little River.

Ord. John Simmons be Constable on upper part of Little River.

John W_____ and wife to Thos. Megginson, deed, pr. by Benj. Megginson.

Wm. Daniel to James Auld, 212 acres, pr. by Geo. Wilson.

John Cartwright and wife to Wm. Coleman and James Pickett, deed, pr. by Joseph Hindes.

Patrick Sanders to Jonathan Llewelling, deed, pr by Thos. Dockery.

Thos. Dockery to Simon Thomas, deed, acknowledged.

Simon Thomas to Daniel Thomas, deed, acknowledged.

Chas. Medlock and wife to Sam'l. Spencer, deed, pr. by Wm. Pickett.

Wm. Pickett, Jr. to Samuel Spencer, deed, acknowledged.

Hannah Cheek to Wm. Pickett, deed, pr by Joel McClendon.

Wm. Mask and wife to Wm. Leak, deed, pr. by John Turnage.

[17 April 1774] (cont.)

James Allen and wife to Solomon Gross, deed, acknowledged.

Solomon Gross and wife to John Almond, deed, acknowledged.

Luke Roberson and wife to Wm. Lucas, deed, pr. by Isaac Armstrong.

p. 117--Ord. Rice Henderson, John Hathorn, Stephen Herrin, Aaron Herrin, John Turnage and William Smith who being in custody of John Cole, constable, be discharged.

Thomas Brigman and wife to Darby Hennigin, 100 acres by Jno. Coleman.

Ordinary license gr. Nathl. Curtis; Bond: John Hamer, James Auld.

Saturday [18 April 1774]

Present: Chas. Robertson, Chas. Medlock, Wm. Blewett, ... Esquires.

On motion of Chas. Spencer, ord. that Wm. Blewett and Thos. Wade take relinq. of dower of Agatha Medlock, wife of Chas. Medlock, to 100 a. from sd Chas. Medlock to Spencer.

Ord. that Wm. Thomas be overseer of road in room of John Husbands.

Ord. that Thos. Dockery continue as overseer of road for ens. yr.

Ord. John Cole be overseer of road from Drowning Cr. to Philemon Thomas.

Ord. that Robert Thomas be overseer of road from Philemon Thomas to province line.

Ord. that Wm. Leggett be overseer of road from Rocky Fork of Hitchcock's Cr. to McAhey's Bridge.

Ord. David Snead be overseer of road from C.H. to Brown's Cr.

Ord. John Walters be cont. overseer of road fr. Little River to Mt. Creek.

Ord. that Daniel Smith be overseer of rd from Mt. Cr to Catfish Road.

ABSTRACTS OF COUNTY COURT MINUTES, 1771-1777

[18 April 1774] (cont.)

Ordinary license gr. Thos. Wade. Bond: James Auld and Chas. Robertson.

Ord. Benj. Kimbell be overseer of rd from C.H. to Blewett's Ferry and that hands of Samuel Spencer, Esq. and Isaac Falconberry work on same.

Ord. Geo. Wilson be overseer of rd fr. the rock at Blewett's ferry road to Morgan Brown's; hands of Joseph Martin, John Jarman, Geo. Wilson, Thomas Downer, John Liles, James Auld, Smith Fields and Thos. Slay work thereon.

Inv: est of Benj. Gordon, decd. ret. by Isaac Falconbery, admr. Ord. that personal est. of Benj. Gordon be sold. (Gardner p. 116)

Ord. Morgan Brown overseer of rd fr. Haley's ferry to Wm. Thomas mill on Jones Cr and from the sd Morgan Brown's house to John Hamer's ferry, and from Brown's house down the river road to Jones Cr. including hands below Island Creek.

Ord. Wm. Pratt be overseer from his own house to the province line.

Ord. John Wall be continued overseer of rd from Hamer's Cr. to Mountain Cr.

Ord. Chas. Robertson, Thos. Wade, Charles Hines, John Crawford, Sam'l Snead, John Colson and Edmund Lilly serve as Jurors to court in Salisbury next June.

Ord. Sampson Williams be overseer to rd from Mt. Cr. to Drowning Cr.

Ord. Wm. McGuire be overseer of rd fr. Mask's ferry to John Smith's.
    Court adjourned.

Tuesday   12 July 1774

p. 120--Present: Matthew Raiford, James Pickett, Samuel Parsons, Charles Robertson, John Colson, Chas. Madlock, Joshua Collins, Thos. Wade.

John Lee to Robt. Lee, deed, acknowledged.

Wm. Pickett, Esq. Commission fr. Gov. appting him Sheriff, dated 5 May 1774. Bond with Thos. Wade, John Walters, Wm. Mask, Solomon Gross and James Pickett; qualified.

12 July 1774 (cont.)

John Rivers to Archibald McCoy, deed, pr. by John Moore.

James Pickett, Sheriff, to Joseph Brown and William Drakewood pr. to Samuel Spencer.

Anthony Hutchins to Joseph Brown, deed, pr. by Samuel Spencer.

Richard James to Thomas Douglas, deed, pr. by John Douglas.

Wm. Morris to Nathl. Williams, deed, pr. by Jonathan Llewelling.

Joel McClendon to William Hay, deed, prov. by James Pickett.

William and Thomas Pickett to James Meredith, acknowledged.

p. 121--David Snead to Thos. Wade, deed, acknowledged.

Thos. Johnson to Niell Blue, deed, pr. by John Blue.

Renatus Downing to James Morris, pr. by James Walker.

Frances Lee to Alexr. Martin, deed, by Collin Campbell.

Arthur Taylor and Francis Lee to Archibald Campbell, deed, pr. by Colin Campbell.

John McCoy to Mary McCoy, deed, pr. by Chas. Medlock.

John McCoy and Mary, his wife to Dunkin Smith, deed, pr. by Alexander Martin.

Solomon Gross and wife to Mak...... Martin, deed, ack.

Samuel Williams to Henry Williams, deed, pr by Wm. Blewett.

Ralph Mason to John Macalman, deed, pr by John Macalman.

George Carter to David Macalman, deed pr. by David Love.

ABSTRACTS OF COUNTY COURT MINUTES, 1771-1777

12 July 1774 (cont.)

William Brooks to Griffin Hogan, deed, pr. by James Hogan Jr.

David Hildreth to Wm. Griffin Hogan, deed, pr by Jas. Hogan Jr.

Samuel Snead to John Snead, deed, acknowledged.

Ord. Roland Kersey, orphan of George Kersey, be bound to Jonathan Llewelling until 21, being now 15 years old, to learn the trade of carpenter.

Thos. Simpson to Henry Rone, deed pr. by Wm. Noble.

p. 122--Admrn. on est. Dunkin Smith ret. and rec. Ord. that perishable est. of same be sold by Sheriff.

Ord. Job Calloway be overseer of rd from County line to Lince's Cr. and that hands of Zacheriah Henderson, Geo. Runnald, James Rogers, Sr. James Rogers, Jr., John Rogers, John Dunn, Edward Moore, John Walker, Robt. Walker, Stephen Treadwell, Wm. Hendley, Tunstall Rone, John Potete, Joseph Henderson, Jacob Bankston, Andrew Bankston, John Calloway, Jacob Carter, John Martin, William Ellis, Lambert Hopkins, Moses Cocks, John Cocks and John Royal work same.

Ord. that Daniel Bankston be overseer of rd fr Lince's Creek to mouth of Huwary and that hands, Thos. Simpson, Mathew Harrold, Adam Rone, Peter Rone, Wm. Noble, David Noble, James Hern, Pursell Hern, Joseph McClester, Samuel Carter, Joshua Carter, Drury Ledbetter, John Allen, Wm. Hern, Joshua Hern, Henry Mounger, Buckley Kimball and George Lee work same.

Ord. Joseph Bell be overseer of rd fr. mouth of Huwary to John Nelsons on Clarke Cr. and that hands Sam'l. Swearingen, Britain Harris, Jesse Christian, Shadrack Hogan, Turner Harris, Christopher Chappell, Henry Queen, Chas. Pritchard, James Sargent, Josiah Taylor, John Schreinsher, John Schrimshire, Jr., Chas. Trysell, Christopher Munday, Wm. Munday, Thomas Cross, Frances Munday, Thompson Clemmons, Arthur Munday, Wm. Clemmons, Sam'l. Munday, Thomas Horn, Nathaniel Bell work same.

Ord. John Wilson be overseer fr. Clark's Cr. near his own house to Mark Allen's store on the Cross [Creek] road near the ford of Little River and that

12 July 1774 (cont.)

hands, Sias Billingsley, Thomas Wilson, Sam'l. Williams, Solomon Williams, John Sheppard, Elisha Thompson, George Brasswell, John Cheek, Wm. Morgan, Isaac Cooper (p. 123) Joseph Morgan and his son, John Morgan work same.

Ordinary license gr. Christopher Butten; bond Sam'l Parsons.

John Webb to Robt. Webb, deed by Edward Smith.

Inv. est. Stephen Thomas, decd. by oath Stephen Thomas, admr.

Wednesday   [13 July 1774]

Present: John Colson, Chas. Medlock and John Jackson.

Wm. Brooks and Jesse Gilbert, deed, pr. by John Colson.

John Hornback to Wm. Hogatt, deed, pr. by John Haley.

Will of Thos. Brigman, decd. exhibited by Solomon Dearman. Isaac Brigman, exor, qualified.

Wm. Adams to Samuel Wise, deed, pr. by Jonathan Wise.

James Oliver and wife to Aaron Tallant, deed, pr by Abraham Belew.

Richard Brasswell to Christopher Christian, deed, by Goin Morgan.

John Wall and wife to John Husbands, deed, pr. by Wm. Lewis.

Admr. on est. Peter Rone, decd. gr. Edw. Moore. Bond: Wm. Noble and James Allen, £ 100.

Robert Jarman and wife to Samuel Spencer, deed, acknowledged. Femme relinquished before John Jackson, Esq.

Chas. Medlock and wife to Samuel Spencer, deed, ack. Femme relinq.

Wm. Dunkin (p. 124) to Robt. Gatewood, deed, pr by Richard Farr.

ABSTRACTS OF COUNTY COURT MINUTES, 1771-1777

[13 July 1774] (cont.)

Grand jury: Sam'l. Snead, foreman, Solomon Gross, Morgan Brown, Wm. Hunter, John Covington, John Thomas, Wm. Pratt, Robert Lee, Joshua Morgan, Abraham Belew, Christopher Christian, Jonathan Llewellen, Geo. Wilson, Geo. Ingram, Henry Williams, Benj. Dumas, and John Wall.

Sam'l. Snead to John McCaskill, deed, pr by Allen McCaskill.

John Swor and wife to John Skinner, deed, pr. by Sol. Gross.

Nicholas White to Francis Parsons, deed, pr by John Parsons.

James Little and wife to Wm. Gulledge, deed, pr by Thos. Creal.

Malachi Watts and wife to Moses Grice, deed, pr by Thos. Creal.

Thos. Creal to Wm. Leonard, deed, acknowledged.

Wm. Scott to Geo. Webb, deed, acknowledged.

Christopher Watkins to Edward Smith, deed, pr. by Marshall Digge.

Henry Adcock and wife to Nicholas Clark, deed, pr. by James Adcock.

Robert Jarman to John Branch, deed, acknowledged.

Wm. McDaniel to James Knotts, deed, acknowledged.

Luke Roberson and wife to Alexr. McLeod, deed, pr. by Mundo McCaskill.

Ord. John Jones be overseer of road fr. Haley's ferry to old School house opposite to Francis Clark and that Randolph Haley and Wm. Haley work same.

p. 125--John Crawford and wife to David Love, deed, acknowledged.

John Downer to David Love, deed, pr by Saml. Williams.

John Crawford and wife to John Kersey, deed, acknowledged.

[13 July 1774] (cont.)

Ord. Isaac Jones, Abraham Jones, Sam'l. Yerkes and negroes be added to hands to work on road under William Ratcliff overseer.

John McLeod and wife to Norman McLeod, deed, acknowledged.

Solomon Gross and wife to John McLeod, deed, pr by John Powell.

Stephen Cole and wife to Wm. Thomas, deed, by Wm. Hunter.

Wm. Terry, Jr. to Matthew Terry, deed, acknowledged.

John Hornback to Wm. Hoggatt, 100 a, pr. by Isham Haley.

John Hoggatt and John Bean, Jr., exrs. of Wm. Hoggatt, to Onesphorus West, 100 a, pr. by Isham Haley.

Onesphorus West to James Auld, 100 a, pr. by Peter Sanders; the femme Margaret West relinq. before John Jackson, Esq.

Richard Adams and wife to Geo. Collins, deed, pr by Jacob Cockeran.

Hopkins Howell and wife to Samuel Howell, deed, pr by Joshua Howell.

Ord. James Roper overseer of road whereof Whitmell Harrington was formerly overseer.

Ord. Walter Ashmore be overseer of road (p. 126) from Moore's ferry to Beaver Dam Cr. and that hands, Edward Moore, Wm. Gray, John Barnett, Richard Warrell, Saml. Billingsly, Thos. Whiteheart[?], Joshua Fry, _____ Powell, Thos. Fry, Jr. Richard Bean Jr., Richard Bean, Sr. John Coggan, Leonard Thomas, Wm. Reaves, Saml. Reaves, Thos. Fry, Sr. Walter Bean, George Fry, Benj. Fry, Roger Williams, Eleazer Burkhead, John Walker and Stephen Treadwell.

Richard Adams and wife to Jacob Cockerham, pr by Jos. Hinds.

Francis Moseley to Wm. Leake by Joseph Hinds.

George Carter and wife to Robert Webb by James Pickett.

ABSTRACTS OF COUNTY COURT MINUTES, 1771-1777

13 July 1774 (cont.)

Zachariah Smith and wife to Wm. Newberry, by Joseph Hinds.

Mary Gambrill to Dennis McClendon, by Ezekiel McClendon.

William Coleman and wife to Thos. Dockery, acknowledged.

Robert Alexander and Mary Gordon to James Chiles, by Robt. Jarman.

Ord. Walton Harris be overseer of rd fr. Beaver Dam Cr. to Rocky Cr. and that hands Nath'l Steed, Wm. Lacey, Geo. Sanders, Moses Sanders, Aaron Sanders, Wm. Hamilton, Frances Marbary, Philip Steed, Moses Steed, Edward Hurley, Thos. Cross, John Morgan, West Harris, Thos. Briggs, James Sargent, Charles Travers, Turner Harris, Chas. Parker, John Callahann, Thos. Parker, Thos. Hearn, Christopher Munday, James Fry Jr., Holland Higgin, John Hallom, John Morris, Edward Cornwell, John Schrimshire, William Munday, Josiah Tallant and Geo. Kerle work same.

Ord. Richard Green be overseer of road from Rocky Cr. to Little River the (p. 127) following hands Arthur Munday, John Hallom, Wm. Ashley, Wm. Hallom, Edm. Nicholas, John Nicholas, Peter Randolph, Thos. Randolph, Jacob Humble, Andrew Hicks, Gabriel Washman, Heaton Morris, James Campbell, John Hues, Wm. Boling, Reuben Holderness and Spencer Hallom work same.

Ord. Dan'l. Hicks be overseer from Little River to County line near Williams old store, hands Joseph Hunt, Lewis Hunt, David Poor, Chas. Allen, John Burcham, Wm. Jordan, Samuel Parsons, Edward Poor, John Macallam, Joseph Burcham, Francis Jordan, Joshua Buttin, Christopher Buttin, Thomas, Dennis, Thomas Ward, Wm. Bland, Moses Bland, Wm. Spencer, Jona. Gregory, John Sowell, Wm. Sowell, Wm. Ingram, John Simmons, James Cotten, Lewis Sowell, Chas. Sowell, Henry Smith, Thos. Lucas, Saml. Bruton and Thos. Stainback.

John Hamer Sr. to John Hamer Jr., by James Auld.

Admr. on est. Wm. White, decd. gr to John Dickerson. Bond: with James Allen £50.

Ord. Mr. Thos. Chiles be allowed £15 per annum for ferrying people having business at Court elections, musters, etc. Same for William Blewett £50.

13 July 1774 (cont.)

Ord. that James Allen and Mary Allen, his wife, formerly widow of Benj. Ingram be summoned to produce last will of sd Benj. Ingram.

Dennis McClendon to Ezekiel McClendon, acknowledged.

Adjourned.

Thursday [July 14 1774]

Present: John Colson, James Pickett, John Jackson, Justices.

John Martin to Lambert Hopkins, by Edward Moore.

Robt. Poston and wife to Venson Davis, by Jos. Hinds.

Ord. Adm. on est of John Jackson gr. to Stephen Jackson, exr.

John Smith to Wm. Seward, deed, by Wm. Bennett Jr.

Chas. Weatherford to Wm. Bennett Jr. by Solomon Townsend.

Phereby Benton to Priscilla Unity Benton, Chas. Benton and Spencer Benton, pr by Stephen Miller.

p. 129--Wm. Primrose to David Love, acknowledged.

Ord. that John Chiles bring John Hubberd an orphan heretofore bound to him to court to be dealt with by law.

Nuncupative will of Silas Thomas, decd., by Hannah Thomas, William Thomas relinquishing his legacy thereon. Wm. husband of Hannah.

William Coleman and wife to John Cole, by Joseph Strother.

Adjourned.

Friday [July 15 1774]

Present: Chas. Medlock, James Pickett and Wm. Blewett, Esquires.

Benj. Dumas appt. overseer of rd in room of John Mask Jr.

[July 15 1774] (cont.)

Robert Edwards to Luke Robertson by Solomon Gross.

Lydia Mondine vs Wm. Morgan. Jury:- Thos. Dockey, Samuel Flake, Isaac Copeland, Wm. Bennett, Caleb Touchstone, Thos. Ussery, Wilson Williams, Lawrence Franklin, Luke Robertson, Thomas Pickett, John Chiles and Isaac Falconberry. Damages £1; cost £1.

Ord. Joseph Henderson and Jacob Vanhoser be Constables in fork between Peedee and Rocky River for year.

Ord. John Macleval be Constable bet. Brown Cr. and Rocky River.

p. 130--Thos. Hurley to Timothy Hurley, by John Hurley.

Wm. Blewett and wife & John Crawford and wife to James Stewart ack. by Wm. Blewett and John Crawford.

Ord. Chas. Medlock take relinq. of Eliz. Blewett and Ann Crawford.

Mary Allen, wife of James and widow of Benj. Ingram relinquishes right of admr. on est. of sd Ingram and on motion of James Pickett he was given adm. of sd estate with bondsmen: William Pickett, James Auld, John Smith, Sandhill, and Robert Jarman £1000.

Luke Robertson to John Smith, pr by John Skinner.

Ord. that hands work on road whereof John Wall is overseer, viz; David Jernigan, Edward Almond, Richard Lake's hands, John Perkin, Mathew Terry, James Moore, Thos. Moorman, Benj. Moorman, Sylas Hayley, Henry Adcock, Thos. Adcock, Matthew Strickland, Zachariah Moorman, John Clark and George Mathews.

Thos. Wade to Francis Smith by Zachariah McDaniel.

Thos. Wade to Thomas Smith by Zachariah McDaniel.

p. 131--John Poston vs Zachariah Hogan. Jury: Samuel Williams, David Rich. Richard Pemberton, Jacob Paul, John Smith, Wm. Lindsey, Shadrack Hogan, John Branch, David Smith, John Skinner,

[July 15 1774] (cont.)

Stephen Jackson, Wm. Coleman. Verdict: for defendant.

Ordinary license gr Samuel Snead. Bond: Wm. Hunt and John Thomas.

Admr. est. Silas Thomas, decd., with will, to Bexley John Lambden. Bond: Isaac Falconberry and John Branch.

p. 132--John Bostick to John Hickman, by Ezra Bostick.

Ord. John Lee be Constable in room of John Macleval.

John Knotts and wife to James Auld, by James Pickett, Esq.

Ord. road be laid fr. fork of road above Cole's Bridge to province line, the old Bridle way by Thomas Brigman's plantation; Wm. Terry, Jr., John James, Jr., John Crowson, James Bounds, Abraham Freeman, Sam'l Dawkins, Timothy Hurley and George Freeman to work same.

Morgan Brown vs Andrew Duffin. Jury: Solomon Gross, Geo. Wilson, Thos. Pickett, Luke Robertson, _____ _____, David Snead, Lawrence Franklin, John Smith, Isaac Falconberry, Wm. Lindsey, John Bounds, Caleb Touchstone and John Skinner. Verdict: for deft.

Ord. that Morgan Brown bring Mary and Eliz. Brown, orphans of Stephen Brown to next court to be dealt with as the law directs.

Ord that John Hamer bring Morgan and John Brown orphans of Stephen Brown to next court as above.

Adjournment.

---

11 October 1774

Andrew Preston of John Spencer, deed, by Andrew Preston

Wm. Nelson and wife to Wm. Nelson, by Reuben Hay.

Ordinary license gr. David Love. Bond: Samuel Snead, Stephen Jackson.

ABSTRACTS OF COUNTY COURT MINUTES, 1771-1777

11 October 1774 (cont.)

James Cotton, Esq. commission apptg. him Register for Anson; qualified with bondsmen, James Auld and James Pickett.

p. 134--John Spencer and wife to Wm. Spencer, acknowledged.

Richard Worrell and wife to Francis Marbury, by Jas. Cotton.

Wm. King and wife to Richard Worrell, by Moses Sanders.

Wm. Barnes and wife to David Dumas, by Thos. Cross.

Moses Sanders records mark......in right ear.

John Martin Sr to John Martin Jr, by Roger MacDonald

Henry Snead and wife to Joseph Hunt, by Duncan Meacham.

John Polke and wife to Philip Frederick, by Henry Talley.

Thos. English and wife to Wm. Weatherford, by Henry Talley.

Peter Copeland records mark.

Wednesday   12 October 1774

Present: James Cotton, James Pickett, Wm. Blewett, Chas. Robertson, Chas. Medlock, Mathew Raiford, Justices.

Phillip Herndon to Thos. Dickson 100 a, by David Raney.

Thos. Dickson to John Donaldson, 100 a, by_____

p. 135--Stephen Jackson to John Donaldson, by Thos. Wade.

William Benson to John Donaldson, by_____

Morgan Brown and wife to John Donaldson by Richard Farr.

Samuel Parsons and wife to John Burcham, by Wm. Jurden.

11 October 1774 (cont.)

Joseph Martin to Thos. Moorman by Stephen Jackson.

John Coleman to Thos. Simmons, by James Pickett.

Reuben Philips and wife to Henry Hargett, by Joshua Yarbrough.

Darby Henigan to Arthur Dees[?], by John Hawthorn.

Stephen Touchstone and wife to Solomon Alred, by John Alred.

Wm. Holley and wife to Wm. Mediall, acknowledged.

Mathew Ingle to Archibald Monroe, by Henry Williams.

Wm. McDonald to Malcom Monroe, ---

Wm. McDonald to Daniel Monroe, by Archibald Monroe.

John Helms to John Bostick, by Thos. Jowers.

Wm. Warren to John Hagler by Jacob Vanhoose[?]

Thos. Fannin to Jonathan Jowers, by Samson Williams.

Richard Adams and wife to Thos. Mason, by Samson Williams.

Luke Robertson and wife to Murdo McCauley, by Daniel_____

p. 135--Ord. John Bounds be overseer of rd from fork above Cole's bridge to the province line.

Grand jury: David Love, foreman, John Long, Stephen Duncan, Caleb Touchstone, John Richardson, James Benton, James Hutchins, Thos. Pickett, Mark Allen, Samuel Flake, John Smith, Isaac Copeland, Saml. Snead, Wm. Covington, George Carter, Benj. Covington, Jesse Bounds and Owen Slaughter.

Zachariah Moorman and wife and Sarah Hall to David Snead, by Hendley Snead.

Admr. on est. of Elizabeth Johnson, decd., gr. to John Smith, Carp. bond: Samuel Spencer, Samuel Flake.

12 October 1774 (cont.)

Wm. McDonald and wife to Daniel McDonald, by Chas. Robertson.

Joshua Morgan to John Morgan, by John _____

Thos. Fannen to Duncan Macleod by Alexander McLellan.

Alexander Macleod and David McCummins to Murdo Macaskill.

Burford and Howard vs Richard Dickson. Jury: Morgan Brown, Stephen Cole, Thos. Cross, Thomas Chiles, John James, Jacob Vanhooser, Geo. Webb, Josiah Swearingen, Thos. Ussery, Chas. Hines, David Rich and Wm. Bennet.

Ord. Gabriel Davis be Constable in room of Jacob Vanhooser. Richard Suggs Constable.

John Hagler and Jonathan Harry paid for one wild cat scalp and one wolf scalp.

p. 137--To Chas. Robertson for attending Salisbury Ct. £1.12.8 To Cornelius Robertson for same, March Term £1.5.0

Luke Robertson to Alexr. McDonald by Soirle MacDonald.

Ordinary license gr. John James; bond Sam'l Snead, Chas. Medlock.

Will of John Liles, decd. by James Auld and Rebecca Liles,[5] executrix.

Admr. est. Wm. Hamer, decd. by Frances Hamer; bond John Hamer and Hopkins Howell. £1500

Robert Jarman to Thos. Jones, by Thos. Huntley.

John James to Samuel Mimms, acknowledged.

Ord. Buckner Kimbell be Constable in room of Joseph Henderson.

Power of Atty from John Shepperd to David Dumas, ack in Ct.

David Dumas to John Ingram, acknowledged.

Ord. Stephen Wright, orphan of Thomas Wright, be bound to John Brooks till of age, now 15 yrs. old, to learn business of a farmer. John Brooks to give

12 October 1774 (cont.)

him year and one-half of schooling more than the law allows.

Joseph Howell to James Smith, by Thomas Jowers.

Ord. Murdo McKaskill be overseer of road for Sampson Williams.

John Jones, Sr. to Benj. Covington, acknowledged.

p. 138--Ordinary license gr. James Farr. Bond, James Auld, Richd Farr.

An Appeal gr. on motion of Wm. Kennon, Esq. from judgment on guardianship of William Roberts.

Thursday [13 October 1774]

Present: James Cotten, James Pickett, Wm. Blewett, and John Jackson, Esquires.

Isaac Brigman recorded his mark.

Nathaniel Holley to Ebenezer Chevers, by Wm. Nelson.

Jury to Salisbury Sup. Ct. Wm. Hunter, James Cotton, James Pickett, Sam'l Snead, Samuel Parsons, Wm. Mask and Moses Sanders.

Will of James Hildreth pr. by John Jeffery and the exor qual.

Ordinary license gr. to Wm. Collson, bond given.

Thomas _____ to Edward Black, by Wm. Rushing.

Christopher Buttin to John Smith, by Wm. Johnson.

p. 139--Philemon, James, and Benj. Thomas, orphans of Stephen Thomas, decd., made choice of John Thomas for their guardian.

Bond with Robert Thomas and Joseph Howell, £ 100.

Ord. that Winnie Harrison, orphan of Joseph Harrison, be bound to Lawrence Franklin till of lawful age, now seven years old.

Joshua Collins and wife to Jermiah Strother, by Wm. Coleman.

ABSTRACTS OF COUNTY COURT MINUTES, 1771-1777

13 October 1774 (cont.)

Simon Hooker and wife to Wm. Coleman, acknowledged.

Vann Swearingen to Josiah Swearingen, by John Jennings.

James Liles to Eliz. ____ by Holden Wade.

Allowances for scalps of wild cats and wolves: Henry Burcham (1), Thos. Ward (3), Chas. Allen (1), Edmund Nichols (1), James Purnell (1), Henry Deberry (1) Lawrence Franklin (4).

Friday [14 October 1774]

Present: James Cotton, Chas. Medlock, Wm. Blewett, Stephen Miller.

p. 140--Accts of Sales of estates of Stephen Thomas, Richard Fanning and Whitmell Harrington returned by Sheriff.

Wm. McNatt to James Benton, by Stephen Miller.

Jerome Miller to Jesse McClendon, by Stephen Miller.

James Terry to Richard Leake, by Robert Webb.

Richard Farr, by motion, objected to bail in his suit vs John Rusk; ord that bail insufficient and Joseph Hines, Coroner, stand bail and be liable.

Ensiant Bettis to Daniel Leonard by John Jackson.

Elijah Bettis to Ensiant Bettis, by John Jackson

Ord. road to be laid from Mecklenburg road near William Leverett's to cross PeeDee at Moorman's Ferry above mouth of Hitchcock's Cr to join road to Cole's bridge on Drowning Cr. Following to lay this out: Wm. Leverett, Lawrence Franklin, John Harnis, Robt. Gatewood, John May, David Rich, Burlingham Rudd, Wm. Fielding, John Knotts, John Jarman, Geo. Wilson, Richard Leake, John Wall and Henry Adcock.

Ord. John Clay, poor aged and infirm, be rec. to be exmt fr tax.

(14 October 1774) (cont.)

William Roberts, orphan of Wm. Roberts, decd, came into court and (p.141) made choice of James Terry for his guardian, who made bond with Caleb Touchstone, Isaac Falconberry and Wm. Terry £500

Tomorrow [15 October 1774]

Present: John Colson, James Cotton, Wm. Blewett, Stephen Miller.

John Batts Baird to Thomas Jennings, by John Jennings.

Admr. on est. of Wm. Watts, decd., gr to John Watts with bond, John Preslar, James Long. £100.

Chas. Thompson to James Cotton, by Bexley John Lambden.

Samuel Spencer and wife to Samuel Flake. Femme relinq before Wm. Blewett.

Ord. James Adcock have license to keep ferry over Peedee at (p.142) Moorman's old ferry where new road ordered to be laid; bond Henry Adcock and John Cole.

Deed of gift. Sarah Harrington to John, Mary, and Whitmell Harrington, pr by John Collson.

Ordinary license gr. James Cotton; bond Saml. Williams, James Auld.

Ord. that Mary and Eliz. Brown, orphans of Stephen Brown, decd., be bound to Morgan Brown till of age. Eliz. now 7 yrs and Mary 11 yrs. Ord. that John Brown, orphan of Stephen Brown, be bound to Stephen Jackson, to learn the trade of blacksmith, till of age; now 15 years.

Christopher Munday, John Schrimshire and Wm. Munday added to lists of hands to work on road whereon Walton Harris is overseer.

Ord. that Samuel Skipper be summoned to bring Henry, William and Chas. Woodward, orphans of Chas. Woodward, decd., to next court.

Ord. Ann Wright be summoned to bring James Weaden an orphan to next court.
p. 143-- Adjourned.

Wednesday   11 January 1775

Present: Wm. Blewett, James Cotton, John Jackson, Esquires.

John Polk and Anna, his wife, to Chas. Ray, by Middleton Pool.

Renatus Downing to Samuel Wilkins, by John Grimes.

George Webb to Allen Martin, acknowledged.

Duncan Curry to Anens (?) Curry, by John McAlmon.

Jesse Wallace and wife to Angus McInnis, by Murdo McInnis.

Robt. Webb to John McAlmon, acknowledged.

Luke Robertson and wife to Soirle McDaniel, by John McLeod.

Sampson Williams and wife to John McLenon, by Roderick McKinnon.

Sampson Williams to Roderick McKinnon, by John McLenon.

John Spencer to Wm. Culpeper by Daniel Culpeper.

Frederick Gibble to Nathl. Halton, by Archibald Holmes.

Mathew Stevens and wife to Nath'l. Ashley, by Abraham Belew.

p. 144-- George Webb to John Mathews, acknowledged.

John Sego and wife to Robert Sego, acknowledged.

John Smith and wife to Nicholas Christian,⁶ by Christopher Christian.

Stephen Jackson to Wm. Blewett, acknowledged.

Josiah Swearingen to John Jennings, acknowledged.

John Lucas and wife to Alexander Beard by John Jennings.

Stephen Cole and wife to Geo. Webb, by Geo. Webb, Jr.

John Cole and wife to Geo. Webb, by Geo. Webb Jr.

Aaron Tallant to John Ingram, by John Smith.

11 January 1775 (cont.)

Shadrack Denson and wife to James Oliver, by Thos. Gower.

John Poston to Jacob Collins, by Wm. Newberry.

Robert Jarman to Wm. Burt, by Wm. McDaniel.

Adm. on est. Henry Chambers, decd., gr. to Solomon Gross. Bond, William Pickett, Caleb Touchstone. £1000.

Ord. that Caleb Touchstone have leave to build water grist mill on Mountain Creek.

Henry Williams to Daniel McDaniel, acknowledged.

Grand-jurors: Morgan Brown, Geo. Wilson, Isaac Falconberry, John Smith, Richard Downs, Lambert Hopkins, (p.145) William Coleman, Christopher Christian, Robt. Webb, Cornelius Robertson, Charles Hines, Wm. Moseley, Caleb Touchstone, Isaac Armstrong, Luke Robertson and Goin Morgan, Wm. Newberry, Jr.

Thomas Gower and wife to Solomon Gross, by Griffin Haywood.

Josiah Swearingen and wife to Duncan McNabb, by Solomon Gross.

Ord. that Zilpah Hopkins, dau. of Priscilla Poor, wife of Edward Poor be put in custody of John Powell and that sd Powell bring sd orphan to next court.

Ordinary licence gr to Samuel Yerkes. Bond, Richard Farr and James Cotton.

Thomas Shelton to Benj. Fuller, by John Jackson, Esq.

Ord. that David Smith be appointed Constable for ensuing year from dist. from Huwarry to Little River.

Edward Smith, an apprentice, pet. for freedom from Edward Crossland (master). Ord. that Edward be discharged on paying the cost of this suit and that William Smith become security for him.
                    Adjourned.

Thursday.   [12 January 1775]

Present: Chas. Medlock, James Cotton, James

ABSTRACTS OF COUNTY COURT MINUTES, 1771-1777

[12 January 1775] (cont.)

Pickett, John Jackson, Mathew Raiford, - Justices.

Nicholas White to John Lefevar, acknowledged.

Alexr. Gordon to Nicholas Green, by Chas. Medlock, Esq.

Power of Atty. from Gibbons Jennings to Richard Farr, by Samuel Spencer, Esq.

Lew Lowry and wife to John Street, acknowledged.

Thos. Mason to John Mason by Sampson Williams.

Jacob Cochran to George Collins, by Sampson Williams.

Robert Edwards to Wm. McKahey, by Sarah McKahey.

John Rush to Samuel Yerkes, by Thos. Dickson.

Jasper Smith to John Mitchell, by John Smith, Carp.

John Smith, Sandhill, and wife, to John Mitchell, by John Smith, Carp.

Thomas Mitchell to John Mitchell, by John Wishart.
Adjourned

Friday   [13 January 1775]

William Terry, guardian of Short Long returned acct and the balance due ward #3.6.3.

Ord. road to be laid out the nearest way from Cross Creek road near John____ to cross Mt. Cr, at Bexley John Lambden's ford, from there to widow McKahey's on Drowning Cr. To lay out same: Jacob Cockran, John Jenkins, William Burns, Thomas Jowers, Wm. Jowers, John___, James Bostick, (p.147) John Bostick, Mathew Raiford, Sr., Ezra Bostick, William Coleman, Mathew Raiford, Jr., Jesse Williams, Wm. Chaplain.

John Almon to Hugh____, by Solomon Gross.

Stephen Cole to Wm. Coleman, acknowledged.

Saturday   14 January [1775]

Present: Chas. Medlock, Wm. Blewett, James

14 January [1775](cont.)

Cotton, James Pickett, Esquires.

Ord. a road laid out from Samuel Parsons to James Allen's. To do so: Luke Robertson, Solomon Gross, Caleb Touchstone, Samuel Bruton, John Swa [Swor] Jr., John Broff, Alexr. Beard, Thos. Gower, John Ussery, Thos. Ussery, James Allen, Soirle McDaniel, John Jennings, Thomas Jennings, Thos. Stanback, Isaac Armstrong, and Benj. Sermner [Sumner?]

Lurang [?] Cannon vs Caleb Touchstone by Jury: Thomas Jowers, Lawrence Franklin, Henry Williams, John Barnett, Samuel Flake, John Jennings, Wm. Coleman, Duncan McNatt, Richard Farr, David Love, James Allen, Abraham Belew. Verdict: for defendant.

Ord. John, Thomas and Leonard Higden, (p.147) and Anna Higden, orphans of Leonard Higden, decd., now in the house of Mary Higden, suffering from want of necessarys of life, be removed and put in the hands of, John Higden with Wm. Blewett, Thomas with John Douglas, Leonard with William Moody and Anne with James Pickett, to be brought to next court.

Jacob Paul and wife and Phillip Paul to James Wild, by Mary Wade.

Rebecca Liles, extrx. John Liles, decd., to James Auld, by Morgan Brown.

Morgan Brown and wife to John Chiles, acknowledged. Femme relinq. before James Cotton, Esq.

Bond from Jacob and Phillip Paul to James Auld, £500, by Mary Wade.

Admin. est. John Simpson, decd., gr. to Thos. Harris. Bond: Richard Farr and Morgan Brown, £150

Mark Allen to Solomon Gross, by Luke Robertson.

Ord. Road be laid out from Huwarry to Anson C.H., to cross the PeeDee at William Pickett's plantation and falling into Salisbury Road at Savannah Cr. To do this: Wm. Pickett, James Hutchins, David Dumas, Benj. Dumas, Cornelius Robertson, John Mask, Jr., James Pickett, John Ingram, Owen Ingram, Moody Ingram, Abraham Belew, Nath'l

(13 January 1775) cont.

Ashley, and Shadrack Denson. Adjourned.

(p.149)
Tuesday   11 April 1775

Present: John Collson, James Pickett, Mathew Rayford, Justices.

Wednesday   12 April 1775

Present: John Collson, Chas. Robertson, and James Pickett.

Neill Brown to Daniel Macduffie, by John Alred.

Robert Jarman to William Yew, by John Smith.

John McLeod and wife to John Manly, by Duncan McNabb.

Commission of Peace: John Colson, Chas. Robertson, Henry Mounger, Soirle MacDonald, James Pickett, Mathew Raiford, James Auld and James Cotton, Esq.

Neill McQueen and wife to William McQueen, by John Martin.

Shadrack Denson to David Dumas by John McClendon.

p. 149--Wm. Hunter and wife to Henry Covington, acknowledged.

Benj. Covington and wife to Henry Covington, by Wm. Hunter.

Jeremiah Gulledge to Dugald Blue, acknowledged.

Jeremiah Gulledge to Edward McNair, acknowledged.

John Long to Thos. Dockery, by Daniel Smith.

Ord. W. Avery, Esq. be appointed attorney for King in absence of Alexander Martin, Esq.

Dan'l. Short to William Short, acknowledged.

Adm. est. Joseph Hough, decd., gr. Joseph Hough Jr.; bond with Henry Williams; £200.

12 April 1775 (cont.)

Ord. John Miller be Constable in room of Wm. Gulledge.

Robert Thomas to Benj Thomas, acknowledged.

Alexander Baird to Andrew Ingram, by James Cotton.

Ord: Roger Williams be Constable in room of Buckner Kimball.

Jesse Wallace and wife to Jeremiah Hendrick, by Sampson Williams.

Ord: Nath'l Carter be overseer of rd. in room of Chas. Hinson; that Robt. Thomas continue overseer of rd fr Falling Creek to Solomon's Cr. and Speed be overseer of road fr Solomon's Cr to province line.

Court Elections for Sheriff: Henry Mounger (3); Mathew Raiford (3), James Cotton (3), James Pickett, Chas. Robertson, John Collson, James Auld. Ord. Solomon Gross, William Terry and James Pickett be recommended as Sheriff for ensuing year.

Jurors to serve next court at Salisbury, June 1st: John Collson, Chas. Robertson, James Cotton, Solomon Gross, James Pickett, Wm. Collson and Buckner Kimball.

John Hornbeck to Wm. Fielding, by Wm. Bennet.

Wm. Fielding to Henry Bailey, by Wm. Bennet.

Penelope Shepherd to Wm. Burns, by Daniel Thornton.

Grand Jury: Saml. Snead, foreman, Shadrack Denson, George Ingram, Solomon Gross, John Hamer, Thos. Baly, Joseph Martin, George Webb, John James, Sr., Duncan Macnabb, Thomas Conner, George Lee, Samuel Flake, John Martin, John McLeod, Norman McLeod and John Smith.

Alexander McDonald to Norman McLeod, by Murdo McCaskill.

John McLeod to Wm. McLarman, acknowledged.

John George to _____

M. Gustavus to Daniel Murphy, by John Downer.

12 April 1775 (cont.)

Mijah Gustavus to Wm. Cox, by John Downer.

On motion of Wm. Hay by Wm. Kennon, Esq. atty, ord that £20 inflicted last court be £3. ; for Edward Davidson £10 be remitted to 30 sh. Present: John Colson, Chas. Robertson, James Cotton and Soirle Macdonald, who remitted the above fines.

Adjourned

Thursday [13 April 1775]

Present: John Colson, Chas. Robertson, James Auld and Soirle Macdonald, -- Justices.

Ord. James Bennet be Constable in room of John Knotts.

John Leveret to Jas. Ray, by Patrick Boggan.

John Hopkins to West Harris, by Walton Harris.

John Richardson to James Ray, by John Long, Jr.

Thos. Wilson to Henry Mounger, acknowledged.

Goin Morgan to Silas Billingsly, by Thomas Wilson.

Ord: Norman McLeod and John McLeod be excused from serving on grand jury; that James Sanders continue as Constable.

Samuel Davis to John Crawford, by Jonathan Llewellen.

Aaron Sanders to Edward Moore, by James Cotton.

James Cotton vs Daniel Burford. Jury: Alexander _____, Wm. McQueen, John Smith, Stephen Jackson, David Smith, James MacDonald, Caleb Touchstone, John Chiles, Joshua Morgan, Ezekiel McClendon, James Fletcher and Burlingham Rudd. Verdict; £20.

Ord. Jonathan Harry be paid for one wolf's scalp.

Thos. Megginson and wife to Wm. Meguire, by Wm. Mask.

Ord: Mathew Raiford, Jr. be overseer of road in room of Wm. Meguire.

Ordinary license gr. to John Chiles, bond with Jas. Pickett.

[13 April 1775] (cont.)

Ord: John Chiles have leave to keep ferry over PeeDee River from own land to Hutchins, below Grassy Island.

Deed of gift, James Allen to Eliz. Ingram, acknowledged.

James Farr to Saml. Yerkes, by Richard Farr.

Ord. Thos. Hern be overseer of rd in room of Walton Harris.

Ord. Wm. Liggett overseer of road fr John Chiles landing on PeeDee to Rocky fork near his bridge.

Ord: Jonathan Llewellen be overseer of road from Rocky Fork to old Cheraw Road; that John James be overseer from Old Cheraw Rd. to Robertson bridge on Drowning Cr; that Wm. Holly be overseer of road fr Mecklenburg line to Negro Head; that Thos. Cheaves be overseer of rd from Negro Head to Brown Cr; that Job Benton be overseer fr Brown Cr to Leverett's Cr.; Nathaniel Ashley from Leverett's Cr to Bremengame[?]; John Chiles from Bremengame to said Chiles Landing; Thomas Graves from Cross Creek Rd to Bexley John Lambden's ford on Mt. Cr.; Jacob Cockerham from Bexley John Lambden's (p. 155) to Collin's Cr. and all hands below Widdow MacMullins Cr. to William Colemans and up Will's Cr. to the Ridge be subject to work the same; that Jonathan Llewelling be overseer of road from Collins Cr. to Widow McKahey's on Drowning Creek.

Adjourned.

Friday [14 April 1775]

Present: James Cotton, James Pickett, Stephen Miller, Justices.

Ord: that David Smith be appointed Constable in room of John Douglas; that Silas Billingsley be Constable in room of David Smith.

Benj. Moorman to George Mathews, Thos. Moorman and Francis Clark, by Morgan Brown.

Saml. Snead and wife to Archibald Campbell, acknowledged.

Ord: Malachi Watts be Constable in room of Wm. Gulledge.

[14 April 1775] (cont.)

John Jackson, Esq, with nomination, qualified as Justice.

p. 156--Admn. est. John Alton gr. Mary Alton, with James Cotton and William Alton, bondsmen. £200.

Jury to lay off road from Saml. Parsons to Allens, now Phillip Raifords, in room of Jury appointed last court, John Batts Baird, Alexander Baird, Thos. Stanback, Caleb Touchstone, John Jennings, Thomas Gowers, John McLeod, Robt. Leveret, John _____, Saml. Bruton and Solomon Gross.

Charles Booth to John Miller, by Walter Cunningham.

Amos Huff came into Court and chose Sampson Hull as guardian. Bond, with James Fletcher and Chas. Ray, £300.

George Wilson to John Jarman, acknowledged.

John Jarman and wife to George Wilson, acknowledged.

The King vs Joseph Winfree. Jury: Lawrence Franklin, Isaac Falconberry, Caleb Touchstone, John Downer, Daniel Murphey, James Fletcher, Owen Slaughter, Joseph Ingram, Henry Adcock, Wm. Lindsey, Christopher Christian, and Jesse Wallace. Not guilty.

Ord. that road be laid out from lower ford of Jones Creek to province line, the River Road, by Thos. Tompkins, John Wright, John Parsons, John Lefeaver, Wm. Pratt, Duke Glenn, Saml. Blackford, Thos. Harris, Joseph Howell, Hopkins Howell, Thos. Tompkins, Jr, John Hamer and Morgan Brown.

Ord: that William Pratt be overseer of road from Province line (p. 127) to ford on Jones Cr; Morgan Brown from ford on Jones Cr. to ford of Island Creek.

Richard Pemberton and wife to John Mask, by Humphrey Rogers.

Lott Tallant to Thos. Hall, by Daniel Love.

Edward Moseley and wife to Wm. Leak, by Noah Agee.

[14 April 1775] (cont.)

Ord: Wilson Williams be overseer of road in room of John Batts Baird; that Edward Almond be Constable in room of John Cole.

Saturday   [15 April 1775]

Present: James Cotton, James Pickett, James Auld, Justices.

Ord: Aaron Sanders be Constable in room of Moses Sanders; John Ricketts, Constable, in room of Bexley John Lambden; and Daniel Hicks in room of Thos. Butten.

Deed of Trust; James Allen to Cummings Warwick. (p. 158)   Adjourned.

Tuesday   (11 July 1775)

Present: James Cotton

Wednesday   [12 July 1775]

Present: Chas. Robertson, James Auld, James Pickett, James Cotton.

Moses Hull to James Hogan, Jr. by Wm. Hogan.

Moses Hull to James Hogan, Sr. by Wm. Hogan.

John Simmons and wife to Benj. Simmons, acknowledged.

John Simmons and wife to John Simmons, acknowledged.

Admn. on estate of John Spencer, decd., gr. to Susannah Spencer,' bondsmen Thomas Wilson, Chas. Ray and William Pickett, £500.

Nelson Gibson and wife to John _____ by Nathl. Williams.

John Street and wife to John Eddins, by Nathl. Melton.

John Street and wife to Wm. Eddins, by John Eddins.

William Coleman and wife to Simon Hooker, acknowledged.

ABSTRACTS OF COUNTY COURT MINUTES, 1771-1777

[12 July 1775] (cont.)

Lawrence Franklin to John Stanfield, by Nathl. Melton.

Bill of sale: James Jeffreys Sr. to John Simmons, by Jas. Cotton.

James Fletcher to William Brooks by Charles Ray.

Francis Marbury and wife to Henry Wade, by Saml. Crabtree.

John Smith, Little River, to Isaac Jones, by Jasper Smith.

Wm. Hoy to George Davidson, by Jesse McClendon.

Micajah Pickett to Daniel Smith, by Chas. Hines.

Benj. Dees to Thos. Turner by James Johnson.

Ord: Donald McDonald have leave to build water grist mill on Mt. Cr. on property (late) of Hugh McDonald.

Edmund Hurley to Stephen Heron, by Thos. Wilson.

Will of John Cary, decd., by David Fennell, one of exrs, who qual.

George Webb to John Watson, by Allen Martin.

Jesse Bounds to Allen Martin, by Jesse Martin.

Ord: Wm. Brooks, James Farr, Nicholas Parker, (p. 160) Arthur Dew, Nicholas Green, Thos. Parker, Wm. Thomas, John Walker and Joseph Straughter be fined for non-attendance at grand-jury.

Grand jury: Morgan, foreman, Robert Webb, Isaac Falconberry, Edward Moore, Wm. Leak, William Smith, Joseph Martin, Jonathan Llewellen, Caleb Touchstone, John Cole, Samuel Flake, George Wilson, Abraham Belew, Jack Cockeran and Shadrack Hogan.

Ordinary license to Joshua Carter; bond, Jas. Cotton, Buckner Kimbell.

Isaac Belew and wife to George Belew, by Abraham Belew.

William Bond and wife to Abraham Belew, by Nathl. Ashley.

[12 July 1775] (cont.)

Burford and Howard vs Isaac Brigman. Jury: John Lambden, Chas. Ray, Wm. Brooks, Burlingham Rudd, Lawrence Franklin, William May, Thos. Jowers, John Stanfield, John Jarman, Duncan McNabb, Joseph Huff and Reuben Phillips. Nonsuit.

Ord. John Knotts be overseer of rd. from Adcocks ferry to Jones Cr. Hands: George Wilson, John Knotts, Stephen Jackson, Bartholomew Murphey, David Rich, Benj. Carter, James Leslie, John Hornbeck and Robt. Gatewood.

Ord: John Wade overseer of road from Jones Cr. to cross-road meeting house near May's mill. Hands liable to work same: John Murphy, Thomas Jones, Ovington Cox, Wm. Fielding, James Covington and Wm. Cresp.

Ord: John Crawford overseer of road from Adcock's ferry to George Webbs. Hands liable to work same: Richard Leak, William Jernigan, Wm. Scott, Peter Sanders, Matthew Strickland and George Webb

p. 161--Ord. that Matthew Strickland, poor, aged and infirm, be recommended exempt from tax.

John Perkins to Jacob Perkins, by Owen Slaughter.

Joseph Dunham to Allen McCaskill....

Ord. Walton Garner be Constable in upper end of County for year.

Thos. Gibson to Wm. Leggett, acknowledged.

Inventory of Malcom Martin, decd.

Wm. Bennett to James Lile by Solomon Townsend.

Ord: John McIlvail be Constable bet. Rocky River and Brown Cr.

Soirle McDonald and wife to Donald McDonald, by Roderick McDonald.

Ord; William Newberry, Jr. be Constable.
Adjourned.

Thursday [13 July 1775]

Present: Chas. Robertson, James Cotton, James Auld, James Pickett, Justices.

[13 July 1775] (cont.)

p. 162--Ord: Edward Moore be overseer of road from Moore's ferry to Beaver Dam Cr. in room of Walter Ashmore.

Benj. Baird to Wm. Thomas, by Thos. Wade.

Ord: Wm. Blewett be overseer of road from the Court House to his ferry, hands liable to work same: Isaac Falconberry, Saml. Spencer, David Love and Wm. Blewett.

William Coleman to James Cotton, acknowledged.
Adjourned

Friday   [14 July 1775]

Present: James Cotton, James Pickett, Stephen Miller, and James Auld, Justices.

Ord. Zilpah Strickling, dau. of Edward Poor be bound to Jas. Cotton till she is 18 (p. 163) (She is now 12 years and 6 mos.) to learn business of a house-wife.

Ord. David Dumas be overseer of road fr forks of Hamer's Cr. to where the new road comes into the old.

John McNatt to Patrick Boggan by Thos. Wade.

Wm. Lawrence to Thomas _____, by Andrew Ross.

Samuel Snead relinquished gdnship of Wm. Watkins.

Theodorick Webb to Stephen Miller, by James Webb.

Will of Jeremiah Strother, decd., pr. by Wm. Coleman.

Henley Snead to John Bounds, by Wm. Briley.

William Lewis Sr to William Lewis Jr, by Isaac Armstrong.

Ord. John Parsons be overseer of rd fr Robins Cr. to Province line.

Stephen Thomas to Philemon Thomas, acknowledged.

Ord: the following persons be appointed searchers in the several districts: John Parsons, John

[14 July 1775] (cont.)

Arthurs, and John Hinson from Province line to Jones Creek......, John Hamer, Stephen Thomas, and Morgan Brown from Jones Cr. to George Wilsons.... George Wilson, John Jarman and Isaac Falconberry fr Geo. Wilson's to Wm. Terry's....... James Terry, Joseph Ingram and Andrew Ross from William Terry's to Cedar Cr. .... John Lyons, Wm. Hicks and Stephen Parker from Province line to Hitchcock's Cr..... John Wall, Mathew Terry, and David Snead from Hitchcock's Creek to Mt. Cr. .... Wm. Leak, Josiah Strother and John Cockran up on Little River near Mask's ferry..... Wm. Mask, John Mask Jr., and George Walters from Little River to James Hutchins .... Burwell Lanier, John Leveret and Joshua Morgan from Mr. Collson's to Mr. Lanier's ...... Stephen Miller, Joseph White and Job Benton from Mr. Lanier's to Stephen Miller's....... John Jackson, William Rorie and Isaac Nichols from Stephen Miller's to the County line.... Edward Moore, Daniel Bankston and George Lee from Mary (sic) to Guilford ...... William Collson, Robert Lee and John Hall from Widow Fanning's to Edmund Lily's upward. . ... Saml. Parsons, John Simmons and Francis Jordan for Little River Dist...... John Smith (Sandhill), Nicholas Christian and Benjamin Baird from up Little River District.

Ord. the following hands be added to work on road whereof Jonathan Llewellen is overseer: Mr. Kahey's, Wm. Ashley, Wm. Alred's and John Cole's.

Ord: Mathew Raiford Jr. be overseer from Hamer's Cr. to Little River, and that John Cole be Constable for ensuing year.

p. 165--Jonathan Llewellen to Robert Webb, acknowledged.

William Legget to Henry Taylor, by Robert Webb.
Adjourned.

10 October 1775

Present: James Auld.

11 October 1775

Present: James Auld, Stephen Miller and John Jackson.

ABSTRACTS OF COUNTY COURT MINUTES, 1771-1777 105

11 October 1775 (cont.)

p. 166--Sampson Williamson and wife to Thos. Stainback, by Thos. Jennings.

George Webb and wife to Jesse Bounds, by Matthew Watson.

John Canfield, poor, aged and infirm, rec. exempt from tax.

George Webb to Mathew Watson by Jesse Bounds.

John Powell and wife to Luke Robertson, by Welcome Ussery.

Admr. est. Joel Chivers gr. Sarah Chevers. Bond: Wm. Nelson and Patrick Boggan.

Arthur Dew and wife to John Bounds by John Hawthorn.

Robert Jarman to John Jarman, by David Love.

Smith Fields to John Jacob, by John Auld.

Joseph Hough to Wm. McHenry, by Stephen Miller, Esq.

Isaac Falconberry vs Nelson Kelly, the bail surrendered the principal. Thos. Wade and Joseph Martin entered bail.

Thomas Mitchell to George Mitchell, acknowledged.

William Hunter, pd for attending Salisbury Ct.

John Jarman to George Wilson, acknowledged.

Joseph Hall Sr. to Alexander Love....

p. 168--Ord: John Crowson Jr. be Constable in room of Joseph Hall.

Luke Williams to John Mathews, by John Dickson.

John James Sr. and wife to John James Jr. by Wm. Love.

George Ingram to Humphrey Rogers, by John Walter.

Will of George Ingram by James Burns. John Walters ex. qual.

Adjourned.

Thursday [12 October 1775]

Present: James Auld, John Jackson, Wm. Blewett.

Jacob Perkins to Solomon Fisher, by John Cole.

John Smith to Isaac Jones by Robert Lee.

Aaron Tallant and wife to Henry Belew, by Abraham Belew.

Henry Blewett and wife to Moses White, by Abraham Belew.

Drury Simms and wife to Zacheriah Moorman, by Silas Haley.

Will of Chas. Morris, proved by Wm. Lacey.

Grand jury: Thos. Wade, foreman, Chas. Medlock, John Chiles, Solomon Gross, Saml. Snead, Robert Lee (River), Richard Farr, Lawrence Franklin, William Mask, (p. 168) John Hornbeck, Burlingham Rudd, Robert Webb, John Cole and John Walters.

Bill of Sale: John Fowler to Robert Fenner, by James Cotton.

James Mode to Moses Bland, by James Cotton.

Christopher Christian to Henry Burcham, by James Cotton.

Saml. Snead to James Cotton, acknowledged.

Wm. Carter and wife to David Love, by Wm. Blewett, Esq.

Moses Bland to Thos. McClendon, by James Cotton.

Archibald Campbell to Murdo McCaskill, by James Cotton.

Hopkins Howell to Wm. Benson, by Morgan Brown, Jr.

Admr. est. Neill McInnis, decd., by Murdo McCaskill. Bond: James Cotton and John Batts Baird. £80.

Shadrack Hogan to Edmund Lilly, by Nathl. Lilly.

Thos. Parker and Nicholas Parker to be excused as grand-jurors.

[12 October 1775] (cont.)

David Dumas to Edmund Lilly, by Nathl. Lilly.
Adjourned.

Friday   [13 October 1775]

p. 169--Ord: John Parsons be overseer from Baber's Creek.

Deed of gift. John Crawford to Thomas Crawford, acknowledged.

Ord. John Coleman be overseer of road in room of John Walters.

Ord: road be laid out from Wm. Holly's crossing Brown Cr at Wm. Johnson's to road leading to the Province line by: Wm. Rushing, Wm. Johnson, Richard Rushing, Solomon Rushing, Wm. Holley, John Jackson, Robert Rushing, James Lowry, Jesse Bates, Benj. Fuller, Thos. Chivers, Moses Green, John Rushing and Malachi Watts.
Adjourned

Wednesday   January 10 1776

p. 170--Present: Stephen Miller, James Auld, Wm. Blewett.

John Campbell to Burwell Lanier, by John Sulivan.

Joshua Morgan and wife to Burwell Lanier, by Micajah Stenson.

Wm. Leverett to Abraham Strickland by Malachi Watts.

Robert Webb to Henley Webb, acknowledged.

Wm. Morris to Leeklin Curry, by Robert Webb.

Robert Webb to William Webb, acknowledged.

John Chiles to James Auld, by Lawrence Franklin.
Adjourned.

(2nd Tuesday)   April 1776

Present: James Pickett, James Auld, and Matthew Raiford.

Ord. Joshua Morgan have leave to build a public grist mill on his own land on Grindstone Cr.

April 1776 (cont.)

Henry Adcock and wife to Nicholas Clark by John Thomas.

Phillip Dill and wife to John Swor, Sr. by James Smith.

Wm. Irby to Shadrack Hogan, by Nathan Hogan.

David Dumas to Shadrack Hogan, by Nathl. Lilly.

John Hamer to Edward Crosland by Stephen Jackson.

Thomas Fry to Thomas Jones, by Roger Williams.

Thomas Jones to West Harris, Sr., by Roger Williams.

Ord: Duke Glenn be overseer in room of Wm. Pratt.

Ord: on pet. of Frederick Hern in that Joseph Thompson to whom Hern was formerly bound an apprentice, be summoned to next court to answer complaints.

Ord: that David Love's hands be added to work road of wh. George Wilson is overseer; Nathaniel Scott's hands added to work road whereof Wm. Blewett overseer.

p. 172--Francis Clark to Henry William Harrington, acknowledged.

Wm. Leak overseer of road in room of John Coleman from Little River to Mt. Creek, and Zachariah Smith be overseer of road in room of John Wall.

Ord. James Meredith Jr. be overseer of road fr fork of road to Mask's ferry, to be worked by hands of Thos. Megginson, Humphrey Rogers, James Pickett, Joseph Isham [Ingram?].
Adjourned.

---

9 July 1776

Present: Chas. Robertson, James Auld, Mathew Raiford and Stephen Miller,... Justices.

Stephen Tomkins to Richard Worthen by John Carruth.

ABSTRACTS OF COUNTY COURT MINUTES, 1771-1777

9 July 1776 (cont.)

Wm. Pratt to Wm. Hamer, by John Hamer.

p. 173--John Hamer to James Auld, acknowledged.

John Parsons to Thos. Ratcliff, acknowledged.

Robert Liles to James Auld, by Jeremiah Jordan.

Wm. Leake to Thos. Megginson, acknowledged.

Will of Gibbons Jennings, decd., gr. Ann Jennings; bond, Richard Farr and Thomas Harris £600.

Bexley John Lambden to Cornelius Robertson by Wm. Bennet.

Richard Worthen to have leave to build a bridge on an old Mill Cr.

Jacob Self and Wm. Self be apptd. to view and condemn one acre of land on Rockey River adj. for use of a mill built by Goin Morgan.

Ord: that John Neil Crowson be overseer of road from the fork above Falling Cr. to Solomon's Creek.

Ord. Chas. Hinson be overseer of road from Jones Cr to Province line.

Ord: John Knotts be overseer of Cheraw road from Anson C.H. to Jones Cr.

John Downer to David Love, acknowledged.
Court adjourned.

14 January 1777
STATE OF NORTH CAROLINA, Anson Co.

p. 175--Whereas by a resolve or an ordinance of this State for establishing inferior courts of pleas and Quarter Sessions, etc., a Commission of Peace and a Dedimus Potestatem for the County of Anson directed to William Blewett, Thos. Wade, Chas. Medlock, Mathew Raiford, James Pickett, Stephen Miller, John Jackson, James Auld, Henry Mounger, Wm. Pickett, David Love, John Chiles, George Davidson, Robert Thomas, Cornelius Robertson, John Kimbrough, James Allen, William Hay, William Collson, John Wade, John Carruth, and Thomas Lacey was openly read at the Court House in the said County on the 2nd Tuesday in January, being the 14th day, the first year of the Independence, 1777.

14 January 1777 (cont.)

Present: Thomas Wade, Chas. Medlock, John Jackson, James Auld, Henry Mounger, William Pickett, David Love, James Allen, William Hay and John Wall, Justices.

Deed from Philip Dill and wife to Ezra Bostick, by James Smith.

Ezra Bostick to James Smith, by John Skinner.

John Swor to James Smith, by John Skinner.

Robert Phillips to Smith Fields, by Saml. Phillips.

George Webb to William Thomas, by Abraham Lefever.

Thomas Megginson to John Walters, by George Walters.

Gabriel Davis to Nathaniel Davis, by Shadrack Hogan.

Samuel Phillips to Thomas Slay, acknowledged.
Adjourned.

Present: James Auld, Henry Mounger, John Wall.

John Crawford elected Sheriff. Bond: Richard Farr, Chas. Medlock.

William Love qualified Deputy Sheriff.

Ord. Job Calloway continue Constable on road from Salisbury to Joshua Carter's; Daniel Bankston same from Joshua Carter's to Mounger's ferry.

Hopkins Howell to Abraham Jones, by Morgan Brown.

Joseph Still to Carny Wright, acknowledged.

Carny Wright to Michael Crawford, by Richard Farr.

John Leverett to John Leverett, Jr, by Stephen Miller.

Ord: Joseph Bell continue overseer of road from Mounger's ferry to Clark's Creek; and John Wilson from Clark's Cr. to Mathew Raiford's, and William Speed from Province line to John Thomas; Wm. Blewett from his ferry to Court House; George Wilson from Island Cr. to the fork of Blewett's ferry above Colo. David Love's; Wm.

January 1777 (cont.)

Thomas from Blewett's ferry to Pedler's; Wm. Pratt from Jones Creek to South line.

p. 178--Ord. that Thos. Fry, John Skinner and John Knotts be Constables.

Ord. Wm. Threadgill be overseer of road from Brown's Cr to Rocky River and that the same be turned a small distance above Major Davidson's; that Thos. Vining be overseer from Medlock's to Pedler's Cabbin; and Thomas Gibson from Rocky Fork to McKahey's bridge; and that Thomas Dockery and John Neil Crowson continue overseer of roads.

Ord: that Christopher Watkins be overseer in room of John Knotts from Adcock's ferry to Jones Cr and John Roe from Mathew Raiford's to Drowning Creek.

Jurors for court at Salisbury next month: Chas. Medlock, Wm. Lofton, Daniel Bankston, George Lee, Wm. Colson, Edmond Lilly and Drury Ledbetter.

Ord: Morgan Brown continue overseer of road from Island Creek to Jones Creek.

p. 179--Thos. Megginson to Joseph Ingram, by Humphrey Rogers.

George Davidson, Esq. qualified as Justice of Peace.
                Adjourned.

(2nd Tuesday)   April 1777

Present: Thos. Wade, Chas. Medlock, James Auld.

Matthew Terry to George Matthews, by Morgan Brown.

Will of George Matthews, by Morgan Brown.

John Ussery and wife to Joseph Tarbutton, by Wm. Pickett.

Stephen Tompkins to Stephen Jackson, acknowledged.

p. 180--Thos. Tompkins to Stephen Jackson, by Richard Farr.

Wm. Moody to Wm. Bennet, by Thomas Dockery.

April 1777 (cont.)

Patrick ____ to ____ Hodgen[?], ack.

Patrick Boggan to Francis Tompkins, acknowledged.

Admr. est. Thos. Tompkins gr. Mary Tompkins, bond John Parsons and Stephen Tompkins £4000.

Ord: Jeremiah Terrell be Constable.

John Ussery[s] and wife to William Pickett, by Philip Raiford.

Adm. est. Wm. Moody, decd. gr. Wm. Blassingham; bond Duke Glenn and Richard ____ £400.

Ord: Eliz. Cardall be summoned to bring her eight children to next court.

Ord: Valentine Morris be overseer of road in room of Thos. Dockery.

Ord. that Henry Wm. Harrington have leave to turn the road leading from Haley's ferry down by Colo. Chas. Madlock's. To view same: Chas. Medlock, Wm. Speed, Benj. Skipper, Henley Snead, John Wall, Israel ____, John Jones, Shadrack Bagget, David ____, Richard Leak, Zachariah Morris, ____, Edward Almond, George ____, James Baggett.
                Adjourned

Wednesday   April 1777

Present: Chas. Medlock, Thomas Wade, James Auld, Wm. Pickett, Esquires.

Grand jury: Thos. Dockery, foreman, Geo. Wilson, George Webb, Duke Glenn, Joseph Howell, Morgan Brown, John Crowson, Thomas Slay, Josiah Martin, Henry Knotts, Wm. Mask, Lawrence Franklin, Burlingham Rudd, Frederick Temple.

Eliz. Cheek to Wm. Pickett, by Wm. Threadgill.

Francis Stevens to Wm. Pickett, by Edwin Ingram.

Robert Webb to Isham ____, (p. 182) by Chas. Medlock.

Thomas Thomas to Stephen Thomas, by Wm. Thomas.

ABSTRACTS OF COUNTY COURT MINUTES, 1771-1777   109

April 1777 (cont.)

William Webb to Burwell Streetter(?)............

John Walters to George Walters, by Wm. Mask.

Ord. Saml. Spencer be atty for county during this court.

Nicholas Bond to John Cole, by Robt. Webb.

John Perkins to Solomon Fisher by John Cole.

Stephen Miller and John Chiles qualified as Justices.

Ord: Phillip Rushing be overseer of rd fr Jackson's old path, hand for same, William Rushing, Thos. Ford, _____ _____, Eliz. Bostick, John Beck, Abraham Jones, Kell Grover and Jacob Jones.

Ord: James Langford be overseer of rd. in room of Lewis Lowry.

Ord: Following hands work road whereof Geo. Wilson is overseer, from Island Cr. to fork of Blewett's ferry road: James Auld, John Jarman, John Auld, Joseph Martin, Jeremiah Terrell and David Love and sd Geo. Wilson's hands.

Ord. that Sheriff summons Henry Kee to next court concerning his holding and detaining Henry Phillips and ____ Phillips, orphans now in his possession.

Ord. David Collier[9] be Constable in dist. he now lives in.

Ord. George Andrews be overseer of road from C.H. to fork of Mask's ferry road and hands of Thos. Wade work under him, and that Henry Wm. Harrington keep road from Haley's _____ to Chas. Medlock's with own hands; also that following hands work on road whereof Thos. Vining is overseer from Pedlar's Cabbins into road below Solomon's Creek, viz: John Webb, Wm. Haley Jr., Silas Haley, Benj. Moorman, Benj. Moorman Jr., John Moorman, Archelus Moorman, William Williams, the young man who lives at Mr. Wall's, Zachariah Moorman, William Lewis, Wm. Webb, Wm. Jernigan, Walter Slaughter, Richard Leake, Wm. Parmer and Wm. Wade's hands at the mill, also James Moore, William Haley, Andrew Moorman, Thos. Moorman and Thos. Moorman, Jr.

April 1777 (cont.)

Ord. that John Chiles be overseer of road from his ferry to Charles _____ with the following hands to work same: William Terry, _____ _____, _____ Long, James Pickett, Abraham _____, J____ Duglass, Thomas Duglass, ____ _____, John Booth, John Newton, James Vanderford, Chas. Br......, William Yew, Wm. Ross, Andrew Ross, John Hendricks, Richard James, Daniel Vine, Joseph Ingram.

Ord: John Cole be Constable in room of Edward Almond and Nicholas Green the same in district he now lives in.

Ord: Robert Webb be overseer (p. 184) of road from Liggett's bridge to Cartledge's Cr. at Thomas Thomas' and the fol. hands assist in opening same from mouth of Lick Branch to George Carter's, to Jonathan Llewellen and Little Mountain Creek, to head of Grimes fork of Rocky fork of Hitchcock's to Chiles' ferry.

Ord. that twelve of following lay out rd from Adcock's ferry to Mecklenburgh road, near old meeting house: John Wade, Daniel Murphy, George Wilson, _____ Fielding, Christopher Fielding, _____ Smith, John Downer, Robert _____, _____ Cox, Thomas Jones, _____ _____, John Karboo, Frederick Temple.

Adjourned.

Thursday   April 1777

Present: Thos. Wade, James Auld, Wm. Pickett, Chas. Medlock.

Ord: John Cole be overseer of road fr Cole's Bridge to Brigman's; Thos. Gibson from Brigman's Cabbins to Chalkfork; John Mathis from Chalk fork to ford of Hitchcock's near Falling creek and John Cowan from Hitchcock's to George Wilson's.

Joseph _____ to _____ Pickett, by James Terry.

Ord: that Isaac Falconberry be fined £10 for contempt and give security for his good behavior toward Samuel Spencer. Bond, Wm. Blewett and Nathaniel Scott.

Ord. that John Parsons and Robert Gordon be patrolers the ensuing year; also Wm. Threadgill,

ABSTRACTS OF COUNTY COURT MINUTES, 1771-1777

April 1777 (cont.)

Dennis McClendell, John Ingram and Thomas Howlett; and Edward Williams and William Baker the same.

Ord. John Carpenter be overseer of road called Crawford's Old Road, from Williams old cabbins to Charles Powell's; Henry Covington from Charles Powell's to Pedlar's Cabbins; Robert Smith from C.H. to Jones Creek; Chas. Hinson from Jones Creek to Province line.

p. 187--State of N.C. vs Soirle McDonald. Bond: Wm. Pickett security for good behavior £200.

Ord: Wm. Garner and Jasper Smith be patrolers in Little River District.

Ord: John Thomas be overseer in room of Jehukel Crowson on road from Philemon Thomas's below Solomon Creek.

State of N.C. vs Isaac Falconberry for appearance in next court to answer for a misdemeanor. Geo. Wilson, Joseph Martin, sec.
Court adjourned.

Present: Thos. Wade, James Auld, John Wall.

Mr. Wm. Love (Deputy Sheriff) came into court and paid to Thos. Wade, Esq. £10, a fine on Isaac Falconberry for contempt.

p. 188--The Court overlooked acct. of Wm. Pickett, Esq. Sheriff of Anson 1772, certified by Thos. Wade, Stephen Miller, James Auld and John Wall; same for 1774, signed by the same.
The Court adjourned.

(2nd Tuesday)   July 8, 1777

Present: James Auld, Stephen Miller, John Wall, Justices.

Commissions as Esquires for _____ _____, _____ Miller, James Love, John Chiles, _____ _____, Duke Glenn, Wm. Thomas, Wm. Leggett, Jonathan Llewellen, Wm. Mask, Esquires, -- qualified.

p. 189--Ord: John Knotts be overseer of road from Adcock's ferry to Cheraw Road; and Christopher Watkins from Cheraw Road to Jones Creek; Thomas Jones from Jones Creek to Mecklenburg.

John Wall, Esq. commission as Justice; qualified.

Ord: George Jefferson have leave to build a public water grist mill on the thoroughfare of PeeDee River below where it comes into Mountain Cr. at the Grassy Island.

Patrick Boggan to Wm. May, by William Pickett.

Ord: James Moore be appointed Constable; also John Stringer.
Adjourned.

Wednesday _____

Present: Thos. Wade, John Wade, Henry Mounger, Wm. Thomas.

The End.

[Next Minutes July 12, 1848]

---

1. This is probably "Coroner" not "Colonel". See p. 139 of the Minutes for Friday, Oct. 14, 1774.
2. George Bagby in the Land Grants.
3. This deed was not recorded but is mentioned in Bk 7-19 with reference to prob. in Inf. Court. Sam'l. Swearingen was prob. born in Edgecombe Co. (N.C.) A Saml. Swearingen bou. tract in Bertie Prec. (later Edgecombe Co.)11 May 1728 fr. Jos. Lane, Jr. and wife, Patience, ack. in May Ct. by Lane and by Mathew Raiford by virtue of Power-of-Atty from Patience Lane. (Bertie D.B "B"-399). Saml. Swearingen and wife, Eliza, sell this land back to Lane in 1733. He also makes deeds to Thomas Swearingen (D. B. 2-173 and to Samuel Swearingen, Jr. (D.B. 5-15) in Edgecombe Records. Pension claim (W. 6113.) of a Thomas Swearingen states that he was b. in Edgecombe Co. N. C. 13 May 1761; entered service fr. Edgefield Co. S. C.; had bros. John and Van also in service. In Anson, Thos. Swearingen makes deed to Vann Swearingen in 1767, Saml. Swearingen Sr. and Samuel Swearingen Jr. witnesses. (Anson D.B. "H#1"-10)
4. "This court annually recommends to the governor three persons out of whom he is to choose one to be sheriff of the county..." N. C. Col. Rec. Vol. VII, p. 480

5. Rebecca Liles was a dau. of Mathew Raiford, Sr. and wife, Mourning, of Cumberland Co., formerly of Edgecombe Co., whose will, dated Bladen Co. 21 July 1752; prob. Apr. Court 1758 in Cumberland (org fr. Bladen 1753)., the original will at Dept. of Arch. and Hist. Raleigh, N. C. Children: Matthew Raiford Jr. (m. Judith, Cumb. D.B. 1-319); Robert Raiford (m. Susannah, Anson D.B. 7-256); William Raiford (m. Mary, Anson D.B. 7-267); Mary Raiford m. in Edgecombe Co. (William Terry, Anson D.B. "C#1")-435); Anne Raiford (m. another William Terry-D.A.R. Rec.); Mourning Raiford, (m. (1) Wm. Robards, Cumb. Co. D.B. 1-382, (2) William Pickett, Anson D.B. 7-574); Rebecca Raiford (m. John Liles, Fam. Rec. Isaac S. London Coll.) Grace Raiford (m. John Stevens, Cumb. D.B. 1-415); Phillip Raiford (m. Jane Armstrong, Cumb. D.B. 3-529); and Druscilla Raiford (m. John Mask, Isaac London Coll.)

6. The grantors of the above deed are evidently John and Sarah Smith, Sandhill, as, from other records, Nicholas Christian apparently m. their dau. Sarah. This may have been a gift deed of personal property as there is no record of it in the Anson deed index and gift deeds of that period are not indexed in Anson Co. unless for land. However, the deed may not have been recorded as was sometimes the case.

7. Spartanburg Co. S. C. Deed Bk. "B"-431. June 12, 1777. Deed of Gift. Susanna Spencer, of Anson County, N. C. for love, etc. to Jesse Spencer, all her estate for the con. that he keep her three youngest children and raise them as well as he can. Wit: John McIlvaile, Griffin Hogan.

8. July 23, 1822, a John Ussery and wife, Mary, of Posey Co., Indiana, sold for $220, to David Smith, of Todd Co., Ky. a section of land in the State of Illinois appropriated by Congress 1812 for military bounty, witnessed by George B. Crutcher (son-in-law of David Smith) and Ezekiel Saunders, and proved by the latter in Todd Co. the same day. The above David Smith was the son of John and Sarah Smith, Sandhill, who lived in Anson County from 1765 to 1779 when Montgomery County was taken from it.

9. In Christian County, Ky. 25 April 1811, David Smith and wife, Obedience, sell 100 acres adj. David Collier, being a part of Collier's original survey (David Collier's original headright). Christian Co. D.B. "C"-247. Surveyed for Martin Collier 400 acres on Spring Cr. adj. David Collier and John Derush. 13 Aug. 1804, David Smith and David Collier, chain carriers. Survey Bk. 3-88, Christian Co. Ky.

ANSON CIVIL SUITS IN SALISBURY DISTRICT SUPERIOR COURT

Trial Papers (Civil), Superior Court of Law, Salisbury District, at Salisbury (N.C.) Court House.

File 1757-82 (Mch.- Nov.)

Little vs Pickett, writ. 4 June 1757. William Little vs John Pickett, of Anson County, Sen. [?] otherwise called John Pickett[1] son of William Pickett, on a plea of trespass. Damage £200 sterling.

Ack. by Wm. Little to be satisfied and to withdraw suit. 20 Sept. 1757.

****

Trial Papers (Civil) Superior Court. 1757 May.

To James Pickett, Esq. high sheriff of Anson, bond of Andrew Preslar (principal) and Wm. Downs and James Denson. 14 May 1757. Wit: John Pickett.

****

Same. Robinson vs Coleson. 22 Sept. 1764. Warrant for David Dumas, Cornelius Robinson, James Gaddis and Joseph Dunham to appear 22 March next as wit. in behalf of plaintiff, Chas. Robinson vs John Coleson. Signed by John Frolock, clk.

****

Command to Salisbury (Sheriff) to summon Gilbert Gibson to appear at Salisbury 22 Sept. next and declare on oath what you have or heard of the rights, credits, goods and chattles of Stephen Cole, of Anson. 22 Mch. 1761. John Frolock, clk.

****

Summon to David Dumas, of Anson Co., admr. of est. of Benj. Dumas, late of Anson, decd., to appear at Court 22 Sept. next and to answer those things objected to in suit by Joseph and John Culpeper, exrs. of will of Martha Dumas, wid., decd. March 2, 1766.

****

Anson Co. Command to summons Temple Coles, of Rowan, merchant, to appear before the Inf. Ct of Com. Pleas and Q. Sessions to be held at Anson C.H. 4th Tuesday in January next to give evidence for the plaintiff in case John Wade, pltff vs Thos. Downer. 5 Oct. 1764. S. Spencer, Atty. Thomas Frolock, clk.

****

Summons from Salisbury to Thos. Boldin, James Long, Cornelius Robinson and Elinor Sutton, all of your county (Anson) to appear at Sup. Ct. 2 Sept. next. Controversy Sampson Thomas, plaintiff vs Chas. Robinson, defendant. Mch. 25, 1765.

****

Same summons dated March 6, 1766.

Same summons to Morgan Brown; and to William Terry and Thos. Baldwin (Boldin?).

****

James Pickett vs Philip Herndon. Summons to Hopkin Howell, Nicholas White, Thos. Dixon, and John Pickett of Anson Co. to appear at Salisbury, 22 Sept. 1765. 30 March 1765. Wit: Chas. Berry, Esq.

****

William Little and Alexander Gordon to appear as wit. in above case on same date. March 1, 1765.

****

1. As John Pickett is apparently a brother of James Pickett, Sr., who was in Anson as early as 1751, this may have significance. The question mark, in brackets, is on the original paper. William Pickett, of Anson, was born in 1725, according to family records, so he could not be father of this John. Did William Little know the Picketts before they came to Anson County?

ABSTRACTS OF WILLS

WILL BOOK I

Page 1--Will of Thomas Smith, of Anson Co.; weak in body; wife, Sarah, whole est, after debts are paid, during her widowhood; she to give the children good learning; but when she marries again to deliver up estate to the use of the children to be equally divided between Ann J., Elizabeth, and Charles. The two orphan boys to have their dues. Exrs: Jonathan Hunt and Sarah, his wife. 12 Aug. 1751.
Wit: Robt. Hoaton, Martha Hoaton,
Aaron Vandeavers (signed) Thomas Smith

Page 2--Will of Chas. McDowell, of Anson Co., weak of body; Rachel, wife, extrix, and good friend and neighbor, George Cath...her assistant. Wife, Rachel one-third, her daughter Hannah Caller, son John McDowell £10 Va. Money; daughter Rachel Eagan, in Augusta Co., Va. 200 acres of land on Broad River in N.C. in Anson Co.; brother Joseph McDowell, of Frederick Co., Va. one brown cloak and one beaver hat and one pair of shoes boots. All rest of personal estate to be divided between four daughters; Ann Evans, Eliz. Barns, Mary McPetre and Hannah Caller. Jany. 24, 1754.
Wit: Evan Morgan (signed) Chas. McDowell
John Davis

At a Ct held at Frederick Co. Tuesday 4 June 1754, Evan Morgan and John Davis subscribing evidences of above will, in open court, made oath that they were present, etc.
Test: J Wood, Clk.

Page 4--Will of John Coburn, of Anson Co; sick; to my dear and well-beloved bro. Jonathan the least thing the law will allow him; to my dear and well-beloved bro. Samuel Coburn tract of land I had of my sister, Judah; to my sister Mary one english shilling; my sister Rebekah one english shilling; to sister Judah the mare I had at ye fork; to sister Sarah one english shilling; to brother Jacob my black mare that I had of my brother Samuel. to bro. Isaac the plantation that joins my brother Samuel; to Samuel Cockendal a sorrel mare and colt.
Nov. 26 1754. John X Coburn
Wit: Chas. Betty [S.C]

Page 5--Will of Richard Hough, of Anson Co., sick and weak; my beloved wife, <u>Matthew</u> Hough, my cows and cattle and £100 Pa. money, etc.; to son, Wm. Hough, dwelling and plantation, 300 acres; son, Thos. Hough £100 Pa. money when it comes due in Pa. and one set of plow lines; to dau. Hannah Croah £150 Pa. money; dau. Elizabeth Sharpe £5 Pa. money; dau-in-law, Sillpey Stall £5 Pa. money; son Richard 300 acres belonging to the aforesaid tract, joining the ford of Broad River and £200 Pa. money. Wife and son, William, exors. Sept. 9, 1754.
Wit: James Love Richard X Hough
Gabriel Brown [S.C.]

Page 6--Nuncupative will of John Moore, killed at the <u>Eakown</u> in the middle settlements of the Cherokee Nations of Indians, take by me Peter Kockindolph, at the time, before the said John Moore dyed he sent for me and told me he wanted to let me know how he would have his estate disposed of. John Moore then said it was his will and desire that his brother Mose's son, John, should have the place which he bought of Jeremiah Potts and the remainder of estate of all kinds he left his own wife, Mary. 6 Aug. 1760.
signed Peter Kuykendal

Page 7--Will of Alexander McConnell, of Anson Co. weak of body; to my cousin Andrew McConnell of Roan Co. my case of pistols and cutlash, and my black broadcloth jacket and beaver hat to his son, John McConnell; to my cousin, John McConnell, of Roan Co., my silver Stock buckle, and to his son, John McConnell, Jr. my straight bodied blue broadcloth coat; to my two Step children, viz: Thos. and Jane Black...I will that my man, Alexr. H. Henderson, do serve out remainder of time to my loving wife, Catherine, and receive a suit of new clothes, a horse, or more value in pounds. Remainder of estate div. between wife and my daughter Agness McConnell. My Wife, and cousin, Andrew McConnell exors. 2 June 1760.
Wit: Chas. Moore, Chas. M. Pealiers,
James Sharp

Page 8--Will of James Armstrong, of Anson Co., weak in body; son Wm. Armstrong, son, John, son, Martin, sons James and Joseph, two youngest sons,

---

1. Land on Buffalo Cr. that formerly belonged to Peter Kuykendal mentioned in York County, S. C. Deed Bk "A", pp. 51, 205. (1782, 1786)

ABSTRACTS OF WILLS

Benj. and Matthew, dau. Mary. John Armstrong and Thomas Betty overseers of will. 11 May 1760
Wit: Chas. Moore, James Price,
John Betty   Signed James Armstrong

Page 9--Will of David Farguson, Anson Co. Samuel Neely and Peter Kulp exors, with wife. Sister Mary Farguson £ 8; Sister Jane £ 2. If my wife has a child, I bequeath it one-half and allow one-fourth for taking care of the child and the remainder to be divided in four equal parts, for my wife, my sister Mary, my sister Elizabeth and my sister Sarah. If so be that there is no child, the estate to be div. as aforementioned. 22 Dec. 1761
Wit: Robert McCreary   David X Farguson
Robert Walker

Page 10--Will of John Hicks, of Anson Co. good health; wife, Obedience Hicks, son William, son, John, dau. Frances Hicks, dau. Mary Hicks, gr. dau Sarah Hicks. 24 April 1760
Wit: Alex. Gordon,   (signed) John Hicks
Wm Hicks   May Ct. 1761 pr. by Alexr. Gordon
John Frolock Clk.

Page 11--Will of John Vanhosen, of Anson Co., son John, Dau. Yonkey, son Valentine, dau. Catherine, dau. Christian, dau. Mary, son Jacob, 150 acres, son Abram 150 acres, dau. Elizabeth tract I bou. of John Davis. Jany 21, 1762.
Edmund Lilly   John X Vanhosen
John X Watson

Page 12--Will of Robert Lee, of Anson Co., very sick; Sarah Lee, my wife, my three ch.: William and Judith, and Richard Lee my negro Jack; son James, son Robert, son John, dau. Millie, my three daus. May Yarbrough, and Mittry, and Elizabeth Lee, £ 10 each; dau. Sarah Crittenden 10 sh. Wife and son, Robt. Lee and brother, John Lee exors.
9 Nov. 1766.   signed Robert Lee
Wit: John Colson, Mary X Colson,
Sam'l. Cooper

Page 16--Will of Jason Meadors, of Anson Co., wife Elizabeth; eldest son Lewis, 5 sh; and also Drucilla Marion and Thomas one sh. each; after death of wife, my plantation and land and other substance to be div. amongst several ch; Lewis, Jason, Job and Mariah. Wife and sons Lewis and Job exors. 3 Mch. 1774
Wit: William Eves, Chas. Boll,
Job Meador   signed Jason Meadors

Page 17--Will of Jennett McLead, of Anson Co., perfect health: nephew Norman McLead my goods and gear, silver and gold, cloth and linen and all other articles etc.: to be sole exor of will.
Feb. 2 1773   Jennett X McLeod
No witnesses   John McLeod

Page 19--Will of John Husbands, of Anson. Loving wife, Tabitha, whole of moveable estate, after debts and bringing up the children. Children, male and female, to be co-heirs of lands and other estate at the death or surrender of their mother.
12 Oct. 1773   Anson Ct April 1774 pr by Wm.
Wm. Blewett   Blewett, and Wm. Thomas and
Joseph Martin   Tabitha Husbands qual. as
Wm. Thomas   exrs. J Auld, clk.

Page 20--Will of Wm. Love, of Anson Co. May 7, 1753. Very sick; to my loving father all entryes of land made in my own name. John Clark told me that he paid for the surveying of four tracts of sd land.
Wit: Robt. X Love   signed William Love
Benj X Love

Page 21--Will of John Giles, of Anson; to Phereby Pool alias Giles, dau of Jere Pool late of Wanamaw(?) my young negro wench called Bass; to my wife, Mary, all rest of my estate, real and personal; wife and trusty friend Hezekiah Rees exrs.
5 July 1766   signed John Giles
Thomas Dickson, Charity X Dickson

Page 22--Will of Charles Morris, late of Virginia and at present a resident of N. C. and dweller in Anson Co; sick in body; to wife, Elizabeth Morris, estate in Va. and in Carolina and elsewhere 27 Dec. 1774.   Charles X Morris
Wit: John Morris, Wm. X Suy [?]
Samuel X Rees

Page 23--Will of George Ingram, of Anson Co.; sick; I leave my land I bou. of Cornelius Robertson (300 acres) and 180 acres William Leak is to make a right to, to be equally divided between my four children: John Ingram, Tabitha Ingram, Jesse Ingram and Nancy Ingram to be sold or divided as my executor thinks most advantageous to my children. My other estate to be divided the same, and to be paid to each child as they come of age, the boys to have their parts at the age of 21 and the girls at the age of 18. John Walters, sole executor. 2 Aug. 1775
Wit: James X Burn   George X Ingram
Chas. X Turner   Anson Ct Oct. 1775 pr by
Rebecca X Leyton James Burn. J. Aulk, clk.

Page 24--Will of Samuel Snead, of Anson Co. In good health; sons: Israel, David, Phillip Burford Snead, William Snead, Daniel Snead, tract I live

on joining John Coales (Cole), John Snead, and my father and Francis Clark; dau. Ann Crosland one shilling; daus. Caty, Patty and Betty Snead 500 acres on Cape Fear Branch. 14 Mch. 1775. Wife, Temperance Snead and gr-dau. Temperance Crosland.   signed Samuel Snead
Wit: Chas. Medlock Tweat,
Nicholas Green, Dempse X Grant

Page 26--Will of William Ratcliff, of Anson, planter. Wife, Susannah, during her widowhood, sons William, Zachariah, Thomas, James, John, Robert Clothen Ratcliff. Elizabeth Curtis £ 30 proc. My friend Mr. William Thomas, son of Philemon Thomas, and Mr. Robert Thomas my exors. 10 Feb. 1777.   Wm. X Ratcliff
Wit: Thomas Dickson, Samuel Curtis,
G. Jefferson

Page 28--Will of John Ryles, of Anson Co.; weak of body; son James, dau. Elizabeth, son John, wife, son Whitmell, son Larkin, dau. Mary, my six children. Jany 8, 1777
Test: Wm. Remy (signed) John Ryle
Henry Pleas Anson Co. Jany 6, 1778 by
Hannah X Hawkins Wm Remy
John Auld, clk.

Page 29--Will of John Presler, of Anson Co., Haberdasher, very sick, wife, Mary, dau. Elizabeth Maness, son John Preslar, dau. Morgan, dau. Ann Nonaih(?), dau. Mary Basley, dau. Susannah Preslar, son William Preslar, son Elias Preslar, dau. Jane Preslar, son Levi Preslar. Wife Extrx. Dec. 6, 1777
Sampson Hough Anson Co. Jany Ct 1778 pr by
John Preslar Sampson Hough and John Preslar
John X Preslar John Auld, Clk.

Page 31--Will of Priscillah McPherson, of Anson Co., son Shadrack Denson all my land, gr-dau. Betsey Denson. Shadrack Denson sole exor. 23 Mch. 1778.
A true copy of Priscillah McPherson's last will and testament. Thos. Wade, clk.

Page 32--Will of John Haymes, of Anson Co., 8 Sept. 1779; dau. Betty Ann Hamock six negroes; dau. Charity Thomas two negroes; son William Hames 5 sh; wife, Ruth Haymes; at her death to be divided bet. two daus. above; wife and friend, William Hammock exrs.
Wit: David Jameson John X Haymes
James Jameson Pr. Oct. Ct. 1781 by
James Jameson,
Thos. Wade, clk.

Page 34--Will of John Lee, of Anson Co.; weak; wife, Elizabeth; son, Richard; son, Anthony; dau. Elizabeth a gray mare and note on Richard Yarbrough for £ 8, etc. Sept. 10, 1778
Wit: Robert Lee John X Lee
Richard Lee

Page 35--John Roper's Will, of Anson Co., very sick; dau. Martha Roper, 300 acres in Montgomery Co. where I formerly lived; dau. Lucy; son Green Roper; dau. Mary Roper; son, William Roper; dau. Susannah Roper; loving wife, 50 acres. She and John Lylly exrs. 17 Aug. 1781
Wit: Vann X Swearingen, signed John Roper
John Jonson, Dennis X McLendon

Page 37--Will of William Terry,[?] of Anson Co.; very sick; dau. Martha Pickett one negro named Tom and £ 20; son, James, all my lands, one negro man named Bob; dau. Mourning Coleman, one negro boy named Sharper; dau. Margaret Smith negro girl named Jude; to Elizabeth Hellams one cow and calf, one feather bed and furniture; then after my lawful debts are paid I lend all the rest unto my wife, Mary Terry, during her natural life and after her decease sixty pounds to be raised out of the estate and equally divided between my three daughters, Martha, Mourning and Margarett and the rest to be equally divided amongst the four children above mentioned, to wit: Martha, James, Mourning and Margarett. Lastly, I appoint my son, James Terry, and my wife, Mary Terry, exors. of this my last will and testament. 6 Sept. 1775.
Wit: John Coleman signed William Terry
Wm. Roberts

Page 38--Will of Mathew Clements, of Anson Co.; very sick; Mary, wife, whole estate, and sole exr. 27 Nov. 1782.

2. All of the above children of William and Mary Terry were married in Anson County. Martha, the oldest, m. bef. 5 Oct. 1765 (D.B. 3-331) James Pickett, son of James Pickett, Sr. decd. James Terry m. Ann Robards Jany. 24, 1771 (Fam. Bible). Mourning Terry m. James Coleman, son of William and Elizabeth Coleman. (Family Sketch by Miss Patton and C. E. D. Egerton, in Collection of Isaac S. Longon.) Margaret Terry m. 1773 David Smith, son of John and Sarah Smith, Sandhill. (Obit. in Mississippian (Jackson, Miss.) 18 Dec. 1835); Spanish Rec. Natchez Dist. (Miss.) Bk. 5-134; 14-18. It is possible that Elizabeth Hellams (Helms) was a gr. dau. or perhaps a niece.

ABSTRACTS OF WILLS 117

Wit: William X Morriss
Roland X Williams
Elizabeth Morriss
    Mathew X Clement
    Anson Ct. April 1783
    Michael Auld, clk.

Page 39--Will of George Wilson, of Anson Co; sick; son, Robt.; gr-son, George Wilson, son of sd Robt.; son, George; sons, Samuel, Solomon, Andrew, and John; loving wife; my younger children. 9 Apr. 1779
Wit: John Auld, James X Helms,
    Morgan Brown   signed George Wilson

Page 42--Will of John Stephens, Anson Co.; in health and mind; my land on Carren Creek on Cape Fear River, 150 acres, and all my other lands to my two sisters, Nancy Stephens (or Cain) and Sarah Stephens and all the residue of est. also; friend, Robt. Raiford and John Cain Exrs. 12 July 1781.
Wit: James Terry, Ann Terry,
    Hardy Hooker   signed John Stephens
    Note: This same will p. 65 with John Stewart substituted for John Stephens and "A true copy. Test Mich. Auld, clk. Anson Co. July 27 1783

Page 43--Will of James Auld, late of PeeDee in Anson Co., now of Mecklenburg Co., Va.; to son, John Auld, 3 tracts on south side of Pee Dee; the remainder of my est. to wife, Rosanna; after her death to be divided equally bet. son, Michael, and daughters, Ann, Mary and Elizabeth; wife, son Michael, and Henry Wm. Harrington exors. 9 Dec. 1780
Wit: Abram Mitchell, H. Wm. Harrington,
    John X Jones

Page 44--Will of John McClendon, of Anson Co.; my eldest dau., Ann; son Dennis; son Samuel; dau. Rebekah 200 acres part of a pat. to Benj. Smith containing 300 acres on west side of Peedee, east of Gold's Fork; son Simon land in Cumberland; residue to be used for raising of my children above mentioned at discretion of William Morris and Joseph Colson whom I appoint exors. 9 Apr. 1784.
Wit: Isham Ingram,   Pr. Anson Co. July 6 1784 by
    Joseph Lanier   exrs. and oath of Isham Ingram
    Dennis McLendon   Michael Auld, clk.

Page 46--Will of Samuel Blackford, of Anson Co.; wife, Rachel; eldest son, Manning; son Mathew, dau. Keziah Andrews; daus., Sarah and Ruth; exrs. Wife and Mr. Duke Glen. 20 June 1781
Wit: Thos. Dickson   Anson Co. Apr. Ct 1785 by
    John Dickson   Thos. Dickson.
    Reuben Braswell   qualified Mich. Auld, Clk.

Page 48--Will of Stephen Vaughn, of Anson Co.; weak; son, William 1 sh; dau. Sarah Vaughn 1 sh; rest to loving wife, Mary Vaughn. 5 Mch. 1785.
Wit: Jeremish Lewis   signed Stephen Vaughn
    Thomas Lewis

Page 48--John Seago's Will, of Anson Co.; weak; son William 200 acres near May's Mill; son, Robert, home plantation for 6 years; son John at end of 6 years my home plantation; gr-son, James Seago, son of Abraham Seago, decd., 100 acres joining Geo. Lindsey; dau. Ann one-third of my movable estate; dau. Elizabeth two-thirds of same; son, Robert, Exr. 6 Dec. 1784.
Wit: Wm. Bennett   John X Seago
    Chas. X Burmingham   Exr. Qualified (sic)

Page 49--Will of James Meredith, of Anson, sick; wife, Elizabeth, one-third of land I now live on containing 500 acres; son, Sanders Meredith remainder of estate; my beloved father, James Meredith, and friend John DeJarnett exrs. 14 Mch. 1785.
Wit: Daniel Perryman   James X Meredith, Jr.
    Arnold Thomason

Page 51--Will of Christopher Davis, of Anson Co.; weak; son, Arthur; son, Thomas: dau., Sarah Benton; dau. Mary Baker; dau. Dicey Brazzell; son, John Davis; son, Lewis Davis; dau. Eliz. Davis; wife, Mary Davis, youngest ch: Lewis, John and Elizabeth. Joseph White exor. 5 Nov. 1785
Wit: Wm. Boggan, Joseph White,
    Mary Preslar   Christopher X Davis

Pages 51-2--Will of Thomas Wade, of Anson Co., merchant. I have given my five children: Holden Wade, Mary Vining, Thos. Wade, Sarah Wade, and George Wade, by deeds of gift a part of my estate, and I hereby bequeath to them £10 and to Sarah Wade one feather bed, a brown mare, two coalts and 200 acres of land on the Long Br. of Jones Cr, now entered by lease to Peter Brown for one year; to son, George, a bay mare and two colts and feather bed and furniture. I lend to wife, Jane Wade for lifetime, for her maintenance London, Ben and Hannah and their family and the residue of household and kitchen furniture, at her death to be divided amongst my five children or their representatives. My wife and my sons, Holden and Thomas Wade, and my friends, Patrick Boggan and James Boggan my exrs. June 2, 1786.
    signed Thos. Wade
Wit: Morgan Brown. Eliz. Brown
Page 54--Will of Thos. White, of Anson Co. 14 Feb. 1785; sick; dau. Unity Purnal, all my estate; Jesse

Gilbert, exr.; to be delivered to her when she comes of age. I desire that Mary Purnal shall have possession of sd child.
Wit: Hum. Yarbrough   Thos X White
    Willa X McCrakin

Page 56--Will of Joseph Marton, of Anson Co.; sick; son, Jesse Martin, all that land I now live on which is not given by deed to John Hail Martin, at his mother's death or marriage; dau. Nancy; son, John Hail Martin; wife, Catherine. Feb. 13, 1787
Wit: Buckner Nance   signed Joseph Martin
    James X Vanderford

Page 58--Will of Wm. Johnson, of Anson Co.; July 29, 1786; weak and low; son, Hugh Johnson, and wife to settle estate between Mary Ann Johnson, Wm. Johnson, Daniel Johnson, Malcom, John, and James Johnson in equal parts. My dau. Katherine Kennedy to have 4 sh and tract of land I purchased of Richard Odem.
Wit: John McRa   signed Wm. Johnson
    John Johnson

Page 59--Will of Joseph Colson, of Anson Co.: wife, Nancy; son, Joseph; dau., Mary Colson; dau. Martha; dau. Charity; dau. Fereebe; dau. Nelle; son, Sanders Colson; son Jacob Colson; son, Thomas Colson; 8 July 1788.
Wit: Wm. Threadgill, Jr.,   signed Joseph Colson
    John Ryle, Wm. Howlett, Jr.

Page 61--Will of Michael Auld, of Anson Co.; to my three sisters, Ann, Mary, and Elizabeth all my share of my Father's estate, also my lands on the Long Br. of Jones Cr.; I lend to my Mamma, Rosannah Auld, one negro woman, etc.; 640 acres to be sold to settle my public accounts with the Treasury; to my loving wife, Sidney, 500 acres; my son, John Fields Auld lands I bou. of my brother, John Auld; my wife, my mother and my sister Mary and my friends Henry Wm. Harrington and Col. John Stokes exors. 17 Sept. 1789
Wit: Smith Field, R. Harrington,
    Benj. Carler   signed Michael Auld

Page 65--Will of John Stewart, Anson Co.; sound health; ["The rest of this will is a duplicate of the will of John Stephens on page 42 of this same will book and testified to as a true copy by Mich. Auld, Clk of Anson Co. July 27, 1783.]

Page 66--John Jackson's Will, of Anson Co; sick; daus., Eliz., Mary, Sard and Rebeccah, each 5 sh; my lands and all my movable est. to be sold to the best advantage and the money to be paid as follows:

to daus. Phebe, Jemimah and Hannah to have it, equally div. bet them. Stephen and John Perkins, exrs. 15 Apr. 1768.
Wit: Job Meadow   Oct. Term 1772, Anson Ct. pr. by
    John May   Job Meadow and
    Charles Booth   Charles Booth

Page 70--Will of Sampson Lanier. Wife, Elizabeth; son, James; if son should die to brothers and sisters; Burwell Lanier, Wm. Lanier and Col. John Stokes exors.
Wit: John Jennings,   signed Sampson Lanier
    Benj X Selby, James Porter
****

Anson County Wills from the Secretary of State's Office. The originals are now in the Dept. of Archives and History, at Raleigh.

Will of William Coleman, of Anson Co., 1 May 1750. Three eldest sons: William, Thomas and John Coleman, the plantation I live on; to be put in their possession as they arrive to the years of twenty-one; my two youngest sons, James and Samuel Coleman, my plantation on Mountain Cr.; to all my five children aforesaid all my breeding mares, etc. Wife Elizabeth; provision for education of children. Wife and fr. Joseph White exrs.
Wit: Jno. Hamer, Anthony Hutchins,
    Mary Coleman
    signed
    At Court held June 4, 1750, present James McCowan, Chas. Robinson, Joseph White, Sam'l Davis, Alex Osborn, Esquires, John Hamer, Anthony Hutchins and Mary Coleman ack. wit. etc. Eliz. Coleman qual. as extrix.

Will of Joseph Reed, of Anson Co.,___1750. Son, William, wife, and other children, (not named). Exrs. John Brandon and John Nesbet. Wit: Joseph Cate, John Raily, and John Artledge; land near Catawba. [Prob. Lancaster Co. S.C.]. July Court, 1751.
M. Brown, clk.

Will of William Kemp, of Anson Co., Apr. 20, 1750. Sons, John, William, Joseph, Steven. Dau. Sarah Kemp. Wife, Elizabeth and sons, John and William exrs.
Wit: Andrew Moreman   April Court, 1753,
    Anthony Hutchins   Jno. Dunn, clk.

Will of Andrew Pickens, of Anson Co., Nov. 4, 1756 Sons, John and Andrew; dau. Jean Pickens. Wife, Nancy, extrix.
Wit: Robert McClenachan   [No probate.]
    John Pickens

ABSTRACTS OF WILLS

Will of Robert McCorkel,[3] of Anson Co., (no date). Sons, Archibald and Robert. Wife, Margaret, James McCorkel and James Linn exrs. Land on Catawba River. (S.C.)
Wit: John Crockett [No probate.]
Robert McClenachan

Will of Charles Robinson, Anson Co., 29 Dec. 1754. Son, Cornelius, as soon as he is of age, to make a title to Adam Readon, in Va., to land already sold, and with money and int. due me buy for his mother one or more slaves to render the remainder of her life more comfortable; daus. Sarah, Eliz:; dau. Cathern Moorman; sons, Cornelius, Townsend and Charles; land to all the above.
Wit: Wm. Downs, signed Charles Robinson
John X Stone, James X Denson

Will of John Little, Anson Co., 8 Dec. 1755. Sons, Thomas, of Rowan Co., William, John, Archibald, James and Alexander; daus. Margaret Little and Martha Reed, wife of John Reed. Grandson, Thomas Little. Son John and John Cathey, exors.

Wit: Chas. Moore, Mary Renick,
Henry Johnson [No probate.]

Will of Thomas Sprat, of Anson Co., 15 Jany. 1757. Daus: Mary, and Ann Barnett and Jean Neel, Susannah Polk, Martha Sprat; sons, Thomas and Thos. Polk. Land on Sugar Cr. and Twelve-Mile Cr. (S.C.)
Wit: William Barnet, James Campbell,
James Sprat [No probate.]

Will of John Leeth, of Anson Co., 21 July 1757. Legatees: Joseph Leeth, son of George, Mary White, dau. of Joseph White. Exr: Anthony Hutchins
Wit: John Thurman, Antho. Hutchins,
Samuel Smart, Mary Thurman
[No probate.]

Will of John Ashley, of Anson Co., 1 Feb. 1759. Sons: John, Francis, William and Jurden; daus. Mary Ann Franks, Elinor Sutton, Rose Touchstone and Sarah Ashley. Wife, Mary, extrix.
Wit: Richard Yarborough.
Christopher Touchstone
Frederick [Touchstone] [No probate]

WILL BOOK 2

Page 2--Will of Henry Adcock, of Anson Co.; low in health; two sons, John Adcock and Thomas Adcock my land whereon I now live; Henry Adcock $65.00; son, James Adcock $65.00, $10.00 of which to be paid out in schooling for him; dau. Elender; wife; dau. Nancy Adcock; dau. Saphira Adcock; to my step-dau. Sarah Dawkins; sons John and Thomas exors; July 26, 1802. Henry X Adcock
Wit: Marshall Digge Oct. Session 1802 pr by
Wm. Wall Wm. Wall
Archelaus Moorman Tod Robinson, clk.

Page 3--Will of Thomas Baly, Oct. 17, 1799. Son, John Baly 200 acres whereon he now lives, one-half of tract of 400 acres; son Jacob 200 acres, whereon he now lives, the other half of above tract and negro boy, Jim; son William 340 acres whereon I now live, one-half of 680 acres; son James Baly, 340 acres, the other half of land whereon I now live, after the death of his mother; wife Jenny Baly, land I live on and three negroes during her nat. life; certain negroes to above sons and to dau. Polly Baly; dau.

Elizabeth Hildreth 10 sh; to dau. Milly Plunkett 50 acres whereon she now lives; the rest of estate to be equally divided amongst son James Baly, and three dau. Caty Baly and Sally Baly.
Wit: James Douglas Thomas X Bailey
Nevel Bennett Oct. Ct 1802 by
Wm. Bennett Nevill Bennett
Tod Robinson, Clk.

Page 4--Thos. Barrett's will, of Anson Co.: sick; crop of cotton and corn, after leaving sufficiency for the support of my family, and my stock of cattle and hogs to be sold, after paying all just debts, the overplus to be equally divided among all of my surviving children, excepting my son, Holden; wife, Jane, negro, etc. for her lifetime; son Holden tract whereon he now lives, 250 acres; and all property by me previously given him; balance of property to be kept together until my daughter, Fanny, is 8 years old, then sold and div. equally bet. surviving ch. except Holden; sons Holden Barrett and Wade Barrett exors. 16 Aug. 1720.

---

3. Inv. of Robert McCorkell presented by Margaret McCorkell and James Linn, 23 July 1757. Probate Rec., p. 123.

ABSTRACTS OF WILLS

Wit; Joseph White   Oct. Term 1826 pr in Court.
Thos. Crowder   Tod Robinson, clk.

Page 5--Will of Katherine Belyew, of Anson Co.; 22 Dec. 1819. Dau. Jane Smith; son William Henry, Esq. $2.00; son John Henry $2.00;rest of estate to George Henry, Philip Henry, and Eliz. Bittle; friend, Samuel Smith exor.
Wit: Nathl Turner, Joshua Seagoe,
Joshua Taylor

Page 6--Will of Nevill Bennett, Sr. of Anson Co; low state of body; beloved wife for her nat. life; my nephews, Wm. N. Bennett and James Bennett, sons of my brother, James Bennett; John Chester who lives in Tennessee, the son of Eliz. McHenry and they moved from this county some years ago; stock in the Bank of Cape Fear to two grand-nieces, Elizabeth and Sarah Bennett, daus. of James Bennett, Sr.; at death of wife, land to Cary or Micajah Bennett, son of Wm. Bennett; Wm. N. Bennett and James Bennett exors; 6 June 1820.
Wit: Martin Pickett   Anson Co. Ct Oct. 1820,
Jno King   by both witnesses
Tod Robinson, Clk.

Page 7--Jesse Bittle, of Anson Co., Oct. 8, 1811; dau. Sarah Kinchen Jones $10.00; son, John Bittle two negroes; and 150 acres etc.; wife Tabitha Bittle.
Wit: Buck Nance   July Ct. 1818
James Chester   Tod Robinson, Clk
Charles Haley

Page 8--Will of Nathaniel Bivens, Sr., of Anson Co., May 9, 1816; weak; son Abel and other nine children, by name: William, Sarah, John, Unity, Moses, Elijah, Lyda, Stephens and Nath'l. to be equally divided. John and Nath'l exors.
Wit: John Bennett, Sr.   Apr. Ct. 1818
John Bennett, Jr.   John Bennett
Wm. Bennett   Tod Robinson, clk.

Page 9--Will of Capt. Patrick Boggan, of Anson County, of an old and advanced age, 12 Oct. 1801. Wife, Mary, tract conveyed to me by John and William May and all my estate and at her death to devise as she may think proper. Wife, Mary, exor.
Wit: Francis Locke
Robt. Coman
Codocil 16 Nov. 1803.
Wit: Robt. Troy   April 1817
Jacob Adams   by Francis Locke
Tod Robinson, clk.

Page 30--Will of John Cortney, wife Mary; two youngest sons, Emanuel and John; son Stephen; dau. Rebecca; dau. Peggy Coutney, dau. Sarah Courtney. 30 Dec. 1799.
Wit: Daniel Gould   pr. Anson Co. (no date)
Jemima Gould   Tod Robinson, clk.

Page 103--Will of John McKay, of Anson, 20 July 1808. Sick; wife, Jean, one-third; rest equally divided among my children.
Wit: Duncan McKay   Prov. Oct. Ct. 1808
Neill McLaurin   by Duncan McKay

Will of William Medcalf, of Anson, Feb. 13, 1797. Sick; wife, Amelia; son John, dau. Anny Brumloe; son William; son Joel; son Emanuel, son David, my other three daughters, Miriam Thomas, Amelia Adams and Lidia Brumloe; my eight youngest children; three sons to make bread for my wife and youngest son; my sons not to sell their land without giving their brothers the refusal.
Wit: Moses X Tomerlinson   Signed
Rebecca X Billin   William Medcalf, Sen.
Elizabeth X Medcalf   July Court 1798

Page 105--Will of John Mills, of Anson, 16 Dec. 1801. Wife, sons, William, David, Joel, Mary Mason and John Haloday share and share alike; wife, Mary, and Samuel Mills exrs.
Wit: Stephen Pace, Senr., Benj. Allen,
William Dabbs   (No probate.)

Page 106--Will of William Morris, of Anson, Jany. 2, 1804. Weak; sons, Nathan and Jeptha; dau. Patsy Morris; son William Airly Morris; my seven children, namely; Molly Yarbrough, Betsy Hanby, Fanny Beverly, Nathan Morris, Sally Yarbrough, Jeptha Morris, and Lydia Pistole. Nathan Morris exr.
Wit: James Marshall, Nancy Segraves,
William Farris   Jany Court 1806

Page 109--Will of Benj. Moorman, of Anson, 26 Mch. 1798. Sons; William, Benj., Michal, as they come of age; Joseph Clark and William Moorman exrs.
Wit: Chas. Hinson   July Court 1798
Armche(?) Crew

Page 113--Will of Judah Murrel, of Anson, Apr. 17, 1816. Money due me of my son's estate, collected by Mr. Goosby before last January to be divided bet. Eliz. Goodson and my two gr-ch. Wm. and Eliz. Threadgill; my son-in-law, John Threadgill, to have that part of my son's estate which has not been collected; dau. Tempe Threadgill.
Wit: Benja. Boykin   July Session 1816
Bryan _____

ABSTRACTS OF WILLS 121

Page 114--Buckner Nance, of Anson, 8 June 1812. Weak; wife Ann; daus. Henrietta Murphy, Olive May Nance, Harriet Nance, Patsy Nance, Betsy Ann Nance, Winifred Nance; John Hinson and Francis Clark exrs.
Wit: Keziah Cox   April Court 1813
William Jernigan

Page 118--Will of Richard Odom, of Anson, 4 Sept. 1797. Weak; Wife Honour Odom; wife's Honour Odom's sons, William Odom, Nancy Odom, James Odom; to Eliz. Franklin for life 50 acres I live on and my dwelling house; my son David; my son Richard; son Isaac Odom's Ch; son Jacob; dau. Lucy Fair; dau. Charity Rutherford.
Wit: Robert Lee, John Scott,
Jno. Davidson   (No probate)

Page 121--Will of William Pratt, of Anson, Oct. 2, 1817. Sons: Benj., John, William; grandson William Fair; son Samuel Pratt; dau. Sarah Adams.
Wit: J. J. Schrater   Jany. 1818

Page 127--Will of Martha Pickett, of Richmond Co, May 25, 1803. Dau. Polly Robards; other children Martin, Joseph, William R., and Frances H. Dejarnett.
Wit: Gilbert Gibson   Jany. Court, 1809
Mourning Gibson   Pr. by Gilbert and
Mattie Covington   Mourning Gibson

Page 128--Will of James Pickett, of Anson, 15 Sept. 1795. Weak; wife Martha; dau.Mary Robards sons Martin, Joseph and William R.; dau Franky Hannah.

Wit: Gilbert Gibson   Anson Court July 1798
Mornie Gibson

Page 132--Will of John Ricketts, of Anson, 7 May 1820. Low health; sons, Reason, John, Wilson; daus. Mary Rickett, Nancy Ricketts, Sarah Ricketts wife Peggy.
Wit: Richard Patishall[4]   Pr. by Hannah Smith
Hannah Smith   July Ct. 1802
     Tod Robinson, clk.

Page 150--Will of Edward Streater, of Anson, Nov. 7, 1820. Wife; son James R. Streater; son Sheppard; son William K. Streater; sons William and Reddick exrs.
Wit: Chas. Hurt, Dan'l L. McRae,
John Hinson   [No probate]

Page 151--Will of Benjamin Smith, of Anson, 15 Nov. 1811. Wife, Sarah; sons Benjamin, Archibald; daus. Mary Morris and Martha May.
Wit: Thos. Everett   Oct. Term. 1817
Ann Everett

Page 152--Will of James Smith, of Anson, 4 Dec. 1817. Wife Lucy; sons James N. and Charles A. Smith in Murray Co., Tenn; child wife is pregnant with.
Wit: Saml. McCullock   April Term 1818
Polly Cook   Tod Robinson, clk.

Page 161--Will of Nancy Tindol, of Anson, 13 Mch. 1811. Whole estate to my sister Mourning Lisles. Toddy Robinson exr.
Wit: John Dudley
D. Graham
April Session 1811

WILL BOOK "A"

INDEX

Page	Page	Page	Page
*Christopher Clark......1	*Benjamin Faulkner.15	*James Bennett........ 24	*Hugh Ross............ 37
*Robert Gatewood........4	*Stephen Wright......16	*Thomas Lacy.......... 25	*Joseph Dunham..... 40
*John Proctor.............5	*Francis Curtis......17	*Jeremiah Lewis...... 30	*Chas. Harrington .. 42
*Francis Smith.......... 7	*William Martin 19	*Nathaniel Edwards... 31	*William Yoe or
*John Colson............ 11	*Melton Perryman...21	*John Jackson.......... 32	Loe 42
*Thos. Finney........... 14	*James Hogan 22	*William Blewett...... 34	*Peter Lowry......... 47

4. Richard Pattishall is a name prominent in 17th century York Co., Maine, and Boston records. N. C. 1790 Census Wake Co. Richard Patishall 1 male, over 16, and one female.

ABSTRACTS OF WILLS

	Page		Page		Page		Page
*Richard Edgeworth..	49	William Shepherd...	88	Wm. Spear............	114	John Flournoy......	139
*Thomas Wade........	53	Elisha Kindred......	90	Daniel McCollum....	115	Joseph Ingram,Sr..	141
*Beverly Clark.........	55	Wm. Carr, Esq.	92	Stephen Taylor.......	120	Lemuel Ingram....	145
John McGregor.......	68	Redding Sims........	94	Joseph Williams.....	118	William Benton....	146
Mary Clark............	71	John Knotts..........	96	Phillip McRae...	112-125	Jasper Turner.....	149
John Garman..........	72	*Mumford DeJarnett.	91	John C. Threadgill..	126	Odom Cocks........	151
Mary Lanier	79	James Sinclair......	98	Martha Rutland...	127-8	Nancy Curtis.......	153
Lawrence Moore.....	77	Allen Chapman......	99	Simon Edwards .129-130		*Col. Joseph Pickett	155
Reuben Medley........	80	John Smith...........	103	Jeremiah Smith,Jr..	131	Daniel Gould	162
Asa Pearse............	75	Anthony McGregor	104	*Sarah Chiles..........	132	Wm. Covington	163
*John Smith	82	Drury Allen.........	107	John Sinclair.......	133-4	Rosa Harrington...	164
Thos. Adcock...........	84	James Hough.......	108	James Slaughter...	135-6	Joseph Tanner.....	167
Godfrey Burnett......	96	John Permenter...	111	Charles Winfree.....	137		

*Abstracted in these records.

pp1-3--Will of Christopher Clark, of Anson Co., Dec. 25, 1798? Sons Joseph and Francis; daus. Ann Moorman, wife of Benj., Agniss Henson, wife of Charles, Mary Stitt; gr-daus. Eliz. and Ann Stitt, daus. of Mary Stitt; exrs. sons, Joseph and Francis, and Benj. Moorman.
Wit: Cornelius Clark July Ct. 1790 by
  Marshall Digge Marshall Digge.
         Wm. Johnson, clk.

p. 4--Will of Robert Gatewood, of Anson, Mch. 5, 1790. Son, Gabriel; sons Griffin and Thomas exors; daus. Gleesy(?), Polly, Sally (5 sh), Elizabeth (5 sh).
Wit: Lewis Lanier
  Thomas X Ellis (No probate)

p. 5--Will of John Proctor, of Anson, 29 Oct. 1790. Wife, Lenny; sons William and Sterling.
Wit: Wm. Henry Proved (no date)

p.7--Will of Francis Smith, of Anson, Dec. 14, 1790. Weak; son, Richard; dau. Unity Hammond; dau. Sarah Pemberton; dau. Elizabeth Buchanan; son Francis; son David; son Nath'l; son John; my five sons; wife Frances.
Wit: Lewis Atkins (signed) Francis Smith
  John Howlet   Frances X Smith
  Sarah Howlet
  Jany. Ct. 1791 pr. by all three witnesses
        Rec. Jany. 26, 1791.

p. 11-- Will of John Colson, of Marlborough, S.C., 20 Sept. 1789. Weak; wife, Margaret Colson; gr-son John Colson Hyde; gr-dau. Mary Colson, dau. of John Colson, decd.; gr- dau. Jane Hyde; son-in-law, Stephen Hyde, of Anson Co. N.C., and friend, Stephen Parker, of S.C., exors.

Wit: Moses Knight, Aaron Knight
Prov. Anson Co. July Ct. 1791. Citation to Hon. Wm. Thomas or Morgan Brown, Esq., of South Carolina, to examine Moses Knight and Aaron Knight concerning execution of above will. July 17 1791. Their deposition before Wm. Thomas, of Marlboro Co. S.C. dated 21 July 1791.

p. 14--Will of Benj. Falkner, of Anson Co. Oct. 18, 1783. Sons John and Henry as soon as they are of age; wife, Eliz., Lewis Rows and Abraham Lewis exrs.
Wit: Nathan Falkner Anson Co. Oct. 1791
  Sarah Falkner Rec. Oct. 22, 1791

p. 16--Will of Stephen Wright, of Montgomery Co., 12 Feb. 1782. To my cousin, Henry Hardy, son of John Hardy, Jesse Gilbert's note for £ 25, also £ 40 due by note of Benj. Dumas, Jr., with Wm. Marsh and Andrew Dumas, Sr; also my lot in town of Halifax in N.C. etc. and all my real estate. Exrs. Henry Stokes, Sr. and John Stokes.
Wit: Shad. Hogan Oct. Ct. 1791
  John Lilly pr. by John Lilly.
  Henry Stokes

p. 17--Will of Frances Curtis, of Anson, 11 Oct. 1790. Sick; sons, John Hamer, William Hamer, and Nathaniel Curtis; daus. Frances Hamer and Susannah Curtis; son, John Hamer, Beverly Clark, Lewis May and John Auld exors.;
Wit: John Auld, Hopkins Howell, Anson Co.
  Phillip Paul, Joseph Howell. Jany 1792

p. 19--Will of William Martin, of Anson, 18 Sept. 1793. Sick; wife, Rebekah, for herself and for raising my young children; my young son, James; dau. Sarah Martin; dau. Nancy; my first children;

ABSTRACTS OF WILLS

William, John, Thomas, Abraham, Cathern, Lewis, Andrew, Isaac; Thos. Vining and Thos. Martin exors;
Wit: Wm. Lindsley (no probate.)
John Smith

p. 21--Melton Perryman, of Anson, Sept. 4, 1793. My three bros. and one sister; Mumford Perryman, Mary Perryman, John Perryman and J. Samuel Perryman; exrs; Daniel DeJarnett, Daniel Gould.
Wit: Mumford DeJarnett, Rachel X Smith, Elizabeth X Stinson

p. 23--Will of James Hogan, of Anson, 11 Sept. 1793. Weak; Son, David; gr-dau. Susannah Hogan; wife, Silmee(?), son Elijah Hogan; all my ch: William James, Griffin, Edmund Hogan, Elijah, Elizabeth Ryle, Nannie Lee, Sarah Ryle and David. Wife, James Marshall and James Exrs:
Wit: Wm. Roper, Green Roper, Henry Marshall

p. 24--James Bennett, Anson Co., 23 Nov. 1793. Wife, three daus., sons William, Minard, John, James, Silas; wife and Nevil Bennett exrs.
Wit: William Bennett (no probate)
William Bennett, Jr.

p. 25--Will of Thomas Lacy, Anson Co., Oct. 1, 1793. Wife, Keziah; two oldest dau s. Mary and Sarah; sons, Stephen, Thomas; dau. Eliz., son Jesse, dau. Anna; son Griffith, dau. Lucretia; exrs. Theodore Webb, and sons, Stephen and Thomas.
Wit: Richard X Manus (No probate)
John Manus
William Manus (Maness?)

p. 30--Will of Jeremiah Lewis, of Anson, 9 June 1794. Weak; wife Sarah; sons Jeremiah, Thomas and Philip; dau. Martha Dyer; gr-son William Lewis:
Wit: Maryann Jarman (No probate)
Daniel Lewis
Jeremiah Lewis

p. 31--Nathaniel Edwards, of Anson, 8 Oct. 1793. Very weak; sons Nath'l Edwards, Isaac Edwards, and gr-son, Zach. Edwards each 5 sh; son Joshua rest of estate and exr.
Wit: James Marshall (No Probate)
James Ryle

p. 32--Will of John Jackson, of Anson, 28 Mch. 1794. Very weak; wife; dau.Sarah Stansill; son Jonathan Jackson; son Samuel; son Isaac, dau.

Mary White; dau. Eliz. White; dau. Rebekah Jackson:
Wit: Wm. Gulledge (No probate)
Elias Honey

p. 34--Will of William Blewett, of Anson, June 15, 1790. Sons: Thomas, William, Eli, Morris, David, James, my six sons my fishery; to Thos. Watkins one-seventh of fishery above; wife Elizabeth; daus: Susannah, Ann. Exors sons, Thos., Wm. and Eli.
Wit: Thos. Smith, Hardy Hooker, Jacob Morris, John Smith, Carpenter

p. 37--Will of Hugh Ross, of Anson, 18 Nov. 1793. Sick; wife, Margaret; sons Donald and Hugh; daus. Mary, Jean, Katherine and Margaret Campbell.
Wit: Chas. Porter (No probate)
John Tison

p. 40--Will of Joseph Dunham, of Anson, (no date) Sick; dau. Lueresy Seago (wife of John), daus.-in-law Margaret Burk and Mary Collins.
Wit: Ezra Bostwick   Anson Court July 1796
Drusilla Bostwick

p. 42--Charles Harrington, of Anson, 24 May 1796. Wife, Bena Arrenton, son William Arrenton, daus: Nanse Crosswell, Nelly Hudson, Mary Stegall, Sukey; sons John Arrington, Whitmell Arrington; Richmond Crosswell and Solomon Stegall exrs.
Wit: Bryant Lee   Anson Ct July 1796
Richard Crosswell

p. 45--Will of William Loe, of Anson, 12 May 1795. Wife, daus. Nancy, Franke; son John; brother Thos. Loe land from father, Daniel Loe; brother Daniel Loe exr.
Wit: Thos. Pattent   Anson Ct. _____ 1796
Mary Pattent

p. 47--Peter Lowry, of Anson, Dec. 11, 1796. Wife Mary and friend Jason Meador exrs.; daus. to the amount of Mary; son, William Leonard's legacy.
Wit: William Leonard   Anson Ct. Jany.
Suffiah Meador   Sess. 1797

p. 49--Will of Richard Edgeworth, of Cheraw Dist., S.C. 3 Nov. 1792. Wife Elizaebth property in N.C. and S.C.; son Sneed Edgeworth and my children that may be born, land in Anson Co.; my son Lovel all my property in Europe; after my death, it my will that he be given up to my friend, John Hardwick, and by him conveyed to my father, Richard Lovell Edgeworth, Esq. of Edgeworth's Town, County of Langford, Ireland, for which purpose I bequeath to sd Hardwick £100, to be paid out of my

property in Europe. Exrs: my father, Richard Lovell Edgeworth, Esq., Capt. Cladius Pegues of Marlborough Co., S.C. John Boone and John Hardwick, of Georgetown.
Wit: Smith Tompson, Thomas Edgeworth, James Pearson
Proven in Anson Co. from Georgetown District. 16 Jany. 1797. Rec. in Anson Jany. 1797.

Page 53--Will of Thomas Wade, of Anson, 8 June 1793. Having taken an infection of small pox and being about to start to Cheraw Hill in order to undergo the operation thereof...My will is that my estate be equally divided among wife, Eliz. and my children Thomas McRose (?) Wade, William Hambleton Wade, and dau. Judith Leak Wade; wife and friends Walter Leak, Thomas Chiles, Sr. and John Pemberton, Esq. exrs. [No wit. and no probate.]

Page 55--Will of Beverly Clark, of Anson, 15 Dec. 1795. Weak; wife, Carey Clark; youngest son Benj. Clark, son John, dau. Lucy, son Robert. Wife and son Robert exrs.
Wit: Francis Clark, Joseph Crew, William Haymore [No probate]

Page 82--Will of John Smith, of Anson Co.,⁵ 1 Nov. 1822. Wife Mary; William Smith, my oldest son; Mary Cooper, my oldest dau.; son Daniel; dau.

Sarah; son John; my younger children Trissah, Kerr, Elizabeth, Patsy, and Henry. D. Cuthberson exr.
Wit: Joshua Books, Elijah Price, Daniel Smith

Page 132--Will of Sarah Chiles,⁶ of Anson, 7 June 1827. Legatees: Mary R. Tindall and Mary P. Terry (wife of Thomas Terry, of Ala.) Abraham Myers exr.
Wit: John C. McKenzie   Prob. July 1827

Page 91--5 Aug. 1823. Will of Mumford Dejarnett.⁷ Wife and four children all my estate; wife, Franky H. Dejarnett and son John P. DeJarnett exrs.
Wit: Thos. D. Parke   Signed Mumford Dejarnett
  J. M. Rutland   by J. B. Billingsley
               at his request

Page 155--Will of Joseph Pickett, of Anson County, 24 Apr. 1828, wife Flora, 16 slaves, 8 to her choice the others to be of equal value as those to be div. among children; estate kept together until son, Martin, comes of age; daus: Martha King, Ellen Bates; Frances, Glovinia and Evelina; lands, my Gould's Fork plantation; 200 acres at the Big Falls, and the Mt. Pleasant plantation. Codocil, Montgomery Co., Va. Brother Martin and Absolem Myers executors.
               Prob. July 1828

---

5. 8 Jany. 1780, the above John Smith, as of Northampton County (N.C.) bou. 475 a in sw part of Wayne County (Wayne Co. D.B. 1-2) and from 1792 to 1807 was guardian of the five children of Andrew Bass III, decd., and his wife, Christian — who m. (2) William Bennett, also of Wayne Co. (Wayne Co. Wills 1793-1807). John Smith sold this tract and others he had acquired in Wayne Co. in 1794 and bought land in Cumberland Co. In 1797, William Bennett, "of Wayne Co.", bou. land adj. John Smith in Cumberland, John Smith and Alexander Scull witnessing the deed. It is not clear whether either of these families lived in Cumberland. However, Ann Bass, the second step-dau. of Wm. Bennett, married John Holton of Cumberland, prob. by 1799. In 1799 William Bennett sold the tract he had bought in Cumberland to John Smith and they are both recorded in the deed as "of Wayne Co.". Uriah Bass and John Holton were witnesses to this transfer. In 1807 there was a final settlement of the estate of Andrew Bass III, a jury dividing the land and personal property among the heirs; Eliz. Bass, Ann Holton, Uriah Bass, Thos. Alexander Bass, Sally Thompson and their mother, Christian Bennett, wife of Wm. Bennett. In 1808, John Smith made gift deeds of the adj. tracts he and William Bennett had owned in Cumberland to his son, William Smith, and Wilson Cooper, husband of his dau. Mary., and in 1812 he sells the remainder of his holdings in Cumberland. as of Anson County. His first wife had evidently died and he had remarried.

Alexander Scull was a private in the N. C. Continental Line from the Hillsborough District and in the 1790 census was a single man at the head of a household in Wayne County. In 1794, he bou. 200 acres in Robeson County as "of Robeson" and in 1799 he bou. a tract in Cumberland on Rockfish Cr. near the Robeson line, where he made his home. In 1810 Census he is married, both wife and self over 45, and another male under 16. If this last was a son, he died, for by his will (Bk "A" p. 242), dated 15 Aug. 1814; prob. Dec. Ct. 1817, Alex. Scull left personal property and his home place to his wife, Mourning, which after her death was to go to Lewis Bennett, son of William and Bidy Bennett; the 200a tract in Robeson to William Bennett, son of William and Bidy Bennett; to Bidy Bennett, in trust, one bed and furniture, to give to which daughter she pleases, of those she had by William Bennett; to Nancy, Bidy, Polly and Edna Bennett, each a heifer; to William Smith 60 acres in Robeson; to Wm. Smith and Wilson Cooper the rest of cows and a mare; to Sarah Smith, a bed and furniture; the pork to be sold and the proceeds div. bet. Daniel and John Smith, sons of John Smith now living in Anson Co., to Wm. Bennett, son of William and Bidy Bennett, his shot-gun; wife, Mourning, and William Smith, exrs. Wm. Smith relinq. right as exr. and Mourning Scull qualified. (Cumb. Co. D.B. 14-310; 16-354; 25-132-3; 26-494; 27-230; Bladen Co. D.B. 13-361; Robeson Co. D.B. "E"-152)

From the above, it would seem that Alexander Scull was the brother (or possibly the father) of the first wife of John Smith and of Christian, whom he called "Bidy" (or Biddy), a nickname, who married (1) Andrew Bass III, (2) William Bennett.

6. Thomas Terry's estate was administered in 1835-6-7 in Autauga County, Alabama, and the sons of Eli Terry, gr-son of William and Mary (Raiford) Terry, were buyers at sale of part of estate. Any relationship bet. these two Terry families does not appear in the records, except the apparent Raiford descent of Thos. Terry's wife, Mary P., through the Tindalls.

7. In an altercation, Mumford DeJarnett struck a man with the butt of his loaded pistol and it was discharged, fatally wounding him. (The Messinger and Intelligence, Wadesboro, N. C. Aug. 27, 1937; article "Capt. Paddy Boggan and the Olden Times" by Kate Shepherd Bennett (Mrs. R. T.).

ABSTRACTS OF PROBATE REPORTS, 1749-1789

WILL BOOK 1

Page 80--24 Apr. 1756. William Love's inv. by James Love, admr. sworn to bef. Adam McCoale, Esq. Justice. [Clothes, horse and saddle].

Page 81--12 July 1760. James Armstrong's inv. by James Armstrong. Among items: "What cash is in the Black Trunk £10-10-6."

Page 82--13 July 1774. John Hamer's inv. by John Hamer.

Page 83--[no date] Robert Lee's inv. by Maryan Lee.

Page 84--1 Oct. 1775. Charles Morris' inv. by Charles Morris. George Ingram's inv. by John Walters and Humphrey Rogers.

Page 86--[no date] John Lee's inv. by James Gray.

Page 87--17 Apr. 1786. James Meredith, Jr's inv. by James Meredith.

Page 87--13 Oct. 1786. William Johnson's inv.

Page 88--10 Dec. 1786. Thomas Wade's inv. [not signed; 3 pages]

Page 91--14 Oct. 1777. Edward Davidson's inv. by Geo. Davidson, admr. [n.d.] John Henry's inv. by Catherine Henry, adm.

Page 92--[n.d.] Wm. Cox's inv. by Mary Cox.

Page 93--_____1775. Henry Chambers' inv. by Solomon Gross, admr.

Page 94--4 Apr. 1775. John Spencer's inv. [not signed]

Page 95--[n.d.] Wm. Price's inv. by Elinor Price, Thos. Price.

Page 95--_____1774. Elizabeth Johnson returned _____.

Page 96--14 Jany. 1778. Alexander McPherson. Inv. [not signed]

Page 97--[n.d.] Joel Cheevers. Inv. by Sarah Cheevers. 1 Jany. 1774. Benj. Gardiner by Isaac Falconberg.

Page 98--Jany. Term 1775. Wm. Hamer, 1774, Inv. by Frances Hamer.

Page 99--1 Apr. 1767. William White. Inv. by Jamima White, admx.

Page 99--8 July 1775. Malcom Martin. Inv. [not signed]

Page 100--Jany. Ct. 1775. Frances Moseley. Inv. by Margaret Moseley.

Page 101--Oct. Ct. 1784. John Stanfield. Inv. Test. Mich. Auld, clk. 12 Jany. 1774. Benj. Ingram. Inv. by James Pickett, admr.

Page 102--[n.d.] William Moody. Inv. by Wm. Blassengen, admr.

Page 103--7 July 1784. Aaron Baxley. Inv. by Mary Baxley, admx. 4 Apr. 1775. Joseph Hough. Inv. [not signed]

Page 104--1 Oct. 1781. Moody Ingram. Inv. by Martha Ingram.

Page 105--25 Jany. 1788. Solomon Townsend. Inv. [not signed]

Page 106--8 Jany. 1771. Violet (male) Primrose. Inv. by Mary Primrose.

Page 107--[n.d.] Stephen Thomas. Inv. [not signed]

Page 108--July 1753. Moses Dickey. Inv. [two pages, not signed]

Page 110--[n.d.] James Long. Inv. by Eliz. Long.

Page 111---20 July 1754. John Snoddy. Inv. by Agness Snoddy.

Page 112--[n.d.] John Brasfield. Inv. by Isaac Jackson, exr.

Page 113--9 July 1777. Thomas Tomkins. Inv. [not signed]

Page 115--_____1757. Andrew Pickens. Inv. by Ann Pickens and William Davis. Horses, mares and colts 12; cows and calves 10; other dry cattle 10; hogs 15 or 20; a still and vessels; a cart; plow and tackler; 3 weeding hoes; mattocks, mall, rings and wedges; 2 axes; 2 cleaves; 3 iron forks; 1 gun; 1 broad ax; hand saw; hammer, 2 augers; 3 beds, furniture and bedsteads; 2 chests; a trunk; dresser with pewter and wooden ware; 4 pots and kettle, 1 pr stilliards; 3 sickles, 2 sithes; a small quantity of books.

Oct. Ct. 1783. John Bailey. Inv. by Lydia Bailey. 28 Sept. 1784 Ord. that perishable estate be sold according to law; David Hildreth or Thomas Bailey, Sen. to sell it Sept. 28. Signed S. Miller, Sheriff.

Page 116--James Pickett, Sr.[1] Notes and accounts due estate: Est. of Stephen Brown, note Preswood to Creeg, George Renck, James Davis, Wm. Phillips, John Betty, James McNick, Joseph Culpepper, Thos. Harrington, Wm. Harrington, Robert Patrick, Thos. Davis, order fr. Crawford to Dumas, and Lawrence Franklin [n.d.]

Page 117--[n.d.] John Hall. Inv. by Elizabeth Brooks, exr.

Page 118--6 Jany. 1758. Joseph Hollinsworth by Martha Hollinsworth.

Page 119--[n.d.] Israel Pickens. Inv. by Martha Pickens, William Pickens.

Page 120--Jany. 1760. Philip Henson, Jr. Inv. by Penelope Henson.

Page 121--[n.d.] Andrew Berry [Barry]. Inv. by Richard Berry [Barry]

Page 122--[n.d.] Avington Sherrill. Inv. by Pirshanna Sherrill.

Page 123--23 July 1757. Robert McCorkall. Inv. by James McCorkall, Margaret McCorkall and James Linn, exrs. [S.C.]

Page 124--27 Dec. 1749. John Davidson. Inv. by Jas. McHilwain, Hill Moregan.

Page 126--[n.d.] Chas. Robertson. Add. inv. by Caleb Howell and Sarah Robertson, exrs.

Page 127--[n.d.] Joseph Weaver. Inv. by Gabriel Davis. Oct. 1783. Joseph Thompson. Inv. [not signed] [n.d.] Richard and Sarah Touchstone. Add. inv. by Henry Touchstone.

Page 128--6 Jany. 1783. William Terry. Inventory by Mary Terry, one of the executors. 8 negroes, to wit: Isaac, Feeb, Bob, Sharper, Jude, Tom, Jacob, and London; 2 mares and colts; 6 cows and calves; 22 heads sheep; 25 hogs; 3 geese; 5 feather beds and furniture. 1 large chest, 2 small chests, 2 tables, etc.

Page 129--7 Oct. 1784. John Howard. Inv. by James Howard. 1 Apr. 1782. Aaron Baker. Inv. by D. Jameson.

Page 130--Oct. Ct. 1772. John Hicks. Inv. by John Husbands and Frances Husbands.

Page 131   William Fielding.

Page 132--[n.d.] Richard and Sarah Touchstone. Inv. by Henry Touchstone and Frederick Touchstone.

Page 133--Feb. Ct. 1762. James McManus. Inv. by Mary McManus.

Page 134--28 Mch. 1768. William Stephens. Inv. by John Steel.

Page 135--[n.d.] John Colson, Jr.[2] by Eliz. Colson. 6 Apr. 1768. Moses Harrell [not signed]

Page 136--[n.d.] Goen Morgan. Inv. by Mary Morgan. [n.d.] Reuben Rone. Inv. by Sarah Rone.

Page 137--3 Jany. 1783. Stephen Gardner. Inv. by Vereby Gardner.

Page 138--_____1782. Robert Jarman. Inventory [not signed]

Page 139--[n.d.] James Lowry. Inv. by Elizabeth Lowry.

Page 140--[n.d.] Sam'l Hayward. Inv. by Sam'l Wilson, Sarah Wilson.

Page 141--22 July 1789. Robt. Phillips. Inv. [not signed]

Page 142--[n.d.]_____. Joseph Thompson. Inv. Test. Mich. Auld, clk. July Ct. _____Michael

Belue. The above "killed man's estate inv. by Sheriff, Jonathan Jackson."

Page 143--[n.d.] Charles McDowell. Inv. [not signed]

Page 144--8 Aug. 1774. Peter Roan. Inv. by Edward Moore.

Page 145--27 Sept. 1782. James Roper. Inv. by Mary Roper, admr.

Page 146--[n.d.] John Thurman. Inv. by Mary Thurman.

Page 147--[n.d.] Simon Hooker. [not signed] Apr. 1761 remaining part of est. of Wm. Black.

Page 148--9 Oct. 1758. John Carmichael. Inv. by Wm. Carmichael.

Page 149--8 Nov. 1759. James Goodfellow. Inv. by Moses Alexander, admr. July Ct. 1782. Peter Lewis. Sale of est. by Shff. Jonathan Jackson.

Page 150--[n.d.] Julius Holly. Inv. by Sarah Holly, admx.

Page 151--2 Jany. 1783. George Wilson. Inv. by Missaneah Wilson, Mich. Auld, clk.

Page 153--29 July 1762. John Mills. Inv. by Joseph Harden, Esq.

Page 154-- ____ 1782. Shadrack Denson. Inv. by Patrick Boggan, Jr. and Edward Travis.

Page 155--2 Jany. 1782. Isaac Nichols. Inv. by Honor Nichols.

Page 156--6 Oct. 1771. Timothy Moncear. Inv. [not signed]

Page 157--2 Oct. 1781. Reuben Phillips. Inv. by Stephen Miller. 8 July. 1785. Elizabeth Ryle. Inv. by James Ryle.

Page 158--8 Jany. 1785. Jesse Ivey. Inv. Mich. Auld, clk. Inv. of perishable est. 1 Jany. 1785 by Mary Ivey, John Bloodworth, wit.

Page 159--10 Apr. 1770. Thomas Hunter. Inv. "money due in Ireland"; by Catharine Hunter, Antho. Hutchins.

Page 160--July Ct. 1783. Robt. Keys. Inv. by Solomon Rushing. 9 Jany. 1782. Thomas Trull. Inv. by Charity Trull.

Page 161--9 Oct. 1783. John Bailey. Inv. by Lidia Bailey. 7 Jany. 1783. Inv. Est. Widow Conner [not signed] [n.d.] Wm. McHenry. Inv. by Mary McHenry.

Page 162--[n.d.] David Rich. Inv. by Timothy Rich, Teste Thomas Wade, Jr., clk.

Page 163--Jany. 1783. Isaac Belieu's est. [not signed] [n.d.] Memo of est. of William Bird, by John Smith. 8 July 1782. Matthew Parker. Inv. by James Howard [n.d.] Lewis Lowry. Inv. by Eliz. Lowry.

Page 164--8 Apr. 1783. James Chiles. Inv. Thos. Chiles, admr. Amended inv. same est. 2 June 1783 by Thos. Chiles. admr.

Page 165--15 July 1780. Nath'l Curtis. Inv. by Francis Curtis, admr. Add. inv. of est John Miller by Jonathan Jackson, admr.

Page 166--7 Jany. 1782. John Williamson. Inv. by David Jameson. 24 July 1777. Wm. Bennett, Jr. Inv. by Thos. Wade.

Page 167--[n.d.] Devalt Poff. Inv. by John Thomas, admr.

Page 168--[n.d.] Wm. Remp [Kemp?]. Inv. land in S.C. [not signed]

Page 170--[n.d.] Benjamin Dumas. Inv. [very long] by David Dumas.

Page 175--April 1784. John Ryle. Inv. [not signed]

Page 176--26 June 1787. Thos. White. Inv. by Jesse Gilbert, exr.

Page 177--[n.d.] Thos. Dinkin. Inv. [not signed] 26 Jany. 1788. James Chiles. Inv. by Elizabeth Chiles.

Page 178--5 Apr. 1783. William Holley. Inv. [not signed]

Page 179--13 Apr. 1789. Joseph Colson. Inv. by Mary Colson. [n.d.] Wm. Denson. Inv. by Wm. Boggan, exr. [see p. 182]

Page 179--15 Jany. 1787. Joseph Martin. Inv. by Katherine Martin and John Martin, exrs.

Page 180--[n.d.] Cornelius Evans. Inv. by Ann Evans.

ABSTRACTS OF PROBATE REPORTS, 1749-1789   129

Page 181--Sept. 1782. John Hamer. Inv. by Mary Hamer.

Page 182--July Ct. 1789. Wm. Denson. Inv. [not signed] 6 Oct. 1777. James Denson. Inv. by Jamima Denson, Admx. "copy made out for Wm. Boggan". [signed] M.A. [Mich. Auld]

Page 183--July Ct. 1782. John Miller. Inv. Thos. Wade, Jr. clk. Apr. Ct. 1782. William Benson. Inv. [not signed]

Page 184--14 Apr. 1758. Joseph Hollingsworth. Inv. by Martha Hollingsworth. wit: Adam McCool.

Page 185--23 Nov. 1782. Division of lands of Walter Leak by Edward Moseley, Elisha Leak. [three pages]

Page 198--[next page] 7 July 1750. John Davidson. Inv. by John Brevard, Alex. Ozburn, Matt Carruth.

Page 201--31 Oct. 1750. John Carmichael. Sale of estate by William Carmichael, admr. Elizabeth buys most of items.

Page 202--1 May 1761. Jacob Richards. Inv. Wm. Richards, Johannes Vanhoese, Edmund Lilly.

Page 204--31 May 1783. William Holley. Sale of est. Sabra Holly a buyer. Test. Jonathan Jackson, Sheriff.

List of sales of estate of Peter Lewis, by Burwell Lanier, Col. Thomas Wade. 2 Oct. 1782. Jonathan Jackson, Sheriff.

Page 205--13 Sept. 1783. List of sales of est. Wm. Griffin Hogan. Buyers: Elizabeth Hogan, Hannah Hogan, Wm. Cooper, John Beverley, James McHenry, Shad Hogan, James Shepard, Walter Gibson, Wm. Hildreth. By Jonathan Jackson, Sheriff.

Page 206--15 Feb. 1783. John Colson; Sales [to Elizabeth Colson] Jonathan Jackson, Sheriff.

Page 207--Sales of est. of William McHenry: Most of items to Mary McHenry; other buyers: Arthur Davis, Jesse Miller, Peter Watts, Jesse McHenry, and John McClendon. Jonathan Jackson, Sheriff.

Page 208--Sale of est. Robt. Jarman. 2 Dec. 1783 by Jona. Jackson, Shff. Buyers: Mayan Jarman, Jeptha Vining, Eliz. Rice, Richard Worthen, Carney Wright, Thos. Huntley, Jonathan Jackson. Jonathan Jackson, Sheriff.

Page 209--June 5, 1758. William Price. Inv. Eleanor Price, Thos. Price.

Page 211--Apr. Ct. 1779. Amount of estate of Benjamin Smith (£303/10/7) by John Smith, Sandhill, Admr. Mich. Auld, clk.

Page 212--Sale of est of John Williamson, decd. Buyers: Mary, Rebeckah, Patty Williamson, Ralph Vickers, Burwell Banier, Patt Boggan, John May, Joshua Morgan, David Jameson, Pat. Boggan Jr. Nat Dobbs, Jesse Miller, John Leverett, Geo. Hammons, John Bloodworth, Mary Morgan. David Jameson, admr. [n.d.]

Page 213--6 Oct. 1758. Acct of sales of est of John Snoddy by Agness Snoddy. Buyers: Gideon Thompson, Jasper Sutton, John Moor, Hugh Parks, James Austin, Samuel Watson, Robert Courtney, James Dougherty, Robt. Tinner [?], Joseph Tanner, Samuel Givens, William Sims, William Barr, Wm. Coatney.

Page 214--Est. of James Irwin, decd. sold at Public Vendue by Margaret Irwin, admr. Dec. 22, 1761.

29 Jany 1785. Acct of sale of Est. Jesse Ivy, decd. Buyers: Wm. Wood, David Jameson, Burwell Lanier, William Yew, Frederick Bass, Mary Ivey, Margarett Belieu, Phillip Gathing, Stephen Miller, John Threadgill, Rebekah Dodd, Pleasant May, Elenor White, John Ivey.

Page 216--[n.d.] Sale of est. John Simpson, decd. Buyers: John Parson, Carney Wright, Thad Harris, John Carruth, Richard Worthen, John Murdock, Sam'l Blackford, Thos. Harris, John Jackson, Thos. Dickson.

Page 217--Acct of sales of est John Miller, decd. Phebe Miller buys most of articles. 3 Sept. 1783. Jona Jackson, Sheriff.

Page 218--[n.d.] Acct of sale of est. of Robt. Lee, decd. Buyers; John Poke [Polk], Thos. Preslar, Jesse Gilbert, James Lee, Chas. Medlock, John Smith, Sampson Culpepper, Francis Smith, William Miller, Milli Lee, Sarah Lee, William Arnett, Walter Gibson, Henry Stokes, John Smith, John Hale Gilbert, Neomi Dickson, John Stephens, Elijah Clark, John Colson; certified by Chas. Medlock.

Page 220--Sale of Est. of Thos. Brigman, decd. Buyers: John Bounds (walnut table), Joseph Hall, John Hathborne, Isaac Brigman, Samuel Snead, Jere Touchberry, William Brigman, Chas. Medlock, Dunkin Curry, William Speed, Nicholas Green, by Isaac Brigman. [n.d.]

Page 221--Nov. 4, 1782. Sale of est. of James Roper. Mary Roper bought everything "that was left out of his will." Jonathan Jackson, Shrf.

Page 222--17 May 1774. Acct sales of John Husbands estate. Buyers: "Mr. John James" [a long list]; "Mr. William Blewett" a parcel of pewter, a tankard, a brass kettle; Mr. Robt. Webb, John Wall, John Cole, Jacob Paul, etc. presented by John James, Tabitha James.

Page 223--8 Dec. 1782. Sale of est of Reuben Rorie. Buyers: Sarah Rorie, many things; William Rorie "a cyphering book", John Stanfield, Solomon Rushing, William Hill, and others. Jona. Jackson, Sheriff.

Page 224--[n.d.] Sale of est. of John Harmon, [or Hamon]decd. Buyers: John Hamon, [a long list], Hopkins Howell, Chas. Medlock, John Hamon the rest, William Pickett, Sheriff.

Page 226--Sale of est. of Nath'l. Curtis. 10 June, 1782. Buyers: Frances Curtis bought nine negroes and some horses; Samuel Curtis bou. horses, cows and calves, sheep, and hogs, [quite a number]; Richard Farr [5 sheep] Chas. Medlock bou. a few items, and others.

Page 227--Abram Belieu, decd. Sale of estate. Catherine Belieu bou. everything. 30 Aug. 1782. Jonathan Jackson, Sheriff.

Page 228--29 June 1784. Perishable estate of John Ryle; sale. Long list of buyers, James Ryle the largest buyer. Stephen Miller, Sheriff.

Page 230--Sale of estate of Edward Traves. Mary Traves buys most of items. William Morris buys a sword and a spoon mold. 3 June 1782. Jona. Jackson, Sheriff.

Page 231--10 Feb. 1783. Est. Thos. Conner. Buyers: Ruthey Conner and a few others.

Page 232--John Hamer. Sale of estate. Mary Hamer buys slaves, farm tools, everything but a trunk wh Jona Jackson buys for £ 1, 10 Dec. 1782.

Page 234--7 Dec. 1782. Sale of James Lowry's est. Buyers: Elizabeth, William, Susannah, Nancy, Robert, John and Peter Lowry. Jonathan Jackson, Sheriff.
June 1784. From same estate Susannah and Ann Lowry bou. a slave, each. Stephen Miller, Sheriff.

Page 236--29 Sept. 1752. Inv. of est. of John Elerbee, aprised by E. Cartledge, John Hicks, Phillip Kenney.

Page 237--29 Nov. 1783. Sale of est Jesse Bailes; Martha Bailes a buyer. Stephen Miller, Shff.

Page 240--20 Jany. 1775. Sale of est Henry Chambers. Buyers: Solomon Gross, Wm. Ussery, James Chiles, Jonathan Jones, Griffin Haywood, John Skinner, Donald McFferson, Wm. Pickett, James Allen, Caleb Touchstone, Edward Chambers, Jerry Menasco, Wm. Coleman, Isaac Armstrong, James Picket [a dictionary], James Smith, Murdock McCaskill, John Chambers, William Chambers, Benj. Powell, Thos Gowers, Thos. Ussery. William Pickett, Sheriff.

Page 242--12 Jany. 1788. Sale of est of Cornelius Evans. Ann Evans largest buyer. Jesse Gilbert, Sheriff.

Page 243--3 June, 1783. Sale est. Wm. Fielding. Mrs. Fielding bought most of it. Jonathan Jackson, Sheriff.

Page 244--24 Oct. 1774. Sale est. Francis Moseley by Margaret Moseley. [a long, long list of buyers.]

Page 246--5 Sept. 1774. Duncan Smith's estate. Buyers: Col. Chas. Medlock, Catherine Smith, Thomas Chiles, John Wilson, John Smith, Charles Smith, Mary Smith, Neal Smith, Robt. Webb, Matthew Watson, Peter McCain, John Brown.

Page 249--December. Sold est John Thurman, Mary Thurman purchased almost all. Chas Medlock.

Page 250--25 Oct. 1772. John Henry's estate sale. Abraham Belyeu purchased much of it; Catherine Henry a long list.

Page 252--26 Aug. 1768. Estate of Wm. Stephens.[3] Buyers: Chas. Medlock, Mathew Stephens, John Stephens, Wm. Coleman, James Pickett, Stephen

ABSTRACTS OF PROBATE REPORTS, 1749-1789

Cole, Jacob Cole, Robert Raiford, Joshua Morgan, William Terry, Thos. Ward.

Page 254--6 Aug. 1774. Est. of Stephen Thomas. Sale report Oct. Ct. 1774. John, Stephen and William Thomas and others buyers.

Page 255--28 Mch. 1758. Inv. of Goods and Chattels of est of Thos. Lockard sold at public vendue. [Names of buyers not given.]

Page 256--[n.d.] Inv. of est of Nath'l Dougherty by John Merman[?] E. Cartledge, James Terry.

Page 257--11 May 1750. Est. of John Price. Inv. by Geo. Renox and Geo. Cathey.

Page 258--4 Aug. 1789. Sale est. Robt. Phillips by William May, Sheriff. Buyers: Mary Phillips, a long list; a few other buyers. Morgan Brown, a Bible.

Page 260--4 Dec. 1754. Est. Matthew Patton. Inv. [not signed]

Page 262--[n.d.] William Hackney est. Sale of cattle and stock by Benj. Jackson.

Page 263--4 Dec. 1774. John Poteet. Inventory by Job Calloway, Daniel Bankston.

Page 264--[n.d.] Acct of Sale of est. of Thomas Tompkins, decd. Buyers; Mary, Francis, Thomas, Stephen Tomkins and others. [A large estate]

Page 268--Robt. Kee, decd. Sale of estate. Oct. 1, 1783. William Smith bought all except one hoe.

Page 268--Jany. 28, 1784. For £115, sale of a negro man of estate of Aaron Baker to James Jameson. S. Miller, Sheriff. [n.d.] Inv. of est. of Thomas Dinkins.

Page 270--28 Oct. 1760. Acct of sale of est. of James McCorkall. Buyers: Jane McCorkall a long list , Robt. Davis, Wm. Davis, John Crocket, James Barnett, Hugh Montgomery, James Gambel, John Linn, Samuel Thomson, Andrew Pickens, John Coffee, James Gambel, Alpheus Spain, Hugh McCain, Thos. Davis, John Nutt, Moses Davis. For the vendue, 4 Gallons and 2 Quarts £ 2/5. [S.C.]

Page 273--[n.d.] Perishable estate of James Chiles. Buyers: Wm. May, David Jamison, Eliz. Chiles, John May, Wm. Wisdom, by D. Jamison.

Page 274--10 Sept. 1782. Sale of Shadrack Denson's est. Buyers: Burwell Lanier, Patt Boggan, John Dejarnett, Wm. Threadgill, John Leverett, John Adkins. Jona. Jackson, Sheriff.

Page 275--Peter Rone [Roane] Sale of est. [n.d.] Buyers: Henry Rone, Adam Rone, David Smith, William Pickett, William Noble, Edward More.

Page 276--27 Jany. 1762. Sale of est. of Sam'l Beason, decd., by Solomon Beason, admr.

Page 277--13 June 1749. Henry Johnson. Inv. by John Handby and Henry Dowland before Samuel Davis, esq.

Page 278--[n.d.] Division of estate of McCorkall. Legatees: Wm., Jane, Mary, Andrew, & James.

Page 279--25 Nov. 1760. Acct of sale of est. of Joseph Cloud returned by Mary Cloud, admx.

Page 280--Acct of sale of est. of Matthew Toole, decd. Buyers: Elenor Toole [9 knives and 12 forks, 5 punch bowls, 7 Delph plates, etc.] Samuel Coburn one of buyers. [n.d.]

Page 283--Charles Burnett's estate. Buyers: David Ker, Andrew Burnett, Samuel Burnett, John Burnett. By Ann Burnett, admx.[n.d.] a long list

Page 285--Est. of Moses Dickey, decd., by Margarett Dickey, admx. [no date]

Page 286--Sale of estate of Thos. White, by Jesse Gilbert, Sheriff. 15 Aug. 1787.

Page 287--[n.d.] Estate of Emanuel Eakles by Joshua Bradly by order of Alexander Gordon, Sheriff. [A very long list.]

Page 292--20 May 1784. Perishable estate of Wm. Benson by Elizabeth Benson. [Buyers not given.]

Page 294--7 Nov. 1783. Perishable est. Joseph Thompson, by Elizabeth Thompson.

29 Jany. 1782. Amount of sale of est. of Reuben Phillips, returned April Ct. 1782 by Jonathan Jackson, Sheriff.

Page 295--10 Nov. 1764. List of sales of est. of Robt. Culpeper. Buyers: Henry Stokes, clothing, etc., Elijah Clark a horse, Thos. Presler gun mold, William Culpeper.

6 Nov. 1772. Sales est. John Hicks. John Husbands, a long list, Mathew Terry, James Pickett, a gun, etc.

Page 298--Isaac Lanier in account with James Lanier, 27 Jany. 1793, as guardian.

Page 299--Est. of Robt. Lee to John Lee, admr.: Legacies to Mintry and Elizabeth Lee, £10, each. Allowed Oct. Ct. 1774. J. Auld, clk.

Page 300--Est. Chas. Burnett. with John Patterson and Ann Burnett, exrs. _____ 1762.

Page 302--Jany. Ct. 1772. Acct of Timothy Taylor, admr. of estate of Joshua Weaver. Paid Jany. 1, 1766 for schooling two children, and Bible for Wm. Weaver; Bible for Eliz. Weaver.

Page 304--Est. Ambrose Still, decd., to wife, Ann, admx.: 25 July, 1760 paid Nicholas White for going to Charleston £23/4; pd Hopkin Howell for going to fetch part of estate from Charles Town. Sworn in open court; wit. John Frolock, clk.

Page 305--Acct Burwell Gregg, decd., to Abner Gregg, of Dinwiddie Co., Va. Aug. 20, 1756. Cash to my brother, Jesse Gregg. The above acct sworn to by Abner Gregg Sept. 28, 1756, Anson Co. before Alexander Lewis.

Jany. 17, 1757. I assigned my whole right to property. Test. Mathew Clements. Abner Gregg

Page 306--Acct Thomas Spratt, decd., to Thomas Polk, admr. [no date]

Page 307--26 Sept. 1772. Acct. John Hicks, decd., 11 Jany. 1772 to Richard Dixon, admr. Wit: Chas. Medlock.

Page 309--1773. Acct of Chas. Medlock, gdn. to orphans of John Hicks, decd.

Page 311--7 Jany. 1783. Est. of Peter Lewis to Burwell Lanier, 1779. Stephen Miller, J.P.

Page 316--1767. Estate James McManus, decd., to Mary McManus, admx.

Page 319--1763. Est. Jas Irwin to Margarett Irwin, admx. Cheese and peach brandy at funeral.

Page 314--Acct of est. Burwell Griggs [Gregg] to Preston Goforth, 1752 (Nov.) to 1756.

Page 314--Est. Robt. McCorkell to James Linn, [no date]; pd Margarett McCorkell £26; pd. Thomas McEthing.

Page 313--Est. Wm. Benson to Eliz. Benson adm. Apr. 28, 1784; settled Apr. 1, 1785.

Page 315--26 July, 1758. Acct est John Carmichael to Wm. Carmichael.

Page 301--[n.d.] Andrew Berry [Barry], decd., to Richard Berry; pd to Robt. McClenachan £6/8, on note.

Page 310--John Hicks, decd., to Robert Thomas: Child's coffin 4 sh; making coffin for self 8 sh; Apr. 4, 1774. Wit: James Cotten.

Page 311--Est. Reuben Phillips, decd., to Clement Phillips., Mch. 18, 1782. Paid to Thomas Gaddy, Timothy Haney, Jerry Gulledge, Nathaniel Dobbs, Abraham.Strickland.

Page 312--July 7, 1783. Acct of James Roper's estate with John Lilly.

Page 326--John Gifford's estate to Thomas Burns, 1755. Pd:........ to Andrew Pickens 5 sh.

Page 336--May 17, 1784. Acct of John Covington, Sr. with estate of Wm. Leak for 1783. [Several pages]

Page 338--Received of Mary McManus, admr. of James McManus, decd., £26 on account and partly a debt due me. Apr. 17, 1765. Hugh Montgomery.

Page 338--July 6, 1784. Received of Mrs. Hannah Hogan, admr. of William G. Hogan, decd., £7/5, part of a judgment obtained by Shadrack Hogan agst Wm. G. Hogan by me Ford DeJarnett, Sheriff of Montgomery Co.

---

1. James Pickett died bef. 10 Feb. 1764 when Committee on Public Claims reported that the est. of James Pickett, former Sheriff of Anson Co., was allowed 16 pounds for his salary as Sheriff for the years 1756 and 1757, for which years he had accounted. N. C. State Records, Vol. 22, p. 838.

2. Died bef. 20 Sept. 1789, the date of his father's will.

3. The names of the buyers, Mathew Stephens, John Stephens, Wm. Coleman, James Pickett, Robt. Raiford and Wm. Terry, suggest that Wm. Stephens may have been son of John & Grace (Raiford) Stephens, of Cumb. Co.

PETITIONS, 1770-1789

Petition 1770 to Governor, Council and Assembly by Inhabitants of Anson County against the court at Salisbury, saying that they spent of necessity much gold and silver there which finds its way to Virginia and South Carolina from the Province of North Carolina; asks that a court at Campbellton be established for Anson, Orange and Cumberland Counties.[1]

Signed by:

James Terry	David Cock
Shadrack Denson	Wm. Rorie
D..... Brown	George Collins
Thomas Baley	John Crowson
Hopkin Howell	Wm. McDaniel
John Leverett	John Bound
Wm. Leverett	James Bound
James Smith	Benjamin Barrett
William Seago	Luke Robinson
John Seago	Welcome Ussery
Joel Phillips	John Skinner
Lennard Webb	Wm. Ussery Sr.
Silvestus Walker	Thos. Ussery
John Stuckberry	Wm. Morris
Wm. Lucas	..... Morriss
Edward Morris	Heton Morriss
Jeremiah Stuckberry	William Morris
Chas. Thomas	W. Smith
John May	John Ussery
John Smith [L.R.]	John Flower
John Lucas	Theophilus Williams
Jos. Harrison	John Simmons
Thomas Ward	Christopher Christian
James Allmond	Richard Downs
John Husbands	Saml. Parsons
Wm. Bennett	William Parsons
John Swan	David Smith
George Carter	John Smith[2]
Robert Webb	Thos. Fanning Jr.
Thomas Mitchell	James Adams
Thos. Fanning	Thomas Harper
Lewis Sowell	Arthur Pierce
Thos. Smith	Sampson Williams
Stephen Thomas	Roland Williams
Wm. Moody	Robert Jarman
Benj. Smith	John James Sr.
John Bailey	Jimmey James
Nathaniel Ashley	Van Swearingen
Moses White	Lewis Lowry
Thomas Smith	Francis Jordan

John Westmoreland	William Bonsall
William Bennett	Robert Poston
William Pratt	Jonathan Llewellen
Malachi Watts	Stephen Tutch ?
Jacob H _____	John Henson
Isaac Falconbery Jr.	Samsom Peacock
Owing Slaughter	Isaac Falconbery
Abraham Busham	Joseph White
Richard Bushan	Charles Hines
Robert Rushing	Sylvanus Walker
James Langford	Jason Meador Jr.
Andrew Watts	Jason Meador
Andrew Watts Jr.	Joseph Martin
Isaac Belyeu	Thomas Lacey
_____ Belyeu	John Hamer
George Belyeu	Tilman Helms
Vick Moon	John McNath
Moses Witt	Henry McNath
James Cotton	Isaac Bolen
Benjamin Moorman	William Bond
Archelaus Moorman	Charles Weatherford
Wm. Coleman	John Downer
Abraham Belyeu	Wm. Hickman
Jacob Paul	John Hornbeck Jr.
William Holly	John Hamer Jr.
Charles Smith	Antho Hutchins
Isom Haley	George Wilson
Andrew Falconburg	Thos. Wright
Henry Falconberg	Samuel Snead
John McIlvail	James Denson
Thomas Fee	Francis Clark
Jonathan Hellams	Jeremiah Terrell
Jonathan Falconbery	

Petition of inhabitants of Anson County: 1777 Because of PeeDee River dividing the county, it is very inconvenient to many of the inhabitants; they ask for a division of the county with the river as the dividing line....
.... If you in your Wisdom should judge the division unnecessary then we pray that commission of disinterested persons be appointed to fix Court House in or near the center of the county, as conveniently as it may be. It now stands in ten or twelve miles of South Carolina and is extremely inconvenient.[3]

1. Chas. Robinson	51. William Allman
2. Dan'l. McDonald	52. John Walters
3. Ezekiel Benbrooke	53. Wm. Coleman
4. John McKee	54. John McRae

133

PETITIONS, 1770-1789

5. (torn) w.... d
6. Samuel Usher
7. Jacob Whitehead
8. William Castleberry
9. John Shepard
10. Charles Smith Sr.
11. Joseph Smith
12. John Willson
13. Nathl. Lilly
14. ____ Hunt
15. Elija Thomson
16. Jas. Hutchins
17. David Dumas
18. John MacLeod
19. John Stevens
20. Henery Stevens
21. Richd. Downs
22. Benj. Baird
23. Jonathan Hellams
24. William Smith [S.H.]
25. Ezra Bostick
26. Thomas Hadley
27. James Price
28. Jonathan Harry
29. John Patterson
30. John Cockerham
31. Jonathan New
32. James Bostick
33. David Collier
34. Jobe Willson
35. Thos. Deten
36. Richd Brassel Jr.
37. Richard Brassel
38. Lewis Hunt
39. Joseph (torn) H.....
40. Benager Randol
41. Henry Deberry
42. Benja. Dumas
43. Dd. Smith [S.H.]'
44. Jas. Terry
45. James Hellams
46. William Chaplin
47. John Bostick
48. Benjamin Phillips
49. Jonathan Gower
50. George Gower

55. Jos. Hines
56. Zechariah Smith
57. Edward Chambers
58. Cornelius Robinson
59. James Phillips
60. John Coatney
61. ____ Morley
62. Moses Sanders
63. Richard Green
64. Francis Sanders
65. John Thomson
66. William Morgan
67. Sollimon Williams
68. Chas. Harrington
69. Goen Morgan
70. William Smith
71. John McLeod
72. John Smith Little R
73. Joseph Chase
74. William Maguire
75. William Gowers
76. William Jones
77. Thomas Jowers
78. Wm. Leak
79. Richard Pemberton
80. Wm. Newberry Jr.
81. Stephen Pitcock
82. Vinson Davis
83. Owen Slaughter
84. William Newberry Sr.
85. William Bolton
86. Robert Poston
87. Noah Agee
88. David Cordel
89. Charles Allen
90. Edmond Newell
91. John Morris
92. George Brien
93. Joshua Ussery
94. Nathaniel Covington
95. Colin MacLennan
96. Thos. Gowers
97. Nat. Powell
98. Anthony Mills Parrot
99. Malcom MacLeod
100. John Smith Sandhill

[Signatures not numbered from here.]
Thos. Lacy
Jerome Miller
William Halley
James Blunt
William Johnson
William Shepherd
Jethro Weaver

John Roland
Richard Ford
William Mask
Moses Pearse
Reuben Hay
William Medcalf
John Dunn

Wright Peirce
John Freeman
William Price
John Newman
William Bleakney
Thomas Bleakney
John White
William Smith
Jacob Blunt
Benjamin Fry
Fendal Roland
Benj. Underwood
Nathaniel Renfro
Abraham Miller
John Rasbury
Nath'l. Biven
Jonathan Wever
Stafford Gibbs
John Pelham
John Wright
William Pace
Joshua Martin
Thomas Chivers
Ottwell Weaver
John Redforn?
John Cole
Thomas Truly
J. P. Clark
William Nelson
Joseph Thompson
Thomas Shelby
Jesse Cordell
Isaac Ford
William Bevin
Wm. Nelson Jr.
Thomas Justice
William Nelson Sr.
John Perce
Jesse Cooper
Thomas Creel
Jonathan Jackson
John Stanfill
Samuel Jackson
William Branch
Britten Branch
Moses Griel
James Knots
Joseph White
John Edens
Abram Hill
James Stanfill
Jacob Stanfill
Charles Sisenbee
Malachi Watts
Abraham Strickland

Geo. Clark
John Duncan
Jonathan Turner
Jacob Hill
Moses Tomlin
Jno Jenings
Henry Tippins
Wm. Usher
Arthur Pierce
Benjamin Dicks
Sebastian Inlaws
Richard Leverett
Robert Leverett
Thomas Ussery
John Leverett
Christopher Butler Jr.
Christopher Butler Sr.
David ____
James Butler
Alexander Baird
Thos. Butler
John Jennings
Soirle Macdonald
Richard Powell
Samuel Shang
Samuel Still
William More
Joseph Gad
Daniel McCray
Thomas Bullock Jr.
Reuben Holderness
Edwin Ingram
Samuel Ingram
Peter Ussery
John Sidum Jr.
Welcome Ussery
Jno. Gross
Joshua Gross
Jno. Braugh
Henry Burcham
Jesse Wallace
Joseph English
Joshua Butler
John Sowell
John Ward
Joseph Allen
Thomas McClendon
John Jones
Wm. Rusel [?]
John Swan Jr.
Wm. Sowell
George Bruton
Thomas Lucas
William Henley
Wm. Mask Jr.

PETITIONS, 1770-1789 135

Andrew Dumas	Robert Price	Martin Gonad	John Bennet Jr.
George Walters	James Lionely	John Jebardgin [?]	Joseph Tarbutton
Benjamin Dumas Jr.	Thomas Runtle Jr. [or Huntle]	Mulvaney Beals	Jeremiah Hendrick
John Hutchins	Thos. Stanfill	William Hamer	Thomas Fanning
William Ussery	Wm. Rushing	William Bayles	Sampson Williams
James Almond	Rowland Rushing	James Hagood	John Powell
John Mobery [?]	Jesse McClendell	John Jackson	Alex. MacLennan
John Sowell	Stephen Miller	John Lisonby	Richard Tallear
Thos. Ward	Robert Rushing	Malcolm McDonald	John McRae Jr.
Philip Raspbery	Joshua Hodges	John Smith	Thomas Dockery
Isaac Jones	William May	John Mask	Wm. Leggett
John Batt Baird	John Stanfill	Robert Webb	Benj. Powell
William Powell	Isaac Nickols	Daniel McNeill	John Mason
Robert Kennon	Richard Rushing	Daniel MacAulay	George Slaughter
Samuel Banton	Luke Langston	William Webb	Jeremiah Simpkin
Alex. Cockerham	Frederick Gordon	Chas. Harbert	Randal Cockerham
John McGlown [?]	Mickel Tadrick [?]	Kno. Wilshur	Townsend Robinson
John Almond	Philip Gathings	Henry Covington	James Pickett
John Carpenter	George Hammons	John Long Sr.	John Kimbrough
Wm. McCurry	Peter Watson	John Long Jr.	John Skinner
August McAuley	James Gorden	Daniel MacCormick	George Carter
John McAuley	Thomas Huntle Sr.	Daniel Thomas	Edmund Collins
Donald Bellou	John Beck	Wm. Thomas	----ner Eights
Collin McCray	Thos. Ford	James Smith	Joseph Hoggs
Dudley Mask	Charles Clark	Jacob Morris	Silious Overstreet
Jacob White	John Granade	Daniel Smith	Benja. Maner
Wm. Chambers	Abraham Jones	John Jenkins	B-------- McLean
John Crouch	John Richards	Jacob Cockerham Sr.	Thomas Gibson
Wm. White	Abraham Rushing	Jonathan Lewelling	David McKay
Thos. Stainback	Wm. Gulledge	Wm. Morris	Isaac Eights
Daniel Matson [Watson?]	Joseph White	Henry Taylor	William Taylor
John Johnsend [Johnson]	Jesse Miller	John Dove	James Hayns
John Taler	Cornelius Clark	John Curry	George Collins
Lachlin McKennox	Davis Lennard	John Love	Ishmael Chavers
Norman McLeod	James Tarlton	Nathan Herinton	Demsey Grant
Donald McKenzie	Theoderick Webb	Lawrence O'Bryan	Nelson Gibson
John Simmons	Johnson Rushing	Cooper Clark	Thos. Collins
Murdoch Macaulay	John Rushing	Elisha Collins	Moses Johnson
Stephen Touchstone	Thomas Meador	_____Taler	Wm. Williams
John Murchison	James Harrell	John McCalman	Elisha Sweeting
John Tarbutton Sr.	Jonathan May	Absolem Hindes	Thos. Turner
Jno. Robinson	William McDaniel	James Phillips	William Lochler
Luke Robinson	Peter Lowry	Stephen Gesford	Thos. Smith
John Ferguson	W. Benton	Patrick Sanders	Stephen Maner
John Meguire	James Webb	William Baker	John Maner
Wm. Meguire Sr.	William Strickland Jr.	William McDonald	Mark Deeds
John Hews	Wm. Strickland Sr.	Simon Hooker	John Umphreys
James Yoe	Thos. Stanfill	John English	William Smith
Benjamin Ingram	Samuel Strickland	John Jenkins	Edward Smith
Nathl. Dobbs	Job Benton	Jacob Cockerham Jr.	John Best
Robt. Hall	James Benton	Farquard McCre	Joseph Hiett
John Branch	Gidden Bowen	Isaac Armstrong	Ezekiel Hiett
Emanuel Tarleton	Absolem Ethredge	Thos. George	Thomas Wilson
Reuben Phillips	John May	James Conway	

PETITIONS, 1770-1789

Petition to Governor, Council and Assembly from the inhabitants of the upper end of the county for a division to form Montgomery County. [Two lists] February 1779.[5]

Thomas Wade, Marshall Digge, Lot Tallant, Joseph Howell, Isaac Fortenberry, Alexander McCaskill, Israel Snead, Wm. Love, Henry Adcock, Burlingham Rudd, George Andrews, John Short, John Dinkins, Lawrence Franklin, John Wade, John Franklin, William Liles, Richard Farr, John Smith, Francis Smith, Solomon Fisher, John Cole, Joseph Martin, Duke Glen, Thos. Slay, Thomas Vining, Wm. Boggan, Patt Boggan, Cornelius Ross, Robert Sego, John Sego, Edward Smith, Shadrach Baggett, Daniel Murphy, Jabez Hendricks, Abraham Lefavour, James Nubry [Newberry], John Crawford, John Auld, Delong Bass, Thomas Conner, William Bennett, Neavil Bennett, James Chiles, Thos. Thomas, John Maclendal, Jas. Bogen, Thomas Baly, Wm. Yoe, Theophilus Evans, James Langford, William Langford, William McDonald, George Loundesdell Rudd, Jeremiah Gulledge, John Smith, Robert Jarman, James Little, William Hickman, Micajah Stinson, George Lindsey, Charles Birmingham, John Newton, William Bennett, Jr., Daniel Low, Richard James, Abraham Jegow [?], Thomas Tallant, Joshua Moses, Moses Tallant, Thomas Hall, Aaron Tallant, John Segar Sr., Jacob Falconberry, Will Watts, Peter Watts, Jonathan Davidson, Wm. Rushing, John Murfee, William Fedricks, Wm. Bales, Wm. May, Pat Boggan Jr., John Street, Moses Greel, Thos. Jones, Mark Rushing, Sol Dearman, Arthur Dees, James Dees,___Bohman, Daniel Vines, Thomas Higdon, John Higdon, John Henricks, Wm. Watkins, William White, John Crisnel, Thomas Phillips, David Watts, Joseph Smith, Abraham Jones, Wm. Gulledge, Benj. Fuller, Jas. Talton, Thos. Talton, James Gordon, Absolem Etherage, John Granade, Jesse Brown, John Auk, Jacob Jones, Thos. Ford, James Temple, John Brooks, William Hall, Jacob Blue, James Long, John Edens, Wm. Edens, John Bains, Hugh McCormack, John Dove, Loflin Curry, Donald McDonald, John Watson, Benj. Merritt, Dempsey Grant, Aaron Turner, Nehemiah Randal, Angus Curry, Joseph Brooks

2nd list

William Pickett, Benj. Baird, Thomas Pickett, Joshua Gross, Henry Mounger, Sias Billingsley, Joseph Henderson, Joshua Carter, James Gray, Zedekiah Ledbetter, George Newmane, Stephen Treadwell, Lawrence Bankson, Isaac Callaway, John Callaway, Colby Randal, Wilbun Gray, Gilbert Simpson, Flanery Rone, James Bankson, George Ramage, John Lunn, Peter Jackson, Bolton Sauls, George Tucker, Thomas Pitman, Thomas Vandyke, William Pitman, Samuel Carter, Mathew Jurden, John Martin, Moses Carter, William Wilson, Joseph McLester, Charles Jones, Buckner Kimball, Darby Henley, William Jackson, John Jordan, David Penington, Moses Curtis, William Bankson, Job Callaway, Charles Jurden, David Hawke, Thomas Bankson, William Noble, John Bankson, Simpson Noble, John Bankson, William Loftin, Richard Parker, Thomas Barnes, Moses Loftin, Julius Nichols, Ethelred Harris, Howel Parker, Thomson Clements, West Harris, George Tucker, John Tucker, John Baker, Roland Harris, Nathaniel Bell, Wm. Ballard, William Clemmons, John Galahon, Buckner Harris, Joseph Bell, William Denman, George Kirke, Jesse Clifton, Edward Corneil, Edward Henly, Rusel Curtis, Matthew Cogan, Arthur Harris, John Coggan, Moody Ingram, Jacob Bankson, John Rogers, Daniel Bankson, James Rogers Jr., Henry Harris, Arthur Harris son of Henry Harris, John Jeffry, Josais Wright, Mathew Harrold, George Shankle, Humphrey Ballard, Drury Bennett, William Ballard, Mark Bennett, Cary Prichard, Charles Ledbetter, William Magreger, John Lankaster, John Harris, Bartlett Megreger, John Walker, Randle Jackson, John Randle, Isaac Allen, West Harris, son of Henry Harris, Adam Rone, James Johnson, Mosés Gordon, James Bryant, Josias Randle, Joseph Vickery, Jacob Shankle, Thomas Simson, William Nobles, Sr., Andrew Dennis, Nathaniel Dennis, William Allton, James Runnels, William Morriss, Thomas Newman, Herbert Suggs.

****

Petition of Inhabitants of Anson County who think that notwithstanding the said county was divided the last Assembly, yet the inhabitants labour under the greatest hardships by reason of great distance from the Court House;'the sd County being 90 miles in length and 38 in breath and the River running through near the middle, which seldom can be crossed without expense of ferriages and sometimes not at all passable; pray to have the county divided into two counties with the Peedee River the dividing line. Oct. 1779.[6]

Signers: Thos. Scott, John Scott, Patrick Bogan, William Head, John Smith, Wm. Flanagin, Peter Watson, Thomas Miers, Job Benton, Nathl. Scott, John Stanfill, Richard Odum, Jesse Bales, Charles Medlock, Jas. Lisenbe, Benj. Merritt, Matt Rushing, Sam Jackson, Thos. Gaddy, William Scott, William Ea---, Jesse Miller, Ezekiel McClendon,

David Watts, John Ivey, David Jameson, Frederick Bass, Richard Smith, Wm. Branch, Sam Strickland, Wm. Leonard, Fedrick Gordon, James Hogan, John Swor, Wm. Bevins, John Adams, James Hellams, John Melton, Wm. Sheppard, John Cole, John Roland, John Adams, Nathl. Bevins, Reuben Phillips, John Branch, William Strickland, John Duncan, Jno. Hill, Bretton Brand, Jacob Stanfill, Thos. Stanfill, _____ Hill, John Liles, Abraham Strickland, Wm. Gulledge, Jas. Webb, Nathl. Dobbs, James Money, ... 2nd section: Christopher Williams, Isaac Brigman, Nathan Faulkner, Methuselah Rowland, John Bleedworth, Thomas Foord, James Smith, Robert Hall, William Mason, Moses Greely, Patrick Boggans, Thomas Crile, Thos. Talton Sr., Thomas Talton Jr., Jeremiah Gulledge, James Bahton, Joshua Hodges, William Ricketts, Isaac Nickols, Joseph White, James Boggan, John Gundey, Phillip Griffin, Robert Rushing, Solomon Rushing, Richard Rushing, Martin Granade, James Little, Robert Grise, William Benton, Wm. Rushing Sr., William Rone, Wm. Nickles, Jesse Brooks, Theoderick Webb, James Harrell, Reuben Rorie, Absolem Ethridge, John Lowery, Malachi Watts, Wm. Hammond, William Meggs, William Hammock, John Harris....3rd section: William Speed, John Henson, Elrzer Cutis, John Cole, River Jurden, John Jurden, John Parsons, Thomas Curtis, Samuel Curtis, John Donaldson, James Baggett, Henley Sneed, Thomas Tomkins, Wm. Pratt, Shadrack Baggett, Duncan Rice, James Baggett, John Skipper, Benj. Skipper, Jr., Benj. Skipper, John Martin, Philip James, Capper Clark, Ronald McDonald, John Steley, Zachariah Moorman, George Cole, S*****McIntosh, James West Mac-Lenon, Daniel McCaskel, John Cole Bridge, Israel Medlock, Wm. Mimes, Robert Lamton, John Wall, Benjamin Thomas, John Dickson, John Webb, John Thomas, Joseph Nall, Sr., Isak Nall, Joseph Nall Jr., James Baggett, Jas. McKeachey, Wm. McKenchey, Thomas Deen, Richd. Odom, John Walters, James Thomas, Marling Williamson, Sion Odom, John Ray, John McInnes, Elisha Cottengame, New Carmichael, Donald Carmichael, Dugald Blue, Daniel Shaw, Luke Williams, Zakriah Johnston, Lot Watson, Thomas Hathcock Jacob Bone, James Ivey, George Swot?, Randolph Johnson, William Dawkins, Robt. Wilson, John Covington........4th section: William Morris, Nathaniel Harrington, Richard Adams, Sr., Absolem Hindes, William Adams, John Jenkins, Elisha Collins, Edward Smith, John Mason, John McCray, Alexander McCray, Christopher McCray, Daniel McCrimmon, Owen Slaughter, Jeremiah Henry, Henry Wilason, William Coster, Patrick Sanders, Thomas Cockeran, David Collins, George Pettit, Edward Almond, William Brigman, William Yoe, William May, John Bostick, Shem Thompson, Nathan Dobbs, Jethro Wever, Jesse Gilbert, John Long, George Bounds, Valentine Moss, John James, William Webb, Wm. McDaniel, Vinson Davis, Isaac Brigman, William Smith, George Webb, Bartho Tuny, Mathew Strickling, Andrew Ross, Wm. Hunter, David Rich, Chas. Vivion, Solomon Jones, Jas. Hutchings, John Gowers, Wm. Ross, Joseph Thompson, George Carter, Joel Phillips, James Phillips, Wm. Bennet, George Collins, Benjamin Maner, John Thomas, John Tony, Edward Smith, Jacob Glockerham, Jesse Bounds, Mathew Covington, John Hall, William Jernigan, Benjamin Covington, Richard Leake, Henry Adcock, Wm. Lewis, Walter Slaughter, Simon Thomas, Sr., Daniel Thomas, William Thomas, Edward Williams, John McCalman, Wm. Scott, Jonas Wilsher, John Wilsher, Daniel Smith, Wm. Covington, Thomas Dockery, John Long Jr., Thomas Donaho, Archibald McMillan........5th section: John Martin, William MacQueen, John Curry, Martin Martin, Donald McDonald, John Martine, Allan Martin, Valentine Morris, Angus Curry, Alexander McDonald, Donald Martin, John Curry, Donald M. Covington, Alexander McLeod, Henry Polson, Angus McDonald, Donald McLennon, William Mounten?, Archibald Duffie, Hugh McCormick, Lachland Curry, John McKay, Matthew Terry, Lawrence Bryan, Ephraim Ferrell, Daniel McNeill, John McKay, John Campbel, Norman Duffie, Norman Martine, Isaac Yeats, Thomas Gibson, Stephen Cole, James Paterson, John McIver, William Terry, James Ates, Duncan McKay, Peter Morton, Edward Curry, Mark Pettis, James Watson, Nelson Gibson, Daniel McInnis, John Brown, John Watson, S---- Stricklin, John Covington, Roger McHair, Duncan Graham, Daniel Cony, John Cury, George Collins, Richard Adams, Jr., John Crawford, Charles Lisenby, Henry Taylor, John Long, Bexley J. Lambden, John Astin, John Benet, Ben Smith, P---------- Downs, John Lisonby, William Newberry, William Rand?, William Bennet, Joshua Brasfield, Stephen Maner, John McCaul, Donald McInnis, John Logue, Daniel McCaul, John Vinenen, Moses Turner, John Lowry,_____ Rose, John Rose, Jesse Rose ... .6th section: Cottingham, Lewis Thomas, Keader Heaton, Mark Deese, John Morton, Samuel Pate, John Peck, George Wilson, John Blew, Elleck Watson, James Smiley, Edward McNear, Anguish Blew, Daniel McCann, Malcom McHennis, Midleton Pool, Robert Broadaway, David Jernigan, Timothy Hurley, Joshua Brigman, Daniel Herring, Thomas Turner, Mark Johnson, William Sanford, Arch McKay, Elleck Watts, Jr., Neal Blew, Dugel McBride, John McBride, Hen. Thomson, D--------McMilen, William Hunter, Samuel Hunter, Stafford Grayham,

PETITIONS, 1770-1789

Moses Johnson, Duncan Blew........7th section: More Troy, Richard Worthen, John Chiles, Chas. Harrington, Lewis Caudell, George Hamons, John Hogen, James Downing, Thos. Gilbert, Thos. Lacy, James Downing Jr. Jno. Stanfield, Joseph Ryce, Allen Martin, Robert Webb, George Davidson, Angus Martin, Jno. Carruth, Thos. Hurbert, Martin Martin, John Maclendon, Isham Ingram, Henry Baly, William Best, John Leverett, Thos. Crawford, Josiah Downing, John Williamson, Samuel Bloodworth, Robt. Jarman, Samuel Williamson, William Threadgill, Robert Lee, Benaj. Dumas, Wm. Legit, James Sander, Jas. Burleyson, Wm. Rushing, John Walters, Farquar McRa, Duncan McRa, Geo. Walters, Robert Polson, Jonathan Turner, Stephen Pittcock, John Harse, Jonathan Harre, Joshua Brassfield, William Newberry Jr., Jonathan Newberry, William Bolton, John McRa, Jr., John McRa, Sr., William Turpin, John Dicks, Thos. Megginson, James Bostick, Thos. Hadley, David Love, Joseph Creed, Wm. Love, David Rainey, Josiah Lyons, Noah Rushing, Frederick Gordon, John Jackson, Rowland Rushing, Andrew Dumas, Joseph Gad, James Chiles........8th section: Stephen Miller, Thos. Lacy, Joseph Thompson, Shem Thompason, Wm. Bleakney, John Freeman, James Blunt, Stephen Weaver, Wm. Perce, Nathan Brasell, Shepard Deason, Jesse Cordell, Joseph Burcham, Abraham Miller, Thos. Dunn, Moses Pearce, Isak Wever, Nathaniel Renfroo, William Holley, Thomas Shelby, William Trull, Thomas McKinney, William Pellem, James Blunt, Joshua Mont, Joel Renfroo, Jerom Miller, George Brower, Rich. Moss, William Sneed, Thomas Chevers, William Nash, Thomas Trull, Moses Tomlinson, John White, James Redfern, William Nelson, John Redfern, William Pace, John Dunn, I-- McIlwain, John Jackson, Jonathan Jackson, Isaac Jackson, Samuel Jackson, Joshua Morgan, Evan Vaughn, John May, Aaron Baker.

****

Oct. 23, 1779. Law passed in H.C., dividing Anson County. Richmond Co. created. Commissioners: Henry Wm. Harrington, John Donaldson, William Legate, John Coal, Robert Wells, Robert Thomas and Richard Pemberton, Esquires and commrs., to erect court house, prison, and stocks.

Petition of inhabitants of Anson County [1783] to General Assembly showeth that whereas an act of the Assembly appointed commissioners to fix a place in Anson County to build a courthouse within two miles of the center of sd county, it appears from the plan thereof to be remote from the bulk of inhabitants and a very poor settlement of barren black-jack land unfitting for public roads, etc.; a remedy where of the petitioners pray an act empowering commissioners to build courthouse on plantation of William Bert, which is high, dry land, well-watered, etc. [The end of petition torn off including a few signatures]

Signers: Jas. Boggan, Jas. Boggan Jr., John Boggan, Wm. Boggan, James Jameson, Wm. Booth, Wm. Wood, Thos. Brown, Jesse McHenery, John Flanegin, John Howard, Zedick Evans, Thos. Harlen, Lewis Harris, George Harrell, Abner Pavell, Andrew Tucker, Benjamin Haris, Wm. Cerbo, Thos. Creek, Peter Spradly, James Dunkin, John Hill, Roger Rees, Abraham Strickling, Frederick Bass, Wm. Leveret, Philip Gathings, Joseph White, Hezekiah White, Josiah White, Peter Watts. Second part: Thos. Ratcliff, David Murphey, Jr., Zachariah Ratcliff, Randal Threadgill, Edmund Tallent, Thos. Slay, Samuel Booth, Samuel Flake, George Briley, William Lewis, John Baley, Bat Murphey, Chas. Weatherford, Neavill Bennett, John King, James Lisles, Joshua Burmingham, John Burmingham, Wm. Dinkins, John Knotts, John Deneson, Jesse Ivey, John R------, Smith Fields, Micah Fields, Elijah Fields, John Field, Wm. Wage [?], Hopkin Howell, David Kemp, Joseph Murphey Sr., Saniel Swor, Thos. Wade, Joseph Thompson, Thos. Thomas, William Pratt, John Everitt, Jabez Hendricks, John Avery, John Hendricks, William Yoe, James ---- ford, Henry Everet, Jas. Terry, Hardy Hooker, Hum. Rogers, J. Pickett, Jos. Ingram, Presley Nelms, John Ingram, Benj. Ingram, Sam'l Ingram, D---- H----, William Kirby, John Johnson, John Booth, Wm. Evert, John King, John Mask, John Martin, Wm. Martin, Wm. Miller, George Wells, William Haley, Edmond Hayes, Griffin Gatewood, Bent. Vanderford, Joseph Bretwell, Absolem Sowerd, John Threadgill, Solomon Wright, Frederick Bass, John Atkins, Andrew Ross, Walter Ross, John Ross, Jno. Herring, John Knotts, John Herring, Richard Worthen, James Smith, Benjamin Bell, Richard Odom, Isack Odom, Job Jordin, Robert Huntle, Thos. Medders, Giddin Mason, Frederick Gording, Young Stoaks, John Gurnad, Martin Gurnad, Thos. Huntly, James Gording, William Worthen, Ephraim Atkins, John Jarman, Jr., Stephen Thomas, Duke Glen, Wm. Vanderford, Samuel ---- fort, John Gresham, Jonathan Helms, Beverly Clark, John Hand, Peter Yeats, James Bennett, Stephen Irby, Stephen Wright, John Cook, William Lindsey, Samuel Miers, Nathan Melton, James Barber, Thomas Lewis, John Lowry, Wm. Batey, James Plunkett, Wm. May Jr., Ed Smith, John

Franklin, Greset? Johnson, William Hall, Robert Gordon, John Green, Richard Hill, Thos. Miars, Burrell Rudd, Thomas Talton, John Talton, Abram Rushing, Phillip Rushing, Thomas Wright, John Mills, Isaac Jackson, Thomas Meador, Jason Meador, Richard Rushing, Robert Rushing, Jacob Rushing, Joseph Milton, Hardy Quin, Job Meador, Thomas Jones, Peter Lowry, Lewis Meador, Joseph Alsop, William Mickols, James Little, James Howard, Samuel Bolden, John Lambden, Henry Lisenby, Richard Farr, William Tompkins, Patt Boggan, John Lynton, Malachi Culpeper, John Dedney, Miles Lewis, Drury Nicols, George Wilwood, William Lisles, Lawrence Franklin Jr., John Franklin, Ison Franklin, John Lisenby, Ezekiel Lisenby, Joseph Cambel Jr., Joseph Cambel Jr., Silas Cambel, Joseph John Wade, James Plunkett, Chas. Lisenby Sr., Jeptha Vining, Thos. Howard, Capt., Thos. Tomkins, Francis Tomkins, Reuben Brassfield, Michael Crawford, Daniel Murphy Sr., Daniel Murphey Jr., Marshall Diggs, Odom Cocks, John Henson, Wm. Ratcliff, Joseph Joyet, Elijah Curtis, John Downer, John Wright, Jonathan Wright, John Parsons, Cornelis Clark, Garay Grillass, Thos. Conner, Far Lisenby, Avington Cocks, Stephen Tomkins, Capt., Wm. Tomkins, William Parsons, Joseph Parsons, John Parsons Sr., James Thompson, Stephen Thomas, Philemon Paul, William Bennett, Neavil Bennett, James Bennett, Jesse Ivey, Sr., Jas. Thomson, Edward Brown, Nathan Evans, William May, Evan Von, Pleasant May, James Farr, Major, Richard Farr, Jr., John Harbard, John Arthur, James Smith, Lawrence Franklin, Samuel Thomas, William Vaughan, William May, John Flanegan, William Johnson, David Owens, Thomas Colley, William Owens Jr., John Willins, Lewes May, John Colley, Thomas Wade Jr., Wm. Threadgill, Capt. Patt Boggan, John May, William Hammol Jr., John Leverett, John Davison, Ambrose Davidson, John McClendon, Dennis McClendon, Sr., Dennis McClendon Jr., John Bloodworth, Ralph Vickers, William Bloodworth, South Denis McClendon, Richard Battis, George Dade, William Ratcliff, Isham Ingram, Joseph Saser, Joseph Colson, Lewis Atkins, Davidson Atkins, Francis Smith, Richard Smith, Aquila Williamson, James Meggs, William Meggs, Abraham Godert, John Wright, John Jackson, Jonathan Jackson, Sheriff, John Stanfill, Capt., Sam'l. Jackson, William Guice, William Atkins, William Womack, Thomas Stanfill, Sampson Stanfill, John Stanfill Sr., Abraham Strickland, John Nelson, Solomon Townsend, John Eddens, M. Melton, Joseph Barbour, Peter Ates, William Colley, Malachi Watts, John McGovett [?], Jeremiah Lewis, William Gulledge, James Harrell, John Harrell, Thomas Miers, Jeremiah Quin.

To the honourable the General Assembly of the State of North Carolina, the Humble Petition of the Inhabitants of Anson County sheweth that your Petitioners are informed that a District Court of Law and Equity is erected at Fayetteville, that Town being about the same distance from the other District Towns in the State aforesaid as such District Towns are distant from each other that your Petitioners are sensible of the great advantage that would arise to them in consequence of their being anexed to and composing part of the Fayetteville District, etc., etc. pray that County of Anson be anexed to the District of Fayetteville.

Signers: Thomas Wade, Richard Farr Jr., Henry Everett, John West, William Miller, John Johnston, Daniel McRay, Samuel Flake, Joseph Dunham, Thomas Gower, Joshua Do----, John Armstrong, Wm. Murphey, Charles Birmungham, Josiah Dobbs, John Murphy, Samuel Howell, William Lowry, Arthur Davis, Geo. Lindsey, Benjamin Gray, Hardy Hooker, George Briley, John Knotts, Sr., Kinchem Martin, Daniel Gould, R. Farr, Thomas Thomas, Garrett Watts, James Bennett, Shadrack Denson, Wm. Lindsey, Benj. Vanderford, Jno. Evans, Hezekiah Hough, Geo. Dodd, William Dinkins, Richard Ratcliff, Thomas Bailey, Jas. Benton, Abraham Lafavore, John Ingram, John Davidson, William Stansell, Wm. Phillips, Danl. Treedaway, Arthur Dudney, Daniel Murphy, Morgan Brown, Nat. Scott, Wm. Kirby, James Lowry, Will Crawford, James Brown, Isaac Jackson, John Wright, John Ingram, Joseph Dowell, J.P., Stephen Pace, J.P., Thomas Vining, Clk., William May, Sheriff, Lewis Lowry, John Johnson, James Farr, Major, Nathan Falkner, Charles Hinson, William Cox, Donald McCaskill, Thomas Lewis, Thos. Sparks, Bartholomew Murphy, William Wisdom, William Bennett, Robert Jarman, Joseph Thoms, James Liles, John Maness, Moses Hollis, Willis Hamer, Ezekiel McClendon, William Pratt, William May Jr., William Beacham, John Smith [Sandhill], Reuben Perie, Daniel Murfey, William Richardson, Jacob Bailey, Thomas Smith, Isaac Nichols, Lewis May, Bexley John Lambden, Jacob Still, James Gaines, James ------, Wm. Boggan, Williamson Plantt, George Hamans, John Birminham, James Jameson, Robt. Akens, Wm. Henry, Richard Pemberton, John Byrd, Phillip Gathings, Reuben Hildreth, George Wells, John Simson, Asa Falkner, Hollingsworth Jarman, John Preslar, Patt Boggan Sr., Thomas Wisdom, James Plunkett, William Liles, John Little, John Bellew, Marshall Digge, Peter May, Edward Lindsey, William

Phare, John Bloodworth, William Marshall, Nathan Morris, John Ricketts, Saml. Phillips, John May, John Gathings, John Downer, Jacob Morris, John Booth Sr., David Booth, John Booth Sr., Thomas Baley, Mathew Baley, Cornies Clark, John Dudney, Nathl. Denson, Jonathan Wright, Henery Watts, Reuben More, John Tomlin, Jason Morris, William Lanier, John Kerby, David Jameson J.P., Burwell Lanier, Isaac Lanier, Mathy Rushen, Wm. Robards, John Evins, Abraham Belyeu, Thomas Jinney, William Stuart, John Wright, Jr., Jas. Pickett, Chas. Sparks, Michael Crawford, Joshua Prout, Hugh_____, Thomas Talton, Elisha Kindred, John Naish, Jas. Boggan Sr., Buckner Nance, Bartholomew Chewning, Charles Reford, Joseph Ingram, Wm. Vanderford, Edward Smith.

Passed by the House Nov. 9, 1789 and by the Senate Dec. 11, 1789.

---

1. Legislative Papers, (1770) House of Commons, No. 6. Dept. of Archives and History, Raleigh, N.C.

2. This is the signature of John Smith, Sandhill, the same as in the following petition (1777), number 100. He signed, also, for his son, David Smith, who, born Oct. 9, 1753, was in his fifteenth year, but a man in size.

3. Legislative Papers, House of Commons, Nov. 20, 1777. Dept. of Archives and History, Raleigh, N. C.

4. The signature in this petition is the first preserved signature of David Smith yet found. With two others, as Commissioner of an election in Montgomery County (N. C.) Mch. 10 and 11, 1779, it identifies him as the David Smith in the Natchez Dist. (Miss.) May 1782-1790, and throughout his colorful career as pioneer and Indian fighter. The name following his is that of his brother-in-law, James Terry, of Sav. Cr.

*Dept. of Arch. and Hist., Raleigh, N. C.

5. Legislative Papers (House of Commons), February 1779. No. 22, Dept. of Archives and History, Raleigh, N. C.

6. Legislative Papers (House of Commons) Oct. 18-25, 1779. No. 24, Dept. of Archives and History, Raleigh, N. C.

7. Legislative Papers. House of Commons. Apr. 26, 1783, L. P. 47, Dept. of Archives and History, Raleigh, N. C.

8. Legislative Papers (House of Commons) Nov. 3-13, 1789. L. P. 85, Dept of Archives and History, Raleigh, N. C.

LIST OF MAJOR JAMES COTTON'S ACCTS, 1776

The claim of the Loyalist, Major James Cotton, a former Justice of Anson County, against the British Government, for his losses,[1] contains the following:

A List of outstanding debts in the Province of North Carolina due James Cotton, Esq. by bonds, notes and book accounts Febraury 1776 when the obligations and books fell into the hands of the enemy, which list was made out to the best of his knowledge, together with the help of Capt. Walter Cunningham, his assistant surveyor of land in that province, who for some time lived in his family, was well acquainted with his affairs and also the several debtors here inserted:[2]

John Adams
James Allen
James Auld
John Burcham
John Brown
John Bounds
John Blackwell
Elijah Bettis
Jacob Braveboy
Isaac Brigham
William Brigham
Benjamin Baird
John Batt Baird
Alexander Baird
Wm. Burns
Thos. Bailey
Daniel Burford
Edward Cornell
Charles Chairs
Donald Campbell
John Crosson
John Cole
George Collens
Edward Chambers
William Coleman
John Culpepper
John Chiles
James Campbell
John Dennis, Sr.

Benj. Dumas
David Dumas
Wm. Eaves
Joseph Fry, Jr.
Joseph Fry, Sr.
John Foy
John Fowler
Donald Ferguson
Lawrence Franklin
Richard Farr
James Farr
Gilbert Gibson
John Gibson
Walton Harris
John Holton
James Holtom
Thomas Hearne
Edmund Hurley
Lewis Hall
Enoch Hall
Lewis Hall, Jr.
Rice Henderson
Benj. Herron
Chas. Hynds
John Hall
Mw. Hogan
John Hornbeck
John Hornbeck, Sr.
Joseph Howell

James Hutchins
Wm. Ingram
Ann Ingram
James Jeffreys
John Jennings
Thos. Jones
Robt. Jarman
John Jones
James Knotts
George Lee
Jonathan Llewellun
Wm. Liggett
Robert Lee
William Leverett
John Leverett
David Love
Lewis Lowry
William Mask
John Morris
William Monday
Joseph Monday
Malcolm Morrison
Hector McNeill
Murdock McCaskill
Soirle McDonald
Donald McCrimmon
Benja. Maine
Allen McSwain
Daniel McMullen
Alexander McKay
Duncan McLane
William Morgan
John McDonald
Stephen Miller
Dennis McClendon
John McClendon
Gawin Morgan
Joel McClendon
Archibald McKissack
Duncan McNichols
Benj. Odom
Edward Poore
Augustine Prestwood
Wm. Pratt

Wm. Pickett, Esq.
Joseph Rogers
Luke Robinson
Matthew Raiford
William Reeves
William Rushen
William Rory
William Rushin, Sr.
John Rushin
Thos. Reynolds
David Rushin
Ann Shider [Snider?]
Nathaniel Steed
Moses Steed
George Suggs
Horatio Suggs
James Sanders
Henley Snead
Samuel Snead
William Smith (Sandhill)
John Smith (Sandhill)
John Smith (Adjutant)
John Smith (Carpenter)
John Shrinsheer?
Charles Thompson
William Terry, Jr.
Elizabeth Fuller
Stephen Tompkins
Jacob Vanhooser
John Walker, Sr.
Sampson Williams
Thomas Williams
Nathaniel Williams
Solomon Williams
Thos. Wilson
John Wilson
Robert Webb
Richard Worrell
Moses Sanders
Aaron Sanders
James Meredith
Samuel Lock
Israel Snead
Robert Lowry

---

1. The Loyalists of N. C. during the Revolution, by Robert O. Demond, page 207. Major James Cotton's claim £ 11,241. He received £ 2,032.
2. Transcripts of English Records of N. C. the James Cotton Papers, Dept. of Archives and History, Raleigh, N. C.

MONTGOMERY COUNTY RECORDS*[1]

MONTGOMERY COUNTY, MISC. PAPERS.[2]

Montgomery County, December Session 1785.

Will of John Simmons, decd., produced by Jacob Humble; Elizabeth Simmons and John Simmons qualify as exrs.

Will of John Simmons, of Anson Co., N.C. 7 Dec. 1775; sick; eldest son Benj/; son William part of land whereon I now live, and provided he will stay with his mother one year after my death, my bay stallion for his service in assisting to bring up the younger children for that space of time; son James, land and provided he stay with his mother until 21 years old a young bay horse; but if he refuses, the said land and horse to be equally divided among children at time of my wife's marriage or death; my five daughters, Dinah, Elizabeth, Sarah, Mary and Margaret. Wife, Elizabeth, and son Benjamin exrs. Wit: Jacob Humble, James Cotton.

Inventory exhibited.

April Session, 1799. James Watkins applies for pay as witness in behalf of State vs Edmond Thomas in the Superior Court, (no date stated)..
1th April 1799.   John Davidson, clk.

On Back: Recd. £10 2 sh for use of James Watkins,   L. Bean
June 5, 1799

****

Returns of probates of will and admr. Secy. of State. 1753-1790.

Montgomery County, September Term, 1782.

Letters of Admr. on est. of Aaron Sanders, decd., granted William Miller. Sec: Mark Allen, Esq. and John Hopkins, for £100.
Rec: 12 Nov. 1782. Bk. A. folio 19.
     George Davidson, clk.

Adm. on est. of Lenard Thomas, decd., gr. to Bedenago Moore, with Joseph Moore and Thomas Ward sec. for £200.

Rec:Bk. A. folio 16.   Geo. Davidson, clk.
Nov. 11, 1782.

Adm. gr., to Thos. Wade on est. of William Going, decd., with Joseph Moore and Bedenago Moore sec.   Geo. Davidson, clk.
Rec:Nov. 12, 1782,
Bk. A. folio 18.

Montgomery County Petition, 1788.

(November 1788)
To the Honorable Speakers and Gentlemen of the General Assembly, the Petition of Parte of the Inhabitants of Montgomery County Humbly sheweth that they live very remote from.the Courthouse of sd county, some not less than forty miles and the Peedee River to cross which is sometimes impassable and renders it very difficult and inconvenient to perform the duties incident to a court. Your petitioners further shew that many of them have not more than half the distance to go to Richmond County court and better roads and no waters to interrupt therefore most humbly pray your honours to Pass an act to annex your Petitioners to Richmond County by a line to be run from Coleson's ferry landing on Peedee River direct to the head of Drowning Creek and all that part of Montgomery county east of said line to be annexed to Richmond County and your petitioners in duty bound will ever Pray:

Wm. Mask, John Mask Jr., Christopher Touchstone, Stith Pemberton, Jno. Jennings, Charles Travers, Henry Travers, Alexander Baird, Edmund Singleton, William LeGrand, John Boyd, George Clark Jr., Samuel Clark, Samuel Scott, Thos. Blake, Richard Leverett, Wm. Leverett, Jas. Turner, Thomas Powell, John McAullay, John Kimbrough, Nicholas Christian, David Ussery, George Clark Sen., Jesse Jones, John Wilkinson, William Powell, Isaac Armstrong, Daniel Frazer, Daniel Baton, William Frazer, Dugald McMullin, Williams Edens, John Frazer, Duncan McLain, Ed Chambers Sr., Ed. Chambers, Peter Ussery, Welcom Ussery, Robert Leverett, Cornelius Robinson, John Chambers

House of Commons, Nov. 10, 1788. Bill to annex part of County of Montgomery to Richmond County. Sheriff of Montgomery to collect taxes now due. Commissioners to run dividing line: Cornelius Robinson, James Turner, James Ussery, Dudley Mask and James Smith. Passed. Passed by the Senate 11 Nov. 1788.

****

Will of Christopher Christian, of Montgomery County, Nov. 29, 1781. March Court 1783. Children: John, James, Patty and Lucy. Friend, Patty Colly. Exrs: John Mack [Mask], Nicholas Christian, William Mack [Mask]; wit: Christopher Christian, Drury Collier, Thomas Bullock. Clerk of Court: Geo. Davidson. Page 427, North Carolina Wills by J. Bryan Grimes.

****

Legislative Papers. Tax Lists. 1780-1782 Montgomery County, 1782.

John Almond, Invalid, 100 ac.
James Almond, 250 acres.
Joseph Allen, Invalid, 100 ac.
William Allen..........
Isaac Armstrong... 500 acres
Charles Allen, Invalid 100 a
Spencer Altom [Alton] 400 ac.
Isaac Allen... 200 acres 7 sl.
Mark Allen Esq. 2900 a, 2 sl.
Bryant Austin..........
Alexander Baird, 225 a, 7 sl.
Daniel Baton..........
Anguish Baton..........
James Bolton, 400 acres
Joseph Burcham, invalid.....
Ezekiel B. Brook, 600 acres
James Butler, 250 acres
Thos. Butler, Esq. inv. .....
Joshua Butler, 200 acres...
Elias Butler, inv.
John Butler, 100 acres...
Sias Billingsley, 800 acres
John Ballard, 200 acres
Patty Bradford..........
Randle Blake, single, 200 a...
Sollomon Bennett, 50 a, 1 sl.
Drury Bennett..........
John Baker, 122 a, 10 sl. ..
William Ballard, invalid...
Mark Bennett, invalid, 300 a...
Humphrey Ballard, inv. 411 a.
Richard Bean..........

Nathl. Bell, 100 acres...
James Bond, 150 a, 4 slaves
Joseph Bell, 500 acres...
John Bell, single.....
Richard Bell single.....
Walter Bean, unjuror ( )200a.
Daniel Bankston, 150 a, 4 sl.
Lawrence Bankston 200 acres...
Samuel Boyd 400 acres
John Bolling, inv. 400a, 3 sl.
Wm. Brooks, 750 a (100a Ans.) 5 sl.
Ann Bankston, 100 acres...
Isaac Burleson..........
David Bryant, 50 acres
John Brooks, Sr., inv. 150 a, 1 sl.
Joseph Bowen, invalid
Samuel Bowen..........
John Brooks, Jr. 900 a (100 An.) 4 sl.
Andrew Bankston, 150 acres
Peter Bankston, invalid, 100 acres
John Brooks, Va., invalid, 3 sl.
Robert Bailey, single, 2 slaves
Edward Chambers, Inv. 500 a, 2 sl.
Edward Chambers Jr..........
Thomas Chiles 870 acres 7 sl.
Nicholas Christian 1000 a, 1 sl.
Thomas Crocker..........
Jesse Christian, invalid, 100 a
Drury Colliar, 6 slaves
Christopher Christian, inv. 1450 a, s sl.
James Crump 860 a, 9 sl.
John Crump, Esq. 250 a, 5 sl.
George Colly, invalid..........
John Curtis 100 acres
Samuel T. Clemmons 100 acres
Christopher Chapel 260 acres
John Cope, invalid, 200 acres
Moses Curtis, single.....
Rusel Curtis, single.....
Daniel Cato, 150 acres...
Thos. Chester, inv. 175 ac.
John Calloway 400 acres
Thomas Cope..........
Samuel Carter..........
Milly Coker..........
Ephraim Carter..........
Isaac Calloway
John Cheek, Sr. Inv. 1182 a, 200 a, in Anson.
Joshua Carter, Inv. 1700 a
Job Calloway, 1060 a, 5 sl.
John Cooper, inv. 100 acres
Thomas Crain Inv. 100 acres
George Crewets invalid.....
Jonathan Carpenter 500 acres
John Cheek Jr. 150 acres
Daniel Culpeper 75 acres

Randle [Randolph] Cheek, inv. 300 a
Wm. Culpeper, inv. 300 acres
Daniel Duglass, inv. 50 acres
Richard Dunn..........
Richard Downs, inv. 200 acres
Thomas Dennis, 100 acres
Henry Debery 421 acres
Sarah Duglas..........
Sarah Dudley 500 acres
David Dumas, inv. 2563 a, 11 sl.
Ford DeJarnett single 1 sl.
Andrew Dennis inv. 150 acres
Allen Dennis single..........
Geo. Davidson 100 a (250 An.) 8 sl.
Gabriel Davis..........
Nathaniel Davis, 75 acres...
Williamson Cope.....
Jacob Carter 250 acres
Charles Carter 150 acres
William Carter..........
Thos. Durham 1010 acres, 1 slave
Nathaniel Dennis..........
William Daniel, invalid 50 acres
Bartin Daniel, invalid, 150 acres
Paul Daniel. ....
Ambrose Edwards, 100 acres, 1 sl.
John Edwards, 330 a., 2 sl.
Nathaniel Edwards.....1 slave
Philemon Edwards..... 300 acres
William Earles 250 acres
William Ellis 100 acres, 1 sl.
William Frazer, invalid, 750 acres
Mary Faircloth 300 acres 2 slaves
Thomas Fry, invalid 200 acres
James Frey, invalid 150 acres
Luky Frey. ....
George Frey..........
Thos. Frey, un-juror...100 acres
Joseph Frey, un-juror 600 acres
Joseph Frey, Sr. un-juror.....
Hartwell Freeman, 100 acres
James Frey, un-juror
Lawrence Fox.....
James Fletcher, Esq. 415 acres 1 slave
James Gibson,
William Gibson, invalid, 400 acres
Thomas Gower, invalid, 400 acres
John Gowers, 250 acres
William Gainer 100 acres
Richard Green 350 acres
Alexander Goodwin, invalid. .....
George Goodwin 600 acres
Lenard Green 350 acres
James Gray, invalid, 250 acres
John Gilbert, invalid 195 acres
Jesse Gilbert, ...

Richard Green 640 acres
Daniel Hix 100 acres
Nathan Howard, invalid, 100 acres
William Hollam, Jr. 150 acres, 2 slaves
Mary Hunt 100 acres
Addery Hix 150 acres
John Hill 630 acres, 1 slave
Jacob Hamble 600 acres, 1 slave
William Holton, Sr., invalid, 100 acres, 2 slaves
Ethelred Harris..........
Jesse Harris 300 acres, 2 slaves
Majr. West Harris 88 acres, 3 slaves
Abraham Forrest 250 acres 14 slaves
Brantly Harris 200 acres
John Harris 400 acres
Turner Harris, invalid, 250 acres
West Harris, Sr., 740 acres, 15 slaves
Roland Harris, 139 acres, 1 slave
Arthur Harris, single 60 acres, 1 slave
Parnal Hearn 100 acres, 1 slave
Arthur Harris single 250 acres 1 slave
Edmond Hurly
Thomas Hearn, un-juror, 200 acres 2 slaves
Richard Hopkins
Stephen Hearn, single
Gerner High 100 acres
Matthew Herrill, invalid 100 acres
John Haglet, Jr.
Joseph Henderson, invalid, 516 acres 5 slaves
Reuben Hollyness 275 acres
Bartin Hannon 150 acres
Peter Hamblett, invalid, 100 acres
John Hannon
John Hagler, Sr. invalid, 600 acres
Capt. West Harris 450 acres, 1 slave
James Howell, invalid, 100 acres
Benj. Hathcock..........
John Hall 350 acres
William Hamby.....
Anthony Holland, invalid...
Sarah Hildreth
William Hildreth
Shadrack Hogan, Esq. invalid 1850 acres
James Hearn 300 acres
Reuben Hildreth single 299 acres
John English..........
Francis Jordan 280 acres
John Jordan 50 acres
Joseph Inglish 100 acres
John Jones, invalid, 100 acres 6 slaves
John Hamblett 140 acres
Joshua Hearn 300 acres
William Jordin, invalid 50 acres
Isaac Jones..........
Henry Jacobs, invalid, 100 acres
James Jeffery, invalid, 1 slave

John Johnson, invalid, 130 acres
James Johnson, invalid, ...
Peter Jackson.....
Cornelius Inglish ...
Charles _____, invalid, 150 acres
John Jordan, 200 acres, 2 slaves
Charles Jones, 200 acres, 2 slaves
John Jennings, invalid, 300 acres, 6 slaves
William Jackson, single..........
Thomas Giles..........
William Irby, invalid, 400 acres
William Irby, Jr., ...150 acres
Ann Jefferys, 350 acres, 1 slave
John Kimbrough, 1235 acres, 24 slaves
George Kerk, 1300 acres, 6 slaves
Samuel Kelly, invalid..........
William Kindle, invalid, 100 acres
William Knap, 100 acres
Robert Leverett, invalid, 600 acres
Thomas Laws..........
Richard Leverett 200 acres, 1 slave
John Lightfoot 150 acres 1 slave
Philip Linch, single, 100 acres
Col. Wm. Loftin 920 acres, 15 slaves
Wm. Lacy..........
Zedekiah Ledbetter, invalid, 50 acres, 2 slaves
Drury Ledbetter, 720 acres, 10 slaves
Edmond Lilly, invalid, 1450, 23 slaves
Charles Ledbetter, invalid, 560 acres, 15 slaves
James Lee, 200 acres
John Lawson.....
John Lilly, 300 acres, 2 slaves
Jesse Lanier, 1 slave
Elizabeth Landram, 100 acres
Benj. Lilly, single..........
William Mask, 1850 acres, 9 slaves
Daniel McKincy..........
Malcom MaCaffee, 50 acres
Daniel McClou, invalid, 150 acres
Daniel McCloud, invalid, 50 acres
John McDonald, invalid..........
John Mareskau, invalid, 100 acres
Dunkin McCloud, invalid, 100 acres
John MaCaffee, 50 acres
John Morrison, invalid
Swain McKinclock
Malcom McCloud, invalid...
Anguish McCally 150 acres
John Martain, 100 acres
John McColly, Jr. 50 acres
John McCowly, invalid, 100 acres
Daniel McDonald, 50 acres
Daniel Mathews..........
Thomas McClendon..........
Jeremiah Manesco..........
Mark McClintock..........

Joel McClendon, Esq. 95 acres, 1 slave
Edward Morris..........
Mary McCray........
Inny McCloud..........
Collon McCray, 400 acres
Massey Morgin, 500 acres
Thos. Megginson, 200 acres, 3 slaves
Nancy McCray..........
Alexander McDonald, single.....
Bedenago Moore, 200 acres
John Morris, 200 acres
Isaac McClendon, single, 400 acres
Henry Mounger, 703 acres, 4 slaves
Joseph LcLester, 680 acres
Ezekiel McClendon, 100 acres
John Martain, invalid, 150 acres
Charles Merriman, invalid, 100 acres
William McGreger, 500 acres
Robert Moss. Esq., 388 acres, 5 slaves
William Matheny..........
Jesse McClendon, Esq., 3117 acres, 4 slaves
Aron Mathany, 65 acres
Aman McMillan, 100 acres
Dunkin McCray, 100 acres
Francis Mabery, invalid, 100 acres
Joel McClendon, 75 acres, 9 slaves
Michael Moore, invalid, 300 acres
Daniel Nichols, invalid.....
William Nickols, 200 acres
Edmond Nickols, invalid, 200 acres
John Nickols, 100 acres
David Nobles..........
William Nobles, invalid, 1600 acres, 1 slave
William Nobles, Jr., single, 400 acres
Simpson Nobel, single,
Thomas Nobel, single, 250 acres
Sarah Naron, 300 acres, 3 slaves
William Oziar, invalid, 200 acres
Patty Pond, 400 acres, 1 slave
Benjamin Phillips..........
Richard Powell, 425 acres
John Powell, invalid, 400 acres
David Poore, 200 acres
John Persons, 130 acres
Samuel Persons, invalid, 400 acres, 2 slaves
Nathan Powell, single, invalid, wounded, 100 acres
John Pore, 100 acres
Anthony Mills Parrott, invalid
Cary Pritchard, 665 acres, 3 slaves
Arthur Perce, invalid
Nicholas Parker, single..........
Richard Parker, single, 150 acres
Howell Parker, 200 acres, 4 slaves
Alexander Pool, 100 acres
Henry Powel 58 acres
John Poplin, 250 acres

Robert Pilcher, 200 acres
Thomas Pollard, invalid, 200 acres
Lewis Phillips, 320 acres
Timothy Queen, 100 acres
Luke Robeson, invalid, 1117 avres, 1 slave
Mathew Raiford, Sr., invalid, 200 acres, 1 slave
James Raiford, single, 200 acres
James Ronalds, invalid, 200 acres
Cornelius Roberson, 2006 acres, 11 slaves
John Randolph..........
Benj. Randolph, 125 acres
Mathew Raeford, Jr., 300 acres
William Reves, invalid.....
John Rone, invalid...100 acres
Samuel Reves, 150 acres
Josias Reves, 250 acres
John Riddle, invalid.....
James Rusell, 100 acres
Adam Roan, invalid, 150 acres
George Ramage Jr., 200 acres
Edmond Randle, 136 acres
William Rice, invalid, 250 acres
Richard Randle, 190 acres, 2 slaves
Josias Randle, invalid, 200 acres
Capt. John Randle 700 acres, 3 slaves
Colby Randle, 400 acres, 1 slave
William Roberds, 460 acres, 6 slaves
Samuel Rogers, 100 acres
George Ramage, invalid, 110 acres
Peter Randle, 190 acres, 11 slaves
John Randle Jr., 200 acres, 6 slaves
Henry Road, 311 acres
Augustus Roland, invalid, 200 acres
Sherwood Roland, 200 acres
John Robins, invalid, 100 acres, 3 slaves
Hacia Roland.....
John Rogers.....
Tyree Roberson, invalid, 400 acres
Richard Roland 323 acres
Richard Renolds, 200 acres, 7 slaves
Thomas Renalds, invalid, 100 acres, 7 slaves
James Roland, 100 acres
George Roland, invalid, 100 acres, 1 slave
John Sewell, 200 acres
John Swor, 500 acres
Benj. Sumner, 200 acres
John Smith L.R., invalid, 100 acres
William Smith, 100 acres
William Sewell.....
Charles Sewell.....
Benjamin Simmons, 175 acres
John Smith S.H., invalid, 1300 acres
John Sewell.....
John Stagner, single. .....
John Stevens, invalid, 200 acres
Rasha Siggs, invalid, 200 acres

Joseph Stacy, 100 acres
Job Self.....
Ruth Smith..........
John Shepperd, invalid, 350 acres
Harberd Suggs, invalid, 600 acres, 1 slave
Drury Sims, invalid, 260 acres
William Stewart, 200 acres
James Suton..........
James Sanders, invalid, 100 acres
Moses Steed, 3113 acres, 7 slaves
Isaac Sanders, invalid, 200 acres
Nathaniel Steed, 430 acres, 6 slaves
George Sanders, unjuror, 100 acres
Samuel Swearingen, invalid, 150 acres
Thomas Simpson, invalid, 196 acres
Jacob Shankell, 150 acres
Gilbert Simpson, 48 acres
Van Swaringen, 100 acres
Robert Spears, 200 acres
George Shankle, invalid, 300 acres
John Shankell, 850 acres
John Swearingen, 75 acres, 1 slave
Henry Stoke, invalid, 610 acres
Joseph Tarbutton, invalid, 175 acres
William Trent, 100 acres
Caleb Touchstone, invalid, 500 acres, 1 slave
Jesse Tillis, 150 acres
Lucy Taylor..........
Joseph Tarbutton Jr., 100 acres
John Thompson, 250 acres
Richard Tilman, 500 acres
George Tucker, 200 acres
Thomas Tallent, invalid. .....
John Taylor, 150 acres
Chas. Travers, 150 acres
James Tindle, 900 acres, 10 slaves
Stephen Treadwell, 100 acres
William Taylor, invalid, 300 acres, 1 slave
Henry Tally, 40 acres
James Trull..........
Nimrod Taylor, 100 acres, 1 slave
Edmond Tayler, 130 acres
William Ussery, 250 acres
John Ussery Sr., 300 acres
Thos. Ussery, Esq., 240 acres, 3 slaves
Elizabeth Tillis, 150 acres
Eliz. Ussery, 500 acres
Joshua Ussery, 300 acres
David Ussery..........
Valentine Vanhooser, 750 acres
Joseph Vickory, 100 acres
Jacob Vanhooser, 200 acres, 4 slaves
Thomas VanDike, 200 acres
John Wright, invalid, 250 acres
William Wooley..........
Jesse Wallice, 200 acres

MONTGOMERY CO. LAND ENTRIES 147

Thomas Ward, Sr., Invalid, 200 acres
Thomas Ward, invalid.....
John Ward..........
Solomon Williams, invalid, 300 acres
Stephen Williams..........
Seth Williams, 450 acres, 4 slaves
Isham Williams, 400 acres, 2 slaves
Mary Whitehead, 200 acres
William Wever, 100 acres
Samuel Williams, 600 acres
Roger Williams..........
Ewel Watkings, invalid, 100 acres
William Williams, single, 100 acres, 6 slaves
Josias Wright..........
William Wright..........
John Wray..........

Peter Ware, invalid, 150 acres
Thos. Ware, 2 slaves
Roland Ware, single.....
George Whitly, invalid, 200 acres
Exodus Whitly, 100 acres
George Whitly, Jr., 100 acres
Moses Wimbly, 100 acres
Edward Young, invalid, 750 acres

Persons subject to two-fold tax:
John McCaskil
Malcom Furguson

by George Davidson, Clerk of Court.
25 November, 1782.

---

*1. See Preface.
2. SS 884. Department of Archives and History, Raleigh, N. C.
3. Legislative Papers. House of Commons. Nov. 3-15, 1788. L. P. 80. Dept. of Archives and History, Raleigh, N. C.
4. Legislative Papers. L. P. 46. 1, Dept. of Arch. and Hist., Raleigh, N. C.

MONTGOMERY CO. LAND ENTRIES*

Benjamin Baird, entry-taker. 1779

Apr. 6--George Gooding, 150 a SWPD, Jacob's Cr, adj. John Swaringhams.
Apr. 6--John Randle, 150 a SWPD adj Sarah Suggs
Apr. 6--Bryant Whitfield, 300a Salisbury Road adj Wm. Taylor.
Apr. 6--Needham Whitfield, 640a Salisbury Road adj Wm. Colson.
Apr. 6--William Whitfield, 300a adj. Wm. Hildreth.
Apr. 6--John Heritage, 640a on head of Cattail Br. and Cedar.
Apr. 6--Josias Wright 100a adj. Chas. Bellus, Joseph McClesters and James Farr.
Apr. 7--Reuben Clanton, 250a adj. Wm. Annton.
Apr. 7--Henry Mounger, Esq.... out.
Apr. 7--John Bagsdale, 100a est of Uwhary Riv. by James Cotton.
Apr. 7--David Pennington, 200a adj. Peter Bankston.
Apr. 7--Cary Prichard, 100a adj. Drury Collier.
Apr. 10--James Whitfield, 100a Timothy Br.
Apr. 10--John Allen, Esq. 640a Island Cr. of Rocky Riv. adj. Philip Self.

Apr. 12--Blake Bryant, 300a adj. Solomon Gross on Thickety Cr.
Apr. 12--Drury Collier, 50a east of the Mt. s. side of Woodin Cr.
Apr. 14--Arthur Taylor, 50a on Big Cr. of Little River.
Apr. 14--William Gibson,___Br of Cedar Cr, inc. improv. where he lives
Apr. 14--Joshua Butler, 50 a same as above.
Apr. 14--William Mask, Esq. 200a adj. Blake.
Apr. 16--James Butler 100a Cedar Cr. inc. own improvement.
Apr. 16--Jesse Walles 50a Cedar Cr. inc. land where he now lives.
Apr. 17--Tabatha Bostick near Hamor's Cr.
Apr. 17--John Gower, 50a on Big Cr.
Apr. 17--Thomas Tower, 100a below mouth of Long Br. of Drowning Cr.
Apr. 21--John Johnson,___Middle Cr. SWPD adj. Elijah Ham.
Apr. 24--Caleb Touchstone, 100a on waters of Cheek Cr. inc. Frazer's improvement where he lived.

MONTGOMERY CO. LAND ENTRIES

Apr. 24--Thomas Stanback 100a on waters of Creek's Cr. inc. imp. George Lamd Lived.
Apr. 26--Josias Randle, 75a adj. McCulloch, Johnson and Meredith.
Apr. 26--John McCaskel, 50a adj. Murdock McKimon's line.
Apr. 26--Daniel Duglas
Apr. 29--Arthur Tayler, 50a on Riggs Cr. waters of Little River.
Apr. 30--Christopher Butler 100a

1779
May 5--William Griffin Hogan, 100a on water of PD and Rocky River, own line and James Roper's.
May 13--Valentine Vanhooser, 100a
May 13--John Vanhooser, 50a adj. own line.
May 20--Edward Young 600a NE Yadkin, adj. Wm. Hamilton.
May 21--Joe McClendon, 400a adj. Little River near Wm. Spencer.
June 7--Edmond Taylor, 50a
June 24--Benjamin Baird (out) 100a adj. Shadrack Hogan and Swearingen's.

June 24--William Rush, 200a Thickety Cr.
June 28--Going Morgan, 50a adj. Alex. Poole.

1779
Sept. 28--Benj. Baird, 100a Long Cr.
Sept. 28--Elenor Baird 150a Lick Br of Jacob's Cr. waters of PD.
Sept. 28--Ann Baird, 100a Long Cr. near Little Bear Cr. imp. formerly Joseph Howell's

1779
Sept. 28--Patsy Baird, 100a Clover Fork bet. James Ham's and Thos. Spear's inc. his improvement.
Oct. 1--Benj. Baird, 100a adj. John Carpenter's old survey on Cabbin Cr.
Nov. 10--John Smith, S.H. 100a adj. Samuel Williams, Thos. Wilson's inc. Sam'l Swearingen's improvement.

1780
Jany. 8--John Smith, Sandhill, 100a at head of Big Cr. on Crawford's Road.
Mch. 11--William Baird 200a Long Cr., inc. Andrew Bankston's imp.

****

---
*1. Dept. of Archives and History, Raleigh, N. C.

RICHMOND COUNTY RECORDS

DEEDS

Deed Book B, page 10. 22 Oct. 1783. William Robards, of Montgomery County, to John Cole, of Richmond County, for £5, 200 acres, in Cumberland County, on both sides of Drowning Cr. at a place called old pine ford, granted Wm. Roberts,[1] father of grantor, dated 1 July, 1758.
Wit: James Terry   Signed William Robards
    Ann Terry   Proved in June Session 1784
                                by James Terry.

Deed Bk. B, page 14. 8 Dec. 1783. William Ashley to Sampson Sellers...
Wit: Benj. Baird, Miche Bierd,
    Alexr. McCay

Deed Bk. B, page 28. 31 Dec. 1784. Solomon Gross of Richmond Co. to John Dejernett, of Anson, for £80; one-third part of a tract of 460 acres, formerly the property of James Hutchins, which was conveyed by John Leverett and Elizabeth, his wife, to Solomon Gross, as her dower and so laid out.
Wit: Wm. Love   December Court 1784.
    John Pemberton

Bk. B, page 29. River Jordan to Henry William Harrington.

Bk. B, page 70. 15 Nov. 1783. Edward Smith to John Ezell, both of Richmond Co., for £65, part of 300 acres gr. to Benj. Maner, 21 Oct. 1758 and conveyed by him to Smith.
Wit: Robert Webb, James Cammill

Bk. B, page 108. 27 May 1783. Mathew Terry, of Bladen Co., to William Terry, of Richmond Co., for £150, 200 acres on an upper branch of Hitchcock's Creek.
Wit: Benj. Ingram   April Court, 1786
    J. Pickett

Bk. B, page 314. 10 Oct. 1789. Moses Hurley of Richmond Co. to James Terry, of town of Rockingham; for £75; 120 acres near Richard Bradford's line.   Oct. Ct. 1789,
Wit: John Cole   prov. by John Cole, Sr.,
    Robert Raiford   Wm. Love, clk.

Bk. B, page 316. 19 Jany. 1788. The Commissioners of Rockingham to James Terry, lots 26 and 29, nearly one-half acres each, in the Town of Rockingham.   Signed Robert Webb
Wit: Wm. Johnson   John Cole
    Jesse Bounds   Henry Wm. Harrington

Bk. B, p. 317. 15 July 1777. Zachariah Smith[2] and Frances his wife, to Samuel Usher, all of Anson Co.; for £190; three tracts east of Little River... adj. James Jowers,...Wm. McDaniel...signed by both.
Wit: Joseph Hines, Thomas Gowers

Bk. C, p. 348. 5 Oct. 1789. James Pickett, of Anson, to James Terry, of Rockingham, for £200, 140 acres in Richmond County on east side of Hitchcock's Creek, supposed to be Thomas Stafford Williams' corner, part of a tract granted Richard Bradford 15 March 1756, by deed to James Pickett; now to James Terry.
Wit: Wm. Robinson   Prov. Richmond Co.
    Tod Robinson   Oct. Ct. 1789
                        by Wm. Robinson.

---

1. 18 Nov. 1760, William Robards, Sr. of Cumberland Co. made gift deeds, in the nature of a will, to his four children, William, Mary, Sarah and Ann, which were proved Nov. Ct. 1760. Cumb. Co. Deed Bk 1, pp 282-3. Ann, who m. 24 Jany. 1771 James Terry, son of William and Mary (Raiford) Terry, was born 13 Feb. 1756. (Family Bible) William, Jr. was younger. He came into court (Anson Co.) 14 Oct. 1774 and chose James Terry as guardian. Mourning (Raiford) Robards, the wid. of Wm. Robards Sr. m. (2) William Pickett of Anson Co.

2. Zacheriah Smith was born 19 Apr. 1734; m. Frances — b. 27 Mch. 1741; moved from Anson Co. to S.C. and was in the Natchez Dist., West Fla. (Mississippi), in the Spanish census of 1792. Ref: Mrs. Hugh M. Rush (Alma McKay), a desc.

Bk. C, p. 683. 14 May 1797, Edwin Ingram and James Pickett both of Richmond County, to Alex. McRae; for £ 35; parts of two tracts, one surveyed for Simon Hooker; the other for Edwin Ingram, 60 acres. Ack. July Session 1797.
Wit: James Terry Tod Robinson, dep. clk.
R. I. Steel James Terry,³ clk.

Bk. C, p. 254. 27 Oct. 1777, Micajor Pickett, of S.C. to William Pickett, of Anson Co.; for £60, land in Anson, ne of Peedee, adj. Henry Hargett, 100 acres.
Wit: John Lewis Proved by J. Pickett,
Francis Lewis June Court, 1783,
J. Pickett Wm. Love, clk.

Bk. C, p. 524. 7 Nov. 1795. Wm. and Toddy Robinson, of Richmond Co. to James Terry, Sr., of same, for £ 250, Lot #25, with all houses, barn, etc. Jany. Session 1796,
Wit: Eli Terry Tod Robinson Clerk for
Wat Leak J. Terry, clk.

Bk. C, p. 351. James Paterson, of Richmond, to James Terry, of Anson, Nov. 17, 1787; for £35; 74 acres on east side of Hitchcock Cr. at Thos. Stafford Williams 3rd line, adj. John Bounds, John Tate?
Wit: Mathew Terry Prov. Oct. Ct. 1789
James Curry by James Curry.

Bk. C, p. 474. John Cole, Sheriff, to William Robards, 18 Sept. 1795. Whereas Mourning Pickett, admx. of William Pickett, decd. filed application to recover £71-6-6 agst James Pickett, heir-at-law of Wm. Pickett, who set up 10 lots in Rockingham April Session 1795; sells same at public sale 30 May 1795; William Robards highest bidder on lot #31, £ 3-15. Oct. Session 1795.
Wit: W. Terry John Macalester, D.C.
Moses Chambers for James Terry, Clk.

p. 520. James Terry Sr. highest bidder for Lot #22 at above sale, for £ 5.
Wit: Tod Robinson 8 Jany. 1796.
Eli Terry

Bk. C, p. 323. 14 Nov. 1794. James Terry to Eli Terry, his son, both of Richmond County, for love and affection, Lot #29 in Rockingham and negro boy named London.
Wit: Tod. Robinson, Jany. Ct. 1795.
Peter H. Cole, James Long

Bk. C, p. 417. 14 Nov. 1794. James Terry to William Terry, his son, both of Richmond County, for love and affection, Lot #26 in Rockingham and negro boy named Tom. Same wit. as in above deed. Jany. Session 1795.

Bk. C, p. 878. 10 Dec. 1798. William Terry to James Terry, his son, for 5 sh. two surveys, 30 June 1797 and 22 December 1770.
Wit: Mathew Terry, Thomas Covington

Bk. C, p. 909. 7 Jany. 1799. Wm. Terry to Champ Terry, his son, for 5 sh. parts of two tracts, one surveyed for Wm. Terry 5 Feb. 1754, the other 22 Dec. 1770, lower side of Hitchcock Cr.
Wit: John Bounds, John Denson

Bk. F, p. 128. 22 Jany. 1802. Toddy Roberson, of Anson, to Mourning Pickett, for $20, Lot #20 in Rockingham.
Wit: Wat. Leak, Wm. Robards

Bk. F, p. 210. 17 Apr. 1802. Eli Terry, of Richmond Co., to Martin Pickett, of Anson, Lot #11 in Rockingham, for £10.
Wit: James Pickett Ack. June Session,
Eli Terry, Clk.

---

3. This is prob. James Terry formerly of Savannah Cr. Anson Co. who mov. to Richmond Co. after 17 Nov. 1787. Tod Robinson was his son-in-law, who m. 8 Mch. 1792, his dau. Martha Ann Terry. (Fam. Bib.)

4. Eli Terry, the son of James and Ann (Robards) Terry married 17 Dec. 1799 Polly Pickett, who was, no doubt, the dau. of James and Sarah (Kimbrough) Pickett (see note 6), and moved to Alabama with or shortly after his bro-in-law, Tod Robinson, and their cousin, Wm. R. Pickett. He d. in Autauga Co. Ala. His will, (Prob. Report, Vol. 3, p. 344) 15 Feb. 1836 - 24 Oct. 1838; wife Mary A., sons, James P. decd, William P., Tod R., John K., and Walter (a minor); daus. Mary, w. of Benj. W. Saxon, Ann w. of Christopher Hicks & Appia; gr. dau. Martha, dau. of son Eli, decd; exrs, Benj. W. Saxon, Christopher Hicks and Walter Terry.

5. William Terry, son of James and Ann (Robards) Terry, lived for a time in Old Sneedsboro, Anson Co, then in Cumberland Co. and later moved to Alabama. He was a Methodist minister and died in Autauga Co., Ala. at the home of his bro-in-law, Tod Robinson. (Montgomery (Ala) Journal, Apr. 1828.)

Bk. L, p. 60. 17 Aug. 1813, James Pickett, of Richmond Co. to Benj. Covington, of same, for $200, land on Mt. Cr., adj. Roper.
Wit: Eli Terry Prov. by Eli Terry,
Jane Cole Dec. Term 1817,
Martin D. Crawford, clk

Bk. L, p. 465. 10 Feb. 1821. Eli Terry to William Smith, both of Richmond Co. for $12.00, 37 1/2 acres on north side of Hitchcock's Cr. adj. Wall, gr. James Terry 14 Nov. 1804. Signed in the presence of James Pickett.
Jany. Term 1822 prov. by James Pickett.

Bk. L, p. 527, 8 Jany. 1805. Walter Leak and James Pickett, executors of Solomon Strother, to James Coleman, of Anson Co.; for $1260.
Wit: Eli Terry Ack. by Walter Leak and
Daniel McSwain Jam. Pickett, Sept. 17, 1822, F. Nash, clk.

Bk. C, p. 398. 9 July 1792. Nicholas Christian and wife, Sarah, of Montgomery County, to James Smith, Little River, of Richmond, for £400, 500 acres gr. to John Ashley, Nov. 22, 1746, east of Little River.
Wit: Jas. Turner, M. L. Grand

Bk. I, p. 105. 25 July 1812. Mathew Raiford, Sen., of Baldwin County, Mississippi Ter., power of atty. to son, Mathew Raiford, Jr., of Baldwin County, to transact all my business in N.C.
Wit: Pleasant Mask
James Powell
Prov. by James Powell before Daniel Johnston, J.P., Baldwin County; recorded Bk. A, p. 37. Prov. in Richmond County, Dec. 1814, by Pleasant Mask.

Bk. L, p. 121. 8 Nov. 1814. Mathew Raiford, of Baldwin County, Miss. Ter. to Thos. Steel, for $120, 52 1/2 acres in Richmond Co. at the foot of Cheek's Mountain... Mathew Raiford 'Sr.'s 3rd line..

Wit: Robt. I. Street (Steel?) Jr.
James Raiford Ack. in court Dec. 1814.

Bk. R, p. 29. Montgomery County. 6 July 1841. George Shankle and Oney, his wife, for $10.00, to Robert and Zedekiah Raiford the right of dower of Oney Shankle in lands of her former husband, James Raiford, both in Montgomery and Richmond Cos.
Wit: A. Little

Bk. N, p. 243. 11 Jany. 1822. Thomas Coleman, of Anson, atty. for James Coleman, Sr. of Alabama, quit claim deed to Robt. Steele, to a certain tract in Richmond Co.
Wit: Wm. F. Morton, Christian Charton

Bk. L, p. 343. Mourning Coleman, of Richmond County, for nat. good will and affection, to beloved granddaughter, Mourning Coleman, infant daughter of James Coleman, of same, all and singular my goods and chattles following: one negro woman named Pheby, one negro girl named Sally, one bed and furniture, to have and hold after my decease, together with the increase of the above slaves. Jany. 1, 1796.
Wit: James Coleman
James Pickett, Sr.
Richmond County, Jany. Session 1821. Col. Joseph Pickett came into court and made oath that he was acquainted with the handwriting of James Pickett and James Coleman, the subscribing witnesses to the within instrument and that James Pickett was dead and that James Coleman hath removed to Alabama and their signatures were their proper writing.

Bk. L, p. 298. 21 Feb. 1801. James Coleman to Gilbert Gibson, both of Richmond, for $200, land bet. Rockingham and Falling Creek.
Wit: Wat. Leak Prov. by Walter Leak
Moses Knight July Term. 1820.

MARRIAGE BONDS

William Baird and Eliz. Bostick, Mch. 13, 1804; Sec. Thos. Baird.

Wm. Cole and Martha Bounds Dec. 18, 1790.

Mathew Dockery and Rachel Webb Oct. 22, 1801; Mathew Terry Sr.

George Keachey and Sarah McFarland,_____ sec: Jas. Terry, Sr.

Pleasant Moses Mask and Patsy Hall, Jany. 8, 1800; John Hughlett.

RICHMOND COUNTY RECORDS

John Stricklin and Patsey Cole, Nov. 4, 1801; Jesse Cole.

Lott Stricklin and Lucy Haley, Mch. 17, 1783; Wm. Jernigan and Wm. Webb.

John Strother and Eliz. Gibson, April 1801; Geo. Humphreys.

Eli Terry and Polley Pickett, Dec. 17, 1799; Sec: John Clark, James Love and James McN. Smith.

James Terry, Jr. and Jean Jernigan Aug. 24, 1790; John James Jr.

Sanders Meredith and Patsey Ingram, Mch. 21, 1803; Eli Terry.

Edward Moorman and Charity Stricklin, Dec. 7, 1799; Jesse Stricklin.

Murdoc McInnis and Christian McDaniel, May 6, 1804; Eli Terry.

Jesse Newberry and Dorcas Petuss, Aug. 26, 1791; James Pickett.

Pembroke Robinson and Sally Gainey; July 29, 1800; Eli Terry.

WILLS

WILL BOOK 1 (1779-1830).

Page 4--Will of George Jefferson, of Richmond County, No. Car.; wife one-third for life and at death to be div. as follows: son Peter all my lands on Jones Creek that I have a right to and what I have not yet a right and title to; son George Jefferson all lands contiguous to Grassy Islands, also my library of books; all my other lands whether in Virginia or Carolina to be sold and after debts are paid one-half of money to be laid out in negroes and stock in trade and the other one-half applied toward taking up lands in some back country to be div. between my sons, John, Garland, and Samuel and my daughter Frances Robinson and the child my wife is big with; wife, friends Henry Wm. Harrington, Edmund Williams and Samuel Spencer, my brothers in law, Samuel Garland and John Garland and my son Peter Jefferson executors, 26 Jany. 1780.
Wit: Mary Nichols   Proved March Term 1780
     Susannah Williams   by Susannah Williams
     Wincy Williams   and Wincy Williams.

Page 22--Will of John Walters, 30 June 1781. Ch: George, Pamela, Eunice, Nancy and John Walters, son (in law?) Thomas Megginson.
Wit: John Bostick   Proved Richmond Co.
     James Bostick   Court by John Bostick
     Samson Sellers   and Samson Sellers.

Page 28--Will of Francis Leak, Anson Co., Oct. 25, 1786. Brother Walter Leak____William____ one bond, sister Judith Leak 2 negroes, £100 and one mare and colt; sister Sally Howard Leak 2 negroes and £100.
Proved by James Pickett, Sr., Joseph Ingram and Solomon Phillips.

Page 35--Will of Solomon Strother. Executors: Walter Leak, James Pickett, Jun.; and beloved wife, Nancy Strother. 3 Aug. 1790.
Wit: Thomas Bras
     John Long
     Sarah Pickett[6]

---

[6]. "James Pickett (son of William and Mourning) m. a Miss Kimbrough." Data compiled by Mr. C. E. D. Egerton, Historian of Richmond Co. N. C. and Miss Mary Patton, of Pensacola, Fla., in the collection of Isaac S. London, Ed. of the Post-Dispatch, Rockingham, N. C. Richmond Co. Execution Docket, 1st___1818 to Mch. 8, 1818. Suit: Dudley Mask and others vs Richard Roe and Saunders Meredith. Cost vs plaintiff. Among receipts for claims as witness:" Rec'd $2.93 the amount of James Pickett's tickett in this suit. (signed) Eli Terry". There are two wills of Sarah Pickett on file in the Probate Court of Autauga Co. Ala. (Prob. Reports C, pp 44-45). As the second will disposes only of property acquired since the writing of the first, it was probably considered as a codocil. The first, dated 20 Aug. 1824, Sarah Pickett, of Autauga Co. Ala.; Legatees, dau. Polly Terry, gr-sons Eli Terry, Wm. Terry and James P. Terry; gr-dau. Mary C. Terry; all my grandchildren, heirs of my dau. Polly Terry. James P. Terry exrr.; wit: Peyton Bibb, J. W. Houck. The second will; Sarah Pickett, of Autauga Co., Ala., dated 19 Dec. 1833. Legatees: Sarah Terry, eldest dau. of James P. Terry; Mary Saxon; exrs, Peyton Bibb and Wm. R, Terry. Wit: James H. Crannon, Jas. Mitchell, John W. Price, Robt. L. Pou. (No probate).

Page 37--Will of James Smith Sr., weak; wife Sarah Smith; Mary Ward after death of her mother; my son, John Smith after death of his mother; dau. Sarah Smith; the rest div. among children. 24 Nov. 1790.
Wit: Jas. Turner Prov. by Jas. Turner
Jemimah Boggan July 1791.

Page 38--Will of Catherine Smith, of Richmond Co., weak; mother Catharine McCairn; uncle Alexander McAlpin. 15 Mch. 1790.
Wit: Archibald McCairn Prov. April Ct. 1791
Christian McArn John McCalman

Page 51--Will of John Chiles of Richmond Co.; low in health; my brother Micajah Chiles and his heirs one-half of est.; other half to James, Elizabeth and Lydia Chiles, children of my brother, James Chiles, decd., and Thomas Chiles of Montgomery County. Also that part of my grand-father, Henry Chiles, decd. estate that fell to me by heirship and by purchase that I made of the said Henry Chiles estate of my brothers, Micajah Chiles, James Chiles and Manoah Chiles, to be divided between the above legatees. Now if the said Thomas Chiles died without heir, that part left to him to be equally divided bet. the above James, Elizabeth and Lydia. But in case my brother, Micajah, is dead that part left to him to be divided bet. James, Elizabeth and Lydia. Exrs: Thomas Chiles, Charles Bevine and Col. Samuel Garland, of Virginia. Aug. 8, 1784.
Wit: William Mask Proved in Richmond Court
John White April 1786 by William Mask,
Josiah Lyons Esq. of Montgomery County.

Page 58--Will of Zachariah McDaniel, low in health; wife Lidia; after her marriage to be divided among children; sons James McDaniel and Wm. Capell exrs with wife; 2 Feb. 1795.
Wit: James Pickett Jr. Wm. Rodgers
Micajah Shelton
Proved April 1795 by James Pickett and William Rodgers. Test. Tod Robinson Dep. Clk, James Terry Clk.

Page 64--Will of William Rodgers; low in health; son Benj.; son John; wife Rachel; son Benj. and wife exrs. 11 May 1797.
Wit: James Pickett Jr. William Powell
Prov. Oct. Session 1797 by oath of James Pickett Jr. Test. Tod Robinson D.C. for James Terry Clk. NIN

Page 95--Will of Benjamin Ingram, of Richmond Co., weak; wife Druscilla Ingram all my land, 396 acres, for widowhood, to be released immediately after her marriage, to be rented by my exrs until my youngest son should be of age; to be equally div. among my children. William Terry Jr. and Stephen Cole, exrs. If it is out of the power of the aforesd Stephen Cole to serve as exr. I wish that Walter Leak should act in his stead. 24 Jany. 1803. Prov. by B. H. Covington
Wit: Benj. Rodgers March Session 1803.
John B. Smith Eli Terry Clk. NIN
B. H. Covington

Page 97--Will of Mourning Pickett,[7] widow, of Rockingham, N.C. I give and bequeath to my worthy friends, Walter Leak of this place and William Terry of Sneedsboro, all my estate, both real and personal for the benefit of my loving daughter, Sally Childs, wife of Thomas Childs, of Montgomery Co. He is not to intermeddle neither shall same be subject to his debts; the above Walter Leak and William Terry and my loving son, James Pickett exrs. (Not dated) Prov. March Session
Wit: Wm. Robards 1803 by
Wm. Leak William Robards.

Page 104--Will of William Terry, Richmond County; son Matthew two negroes, the increase to go to Hannah and Druscilla, the two youngest daughters of Benj. Ingram; son William negro and horse; son James two negroes; dau. Nanney Cole negro; son Champness Terry four negroes, bay horse, Salem, and all the household furniture; dau. Betsy Wilson 5 shr.; lands to sons; four sons exrs.
Wit: Wat Leak Prov. Sept. Session 1805
Wm. P. Leak by Walter and William P. Leak.

---

7. On Jany. 7, 1800, Mourning Pickett made deeds of gift, of lots in Rockingham, to her following grandchildren; to Mourning P. Tindle, lot #60; to Lucy Davison Tindle, #67; to Nancy Robards Tindle #61; to Eli Terry lot #11; to Mourning P. Leake lot #16; and on July 12, 1800 to William Leake part of lot #42, on Washington St. The first three deeds were witnessed by Eli and Polly Terry, the one to Eli Terry by Ann Terry (his mother) and N. Tindle, the one to Mourning P. Leake by James Pickett and Wm. Leake and the one to William Leak by Willm. Terry and Walter Leak. Richmond Co. Deed Bk E, pp. 147, 148, 149, 154, 158 and 266.

Page 105--Will of Joseph Hines, Esq., of Richmond Co. 18 March 1803. Legatees: Benjamin Williams and wife Elizabeth, Nathan Jones Hines, grandsons Joab and Joseph Hines, sons of Thomas Hines; Thomas Hines and Senay Hines, his wife, (to her his riding chaise); Son, Thomas Hines and Benj. Williams exrs.
Wit: Jas. Robertson   Thomas Dockery
     Noah Agee
     Proved by Thomas Dockery December Session 1805. Wm. Leak D.C. for Eli Terry. NIIN

Page 151--Will of John Pemberton, Nov. 26, 1811 .... Exrs: Mumford Dejarnett, Walter Leak and James Pickett, Sr.
Proved March Session 1812.

Page 113--Will of Geo. Dougherty, Oct. 6, 1806.
Wit: Eli Terry   James Pickett
Proved Oct. Court 1807 by Eli Terry.

Page 216--Will of Champ Terry, low in health, of Richmond Co., wife: Johannah Terry; sons Eli, Calvin, Stephen, other ch: Nanny Gibson, wife of Samuel Gibson, Mathew, Judy, Druscilla, Champ, Harrod, Walter, Hannah and Jane. July 17, 1820.
Wit: Saml. Terry   John W. Terry
     James Terry, Jr.
     Apr. Ter. 1821.

Page 293--Will of Nicholas Smith, weak; my wife, all lands while she lives at her disposal, mare chaise and harness, etc.; my first born daughter, Mary Ward and my first born son, Henry Smith who have moved to the west $50.00 if they or their heirs demand the same from my exrs or their heirs; grandchildren, Thomas Smith's offsprings, $10.00 each; son Richard and son-in-law $1.00 each as they formerly recd a competent portion of my estate; two sons in law, Daniel Evans and Joshua Fletcher, the value of all my land and that which I gave my wife, at her death, to be div. among their heirs and they are to pay the foreign heirs, viz: Mary Ward, Henry Smith and Thomas Smith's offsprings the portion allotted to them if they ever demand it. Jany. 17, 1828.
Wit: William McD.Shaw   William Bunday
     John Fletcher
     April Term 1828.

Will Bk. 1, page 134. Will of John Covington, 12 March 1803-Jany. 1809. Wife Nancy; nine children, John, Eliz., Benj., Ann, William, Rebecca, Henry, Thomas and James.
Wit: Moses Chambers   Stephen Cole
     Peter H. Cole

Bk. 1, page 83-4. Will of William Wall, probated January 1801. Lucy Wall, wife; children Henry, Sallie, two oldest, not of age, Polly, and Nancy.

Book 1, page 6-7. Will of John Mask, Sept. 1781 - April 1813. my oldest son 5 sh; John Mask, my second son; ch. Dudley Mask; James P. Mask, Walter Mask, Lucy Mask, Druscilla Mask, Phillip Mask, Daus.: Grace Agee, Patty Agee, Mary Ingram, gr-ch: John Mask Jr. and Mary Mask.
Wit: Thomas Bullock   Martha Mask

Bk. 1, p.____. Will of Lucy Mask. Aug.-Dec. 1814. Brothers and sisters: Phillip Mask, Dudley Mask, Pleasant Mask, Druscilla Mask, James P. Mask, Walter L. Mask.

Bk. 1, p. 197. Will of Francis Cole, sick, Mch. 30, 1818. son John; to John Strickland and wife, Patty, and Henry Watkins and wife Rachel, my dearly beloved daughters and sons-in-law I have already given them what I allowed to them. (no probate)

Bk. 2, p. 4-5. Will of James Raiford: wife Oney; sons: Zedekiah and Robert Raiford; daus: Judith Chambers, Mary Ewing.
Jany. 1830.

RICHMOND COUNTY RECORDS

PROBATES

List of administrations returned from Richmond County to Secy. of State's office.[8]

March Session 1780

Jehucal Crowson, admr. of John Crowson, decd. £10,000.
Security: George Bounds   Henry Adcock

December Session 1781

Sarah Crowson admx. of Jehucle Crowson, decd. £100.
Sec: Jesse Bounds   Moses Chambers

June Session 1782

Isabel Burt, admx. of William Burt, decd. £3000.
Sec: Randolph McDaniel   Daniel McDaniel

Elizabeth Hutchins, admx. of James Hutchins, decd. £100.
Sec: Solomon Gross   Wm. McDaniel

March Session 1782

Zacheriah Martin, admr. of Wm. Snead, decd. £250.
Sec: John Sap   Edmond Almond

December Court 1782

Ezra Bostick, admr. James Grice, decd. £50.
Sec: Nathl. Harrington   John Hilyard

Benjamin Beard (Baird), admr. of Solomon Alred, £50.
Sec: Joseph Hines.

March Court 1783

Dugald Blue and Mary Blue, jointly admrs. of John Blue, decd. £100.
Sec: Alex. Watson   Duncan McFarland

December Court 1783

John Crawford, admr. of John Turner, decd. £100.
Sec: William Hunter Sr.

Nancy McLeoud, admx. of Daniel McLeoud, decd. £200.
Sec: John McCaul, Sr.

Mary McCoy admx. of John McCoy, decd. £100.
Sec: John Sneed, Esq.

Edward Williams admr. Wm. Chapplen, decd. £200.
Sec: John Crawford Sr.   William Love, Clk.

Sept. Sessions 1782

Eliz. Hales, admx. William Hales, decd. £50.
Sec: John Long   Burrel Strickland

William McGuire. admr. John McGuire, decd. £50.
Sec: William Mask   Walter Leak

Stephen Cole, admr. Israel Medlock, decd. £200.
Sec: John Chiles   James Cole

The foregoing list contains all the admrs. that have been made in this county of Richmond since the division wherein the administrators name are mentioned first, the names of deceased, and their securities.
Certified this 14 Nov. 1782.   Wm. Love, Clerk

---

8. Secy. of State Papers. SS883. Dept. of Archives and History, Raleigh, N.C.

INDEX

In the List of Land Grants, pp. 1-23, only the names that are given in the descriptions of the grants are indexed. The names of the grantees are arranged alphabetically and are not included in the index. *means that name appears in more than one abstract.

Abrams, Robert 28
Acock, Anthony 44, Charity 44, Odom 44
Adams (Addams), Amelia 120, Jacob 120, James 33, 74,133, John 137,141, Richard 88,92,95, Richard, Sr. 137, Richard, Jr. 137, Robert 35, Sarah (Pratt) 121, William 91,137
Adcock, _____ 108,109,110, Elender, 119, Henry 23,64*,65*,79,83,92,94,97*,102,106,119,136, 137,155, Henry, Jr. 119, James 74,92,97,119, John 119, Nancy 119, Saphira, 119, Thomas 65,94,119,122
Addison, Thomas 33
Adkins, John 131
Agee, Grace 154, Noah 102,134,154, Patty 154
Aikins, Robert 139
Ainsworth, William 38,60
Alexander, Charles 28*, Moses 128, Robert 93
Allen, Benjamin 68,120, Betty 57, Charles 93,97, 134,143, David 68, Drury 68,122, Elizabeth, 65, Gabriel 66, Isaac 136,143, James 48,55, 56,57,74*,85,86,89,91,93*,94,99*,101,102,107, 130,141 John 91,147, Joseph 134,143, Julius 68, Mark 53,55*,73,74*,75,76,79,86,88,91,95,99, 142,143,82, Mary 57,93,94, Nelly 68, Richard 66, Thomas 68, William 68,143
Alley, James 29,32
Allman, William 133
Almond, Edmond 78,155, Edward 71,72,75,94,102, 108,109,137, James 59,72,135,143, John 41,56, 74,81,89,99,133,135,143, William 24
Alred, John 95,100, Solomon 95,155, William 104
Alston, John 71, Philip 60,69
Alsop, Joseph 139
Alton (Altom), John 102, Mary 102, Spencer 143, William 71,72,83,87,88,102,136
Anderson, Mary 57, Dr. Thomas 29
Andrews, George 109,136, Keziah (Blackford), 117, Marcus 86
Annton, William 147
Armstrong, Benjamin 115, James 34,45,114,115, 126, Jean 34, John 45,114,115,139, Joseph 114, Isaac 57,86*,87,89*,98,99,104,130,135,142,143, Martin 34,114, Mary 115, Mathew 115, Samuel 26, Thomas 27,38,40, William 114
Arnett, William 129
Arnold, Samuel 29
Arnoldpender (See Pender)

Arrington (See Harrington)
Arthur, John 104,139
Artledge, John 118
Ashley, Francis 119, John 38,43,44,119,151, John, Jr. 119, Jurden 119, Mary 119, Nathaniel 76, 77,82,98,100,101, Sarah 119, William 44,82,93, 104,119,149
Ashmore, Walter 23*,24,46,85,87,92,104
Astin, John 137
Ates (See Eights), James 137, Peter 139
Atkins, Davidson 139, Ephraim 138, John 138, Lewis 122,139, William 139
Attaway, Joseph 35
Atwood, Jeremiah 30
Auk, John 136
Auld, and Chiles 52, Mr. 82, Ann 45,117,118, Elizabeth 117,118, J. Clk. 53,54*,55*,56*,57*, 58*,58*,59*,115,132, James 45,59,72,73,74,83*, 86,87*,88,89*,90*,92,93,94,95,96*,97,99*,100*, 106,107*,109,116,117,141 John 45*,46,48,60,61, 71,85,86,105,109,116,117,118,122,136, John Fields 118, James, Esq. 101,102*,103,104*, 105,106,107,108*,110, Mary 117,118, Michael 47,61*,62*,117*,118*,126,127,128*,129*, Sidney 118, Rosanna 117,118
Austin, Bryant 143, James 129, Mary 34, Richard 64*, Stephen F. 45
Avery, John 138, W. 40,100
  ****
Bagget, James 74,108,137*, Shadrack 108,136,137
Bagley, George 73,85,110, George, Jr. 76, George, Sr. 81
Baily (Baly), Caty 119, Henry 48,49*,100,138, Jacob 119,139, James 119, Jenny 119, John 119, 127,128,133,138, Lydia (Liday) 63,127,128, Mathew 44,49,63*,140, Mathew, Sr. 49, Polly 119, Rachel 44,49, Robert 143, Sally 119, Thomas 2,3,49,54,61,62,63*,64,82*,100,119, 133,136,139,140,141, Thomas, Jr. 49, Thomas Sr. 127, William 119
Bailes (Bales, Bayles) Jesse 130,136, Martha 130, William 135,136
Baines, John 136
Baird (Beard), Alexander 55*,57*,98,99,100,102, 134,141,143, Baird's 45, Ann 148, Bat 57, Benjamin 23*,24,46,47,48*,52,53,54*,55*55*, 59*,75,79,84,87,104*,134,136,141,142,148*,149,

157

INDEX

155, Elenor 148, Jennie, 57, John Batt 46,55*, 57*,85,97,102,105,135,141, Micha (Miche, Mickey) 52,149, Patsy 148, Thomas 151, William 27,35,148,151
Bagsdale, John 147
Baker, Aaron 127,131,138, Francis 63*, James 60, John 60,136,143, Mary 117, William 110, 135
Baldwin (Boldin), Thomas 113
Baluck, Comfort 60
Ball, Jesse 82, John 62
Ballard, Humphrey 136,143, Jesse 14, John 143, William 136,143
Banks (Bankston?), Andrew 85
Bankston (Bankson), Andrew 85,91,143,148, Ann 143, Daniel 73,85*,91,104,108,131,136,143, Jacob 73,85,91,136, James 136, John 136, Lawrence 136,143, Peter 143,147, Thomas 136, William 136
Barbour (Barber), James 138, Joseph 139
Barnett (Barnet), Ann (Sprat) 119, James 131, John 73,92,99, William 28,119
Barnes (Barns), Elizabeth (McDowell) 114, Thomas 136, William 95
Barr, William 78
Barrentine, William 78
Barrett, Benjamin 133, Fanny 119, Holden 119, Jane 119, Thomas 119, Wade 119
Barringer, Paul 36
Barry (Berry), Andrew 27,28,35,36,127,132, Hugh 27,28, Jeanet 27,28,35, Richard 27,35, 127,132
Barton, James 137
Basley, Mary (Preslar) 116
Bass, Andrew 124,125, Ann 124, Christian 124, 125, Delong 136, Elizabeth 124, Frederick, 81,129,137,138, Thomas Alexander 124, Uriah 124
Bates, Ellen 124
Baton, Anguish 143, Daniel 142,143
Baxley, Aaron 126, Mary 126
Beacham, Alex 74, William 64,139
Beals, Mulvaney, 135
Bean, John, Jr. 92, L. 142, Richard, Jr. 92,143, Richard, Sr. 92, Walter 92,143
Beason, Samuel 36,131, Solomon 131
Beard (See Baird)
Beaty (Betty, Batey), Charles 30,36,114, Chrs. 45, Francis 36,45, John 27,28,115,127, Mary 28, Thomas 115, William 138
Beck, John 109,135
Bedinfield, Henry 30,31 William 31
Belew (Belieu, Bellu, Bellue, Belyeu) Abraham 41, 60,66,74,77,82,84,91,92,98,99*,103*,105,130, 133*,140 Abraham, Jr. 73, Charles 147, Donald 135, George 62,103,133, Henry 105, Isaac 73,103,128,133, John 139, Katherine 120,130,

Margaret 129, Michael 128
Bell, Benjamin 138, John 143, Joseph 91,107,136, 143, Nathaniel 91,136,143 Richard 143, Susanna 84
Benbrooke, Ezekiel 133
Bennett, Bidy 124,125, Christian 124,125, Drury 136,143, Edna 125, Elizabeth 120, James 101, 120,121,123,138,139*, James (Jr.) 123, James, Sr. 120, John 69,137, John, Jr. 120,135, John, Sr. 120, Lewis 124,125, Mark 136,143, Micajah 120, Minard 123, Nancy 125, Nevill 48,49,119, 123,136,138,139, Nevill, Sr. 120, Polly 125, Sarah 120, Silas 123, Solomon 143, William 44, 49*,54,69,72,73,74,94,103,107,108,117,119,120*, 123,124,125,133,136,137,139*, William (Jr.) 123,124,125, William N. 120, Written 60
Benson, Elizabeth 131,132, William 95,96,105,129, 131,132
Benton, Charles 93, James 95,97,135,139, Job 80, 101,104,135,136, Joseph 79, Phereby 93, Priscilla Unity 93, Samuel 135, Sarah 117, Spencer 93, W. 135, William 79,122,137
Berry, Charles, Esq. 113, Thomas 54
Berryman, John 26
Bert, William 70
Best, Bostin 35, John 135, William 138
Bettis, Elijah 97,141, Insign (Ensiant) 82,97, Richard 139
Beverly, Fanny 120, John 129
Bevine, Charles 153
Bevens (Bivens) Abel 120, Elijah 120, John 120, Lyda 120, Moses 120, Nathaniel 120,134,137, Nathaniel, Sr. 120, Sarah 120, Stephen 120, Unity 120, William 120,134,137
Bibb, Peyton 152
Bickerstoff, Samuel 18
Billingsley, J. B. 124, Samuel 92, Sias 52,57,86,91, 101*,136,143
Billing, Rebecca 120
Bingham, Thomas 38
Bird, William 128
Bittle, Elizabeth 120, Jesse 120, John 120, Tabitha 120
Black, Archibald 65, Edward 96, Helen 35, Jane 114, Thomas 114, William 35, William, Jr. 35,128
Blackford, Manning 117, Mathew 117, Rachel 117, Ruth 117, Samuel 71,72,76,78,79,80,84,88,102, 117,129 Sarah 117
Blacksher, Robert 75
Blackwell, John 141
Blake, ___ 147, Randle 143, Thomas 142
Blakely, Luke 26*
Blalock, Lydia 44, John 44,73
Bland, Moses 93,105, William 78,93
Blassingham (Blassengen), William 108,126
Bleakney, Thomas 134, William 134, 138
Bletcherton, George 60

INDEX 159

Blewett ___ 65,87, Ann 123, David 123, Eli 123, Elizabeth 79,94,123, Henry 105, James 123, Morris 123, Susannah 123, Thomas 123, Will 32, William 31,42,55,57,73,74,75,76,79,80,84, 88,89,90,93,94,97,98,99,104,105,106,107,109, 115,121,123,130 William, Jr. 123 William, Esq. 69,71,72,73,74,86,88,89,93,95,96,97,98,99
Bloodworth, John 51,63,64,128,129,137,139*,140, Samuel 51,72,138, William, 139
Blue, Anguish 137, Dugald 100,137,155, Duncan 138, Jacob 136, John 90,137,155, Mary 155, Neill 90,137
Blunt, Jacob 134, James 134,138
Boggan, James 51,117,136,137, James, Jr. 138, James, Sr. 63,138,140, Jemima 49,153, John 138, John, Jr. 61, Mary 120, Capt. Paddy 125, Patrick 49,51,67,69,101,104,105,108,110,117, 120,129,131,136*,137,139, Patrick, Jr. 85, 128,129,136, Capt. Patrick 139, Solomon 65, William 49,85,117,128,129,136,138, 139, William, Jr. 61
Bohman ___ 136
Boldwin (Bolden), Thomas 39,40,113*, Samuel 139
Bolen, Isaac 133
Boll, Charles 115
Bolling, Benjamin 51, John 143, William 93
Bolton, James 143, Thomas 82, William 82,134, 138
Bond, James 143, Nicholas 28,32,36,109 William 53,82,103,133
Bone, Jacob 137
Bonner, Jane 29
Bonsall, William 133
Books, Joshua 124
Boone, John 124
Booth, Charles 53,72,82*,102,118, David 140, John 109,138, John, Jr. 140, John, Sr. 140, Samuel 138, William 138
Boothby, Charles 84
Bostick, Druscilla 123, Elizabeth 109,151, Ezra 58,64,66,94,99,107,123,134,155, James 74,99, 134,138,152, John 69,70,72,74,78,82,87,94,95, 99,134,137,152 Tabatha 147
Bounds (Bound), Anne 42, Elizabeth 44, George 81, 84,137,155, James 23,25,44,58,94,133, James, Jr. 42,48, James, Sr. 48,49,58,84, Jesse 42, 78,95,103,105,137,149,155, John 42,48,49,52, 58*, 77*, 78*, 84*, 88,94,95,104,105,130,133, 141,150*, Martha 151, Mary 48
Bowen, Gidden 135, Joseph 143, Samuel 143
Boyd, Abraham 47, John 142, Samuel 143
Boykin, Benjamin, 120
Bradford, Patty 143, Richard 27,32,149*
Bradly, Joshua 131
Braley, John 26
Branch, Britton 134, John 92,94*,135,137, William, 134,137

Brand, Bretton 137
Brandon, John 13,35,118
Brassfield (Brasfield) John 126, Joshua 136,138, Reuben 139
Brasswell (Braswell), George 56,91, Reuben 117, Richard 56,91
Brassell (Brazzell), Dicey 117, Nathan 138, Richard 134, Richard, Jr. 134
Braugh, John 134
Braveboy, Jacob, 141
Bras, Thomas 152
Brigham, Isaac 141, William 141
Brigman,___ 109, Isaac 88,81,96,103,130,137*, Joshua 137, Thomas 89,91,94,130, William 130,137
Bravard (Brevard), John 35,129
Brelar (Brular) Elisha 60*
Brent, Joseph 38
Bretwell, Joseph 52,138
Bridge, John Cole 137
Brien, George 134
Briggs, Thomas 93
Bright, Albright 71
Briley, George 64,138,139, William 58,104
Brister, Peter 50
Broadway (Brodway) Nicholas 49,54,76, Robert 62, 137
Broff, John 89,99
Brooks, Elizabeth 127, Ezekiel 143 James 21,46, Jesse 137, John 66,96,136, John (Va.) 143, John, Jr. 143, John, Sr. 143, Joseph 136, William 66,75,91*,103*,143
Brower, George 138
Brown, D., 133, Edward 139, Elizabeth 31,33,62,72, 94,97,117, Gabriel 114, Gideon 46, Jacob 45, James 33,139, Jesse 136, John 33,43,94,97, 130,137,141. Joseph 56,90*, M. 24,27,28,29, 30,31,33,36,80,118, Mary 94,97, Morgan 30,31*, 39*,40,41,44*,47,53,55,57,59,62,73,82,86,90, 92,94*,95,84,96,97,98,99*,101,102,104,107,108, 113,117,122,131,139, Morgan, Jr. 38,105, Neill 100, Peter 117, Stephen 94,97,127, Thomas 138
Brumbeloe (Brumloe), Anney 120, Lidia 120
Bruton, David 40, George 134, James 49, Samuel 93,99,102
Bryan, Lawrence 31,42,137, Samuel 32,44
Bryant, David 143, James 136, John 66
Buchanan, Elizabeth 122, James 67
Bullock, Thomas 143,154, Thomas, Jr. 134
Bunday, William 154
Bunts (prob. Baird), Benjamin 47,75
Burcham, Henry 56,97,105,134, John 93,95,141, Joseph 83,93,138,143
Burford, and Howard 96,103, Daniel 101,141
Burk, Edward 44, Margaret 123
Burkhead, Eleazer 92
Burgess, Thomas 43

Burleson (Burleyson) Isaac 143, James 138
Burmingham, Charles 87,117,136,139 John 138, 139, Joshua 138, Phillip 139
Burnett (Burnet) Andrew 131, Anne 28,131,132, Charles 28,45,131, David 29, Daniel 29, Godfrey 122, John 29,35,131,132, Margaret 29, Samuel 45,131
Burns, Darius 24,76,80, James 59*,105,115, Thomas 29,132, William 74,83,99,100,141
Burt, William 38,40,82,98,155, Isabel 155
Buschan, Abraham 133, Joseph 82, Richard 133
Butler, Christopher 83, 148, Christopher, Jr. 134, Elias 143, James 134,143,147, Joshua 134,143,147, John 36,143, Thomas 87,134,143
Butten, Christopher 91, 93, 96, Joshua 86,93, Thomas 102
Byrd, John 139, William 32
****
Cain, John 117, Nancy Stephens 117
Cairns, Archibald, 28
Caldwell, Robert 28
Caller, Hannah 114
Callahan, John 93
Calloway, Isaac 136,143, Jacob 73, Job 73,85, 91,107,131,136,143, John 85*,91,136,143
Cammill, James 149
Campbell, Archibald 90,101,105, Charles 90, Colin 90*, Donald 141, James 79,81,93,119, 141, John 40,137, Joseph 139, Margaret 123, Robert 56, Silas 139
Canfield, John 105
Capell, William 153
Cannon, John 16,41, Lurong 99, Thomas 84
Card, Wm. 28
Cardall (Caudel) Elizabeth 108
Carler, Benjamin 118
Carmichael, Donald 137, Elizabeth John, 128,129, 132, New 137, William 128,129,132
Carpenter, Jonathan 143, John 38,83,110,135,148
Carr, Robert 73,85, William, Esq. 122
Carroway, William A. 66, William T. 67
Carrell, Torrance 30
Carruth, John 106,107,129,138, Matt 129
Carter, Benjamin 80,83,103, Charles 144, Ephraim 143, George 57,80,81,90,92,95,109, 133,135,137, Jacob 73,85,91,144, James 30,66, Joshua 73,85,91,103,107,136,143, Moses 136, Nathaniel 100, Samuel 91,136,142, William 75, 105,144
Cartledge, ___ 58, E. 27,32,130,131, Edmund 30,31, 43,58,60
Cartwright (Cartright), John 36,50,56,74,89
Carey, John 103
Castolo, John 33
Castleberry William 134
Caswell, Richard 41,46,57,85

Cate, Joseph 118
Cathey (Cath--), George 35,114,131 John 119
Cato, Daniel 143
Caudell (See Cardall), Lewis 52,138
Cerbo (Curbo), William 138
Cewin?, Crto. 40
Chairs, Charles 141
Chambers, Edward 47*,85,86,130,134,141,143,142, Edward, Jr. 143, Edward, Sr. 142, Henry 98, 126,130, John 130,142, Judith 154, Nathaniel 61, William 47, 130,135, Moses 150,154,155
Chaplin (Chapplen), William 51,99,134,155
Chapman, Allen 122
Chappell, Christopher 91,143, Elizabeth 46
Charlton, Thomas 79, Christian 151
Chase, Joseph 143
Chavers, Ishmael·135
Cheek, Elizabeth 53,108, Hannah 51,53,89, Jane 38,42, John 10,11,38,41,42,53,87,91,143, John, Jr. 143, Randolph 38,50,66,88,144
Chester, James 120, John 120, Thos. 143
Chew, Joseph
Chewning, Bartholomew 140
Chiles (Childs), Elizabeth 128,131,153, Henry 153, James 93,128,130,131,136,138,153, John 50, 85*,87,93,94,99,101,105,106,107,109,110,138, 141,153,155, Lydia 153, Manoah 153, Sally 153, Sarah 122,124, Thomas 24,51,84,93,96,128,130, 143,153* Thomas, Sr. 124
Chivers (Chevers, Cheves), Ebenezer 96, Joel 72, 105,126, Sarah 105,126, Thomas 81,82,101,134, 138
Christian, Christopher 24,39*,41,45,56*,78,82,91, 92,98*,102,105,133,143, James 143, Jesse 24, 91,143, John 143, Lucy 143, Nicholas 24*, 25, 98,104,111,142,143*,151, Patty 143, Sarah 111, 151
Churchill, Simon 62, Sarah 62
Clanton, Reuben 147
Clark, Benjamin 124, Beverly 122,124,138, Clark's 40, Carey 124, Capper 137, Charles 47,135, Christopher 23,59,76,80,86,121,122, Cooper 135, Cornelius 47,122,135,139,140, David 48,49, Elijah 39,42,129,131, Gen. Elijah 40,52, Elizabeth 47, Fanny 52, Francis 38,65,69,73,74,79, 92,101,115,121,122,124,133, George 134, George, Jr. 142, George, Sr. 142, Henry 106, Isaac 69, John 30,38,42*,43,48,51,54,71,94,115,152, J. P. 134, Joseph 35,66,68,122, Lucy 143, Martha 68, Mary 122, Nicholas 92, 106, Renny 81, Robert 64, Samuel 142, Underwood 22
Claus, Mathias 27
Clay, John 97
Cleghorn, William 35,36
Coatney (See Courtney)
Clemmons (Clements), George 36,42, John 28,36,

INDEX

161

Judith 28, Mary 116, Mathew 116,117,132, Samuel T. 143, Thompson 91,136, William 91, 136
Clifton, Jesse 136, Salathiel 52
Cloud, Joseph 131, Mary 131
Coburn, Isaac 114, Jacob 28,29,35,114, John 114, John B. 29, Jonathan 114, Judah 114, Judith 28, Kitty 29, Margaret 27,35,36,45, Mary 35,114, Rebekah 114, Samuel 27,28,29,35,36,45,114,131, Sarah 114
Cochran (Cockeran, Cockroon), Cockran's 36, Jack 103, Jacob 88,92,99*,137, John 66, 81, 104, Thomas 29,34,137
Cocke (Cock, Cocks) David 133, Francis John, 91, Moses 91, Odam 49,122,139
Cockendal (Kuykendall?), Samuel 114
Cockeral, John 23, 32,
Cockerham (Cockeram), Alex. 135, Jacob 32,58, 74,88,92,101, Jacob, Jr. 135, Jacob, Sr. 135, John 74,86,134, Randal 135, Thomas 87
Coffee, John 131
Cogan, John 136, Mathew 136
Cogdell, Charles 33
Coggan, John 92
Coker, Milly 143
Cole, Elinor 49, Francis 154, George 137, Jacob 130, James 155, Jane 151, Jesse 151, John 38,48,49,51,54,58,70,71,72,75,78,81*,83,84, 87*,89*,93,97,98,103,104,105,109*,115,130,134, 136,137*,138,141,149*,150,154, John, Jr. 33, Nanney 153, Patsy 152, Peter H. 150,154, Stephen 33,35,43,48,49,56,70*,72,76,77,78,79*, 80,81,92,96,98,99,112,131,137,153,154,155, Temple 112, William 38,42,151, Wm. Temple 35,40,75
Coleman, Elizabeth 116,118, James 59,67,116, 118,151*, James, Jr. 67, John 43,46,47,50,51, 54,59,70,73,77,80,82,84,89,95,106,116,118, Mary 118, Morning 54, Mourning 59, 60,116, 151, Patience 48, Samuel 118, Thomas 47,50, 67,118,151, William 44,46,47,48,50*,51,52,53, 54,56*,69,70*71*,72,74,75,76,77,78*,80,81,82*, 83*,84*,85*,86,89,93*,94,96,97,98,99*,101, 102,103,104,116,118,130,132,133,144, William, Jr. 118
Colley (Coley), George 143, John 42,139, Patty 143, Thos. 139, Wm. 139
Collier, David 109,111,134, Drury 143,147, Martin 111
Collins, David 137, Edmund 135, Elisha 135,137, George 92,99,133,135,137,141, Jacob 98, Joshua 72*,74,76,81,83*,85,86,87,88,89,90,96, Mary 123, Thomas 29,135
Colson (Collson), Charity 118, Colson's 53,54, Elizabeth 127,129, Fereebe 118, Jacob 35,118, Jane 56, John 27*,32,33,35,37,38*,42,47,50,

54,61,62,64,70,71,73*,74,75*,77,79,80,88*,90, 91,97,100,112,115,121,122,129*, John, Jr. 118, 127, Joseph 117,118,128,139, Joseph (Jr.) 118, Martha 118, Mary 118, Nancy 118, Nelle 118, Sanders 118, Susannah 118, Thos. 118 Margaret 122, William 39,50,51,56,96,100,104,107,108, 147
Coman, Robert 120.
Condall (Caudall?), John 43
Conally (Conelly), Thomas 33,44,79
Conner, Ruthey 130, Thomas 49,82,100,136,139, Widow 128
Conway, James 135
Cony, Daniel 137
Cook, Anthony 44, John 47,82,138, Polly 121
Cooper, Francis 35, Isaac 91, Jane 56, Jesse 134, John 143, Samuel 115, Wilson 124,125,129, Mary 124
Cope, John 143, Thomas 143, Williamson 143
Cortney (Courtney, Coatney), Emanuel 120, John 66,120,134, Peggy 120, Rebecca 120, Robert 129, Sarah 120, Stephen 120, William 129, Mary 66, 120
Copeland, Isaac 82,94,95, Peter 95
Cordell, David 134, Jesse 134,138
Corneil (Cornell) Edward 136,141
Corwell, Edward 25,93
Coster, William 137
Costillo, Pierce 33
Cotton, James 23,24,45*,46,56,70,71,73,75,93,95, 97*,98,100*,104,105,133,141,142,147, James Esq. 75,76,78,80,82,86,87,88,89,95,96,97,98, 99,101,102,104
Cottingham (Cottengame), Elisha 137
Covington, Ann 154, Benj. 47,66,67,72,95,96,100, 137,151,154, B. H. 153 Eliz. 154, Donald 137, Fanny 47, Hannah 50, Henry 44,47,66,78,100, 135,154, James 103,154, John 50,69,77,78,83,92, 132,137*,154, Mary 50, Mathew 50,137, Mattie 121, Nancy 154, Nathaniel 134, Rebecca 154, Sarah 121, Thomas 150,154, William 55,95,122, 137,154
Cowan, John 109
Cox, Avington 61,103,139, Charles 32, Keziah 121, Margaret 87, Mary 126, William 87,101,126,139
Crabtree, Samuel 103
Craig, William 37
Crane, Junstal 73, Thomas 143
Crannon, James H. 152
Crawford, ___ 127, Ann 72,94, John 5,33,35,37,42,43, 44*,47,57,70,71,72,73,74,75,77,88,90,92*,94, 101,103,107,136,137,155, John Esq. 69,70,72,73 74, Martin D. 151, Michael 107,139,140, Thomas 138, Will 139
Creek (Creal) Moses 136, Thomas 92*,134,137
Creed, Joseph 138, Thomas 72

INDEX

Creek, John 72, Thos. 138
Cresp, William 103
Crew, Armsby (Armsbe) 120, Joseph 120
Crewets, George 143
Crisnel, John 136
Crittenden, Eleanor 32, Sarah 38,115, William 32, 34*,36,38*,39*,41,46,59
Croah?, Hannah Hough 114
Crockett, Arch 28, John 27,28,119,131
Crocker, Thomas 143
Crosland (Crossland), Ann 115, Edward 98,106, Temperance 115
Cross, Thomas 91,93,95,96
Crosswell, Richmond 123, Nance 123
Crouch, John 35,47,135
Crowder, Thomas 120
Crowson (Crosson) Jehucal 110,155, John 77,78, 84*,86*,94,108,133,141,155, John Jr. 105, John Neil 107,108, Nicholas 78, Sarah 155
Crump, James 143, John 143
Crutcher, George B. 111
Culcaster, James 32, John 35
Culp, Caspar 28, Jacob 35
Culpepper, Daniel 98,143, John 32,71,76,112,141, Joseph 39,112,127, Malachi 139, Robert 131, Sampson 51,129, William 69*,98,131,144
Cummings (Cummons) George 50, James 28
Cunningham, Joseph 24, Walter 23*,24,25,37,46, 56,102,141
Curbo, Joseph 60
Curry, Anens 98, Angus 136,137, Duncan 86,98, 130, Edward 137,149, James 150, John 34,135, 137, Loflin (Lackland, Leeklin) 106,136,137
Curtis, Eleazer 137, Elijah 139, Elizabeth 116, Frances 121,122,128,130, John 143, Moses 136, 143, Nathaniel 47,81,89,128,130, Russell 136, 143, Samuel 116,130,137, Susannah 122, Thomas 69,72,73,77,83, 137
Cuthberson, D. 124

****

Dade, George 139
Dammont, William 42
Daniel, Bartin 144, Edward 80, Paul 144, Wm. 89, 144
Darrell, Edward 62
Davenport, Francis 25, Isaac 29, William 61
Davidson, Ambrose 139, Edward 101,126, George 46,50,52,61*,62,103,107,126,138,142*,143,144, Jonathan 136, John 78,121,127,129,139*,142, Major 108
Davis, Christopher 49,117, Arthur 117,129,139, Daniel 41, Eliz. 117, Gabriel 73,96,107,127, 144, James 127, John 74,114,115,117, Joseph 35, Lewis 117, Mary 117, Moses 131, Nathaniel 107,144, Richard 34, Robert 27,131, Samuel 30*,38,41,42,43,72*,73,101,118,131, Samuel, Jr.
41, Thomas 36,117,127,131, Vinson 93,134, 137, William 27,127,131
Dawkins, Samuel 94, Sarah 119, William 137
Dawson, John 69
Dean, Luke 31, Thomas 137
Dearman, Richard 42,58, Solomon 24,58,88,91,136, Thomas 24
Deason, Shepard, 138
Deberry, Henry 97,134,143
Dees, Arthur 95,136, Benj. 47,103, James 136. Mark 135,137
Dedney (Dudney) Arthur 139, John 139,140
Deeton, Thomas 47,81,134
Dejarnett, Daniel 123, Frankie H. 121,124, Ford (Mumford) 63,122,123,124,125,132,144,154, John 46,52,56*,57,63,117,131,149, John P. 124, Richard 63
Denman, William 136
Dennis, Allen 144, Andrew 136,144, John, Sr. 141, Nathaniel 35,136,144, Thomas 93,144
Denson___29,40,48, Betsey 116, Jamima 129, James 23,27*,28*,29,35,40,44,46,73,79,112, 119,129,133, James, Sr. 26*,46,77,82, James, Jr. 26, 27,33, John 138,150, Leonard 55, Mary 75, Nathaniel 140, Sha. 33, Shadrach 29,36,44, 46,47,61,69,73*,74,75,77,78,80,81,82,83,85,98, 100,116,128,131,133,139, Wm. 129
Derush, John 111
Desaussure, David 62
Dew, Arthur 103,105, James 77.78
Dewey, John 75
Dickerson, John 84,93, Michael 60
Dickey, Moses 126,131, Margaret 131
Dicks, Benjamin 134, John 138
Dickson, Batt 8, Charity 115, John 105,117,137, Naomi 129, Richard 96, Samuel Blythe 62, Thos. 72,79,95,99,115,116,117,129, Dr. Thos. 72,79
Diggs,___23, Ann 43, Marshall 26,36,39,42,43,44, 73,78,92,119,122,136,139
Dill, Philip, 106,107
Dinkins, John 136, Thos. 80,128,131, William 138, 139
Dismukes, William 67
Dixon, Richard 132,38, Thos. 38,113
Dobbs, Josiah 139, Nathaniel 49,81,77,84,87,129, 132,135,137, Wm. 120
Dockery, Ann 50,74, Mathew 151, Michael 50, Thomas 50,55,69,74*,77,83,85,86,89*,93,94, 100,108*,135,137,154
Dodd, George 139, Rebekah 129
Donaldson, John 47,95*,137,138
Donohoe (Donaho), John 38, Thos. 137
Doster, William 72
Dougherty, George 154, James 129, Nathaniel 131
Douglass, Benj. T. 67, Daniel 144,148, J. 109, James 119, John 76,77,80,88,99,101, Sarah 144, Thos. 90, 109

Dove, John 135,136
Dowell, Joseph 139
Dowland, Henry 131
Downer, F. C. 35, John 92,100,101,102,107,109, 133,139,140, Thomas 75,88,90,112
Downing, James 28,31,71,79*,80,86,138, James, Jr. 138, Josiah 71,81,138, Joseph 71, Renatus 24,52,90,98
Downs___38,137, H. 39, Henry 27,29,30,32,34,39, 48,54, J. 39, Jonathan 27, R. 33,36,59, Richard 25,30,31,34,39,41,47,53,63,70,74,78,80,81,98, 133,134,144, William 26*,27,28,29,30,39,112, 119
Drakewood, William 90
Dry, Sarah 60,61, Wm. 39,60,61,69,74
Dudley, John 121, Sarah 144
Duffin, Andrew 94
Duffie, Archibald 137, Norman 137
Duland, Ruben 42
Dumas___56, Andrew 135, Azariah 64, Benjamin 27,28,30,44,76,92,93,99,112,128,134,138,141, Benj. Jr. 122,135, Andrew Sr. 122, David 30, 38,44,63,64,71,76,95,96,99,100,104,106,112, 128,133,141,144, Jeremias 27,28,30, Martha 27,112, Obadiah 64
Duncan, James 138, John 45,134,137, Stephen 95, William 91
Dunchow, Charles 81, Thos. 81, Wm. 81
Dunham, Joseph 24,55,69,72,82,103,112,121,123, 139, Mary 55 (see Durham)
Dunlap, Samuel 33
Dunn, John 26,30*,31,78,79,81,82,91,118,134,138, Richard 144, Thomas 138
Durham, Joseph 54, Thomas 23,144
Dyer, Martha 123
Dyson (Dison,Denson). Dyson's 39, Leonard 27*, 41,45, Nicholas 27
****
Eagan, Rachel 114
Eakles, Emanuel 131
Earles, William 144
Eastes, George 53
Eddins (Edens) John 102,134,136,139, William 102,136,142
Edgeworth, Elizabeth 123, Lovell 123, Richard 122,123, Richard Lovell, Esq. 123, Sneed 123, Thomas 124
Edwards, Ambrose 144, Isaac 123, John 38,68, 144, Joshua 123, Nathaniel 121,123,144, Nathaniel, Jr. 123, Philemon 144, Robert 23*,24,25, 46,78,94,99, Sarah 68, Simon 122, Zachariah 123
Ekins, John 39
Eights (See Ates, Yeats), Isaac 135
Elkins, John 36, Joseph 60

Ellerby (Ellerbe)___77, John 130, Thomas 62
Elliott, Archibald, 28
Ellis, Thomas 62,122, Wm. 81,91,144
English, John 135,144, Joseph 134, Mathew 86, Thomas 82,95
Engoss, Joseph 49
Erick (Ereak) Peter 27
Erwyn, Nathan 42
Etheredge, Absolem, 135,136,137
Evans, Ann 114,128,130, Cornelius 128,130, Daniel 154, John 48,139,140, Jonathan 43, Nathan 139, Theophilus 136, Zedick 138
Everett, Ann 121, Henry 138,139, John 57,60,138, Thos. 47,121, William 138
Eaves (Eves), William 115,141
Ewing, Mary 154
Ezell, John 149
****
Fair, Lucy 121, William 121
Faircloth, Mary 144
Falkenburg (Falconberry), Andrew 26,133, Henry 10,30,31,38,133, Isaac 26,69,81,83,84,86,89,90, 94,97,98,102,103*,104,105,109,110,126,133,136, Jacob 136, Jonathan 133, Samuel 75
Fanning,___23,81, Edmund 48,51, Hannah 56,66,88, James 62, Richard 48,51,56,66,72,75,84,88,97, Susannah 56,88, Thos. 71,95,96,133,135, Thomas Jr. 133, Widow 104
Farguson, David 115, Eliz. 115, Jane 115, Mary 115, Sarah 115
Farmer, Henry 34
Farr, James 62,76,78,79*,80*,81,96,101,103,139, 141,147, Major James 139, Richard 71,74,76*, 78*,79,80,85,91,95,96,97,98,99*,101,105,107, 108,130,136,139,141
Farris, William 120
Faulkner,___16, Asa 139, Benjamin 121,122, Elizabeth 122, Henry 122, John 122, Nathan 60*, 122,137,139, Sarah 122
Fee, James 69*, Thomas 69,133
Fedricks (Tadrick), William 136
Fenn, Zachariah 60,69*
Fenner, Robert 105
Fennell, David 103
Ferguson, Donald 141, John 135, Malcom 146
Ferrill, Ephraim 137, William 44
Fielding,___109, Christopher 109, William 44,48,49*, 58,66,72,74,87,97,100,103,127,130, Mrs. 130
Fields, Elijah 138, Elizabeth 66, George 40,138, John 138, Micah 138, Samuel 138, Smith 23,24, 66,75,80,86,87,90,105,107,118,138
Finney, Thomas 121
Fincher, Joseph 39
Fisher, Solomon 105,109,136
Fitzgerald, John 26*
Flake John 25, Samuel 25,54,55,61,69,70,73,75,

INDEX

76,77*,78,79,81,94,95,97,99,100,103,138,139
Flanegin (Flandegin), John 138,139, Sarah 46, William 136
Fleming, William 30
Fletcher, James 101,102*,103,144, John 154, Joshua 154
Flournoy, John 122
Flowers, John 46,54,81,82,86,133, Obedience 54
Fonder, Ephraim 75
Ford, Alex. 40, Edward 84*, Isaac 134, Richard 134, Thomas 79,109,135,136,137
Forrest, Abraham 143
Fox, Lawrence 144
Fowler, John 105,141
Foy, John 141
Francis, John 37,41, Mary Ann 34
Franks, Mary Ann 119
Franklin, Bentley 28,34, Elizabeth 121, Ison 139, John 136,139*, Lawrence 35,72,74,94,96,97*, 99,102,103*,105,106,108,127,136,139,141, Lawrence, Jr. 139
Frazer, ___ 147, Daniel 142, John 142, William 142, 144
Frederick, Philip 95
Freeman (Freman), Abraham 86,94, Cassandra 81, George 81,84,94, Hartwell 144, John 31,134, 138, Thomas 58
French, Samuel 30,32,33,61
Friday, Nicholas 78, Nicholas Jr. 78
Frolock, John 27*,28,79,81,112,115,132, Thos. 40, 42*,112, William 42*
Fry, Benjamin 92,134, George 92,144, James 23, 44,71,144, James, Jr. 93, Joseph 87,144, Joseph, Jr. 141, Joshua 92, Leeky 144, Thos. 92,106,108,144, Thomas, Jr. 92
Fuller, Benj. 98,136, Elizabeth 141
Fullerton, David 6

******

Gad, Joseph 138, Moses 134
Gaddis, James 112
Gaddy, Thomas 132,136
Gaines, James 139
Gainer, William 144
Gainey (Ganey), Micajah 64, Sally 152
Gallahon, John 136
Gamble, James 28, William 33
Gardner, Benjamin 89, 126, Stephen 127, Vereby 127
Gambell (Gambrill), James 131, Mary 93
Garland, David 48, John 152, Samuel 152, Col. Samuel 153
Garner, Walton 103, William 110
Gatewood, Elizabeth 122, Gabriel 122, Gleesy 122, Griffin 122, 138, Polly 122, Robert 91, 97,103,121,122, Sally 122, Thomas 122
Gathings, John 140, Phillip 129,135,138,139

George, John 100, Thos. 24,29,30*,34,37,38*,49, 50,51*,135
Gesford, Stephen 135
Gibble, Fred 56,98
Gibbs, Stafford 134
Gibson, ___ 24, Elizabeth 152, George 52, Gideon 47, 52, Gilbert 112,121*,141,151, Henry 52, James 144, John 141, Jórdan 33,47,52, Mourning (Mornie) 121* Nanny 154, Nelson 42,69,74,77, 86,102,135,137, Samuel 154, Silvanus 77, Thomas 69,73,74,82,86,103,108,109,135,137, Walter 38*, 39,84,86,129, Wm. 144,147
Gifford, John 132
Gilbert, Jesse 91,118,122,128,129,130,131,137,144, John 144, John Hale 129, Thomas 138
Giles, John 33,36,115, Thomas 145, Mary 115
Gillin, Rebecca
Givens, Agnes 36
Givens, Samuel 129, Edward 36
Glen, Duke 51,54,78,86*,102,106,108*,110,117,136, 138
Goddert, Abraham 139
Goforth, Preston 36,132
Gold, John 44
Goldsby (Gouldsbury) James 34,35
Gonad (Gurnad), John 138, Martin 135,138
Goodfellow, James 128
Gooding, George 147
Goodman, Samuel 39
Goodson, Elizabeth 120
Goodwin, Alexander 144, George 144
Goosby, Mr. 120
Gordon, ___ 45,81, Alexander 28,35,79*,80,99,113, 115,131, Benj. 45,90, David 38, Elizabeth 45, Frederick 135,137,138*, James 27,42,46,135, 136,138, John 45, Mary 93, Moses 136, Robert 69*, 109,139, Ruth 45, Thomas 45
Gose, John 73
Gould, Daniel 62,66,120,123,139, Elizabeth 40, George 66, Jemima 120, Malachi 40
Gowers (Gower), George 134, John 137,144,147, Jonathan 134, Thomas 57,85,98*,102,130,134, 139,144,149 William 134
Graham, Bennet 47, D. 121, Duncan 137, John 23,24, Stafford 137
Granade, John 135,136, Martin 137, Sukey 60
Grand, M. L. 151
Grant, Dempse 116,135,136, Dunn 58
Graves, Thomas 101
Gray, Benjamin 138, James 40,88,126,136,144, Robert 46,51, Wilbun 136, William 92
Graig (Gregg)
Greely, Moses 137
Green, Elizabeth 66, Gideon 64, Jacob 64, John 139, Leonard 144, Nicholas 71*,88,99,103,116,130, Richard 93,134,144*

INDEX

Gregory, Jonathan 93
Gregg, ___ 33, Abner 132, Burwell 132, Jesse 132, William 85
Gresham, Betty 57, John 138
Grice, James 155, Moses 92, Robert 137
Griel, Moses 134
Griffin, Andrew 79, Phillip 137
Griffith, Benjamin 85
Griggs (Gregg?), Burwell 132
Grillas, Garay 139
Grimes, Archibald 28, John 43,54,98
Grinnan, John 35
Gross (Groce) Jared (Jarut, Jarratt) Ellison 41,43, 45,55,89, John 134, Joshua 134,136, S. 41,46, Sheppard 45, Soll. 41,46,53,55*,57, Solomon 41*,42,43,44,45*,46,48,50*,53,55,57*,59*,74*, 75,78,79,80,81,83,86,89*,90*,92,94,98*,99, 100,102,105,126,130,147,149,155
Grover, Kell 107
Guice, William 139
Gulledge, Jeremiah 46,88,100,136,137, Jerry 132, Thomas 87, Thomas H. 68, William 45,60,92, 100,101,123,135,136,137,139
Gundry, John 137
Gustavus, M. 100, Mijah 101
Gwin, John 84

****

Hackney, William 131
Hadley ___ 7, Thomas 137,138
Haecker, William 36
Hagler (Haglet), John 43,95,96,144, John, Jr. 144
Hagood, James 135
Hales, Elizabeth 155, William 155
Haley (Hailey), Charles 120, Elizabeth 44,50, Isham 41,44,50,70,76,79,80,46,88,92,133, John 64,91, Lucy 152, Randolph 92, Sela 50, Silas 105,109, Wm. 47,70,73,79,92,109,138, Wm. Jr. 109
Hall, Enoch 141, James 33, John 27,33,43*,87,104, 127,137,141,144, Joseph 55,81,105,130, Lewis 141, Lewis, Jr. 141, Patsy 151, Robert 48,135, 137, Sarah 95, Thomas 102,136, William 136
Hallam, John 93*, Spencer 93, William 29,93
Hallaway, John 63
Halley, William 134
Haloday, John 120
Ham, John 7, Elijah 147, James 148
Hamble (Humble), Jacob 144
Hamblett, John 144, Peter 144
Hamby, William 144
Hamer ___ 39, Charles 64, Frances 96,122,126, John 31,47,75,77,79,87,89,90,94,96,100 102,104,106,107,118,122,126,129,130,133, John, Sr. 69,83,93, John, Jr. 72,81,93,133, Mary 129,130, William 69*,76,81,82,87,96, 107, 122,126,135,139

Hamilton, William 93,148
Hammock, Betty Ann 116, Wm. 116,137
Hammol, William, Jr. 139
Hammond, George 60,129,135,138,139, Unity 122, William 67,137
Hanby, Betsy 120, John 131
Hand, John 138
Haney, Timothy 132
Hannon, Bartin 144, John 144
Hansom, Isom 42
Harbard (Harbert), Charles 135, John 139
Hardin, Joseph 37,128
Hardwick, John 123,124
Hardy, Henry 122, John 122
Hare (Harre), Jonathan 138, Wm. 64
Hargett, Henry 95,150
Harlen, Thos. 138
Harmon (Hamon) John 130
Harnis, John 97
Harper, Thomas 133
Harrell (Herrill), George 138, James 135,136,139, John 139, Mathew 144, Moses 127, Richard 87
Harrington (Arrington, Arrenton), ___ 7, Ann 87, Bena 123, Charles 43,54,57,62,86,121,134,138, H. Wm. 117, Henry William 46,60,106,108,109, 117,118, 138,149*,152, James 48,49, John 54, 57,97,123, Mary 88,97, Nathaniel 137,155, R. 118, Rosa 122, Sarah 97 Sukey 123, Thos. 32, 35,127, Whitmell 79,88,92,97,123, William 77, 123,127
Harris, Arthur 51,136,144, Benjamin 138, Brantley 144, Brittain 91, Bucker 136, Ethelred 52,136, 144, Henry 51,136, Jesse 51,144, John 46,51, 58,136,137,144, Lewis 138, Malcom 52, Robert 32,36, Robt. Jr. 36, Roland 36,144, Roberta 53, Thad 129, Thos. 85,99,102,107,129, Turner 91, 93,144, Walter 53,87, Walton 23,86,93,97,101, 141, West 51,52*,87,93,101,136,144, West, Sr. 106, Major West 144
Harrison, Joseph 44, 93*, 133, William 31, Winnie 96
Harrold, Mathew 91,136
Harry, Jonathan 96,101,134
Harse, John 138
Harvey, John 35, Mary 35, W. 61, William 50,83
Hathcock Benjamin 144, Thomas 137
Hawke, David 136
Hawkins, Hannah 116
Hawthorn (Hathorn), John 95,89,105,130
Hay, Abraham 32, Reuben 94,134, Sarah 52, William 51,90,101,107, Capt. William 46,52
Hayes, Edmond 138, Gilbert 29
Hayley, Sylas 94
Haymes (Hames, Aymes) John 86,116, Ruth 116, William 86,116
Haynes, (Hayns) Harbert 44, James 135

Haymore, William 124
Hayward (Haywood), Griffin 98,130, John 77, Samuel 127
Head, William 136
Healy's 7
Hearne (See Hern), James 144, Joshua 144, Parnal 144, Stephen 144, Thomas 79,93,141, 144
Heaton, Keader 137
Helms (Hellams, Holmes), Elizabeth 116* George 34*,70, James 117,134,137, John 34,95, Jonathan 26,36,37,40,133,134,138, Tilman 31,32, 39,40*,49,82,133
Hemphill, Andrew 37
Henderson, Alexander 114, Joseph 85,91,94,96, 136,144, Rice 2,71,79,82,89,141, Rice, Jr. 71, Zacheriah 91
Hendricks, Jabez 136,138, Jeremiah 100,135, John 109,136,138
Hendry, Henry 30
Henley (Hendley), Darby 136, Edward 136, William 47,73,85,91,134
Hennigan, Darby 89,95
Henry, Catherine 82,126,130, George 120, Jeremiah 137, John 54,74,82,85,120,126,130, Philip 120, William 61,120,122,139
Henson (Hinson), Agnes 122, Charles 100,122, John 133,137,139, Penelope 127, Phillip 127, William 64
Hurbert, Thomas 138
Herinton, Nathan 135
Heritage 147
Hern, James 91, Joshua 91, Purcell 91, Frederick 106, Thomas 101, William 101
Herndon, Philip 72,95,113
Herren (Herrin, Herring), Aaron 89, Benjamin 141, Daniel 137, John 71*,138, Stephen 89,103
Hiatt (Hiett, Hount), Ezekiel 135, Joseph 135, Mary 25, 41
Hickman, John 94, Wm. 133,134
Hicks, Andrew 93, Ann (Terry) 150 Christopher 150, Daniel 71,93,102, Frances 115, Francis 78,83, John 78,82,83,115,127, 130,132*, Martha 83, Mary 115, Obedience 115, Sarah 115, William 104,115
Higdon, Anna 99, Charles 39, Eliz. 73, Jeptha 40, John 62,99,136, Leonard 39,62,99, Mary 40,62, 99, Thomas 99,136
Higgin, Holland 93
High, Garner 144
Highlowerby, Thomas 47
Hilburn, John 80
Hildreth, David 49,91,127, Elizabeth 119, James 96, Reuben 139,144, Sarah 144, William 129, 144,147
Hill, Abram 49,134, Charles 134, Jacob 134, John 49,137,138,144, Samuel 49, Richard 139, William 130,139
Hillen, Mary 44, Nathaniel 26*,35,44
Hilyard, John 155
Hinds (Hines) Absolem 135,137, Charles 56,57,69, 70,73,76,78,81,90,96,98,103,133,141, Easter 50, 54, Joab 154, Joseph 44,46,50,54*,55,56*,74, 75,87,88,89,92,93*,97,134,149,154,155, Nathan Jones 154, Senay 154, Thomas 76,154
Hinson, Benjamin 71,72,73,77,79,88, Charles 79, 88,107,110,120,121,139, Hester 64, John 72,79, 104,121
Hix, Adrack, 86*, Addery 144, Daniel 144
Hoaton, Martha 114, Robert 114
Hodges, George 57, Joshua 135,137
Hogan, David 123, Elijah 123, Elizabeth 129, Edmund 123, Edward 28, Griffin 91,111,123, Hannah 129,132, James 51,88,102,121,123,137, James, Jr. 91*,102,123, John 51,138, Nathan 106, Shadrach 34,38,39,40,69,87,91,94,103,105, 106*107,122,132,144,148, Shd. 52,129 Silmee 123, Susannah 123, Wm. G. 132, William 69,71, 102,123,141, William Griffin 71,80,86,91,129, 148, Zacheriah 54,79,88,94, William 75
Hogatt, John 92, William 91,92
Hoggs, Joseph 135
Holderness, Reuben 93,134,144
Holdings, John 83, Reuben 86
Holladay, Daniel 27
Hollam, William, Jr. 144
Holland, Anthony 144
Hollifield, William 10,61
Hollis, Moses 139
Holloway, William 43
Hollingsworth, Joseph 127,129, Martha 127,129
Holly (Holley), Julius 43,70*,72,128, Sabra 129, Sarah 70,72,128, Nathaniel 75,82,96, William 70,75,81,82,83*,95,101,128,129,133,138
Holmes, Archibald 56,98, Thos. 26,34,50
Holton, Ann, 124, James 141, John 87,124,141, Nathaniel 56,98, William 34,35,39,40,46,144
Honey, Elias 123
Hooker, Elizabeth 55, Hardy 49,61,117,123,138, 139, Simon 47,54,55,86,97,102,128,135,150
Hopkins, John 79,101,142, Lambert 85*,91,93,98, Richard 144, Zilpah 98
Hopper, Thomas 26,29,36
Hornbeck, John 26,46,49,69,73,91,92,100,103,105, 141, John, Jr. 133
Horne (Horn), Benjamin 26,80, John 80, Thomas 73,91
Hough, Hezekiah 139, James 64,122, Joseph 100, 105,126, Joseph, Jr. 100, Matthew 114, Richard 114, Sampson 116, Thomas 114, William 114
Hount (See Hiatt)
Hover, Thomas 78

INDEX 167

Howard, Elizabeth 34, James 51,127,128,139, John 127,128, Nathan 144, Capt. Thomas 139
Howell,___ 49, Caleb 26,30*,62,127, Elizabeth 46, Frances 46, Henry 11, Hopkins 46,47,50,57, 78,79*,87,92,96,102,105,107,113,122,130,132, 133,138, James 144, Joseph 54,71,77,78,79,81, 82,86,96,102,108,122,136,141,148, Joshua 92, Saml 46,51,92,139
Howlett, John 122, Sarah 122, Thomas 110, William, Jr. 118
Hoy, Capt. William 103
Hubberd, John 85,93, Manoah 85, Peter 85
Hudson, Nelly 123
Hues, John 93,135, Solomon 31,46
Huff, Amos 102, Joseph 103
Hughs, Richard 33
Hughlett, John 151
Hull, Joseph 23,50,55, Moses 23*,102*, Sampson 102, Sarah 66
Humble, Jacob 81,93,142
Humphreys, George W. 29, George 152
Hunt, Christopher, 57, John 77, Jonathan 144, Joseph 93,95, Lewis 93,134, Mary 144, William 94
Hunter, Catherine 128, Samuel 137, Thos. 128, Wm. 47,49,61,77,78,92,96,100,105,137*,155
Huntle, Robert 138, Thos. 135, Thomas, Jr. 135
Huntley, Robert, Sr. 68, Thomas 72,78,96,129, 138
Hurley, Edmund 103,141,144, Edward 87,93, John 46,76,94, Moses 149, Thomas 76,84,94, Timothy 44,94,137
Hurt, Charles 121
Husbands, Frances 127, John 49,79*,87,89,91, 115,127,130,132,133, Tabitha 78,87,115, William 58
Huston, Thomas 39
Hutchinson (Hutcheson), John K. 60, John King 7
Hutchins,___ 101, Ann 72, Anthony 30*,31*,32,33*, 37,49,53,56,59,62,70*,71,72,83*,87,90,118*, 119,128,133, James 17,70,74,75,77*,78,80, 81*,82*,95,99,104,133,137,141,149,155,Elizabeth 155, John 135, Samuel 73, Thomas 59
Hyde, Jane 122, John C. 61, John Colson 122, Stephen 61*,62*,64,65,66,122
****
Inglish (See English), Cornelius 144, John 81, Joseph 144, Mathew 81,95, Thomas 84
Ingram, Andrew 100, Ann 141, Benjamin 42,48,60, 70,80,93,94,126,135,138,149,153, Druscilla 153*, Edwin 49,108,134,150, Elizabeth 56,101, George 69,75,78,83,92,100,105*,126,115, Hannah 115, Isham 64,66,69,79,84,138,139, James Moody 49, Jesse 115, John 69,96,98, 99,109,115,117,138,139*, Joseph 46,48,59,61, 69,70,79,104,108,109,138,140,152, Joseph,

Sr. 122, Joseph Moody 69,102, Martha 126, Moody 48,54,99,126,136, Lemeul 122, Mary 154, Nancy 115, Owen 99, Patsey 152, Samuel 54, 134, Richard 79, Tabitha 115, William 93,141
Inkgralds, James 53
Inlaws, Sebastian 134
Irby (Yurby, Yearby), Edmond 30,31, Marget 34,41, Stephen 138, William 25,34,37,38*,41,74,106,145, Wm. Jr. 145
Irwin, James 129,132, Margaret 129,132
Isham, Joseph 106
Ivey, James 137, Jesse 128,129,138, Jesse, Sr. 139, John 129,137, Mary 128,129
****
Jackson, Benjamin 38,131, Capt. 78, Elizabeth 56, 118, Hannah 118, Henry 62, Isaac 56,62,73,123, 126,138,139, Jemimah 118, Job 77*,78, John 53, 70,72,75,76,78,82,83,84,88,93,97,104,107,121, 123,118,129,135,138*,139, Jonathan 62,123,128*, 129*,130*,131,134,138,139, Mary 118, Peter 136, Phebe 118, Randle 136, Rebecca 118,123, Richard 83, Samuel 123,134,136,138, Capt. Samuel 139, Sard 118, Stephen 55,69,72,77,79, 82,83,84,89,93,94*,95*,97,98,101,103,106,108, William 58,136,145
Jacobs, (Jacob), John 105, Josan 43, Patty Brian 36, Shadrach 36*,37
James, Ann 73, Jimmey 133, John 27,33, 70,77,78, 80,87,88,96*, 101,130,137, John, Sr. 58,78,100, 105,133, John, Jr. 58,88,94,105,152, Philip 137, Richard 70,73,90,109,136, Tabitha 130, Timmey 44
Jameson (Jemison), D. 127,131, David 47,116,128, 129*,131,137,140, Chrislars 65, James 116,131, 138,139
Jarman,___17, Alice 60, Eliz. 60, Hollingsworth 139, Jane 58, John 23*,48,57,58*,60,75,76,82, 83,87,90,97,102,103,104,105*,122 John, Jr. 138, Maryann 123,129, Molly 60, Nancy 60, Priscilla 60, Robert 5,25,43,54,55,58*,59,60*, 70,73,75*,76*,81*,82,83*,84,86,88,91,92, 93,94,96,98,100,105,127,129,133,136,138,139,141, Ullis 60
Jefferson, G. 116, Garland 152; George 47,48*,49, 50,51,110,152, George, Jr. 152, John 152, Peter 152, Samuel 152
Jeffreys, Ann 145, James 23, James, Sr. 103,144, John 23,38,44,73,78,88*,96,136,145
Jenkins, John 44,72,73,74,99,135,137
Jennings, Ann 107, Daniel 62, Gibbons 99,107, John 55*,56,57*,58,85*,97*,98*,99*,102,118, 134,141,143,145, Thomas 55*,57,58,97,99,105
Jernigan,___81, David 53,75,79,94,137, Jean 152, William 103,109,121,137,152
Jinney, Thomas 140
Johns___39

168 INDEX

Johnson, ___ 50,148, Daniel 118, Delilah 67, Elizabeth 95,126, Greset 139, Henry 119,131, Hugh 118, James 64,136,118,145, John 70,116,118, 135,136,138,139*,145,147, Malcom 118, Mark 137, Mary Ann 118, Moses 135,138, Randolph 137, William 51,63,64,72,81,82,96,118,122, 126,134,138,139,149, William, Jr. 118
Johnston, Daniel 151, Moses 88, Thomas 88,90, William 75, Zacheriah 137
Jokoy, Benjamin 30
Jones, Abraham 92,107,109,135,136, Charles 136, 145, Isaac 57,92,103,105,135,144, Jacob 109, 136, James 2, Jesse 142, John 48,73,79,81, 92,108,117,134,141,144, John, Sr. 96, Jonathan 130, Joseph 36, Nelson 67, Sarah Kinchen 120, Solomon 137, Stephen 36, Thomas 23, 26,29,43,47,50,60,62,82,96,103,106,109,110, 136,139,141, Walter 46, William 35,134
Jordan, Alex. 73, Charles 136, Frances 71, Francis 93,104,133,144, Jeremiah 107, Job 138, John 136,137,144, Matthew 136, Over 11, Priscilla 11, River 11,137,149, William 93,95, 144
Jowers, James 48,149, Jonathan 95, Thos. 74,95, 96,99*,103,134, William 69,99
Joyet, Joseph 139
Justice, Thomas 134

****

Kahey, Mr. 104
Karbo, John 109
Keachey, George 151
Kebelson, Tillotston 34
Kee, Henry 109, Robert 131
Kelly, ___ 15, Nelson 44,81,83,105, Samuel 145
Kemp, David 138, Elizabeth 118, John 118, Joseph 39,118, Sarah 118, Steven 118, Thomas 118, William 118, William, Jr. 118
Kendall (Kindle), John 45, Wm. 145
Kennedy, John 31, Katherine 118, William 33
Kenney, Phillip 130
Kennon, Robert 134, William 96,101
Ker (Kerr), David 131, Patrick 27,31*, Robert 36
Kerle, George 93
Kersey, George 91, John 92, Roland 91
Keys, Robert 128
Kiker, Nancy 68, Philip 68
Kilpatrick's 27
Kimball (Kimbell), Benjamin 90, Buckley 85*,91, 96,100*,103,136
Kimbrough, Ann 65, Goldman 31, James 65,66*, 68, John 13, 24*,30,47,48,51,59,65,66*,107, John, Jr. 66, Marmaduke 28, Miss 152, Nathaniel 30,66,68
Kindred, Elisha 66*,122,140, Samuel 66
King, John 66,120,138, Martha 124, William 95
Kirby, William 138,139, John 140

Kirke (Kerk) George 136,145
Knap, William 145
Knight, Aaron 122, Moses 122,151
Knotts, Henry 108, James 92,134,141, John 62,64, 83,84,87*,94,97,101,103*,107,108*,110,122,138*, 139
Kulp, Peter 115
Kuykendal (Kochindolph), Peter 114

****

Lacy, Anna 123, Eliz. 123, Griffith 123, Jesse 123, Kesia 123, Lucretia 123, Mary 123, Sarah 123, Stephen 123, Thomas 75,79,82,107,121,123,133, 138, William 93,105,145
Lake (Leak?) Richard 94
Lamb, George 148
Lambden (Lamton), Bexley John 72,73*, 74,76,77, 78,86*,87,94,97,99,101,102,107,137,139, John 66, 78,103,139, Robert 137
Lancaster, John 136
Land (Lants), Benjamin 37, Eleanor 28,32,33,37, James 31,37, John 31,35,37,56, Catherine 35, Thomas 28*,30,31,32,33*,34,35,36,37, William 37
Landram, Elizabeth 145
Lane, Joel 110, Patience 110, Wm. 27
Langford (Lankford), James 72,84,109,133,136, William 136
Langston, Luke 135
Lanier, Burwell 47,50,57,62*,63,104,106,118,129*, 131,132,140, Eliz. 118, Isaac 132,140, James 118,132, Jesse 145, Joseph 117, Lewis 62*,122, Mary 122, Sampson 63,118, William 62, 63, 118, 140
Larrimor (Lorrimer), Hugh 27,29
Lassiter, Robert 83*
Lawrence, George 67, Peter 49, William 49,104
Laws, Thomas 145
Lawson, John 145
Leak (Leake), Pickett and Co., 67, Elisha 129, Francis 152, Judith 152, Mourning 153, Richard 25,54,59,77,97*,103,108,109,137, Sally Howard 152, Walter 46,51,59*,65,124,129,151*,152*, 153*,154,155, Wat 150*,151,153, William 41,42, 50,53,54,56,58*,75,86,89,92,102,103,104,106, 107,115,134,152,153*,154. Wm. P. 153
Ledbetter, Charles 136,145, Drury 53,73,75,84,85,91, 108,145, Zedekiah 62,136,145
Lee, Anthony 116, Bryant 123, Elizabeth 115,116,132, Francis 78,90*, George 73,91,100,104,108,141, James 63,115,129,145, John 33,43*,46,61,73,76, 79*,80,82,90,94,115,116,126,132, Judith 115, Maryan 126, Millie 115,129, Mittry 115,132, Nannie 123, Richard 115,116, Robert 33,34,76, 90,92,104,105,115,116,121,126,129,132,138,141, Sarah 115,129, Wm. 115
Leeper, Robert 45

INDEX 169

Leeth, George 119, John 28,30*,31,32,33,119, Joseph 119
Lefeaver, Abraham 49,107,136,139, Diana 49, John 99,102
Leonard (Linard), Daniel 97, Davis 32,135, John 27,32,33, Thos. 32, William 92,123,137
Leslie, James 103
Leverett, Elizabeth 149, John 51*,57,66*,69,71,72, 101,104,107,129,131,133,134,138,139,141,149, John, Jr. 107, Richard 134,142,145, Robert 76, 79,85,102,134,142,145, Thos. 61, William 45, 57,72*,79,97,106,133,138,141,142
Levina, William 24
Lewis, Abraham 122, Alexander 27,28,35,36,132, Daniel 123, Francis 150, George 150, Jeremiah 117,121,123,139, John 150, Miles 139, Nath'l. 62, Peter 47,62,128,129,132, Philip 123, Sarah 123, Thomas 117,138,139, William 91,104,109, 123,137,138, William, Jr. 104
Leyton, Rebecca 115
Lightfoot, John 145
Liles (Lisles) Edmund 71, Ephraim 47, James 12, 62*,70,97,103,138,139, John 59,86,90,96,99, 111,137, Mourning 121, Rebecca 59,96,99,111, Robert 107, William 136,139*
Lilly, Benjamin 145, Edmund 27,30,36,43,84,86, 90,104,106,108,115,129,145, John 122,132,145, Nathaniel 43,73,105,106*,133, Sarah 30
Linard (See Leonard)
Lindsey (Lyndsey), Edward 139, George 24,62*, 64,80,117,136,139, William 23,53*81,88*94*, 102,123,138,139
Lionely, James 135
Linn, James 9,119,127,132, John 131
Lipham, Jacob 35
Lipscomb, Daniel 75
Lisonby (Lisenby, Lisenbe), Charles 137, Charles, Sr. 139, Ezekiel 139, Far 139, Henry 139, James 136, John 135,137,139
Little, Abraham 34, Alexander 119, Archibald 119, Catherine 78, George 28*, James 61,66, 84,92,119,136,137,139, John 119,139, John, Jr. 119, Margaret 119, Thomas 119, William 28*, 30,31,78,112*,113*,119, W. 68
Llewellyn, Jonathan 32,44,77,81*,89,90,91,92, 101*,103,104,109,110,133,135,141,149, Ruth 44
Lochler, William 135
Locke, Francis 120, Samuel 141
Lockhard, Thomas 131
Loftin, Moses 136, Wm. 108,136, Col. William 145
Long___ 109, Elizabeth 126, James 44,78,80*,97, 113,126,136,150, John 55,74,95,100,135,137, 152,155, John, Jr. 86,101,135,137, Short 44,80, 99, Walter 80
Love, Alexander 105, Benjamin 115, Daniel 102, David 64*,65,84,90,92,93,94,95,99,104,105*, 106,107*,109,138,141, Col. David 107, James 110,114,126,152, John 135, Robert 29,115, William 24*,25,51,62,105,107,110,115,126,136, 138,149*,150,155
Low (Loe),___ 36, Daniel 13,123,136, Franke 123, John 123, Nancy 123, Thomas 123, William 123
Lowry, Ann 130, Eliz. 127,128,130, James 82,84, 127,130,139, Judy 45, 52, Lew 99, Lewis 45,61, 72*,79,84*,109,128,133,139,141, Mary 123, Nancy 130, Peter 61,121,123,130,135,139, Robert 72,130,141, Susannah 45,130, William 130,139
Lucas, Mary 55, John 55,98,133, Thos. 93,134, Wm. 47,86,89,133
Lunn, John 136
Lucy, Edward Avery 64
Lyons, Andrew 104, Josiah 138,153, Richard 77
Lynch, John W. 67, Philip 145
Lylly, John 116
Lynton, John 139

****

McAfee, James 36,37, Robert 37
McAlester, John 150
McAlman (MaCalman) David 90, John 90,98*,135, 137,153
McAlpin, Alexander 152
McAuley (McColly, McCowly, McCally) Anguish 145, August 135, Daniel 135, John 135,142,145, John, Jr. 145, Murdo 95, Murdock 135
McBee, Hannah 52, Vardry 52
McBride, Dugald 137, Hugh 44, John 137
McCaffee, John 145, Malcom 145
McCairn, Archibald 153, Catherine 153, Christian 153
McCain, Hugh 131, Peter 130
McCall (McCaul), Daniel 137, John 137,155
McCamel, John 22
McCann, Daniel 137
McCaskill, Allan 55,92,103, Alex. 60,136, Daniel 137, Donald 139, John 92,147,148, Margaret 55, Murdo 58,92,96*,100,105, Murdock 130,141
McCay, William 60
McClellan, Angus 61, James 35, Jennet 35
McClenachan, Elizabeth 33, Robert 28*,30,32*,33*, 34,35,82,118,119,132
McClendon (McClendall), Ann 117, Benj. 66, Dennis 63,74,83,93*,109,116,117,139,141, Dennis, Jr. 139, South Dennis 139, Ezekiel 47,63,66,72, 93*, 101,136,139,145, Isaac 145, Jacob 54, 52,56,69,87,88,97,103,135,145, Joe 148, Joel 50, 53,56,69*,73,74,76,82*,84,85,87,88,89,90,141, 145, John 51,57,63,100,117,129,136,138,139,141, Rebekah 117, Samuel 117, Simon 117, Thomas 105,134,145
McClerry, Samuel 28
McClevael, John 69*,77,94*

McClintock (McKinclock), Mark 145, Swain 145
McCollum, Daniel 122
McConnell, Agnes 114, Alexander 114, Andrew 114, Catherine 114, John 114, John, Jr. 114
McCoole, Adam 45,126,129
McCorkel (McCorkall), Andrew 131, Archibald 119, James 119,127,131*, Jane 131*, Margaret 119,127,132, Matthew 36, Robert 30,119,127, 132, Robert, Jr. 119
McCormick (McCormack), Daniel 135, Hugh 136, 137
McCowan, James 118
McCoy, Alex. 87, Archibald 90, Ann 60, Alecy 60, Elizabeth 60,69, Frances 60, Mary 90*,155, Molly 60, Mildred 60, John 31,32,43,57,58*, 60,90*,155, Sarah 60
McCrakin, Willa 118
McCre, Farquard 135
McCreary, Robert 115
McCrimmon, Daniel 137, Donald 141
McCulloch,___ 148, Henry Eustace 42, Samuel 121
McCummins, David 96
McCurry, Duncan 77, Wm. 46,135
McDaniel, Absolem 29, Ann 63, Christian 152, Daniel 40,58,98,155, James 153, John 36,63, Lydia 153, Patrick 75, Randolph 155, Soirle 98, 99, William 48,76*92,98,133,135,137,149,155, Zacheriah 54,94*,153
McDonald, Anabella 58, Angus 137, Alexander 58, 84,96,100,137,145, Daniel 96,133,145, Donald 58,103*136,137, Flora 58,87, Florrie 58, Hugh 78,103, James 45,101, John 29,45,78*,141,145, Kenneth 58, Malcolm 135, Roger 95, Ronald 137, Roderick 103, Soirle 45,55,58*,78*,96, 100,101,103,110,134,141, William 54,58†95,96, 135,136
McDowell, Charles 114,128, Eliza 78, John 114, Joseph 114
McDuffie, Daniel 100
McDugal, James 30
McEthing, Thomas 132
McFadden (McFadding), Wm. 75
McFarland, Duncan 155, Sarah 151
McFerson, Donald 130
McKelhenny (McElhoney), Jean 33, Thomas 28,45
McGovett, John 139
McGown (Glown), John 135
McGregor (McGrigger), Anthony 122, Bartlett 136, John 122, William 52,136,145
McGuire (Meguire, Muguaire),___ 70, John 155, Wm. 24,50,69,86,90,155
McHenry (McHenery), Eliz. 120, James 129, Jesse 138, Mary 128,129, William 105,128, 129
McIlvaile, John 103,111,133
McIlwean, Francis 30,32,33,54, I-----138, James 127

McInnis, Angus 98, Daniel 137, Donald 137, John 137, Malcom 137, Murdo 78, Murdock 152, Neill 105
McIntosh, S----137
McIver, John 137
McKahey,___ 108, Margaret 88,89, Sarah 99, Widow 99,101, William 81,82,88,89,99
McKay, Alexander 141,149, Archibald 137, David 135, Duncan 120,137, Jean 120, Michael 68
McKee, John 133
McKennox, Lachlin 135
McKenzie, Donald 135
McKeachey (Kenchey) James 137, Wm. 137
McKincy, Daniel 145
McKindrick, Patrick 45
McKinnie (Kinney) Matthew 39, Thos. 138
McKimons, Murdock 148
McKinnon, Roderick 45,58*,87,98*
McKissack, Archibald 141
McLean, B---- 135, Duncan 141,142
McLarman, Wm. 100
McLaurin, Neill 120
McLellan, Alexander 96
McLennan (Lenon), Alex. 135, Colin 134, Donald 137, James West 137, John 98*
McLeod (McCloud), Alexander 92,96,137, Duncan 96,145, Daniel 145,155, Innis 145, Jennett 87, 115, John 86,87,92*,98,100*,101,102,115,133, 134, Malcom 134,145, Nancy 155, Norman 58*, 92,100,101,115,135
McLester, Joseph 23,91,136,145,147
McMahain, Alexander 16
McManus (McManness)_____ 39, James 127,132*, Mary 127,132*
McMillan, Aman 145, Archibald 137, D---137, Daniel 69
McMullin, Daniel 141, Dugald 142, Widow 101
McNabb, Duncan 57*,58,98,100*,103 William 59
McNair (McNear, McHair) Edward 100, 137, John 81, Neill 87, Roger 137
McNath, Henry 133, John 133
McNatt, Duncan 99, John 104
McNeill (McNeal), Daniel 81,135,137, Hector 141
McNichols, Duncan 141
McNick, James 127
McNish, Henry 77
McPetre, Mary 114
McPherson Priscillah 116, Alexander 126, Robert 26
McQueen, Neal 77,100, William 100,101,137
McRae (McRa,McCray), Alexander 67,137,150, Angus 67, Christopher 137, Colin 135,145, Daniel 134,139, Daniel L. 121, Duncan 62,138, Farquar 138,145, John 118,133,137,138, John, Jr. 135,138, Mary 145, Nancy 145, Philip 122, William
McSwain, Allen 141, Daniel 151
****

Macallam, John 93
Macby (Magbee, Magby, McBee), James 34
  Matthias 34, Samuel 32,34, Susannah 34,
  Rachel 59, Vadry 34, William 34,51,64
Mackelbray, James 26
Mackahey William 71
Maine, Benj. 141
Maness, Elizabeth 116, John 123,139, Richard 123,
  William 123
Maner, Benjamin 135,137,149, John 135, Nancy 70,
  Stephen 135,137
Mandles, Jeremiah 85
Manley, John 100, Richard 61
Marasked (Menasco), Jeremiah 59
Marby (Macby) Rachel 34,51
Marbary, Francis 93,95,103,145
Marchbanks, George 69
Menasco (Mareskau) Jeremiah 145, Jerry 46,130,
  John 145, Jeremiah 55,82
Mark's 39
Marsh, William 122
Marshall, James 120,123*, Henry 123, William 140
Martin, Abraham 123*, Alexander 82,90*,100,
  Alex. Jr. 82, Allen 24,88,89,137,138,103*,
  Andrew 123, Angus 138, Atten 84, Benj. 32,33,
  Catherine 118,123*, Donald 137, George 44,
  Isaac 123* James 122,123, Jesse 103,118,
  John 77,85,91,93,95,100*,123,128,136,137*,
  138,145, John, Jr. 95, John Hale 81,118,
  Joshua 134, Josiah 108, Joseph 58,62,70,73,
  75,76*,77,78,79,80*,81*,82,83,86,88,90,95,100,
  103,105,109,110,115,118,128,133,136, Katherine 128, Kinchen 64,139, Lewis 123* Malcom
  55,103,126, Martin 137,138, Nancy 118,122,
  123, Rebekah 122,123, Sarah 122,123, Susannah
  44, Thomas 123, Samuel 27,29,31, William
  121,122,123, Zacheriah 155
Martine, John 137,145, Norman 137
Mask, Druscilla 154*, Dudley 135,143*,152,154*,
  James P. 154*, John 44,75,102,135,138,154,
  John, Jr. 75,76,93,99,104,111,142,154, John,
  Sr. 44,72, Lucy 154, Martha 154, Mary 154,
  Phillip 154, Pleasant 151*, Pleasant Moses
  151, Rebeckah 41,44,53, Walter 154, William
  25,38,41,42,44*,46*,48*,50,51,52,53,54,56,59,
  69,70,71,74*,75*,78*,80,86,89,90,96,101,104,
  105,108,109,110,134,141,142,143*,145,147,153,
  155, William, Jr. 134
Mason, Gidden 138, John 99,135,137, Mary 120,
  Ralph 76,81,90, Thomas 95,99, William 137
Matheny, Aaron 145, William 145
Mathews, Daniel 145, George 46,70,79,94,101,
  108*, John 98,105,109
Matson, Daniel 135
May, Daniel 66, John 45,60,67,72*,94,118,120,
  129,131,133,135,138,139,140, Jonathan 135,
  Lewis 122,139, Lucy 46, Martha 121, Peter
  139, Philip 82,84*, Pleasant 60,129,139, William 46*,53,78,79,84,103,110,120,131,135,136,
  137,139, William, Jr. 138,139
Mays, Drury 47
Meacham, Duncan 95
Meador, Elizabeth 115, Druscilla 115, Jason, 69,72*,
  74,115,123,133,139, Jason, Jr. 74,115,133, Job
  72,82*,115,118,139, Lewis 72,82,115,139, Mariah
  115, Marion 115, Suffiah 123, Thomas 72,115,
  135,139
Mears, William 41,46
Medcalf, Amelia 120, Emanuel 120, Joel 120, John
  120, William 120, Wm. Jr. 120
Mediall, William 95
Medley, Reuben 122
Medling, John 82
Medlock Agatha 54,55,89, Charles 42,43,44, 54*,55,
  70*,71,73,74*,75*,77*,78*,79,80,83*,84,87,88,
  89*,90*,91,94,96,105,107*,108*,109,129,130*,
  132*,136, Colo. Chas. 108,130, Israel 137,130
Megginson, Benjamin 89, Thomas 46,56,57,59*,79,
  84,89,101,106,107*,108,138,145, Thomas G. 51
Meggs, James 139, William 137,139
Melton, John 137, M. 139, Nathaniel 45,46,102,103,
  138
Menes, John 51
Meguire (Maguire) ___ 70, John 135, William 69,
  83,101,134,135
Mercer, Jeremiah 63
Meredith ___ 147, Elizabeth 117, James 52,90,106,
  117, James, Jr. 126 Sanders 117,152*
Merman, John 131
Merritt, Benjamin 136*
Merriman, Charles 145
Meseles (Meselie) Peter 77*,81
Metland, George 35
Miles, David 24,39*,45,55
Miller, Aaron 76, Abraham 134,138, Charles 134,
  138, David 65, James 9, Jesse 129*,135,136
  Jerome 39,41,97,138, John 100,102,128,129*,
  Phebe 129, S. 127,131, Stephen 41,49,53,72,75,
  76,77,79,81,82,83,84,88,93,97*,104,105,107,109,
  110,128,129,130*,132,138,141,135, Theodorick
  49, William 129,138,139,142
Mills, David 120, Joel 120, John 120,128,139, Mary
  120, Nathan 39,48, Robert 23,30,35,38,39*,41,
  45,46,48, Samuel 120, William 120
Milton, Joseph 139
Mims, Benjamin 36,76,80, John 50,69,75,76, Mary
  50, Samuel 96, Thomas 72, William 80,137
Minshew, Arson 81
Minor, Stephen 40
Mitchell, Abram 117, George 105, James 26,152,
  John 24*,45*,46,55*,60,79,80,82,99*, Thomas
  60*,77,82,99,105,133

INDEX

Moberly, John 135
Mode, James 105
Money, James 137
Monroe (Munroe), Arch. 58,95*, Catron 58, Daniel 95, Malcom 58,95
Mont, Joshua 138
Montseer (Monseer) John 74, Thomas 53,73,80, Timothy 53,73,128
Mondine, Lydia 94
Moody, William 56,72,73,77,78,99,108*,126,133
Moon, Vick 133
Moore, Bedenago 142*,145, Charles 114,115,119, Edward 73,85*87*,91*,92,93,101,103,104*, 128,131, Edward, Jr. 76, James 35,75,76,85,94, 109,110, John 81,90,114,129, Joseph 142*, Mary 114, Michael 145, Moses 114, Lawrence 122, Reuben 140, William 134
Moorman 40, Andrew 25,46,109,118, Archelas 50*,70,72,79*,109,119,133, Ann 122, Benjamin 39,50,70,79,94,101,109,120,122,133, Benj. Jr. 109,120, Cathern 119,Edward 79,152, John 109, Mary 50, Michael 120, Thomas 38,39,43, 50,70,79*,94,95,101,109, Thomas, Jr. 109, Zacheriah 39,46,50,79,94,95,105,109,137, William 120
Morgan, Ann 57, Evan 114, Gawin (Goen, Going) 48,51,56,57,73,74,77,79*,91,98,101,107,127, 134,141,148, Hill 127, John 51,57,91,93,96, Jonathan 64*,66*, James 61, Joseph 91, Joshua 24,43,50,51,57*62,76,92,96,101,104, 106*,129,131,138, Mary 127,129, Massey 145, Nathaniel 4, William 49,57,64,67,73,91,94, 134,141
Morley, 134, Francis 46
Morris, Charles 105,115,126, Eliz. 47,115,117, Edward 55,71*, 133,145, Daniel 58, George 37, Jacob 123,135,140, James 90, Jason 140, John 25,93,115,134,141,145, Joseph 52, Haden (Haten) 40,47,50,71,87,93,133, Jeptha 120, Mary 121, Nathan 63,120,140, Patsy 120, Oston 84, Thomas 76, Valentine 69,84,108,137, William 70,90,106,117*,120,130,133,135,136,137, William Airley 120, Zacheriah 108
Morton, Edward 137, John 137, Peter 137, William F. 151
Morrison, John 145, Malcom 141
Moseley, Edward 102,129,130, Francis 54,70,75,76, 79,83,88,92,126,130, Margaret 49,126, William 98
Moses, Joshua 136, Samuel 64
Moss, James 77*,78, Richard 138, Robert 145, Valentine 137
Mounger, Edwin 52, Mounger's 24,107, Henry 46, 51*,52*,58,85,91,100*,101,107,136,145,147
Mounten, William 137
Mumford's 46
Munday, Arthur 91,93, Christopher 91,93,97,
Francis 91, Joseph 141, Mary 53, Samuel 91, William 91,93,97,141
Murchison, John 135
Murdock, John 129
Murphy (Murpe), Bartholomew 44,71,80,84,86,103, 139, Bat 138, Daniel 44,64,73,100,102,109,136, 139*, David 138, Henrietta 121, John 103,136, 138, Joseph 38*,49,70,138, Valentine 38, Thomas 81, William 139
Murrel, Judah 120
Myers, Abraham 124, Absolem 124, Samuel 138, Thomas 136, 139*

****

Nall, Isaac 137, Joseph 137
Nance, Ann 121, B. 65, Betsy Ann 121, Buckner (Buck) 64,66,118,120,121,140, Harriet 121, Olive May 121, Patsy 121, Winifred 121
Naron, Sarah 145
Nash, F. 151, John 140, William 138
Neals (Neel), George 28, Jean 119
Nelms, Presley 138
Nelson, John 91,139, William 43,75,81,84,94,96, William, Jr. 134
Nesbit, John 35,118
New, Jonathan 134
Newberry, James 136, Jesse 152, John 43,54,72,88, Jonathan 138
William 54,72,74,81,82,86,87,93,98,134,137, William, Jr. 72,75,98,103,134,138
Newell, Edmond 134
Newman George 136, John 134, Thos. 136
Newton, John 109,136
Nichols (Nickols) Daniel 145, Drury 139, Edmund 83,87,97,145, Honor 128, Isaac 83,104,128,135, 137,139, John 145, Julius 136, Mary 49,51,152, Susannah 51, William 49,137,145
Nicholas (Nicolas), Edward 71, Edmund 93, Isaac 8, John 40,93
Nixon, Thomas 75
Noble, David 91, 145, Simpson, 136,145, Thomas 145, William 78,91*,136,145
Nonaih?, Ann 116
Norman 30,31*,38
Nowland (Noland), Dennis 34,40,44,51,59
Nutt, John 131

****

Oats, Joseph 37,40,49
O'Bryan Frances 44, Lawrence 44,48,49*,60,118, 121,136,137,138
Odam (Odom), Benjamin 141, David 121, Honour 121, Isaac 121, 138, Jacob 121, James 121, Nancy 121, Richard 48,49*,60,118,121,136,137,138, Sion 137, William 121
Oliphant, David 48
Oliver, Ann 54, James 53,80,88,91,98, John 58, Mary 53

INDEX

Osburn, Adlai 83, Alexander 14,27,30,118,129
Outlaw, Lodowick 81
Overstreet, Silas 135
Oziar, William 145
****
Pace, Stephen 120,139, Wm. 134,138
Page, William 40,71,72
Parke (Parks), Hugh 129, Robert 33,34,38*
Parker, Chas. 39,93, Elisha 39, Francis 26, Howell 136,145, John 33,36, Mathew 128, Nicholas 103,105,145, Richard 136,145, Robert 24, Stephen 39,104,122, Thomas 24,71, 93,103,105, Parker's 39,48
Parmer, William 109
Parnold, John 34
Parrot, Anthony Mills 134,145
Parsons, Francis 92, James 34, John 71,72,79,92, 102,104,107,108,109,129,137,139, Joseph 139, Rachel 40,47, Samuel 24,27,32,35,36*,40*,41, 47*,48,50,71,74,75,79,81,83,86*,87,88*,91,93, 95,96,99,102,104,133, William 133,139
Pate, Samuel 137, Thorowgood 70,76
Patrick, Robert 127
Pattent, Mary 123, Thomas 123
Patterson, James 137,150, John 35,88,132,134
Pattishall, Richard 67,121*
Patton James 30,32*,33, John 36, Matthew 131
Paul, Jacob 30,38,43*,44,50,94,99*,130,133, Philemon 139, Phillip 42,99*122
Pavell, Abner 138
Peacock, Samson 133
Pealiers, Charles M. 114
Pearce (Pearse), Asa 122, Arthur 145, Jesse 75, John 134, Moses 134,138, William 138
Pearson, 124
Peck, John 137
Pegge, William 79
Pegues, Clauddius 42,71, Capt. 124
Pelham (Pellam), Dorcas 44, John 41,44,75*,76, 82,134, William 34,138
Pemberton, John 62,124,149,154, Richard 46,48, 82,88,94,102,134,138,139, Sarah 122, Stith 142
Pender, John Arnold 35
Pennington, David 136,147, Edward 11, George 36
Pentecost, Dorsey 38
Perie, Reuben 139
Perkins, Jacob 84,103, John 38,84,94,103,105,109, 118, Stephen 118
Permenter, John 122
Perryman, Daniel 117, John 123, Mary 123, Melton 121,123, Mumford 123, Samuel 123
Persons, John 145, Samuel 145
Peterson, John 1
Pettis (Petuss), Dorcas 152, Mark 137
Phare, William 140
Phelan, Daniel 67

Phillips, Benjamin 134,145, Clement 132, Henry 109, Jacob 63, James 76,86,134,135,137, Joel 33,35,62,69,133, John 61, Lewis 145, Mary 131, Reuben 72,75,95,103,128,131,132,135,137, Robert 86,107,127,131, Samuel 53,80,107*,140, Solomon 152, Thomas 136, William 26,30,34, 39,42,46,57*,71,75,127,139, William, Jr. 85
Pickens, Andrew 28,30,31,35,118,127,131,132, Ann 127, Israel 127, Jean 118, John 28,31,118, Martha 127, Nancy 118, William 31,127
Pickett,___39,40,51,109, Elizabeth 42, Frankie Hannah 65,121, J. 39*,41,53*,54,138,149,150, J. Jr. 36, Jam. 65,151, James 40,42,46,48,50, 51,53*56,59,65*,69,70*,71*,73,74,75*,77,83*, 86*87,88,89,90*,92,94*,95,96,99*,100*,101,106, 107,109,112,113,116, 121,126,130*,132*,135, 140,149,151, James (of Richmond Co.) 150*,151, 152*,153*,154, James, Jr. 31,32,33*,35, James, Sr. 33,40,113,116,127,152,154, John 36,39,41, 53,112,113* Eveline 124, Frances 124, Glovina 124, Flora 124, Joseph 65*,67,68,121*, Col. Joseph 122,151, Martha 39,66,116,121*, Martin 65,67*,120,121,124,150, Micajah 38,55,57,103, 150, Micajah, Jr. 42, Mourning 39,51,56*,57, 65,150*,152,153*, Polly 150,152, Sarah 152*, Thomas 46,48,56*,57,59,90,94*,95,136, William 24,25*,35,37,38,39,40,42*,48*,49,51*,53*, 54,55,56*,57,65,71*,73,74,75,77,78,79,80,82,83, 84,85,86*,88,89,90,94,98,99,102,107,108*,110, 111,112,113,130*,131,136,141,149,150*,152, William, Jr. 89, William Raiford 66*,66, William R. 121*, 150
Pierce (Peirce) Arthur 133,134, Wright 134
Pilcher, Robert 146
Pike, John 18
Pistole, Lydia 120
Pitcock, Stephen, 134,139
Pitman, Jesse 64, Thos. 136, Wm. 136
Pleas, Henry 116
Plant, Williamson, 139
Plunkett, James 138,139*, Milly 119
Poe, P. 64
Poland, John
Polk, Andrew 67, Anna 98, Ellender 51, James L. 10, John 51,95,98,129, Susannah 119, Thomas 48,119, 132
Pollard, Thomas 146
Polson, Henry 80,81,137, Robert 138
Poff, Devalt 128
Pond, Patty 145
Pool (Poole), Alexander 145,148, Jere 115, John 39, Mathew 27, Middleton 98,137, Phereby 115
Poor, David 56,87,93,145, Major David 71, Edward 93,98,104,141, John 145, Priscilla 98
Poplin, John 145
Porter, Barnaby 64, Charles 64, James 118,123

INDEX

Poster, John 37
Poston, James 83, John 23,75,78*,82,87,98, John, Sr. 33,94, Robert 86,93,133,134
Poteete (Pettit) George 137, John 91,131
Potts, Jeremiah, 114
Powell, Benjamin 130,135, Charles 79,100, Henry 145, James 151, John 55,87,89,92,98,105,135, 145, Nat 134, Nathan 145, Richard 134,145, Thomas 142, William 35,39,41,61,134,142,153
Pou, Robert L. 152
Powers, James 28
Praton, John, Jr. 69
Pratt, Benjamin 121, John 121, Samuel 121, William 49,50,72,75,76,77*,78,80,84,86,87,90,92, 102*,106,107,108,121,133,137,138,139,141
Preslar, (Presler, Pressley) Andrew 35,36*112, Anthony 116, Elias 116, Jane 116, John 24,77*, 97,116,139, John, Jr. 116, Levi 116, Mary 116, 117, Morgan 116, Peter 34,37, Susannah 116, William 116, Thomas 69,129,131
Preston, Andrew 94
Prestwood, Augustine 43,47,73,141, Elizabeth 47, Thomas 27*,36
Preto, John 69
Prettnett (Bretwell?) Joseph 49
Price, Elijah 124, Elinor 126, 129, James 115,134, John W. 152, 130, Robert 135, Thomas 126,129, William 126,129,134
Prichard (Pritchard), Cary 136,145,147, Charles 91
Pritchet, Robert 31
Primrose, Mary 126, Thomas 31, Violet 31, 126, William 93
Proctor, John 121,122, Lenny 122, Sterling 122, William 122
Prout, Holden 63, Jane 63*, Joshua 63*,140, Joshua, Jr. 63, Lydia 63, Sarah 63
Purnal (Purnell), Charity 117, James 97, Mary 118
****
Queen, Henry 91, Margaret 34,48,63, Mary 34, Timothy 146, William 34,35,40*,41,48,63
Quin, Hardy 139, Jeremiah 139
****
Raiford (Rayford, Reford) 5,50, Charles 140, Anne 59,111, Druscilla 111, Grace 111, James 24*,59,146,151*,154, Jane 111, Judah 59, Judith 111, Mary 51,111, Matthew 24*,29,32*,34,37*, 40*,43,48,50,56,59*,70,73*,74*,75,88*,90,99, 100*, 107*,108,110,141,151, Matthew, Sr. 59, 86,111,146,151*, Matthew, Jr. 24*,59,86,88, 99,101,104,111,146,151, Mourning 29,111, Oney 154, Philip 51,56*,102,108,111, Rebecca 111, Robert 29,47,51*,75,111,117,131,132,149,151, 154, Susannah 47,111, William 39,41*44,47,51, 111, Zedekiah 151,154
Railey, John 118

Rainey, David 138, Robert 24,51
Ramage, George 136,146, George, Jr. 146
Ramsey, Robert 27
Rand, William 137
Raney, David 95, Robert 40,66*,
Randel (Randle, Randall) Barnett 48, Benager 134, Benjamin 146, Colby 136,146, Edmond 146, John 136,146,147, Capt. John 146, Josias 136, 146,148, Nehemiah 136, Peter 93,146, Richard 146, Thomas 35,41,43,93
Rasbury, John 134, Philip 135
Ratcliff, James 116, John 116, Mary 41, Richard 139, Robert Clothen 116, Samuel 35,37,38,39, 41,45,55, Susanna 116, Thomas 107,116,138, William 41,72,80,92,116,139*, William, Jr. 116, Zachariah 116,138
Rattery, Alexander 32, James 32
Ray (Reay) Charles 98,102,103*, James 51,101*, 102, John 48,137, Samuel 39
Reaves (Reeves, Reves), Josias 146, Samuel 92, 146, William 141,146
Redd (Red,Reed), John 43,60, Thomas 29,30,32
Readon, Adam 119
Redley, Brumfield 69
Redfern (Redforn), James 138, John 134,138
Reed, John 119, Joseph 118, Martha 119, William 35,37,118
Rees, Hezekiah 115, Roger 138, Samuel 115
Regny, Charity 38
Remy (Remay) William 62,116
Remp, William 128
Renfro, Joel 138, Nathaniel 134,138
Renick (Renck, Ronicks, Renox), George 30,33,127, 131, Mary 30,33,119
Rennolds (Reynolds) Benjamin 32,33, Richard 146, Thomas 141,146
Renox (See Renicks)
Resnall, James 50, Duncan 137, Dunn 74, Elizabeth 129, Joseph 138, William 146
Rich, David 75,94,96,97,103,128,137, Timothy 128
Richards, Frances 85, Jacob 129, John 135, William 129
Richardson, John 46,87,95,101, William 33,139, Thomas 29
Richman, John 35
Ricketts, John 102,121,140, Mary 121, Nancy 121, Peggy 121, Reason 121, Sarah 121, William 137, Wilson 121
Riddle, John 146
Ridge, Thomas 26
Rivers, John 90
Road, Henry 146
Robards (Roberts) Ann 67,116,149, Benjamin 35, 41, Mary 67,121,149, Mourning 149, Polly 121 Sarah 150, William 66,111,116,140,146,149*, 150,153, Wm. Sr. 149;96,97

Robins, John 82,84,146, William 82
Robinson (Robertson, Robeson), Charles 25,27,28, 29,30,32,34,35,36,37,38,39*,40*,42,43,44*,47*, 48*,58,71,74,75,76,79,80,87,90*,96*,100*,112, 113,118,119,127,133, Chas. Jr. 26*,119, Charles, Sr. 26, Cornelius 24*,25,29,37,39*, 44,50,51*,59,65,70,71,72,73*,74,77*,79,80,84*, 86,88,96,98,99,107,112,113,115,119,134,142, 143,146, Elizabeth 47,50,119, Frances Jefferson 152, Hannah 33, James 27,28,33,154, John 43,135, Luke 44,55*,58,71,72,78,79,80,81,86*, 87,89*,92,94*,95,96,98*,99*,105,133,135,141, 146*, Pembroke 152, Sarah 47,119,127, Sophia 47,51, Tod, Clk. 63*,64*,66*,67*,119* 120*,121, Toddy (Tod) 64,66,67*121,149,150*, 153*, Thomas 68, Tirey (Tyree) 38,146, Townsend 26*,27,29*,31*,33,36,47,51,84,119,135, Tow 27,32, William 65,149,150
Roe, John 47,86*,108,147, Richard 152
Rogers (Rodgers) Benjamin 153*, Humphrey (Hum) 46,48,59,102, 105,106,108,126,138, James, Sr. 91, James, Jr. 91,136, John 91,136,141,153, Joseph 141, Rachel 153, Samuel 146, William 73,153*
Roland (Rowland) Augustus 146, Ezekiel 60, Fendal 134, George 146, Hacia 146, James 146, John 60,134,137, Methuselah 137, Richard 146, Sherwood 146
Ronalds, James 146
Rone, Adam 91,131,136,146, Dunkin 85, Flanery 136, Henry 91,131, John 146, Peter 91*,128, 131, Reuben 127, Sarah 127, Tunstall 85,91, Wm. 137
Roper, Green 116,123, James 51,86*,92,128,130, 132,148, John 116, Lucy 116, Martha 116, Mary 116,128,130, Susanna 116, William 116, 123
Rorie (Rorey), Reuben 130,137, Sarah 130, William 76,78,82,84,104,130,133,141
Rose 137, Jesse 137, John 137,138
Ross, Andrew 61,104*,109,137,138, Cornelius 136, Donald 123, Daniel 66, Hugh 10,61*,63, 121,123, Jean 123, Katherine 123, Margaret 123, Mary 123, Walter 138, Wm. 109,137
Rowan, Mary 61
Rows, Lewis 122
Royal (Ryle) John 77,91
Rudd, Burlingham 87*,70,72,77,97,101,103,105, 108,136, Burlingham, Jr. 27, Burrell 139, George Loundell 77,136
Rundle (Randolph in heading), Thomas 42
Runnels, Giles 83, James 136, George 91
Rush, John 99, William 148
Rushing, Abraham 72,76,82,135,139, David 67,141, Jacob 139, John 135,141, Johnson 135, Mark 87,136, Matt 136,140, Noah 138, Philip 109,

139, Robert 135,137,139, Roland 135,138, Richard 51,135,137,139 Solomon 128,130,137, William 62,72,75,82*,96,109,135,136,138,141
Rusk, John 97
Russell, Joseph C. 68, James 146, William 134
Rutherford, Charity 121
Rutland, J. M. 122, Martha 122
Rutledge, George 45
Ryans, Nichol 67
Rye, Dan 54, Joseph 54
Ryle, Elizabeth 116,123*, James 73,116,123*,130, John 74,80,85,116,118,128,130, Joseph 81, Larkin 116, Mary 116, Sarah 123, Whitmell 116
****
Sallis, John 33
Sanders, Aaron 93,101,102,141,142, Benjamin 82, Francis 134, George 93,146, Isaac 146, James 71,74,77,78*,81*,86,88,101,138,141,146, John 52, Lewis 52, Moses 87,93,95,96,102,134,141, Patrick 74*,76,89,135,137, Peter 92,103, William 86
Sanderson, Patrick 76
Sap, John 155
Saralson, Frances 76, Mary Ann 76, Richard 76
Sargent 71,87,91,93
Sanford, William 137
Sasser, Joseph 139
Sauls, Bolton 136
Saunders Ezekiel 111, James 23,36,69,76,79, Moses 75, Pate 75, Susan 41, William 41
Saxon, Benj. W. 150, Mary 150,152
Schrater, J. J. 121
Schrimshire, John 91,93,97,141, John, Jr. 91
Scisco, John 75
Scoff, John 29
Scott, Abraham 33, John 121,136, Nathaniel 106, 109,136,139, Samuel 142, Thomas 136, William 74,77,92,103,136,137
Scull, Alexander 124,125, Mourning 124,125
Seago, Abraham 117, Ann 117, Eliz. 117, James 117, John 49,69,70*,98,117,123,133,136, Joshua 120, Lueresy 123, Robert 62*,98,117,136, William 78,82,84,117,133
Segar, John, Sr. 136
Segraves, Nancy 120
Selby, Benjamin 118
Sellers (Sealors) Abraham 33, Eliz. 33, Leonard 1, Sampson 149,152
Self, Jacob 107, Job 146, Phillip 147, William 107
Selvey, Mary 44
Selwyn, George Augustus 42, George 42
Severight, John 28
Seward (Sewerd) Absolem 138, Wm. 54,93
Sewell, Charles 146, John 146, Wm. 146
Shankle, George 73*,136,146,151, Jacob 136,146, John 146, Oney 151

INDEX

Sharpe, Elizabeth (Hough) 114, James 114
Shaw, Daniel 137, Wm. McD. 154
Shelby, Reese, Sr. 63, Reese, Jr. 63, Evan 63, Evan, Jr. 63*, Thomas 134,138
Shelton, Micajah 153, Thomas 98
Sheppard (Shepherd), J. 44, Jacob 35,39,42,47,72, James 34,35,38,40,41,42,43*,59,72,129, John 25,39,53,56,86,91,96,134,146, Littlebird 36, Lucy 43,72, Nancy 55,86, Penelope 44,100, Thomas 73, William 41,43,63,122,134,137
Sherrill, Avington 127, Pershanna 33,127
Shirley, William Stoutley 42*,55,57
Short, Daniel 100, James 36, John 136, William 100
Shumak, Samuel 76
Sidum, John, Jr. 134
Simmons, Benjamin 102,142,146, Dinah 142, Elizabeth 142, James 142, John 88,89,93,102*,103, 104,133,135,142, Margaret 142, Mary 142, Sarah 142, Thomas 45,95, William 142
Simpkins, Jeremiah 135
Simpson, Gilbert 137,146, Getbird (Gilbert) 73, John 99,129,139, Thomas 73,91*,136,146
Sims (Simms) Drury 46,105,146, Redding 122, William 129
Sinclair, James 122, John 122
Singleton, Edmund 142
Sisenbee (Lisenby) Charles 134
Skelton, Thomas 76,82
Skinner, John 50,58,59,72,82,87*,92,94*,107*,108, 130,133,135
Skipper, Barnaby 74,81, Benjamin 74,108,137, Benjamin, Jr. 137, John 137, Samuel 97
Slaughter, George 135, James 122, Owen 46,82*, 86,95,102,103,133,137, Walter 109,137
Slay, Thomas 72,73,80,90,107,108,136,138
Sliger, Gasper, Elizabeth 28, George 28,29
Smart, Samuel 119, Smiley 137
Smith, A.F. 30, Aaron 33,36,37,41, Ambrose Joshua 28*, 32, Ann J. 114, Archibald 121, Arthur 63*,64, Benjamin 24*,25,29,30*,34*, 38*,41,49,51,60,61,66,117,121,129,133,137, Benjamin, Jr. 61,66,121, Catherine 130,153, Charles (L.R.) 23,35,39,46,53,59,72,85*,87, Chas. (s of Thos.)114,130,133, Charles, Sr. 134, Chas. A. 121, D. (David) 40,52, Dd (David S.H.) 134, Daniel 55,57,89,100,124,125, 103,135,137, David (s of Francis) 122, David (S.H.) 23*,24*, 25,40,46,52*,54,80,84,94,98,101*,111*,116,131, 133,140 Deborah 42,74, Dunkin 84,90,91,130, Easter 62, Ed 138, Edward 24,37,38,41,43,51, 62,82,86,91,92,98,135,136,137,140,149 Eli 64, Elizabeth 114,125, Fanny 54, Frances 48,122, 149, Francis 28,36,38,54,69,71,76,77,80,88,94, 121,122,129,136,139, George 62, Gun 15, Hannah 121, Henry 93,125,154, James 58,59,61,64, 96,106,107*,121,130,133,135,137,138,139,143, James (L.R.) 151, James N. 121, James McN. 152, James, Sr. 152, Jane 120, Jasper 23*,36, 53,55,59*,78,85,89,99,103,110, Jeremiah 68, Jeremiah, Jr. 122, Jesse 64, John 37,38,42,43*, 45*,47*,54,60*,61*,64,70,75,88*,90,93,94*,95, 96,98*,100,101,122*,123,124*,125,130,135,136*, 153,35, John A. 68, John B. 153, John Curlo 48, John (Carp.) 19,23*24,25,48,53*,55*,61,69,73, 80,81*,95,99*,100,105,123,128,129,136,141, John, Jr. 24, John (L. R.) 19,23,25*,26,27*,29, 34,35*,36,39,44,53,59,63,80,81,85*,87,103,133, 134,141,146, John (Sandhill) 19,23*,24*,25*,38*, 39*,40,41*,45*,46,47,48*,52,53,54,55*,61,66,69*, 70, 71*,72, 75*, 79,80*,84*,87*,94,99,104,111,116, 129,133,134,139,140,141,146,148, John (Wayne Co.) 124,125, Josiah 24,62, Joseph 23,59,87,134, 136, Ker. 124, Lucy 68,121, Lydia 68, Margaret 40,116, Mary 56,61,62,64,124,130, Nathaniel 68, 122, Neal 130, Nicholas 26*,29,31*,35*,37,42, 43,48, Obedience 111, Patsy 125, Peter 31,62, Rachel 123, Richard 62,137,139,154, Richard (s of Francis) 122, Robert 110, Ruth 24,61,146, Samuel 64,120, Sarah 114,121,125,153, Sarah (Sandhill) 45*,54,55*,111,116,60, Sarah (Dry) 61, Susannah 62,68, Thomas 42,61*,74,83,94,114, 123,133,135,139,154, Trissah 125, William 24*, 29,34,37,42,49,51,52,62,89,98,103,124,125,131, 134,135,137,151, W. 133, William (L.R.) 34,53, 59,63,134,146, William (S.H.) 134,141, Willis 82, Zechariah 27*,35,36*,39,47,48*,54,55,57,74*, 93,106,134,149*
Snead, Betty 116, Caty 116, Christopher 116, Daniel 76,115, David 36,44,50,89,90,94,95,104,115, Henley 43,58,70,95,104,108,137,141, Henry 58, 95, Israel 36,44,50*,70,115,136,141, Israel, Jr. 50, John 50,91,116, John, Sr. 155, Phillip Burford 115, Samuel 43*,44,47,49* 70*,71*,72,74*, 75*,76*,77,78,81,90,91,92*,94*,95,96*,100,101, 104,105*,115,116,130,133,141, Capt. Samuel 74, Solomon 44,49, Temperance 116, William 80, 115,138,155, Patty 116
Snoddy, Agnes 126,129, John 126,129
Snuggs, Robert 41,74,85, Richard 85
Sowell, Charles 93, John 93,134, Lewis 93,133, William 93,134
Spann (Span), John 28*, 32
Spain, Alpheus 131
Sparks, Charles 62,140, Thomas 139
Spear, Robert 146, Thomas 148, William 122
Speed, John 61,64, William 81,100,107,108,130,137
Spencer, Daniel 56, John 44,50,69*,71,72,94,95,98, 102,126, Joseph 44, S. 112, Samuel 41*,42*,43*, 44*,50*, 53*,54,55,83,87*,89*,90*,91*,95,97, 104,109*,152, Susanna 50,102,111, Sybil 55, William 83*,93,95,148
Spradly (Spradling) Chas. 49, Peter 138

INDEX 177

Sprat (Spratt, Sprot), James 119, Martha 119, Mary 119, Thomas 119,132, Thomas, Jr. 119
Stacy, Joseph 146
Stagner, John 146
Stafford, Thomas 3, (See Williams)
Stall, Silpey 114
Stanback (Stainback), Thomas 55,85,93,99,102,105, 135,148
Stanfield (Stanfill), Jacob 134,137, James 134, John 103*,126,130,134,135,136,138,139, John, Sr. 139, Sampson 139, Thomas 135,136,139
Stansill, Sarah 123, William 139, Staton, Fred 67
Steed, Moses 93,141,146, Nathaniel 93,141,146, Philip 93
Steel, Ambrose 27, John 127, Joseph 34, Robert I. 151, R. I. 150, Susan 45, Thomas 27,151
Stegall (Steigall), George 1, Mary 123, Solomon 123
Steley, John 137
Stette (see Stitt), Ambrose 47, Ann 47, Joseph 47
Stewart (Stuart), James 24,94, John 117,118, William 140,146
Still (See Stette), Ambrose 132, Ann 132, Jacob 139, Joseph 107, Samuel 134
Stinson (Stenson), Chas. 67, Eliz. 123, Micajah 57*, 104,136
Stevens (Stephens) Francis 73,108, Grace 132, Henry 134, James 25, John 38,40,41,42,51,56, 88,111,117,118,129,130,132,134,146, John, Jr. 40,48,49, Mathew 98,130,132, Nancy 132, Sarah 117, William 47,127,130,132
Stitt, Ann 70*,122, Elizabeth 122, Mary 122, Joseph 70*, Samuel 70*
Stokes, Henry 43*,72,77,122,129,131,146, Henry, Sr. 122, John 122, Col. John 118*, Young 138
Stone, John 28,30,119, Sabey 44, Wm. 25,27,28*,32, 36,41,46,48,50,56,59
Stouchberry (Stuckberry), Jeremiah 133, John 23, 133
Straughter (Strother) Joseph 103
Streater, Burwell 109, Edward 121, James R. 121, Redick 121, Sheppard 121, William K. 121
Street, John 45,99,102*,136
Strickland (Strickling), Abraham 45,106,132,134, 137,138,139, Burrell 155, Jesse 152, John 152, 154, Lott 152, Patty 154, Mathew 94,103*,137, Charity 152, S. 137, Samuel 135,137, William 61,73,137, William, Jr. 135, William, Sr. 135, Zilpah 104, Strickland's 79
Stringer, John 110
Strother, Catherine 56, Jeremiah 23,54,56,84,86,96, 104,152, John 152, Josias 104, Joseph 93, Nancy 152, Solomon 56,151,152
Suggs (Siggs), George 141, Herbert (Harbert) 136, 146, Horatio 141, Rasha 146, Mary 35, Sarah 147, Richard 96, Thomas 35, Sugges 10
Sullivan, Rebecca Ann 61

Sumerall, Jesse 33
Sumner (Sermner) Benjamin 99,146
Sutherland, Ransom 51
Sutton, Elinor 113,119, James 146, Jasper 129, John 42, Phillip 23
Suy (Guy?) Williams 115
Swan, John 133, John, Jr. 134
Swearingen, Eliza 110, John 110,146,147, Josiah 23,56,57*,58,79,96,97,98*, Mary 46,57*,80, Samuel 24*,25,41,45,46,48,50,52,54,59,75,76, 80,81,91,110,146,148, Samuel, Jr. 24,41,110, Samuel, Sr. 57,74,76,110, Thomas 41*,46,57, 73*,74,110, Vann 41*,57,62*,74,76,97,110,116, 133,146
Sweeting, Elisha 135
Swor(Swa), Daniel 138, John 59,92,99,107,137,146, John, Jr. 106
Swot, George 137
Symon, William 53

****

Tabor, John 23
Tadricks (See Fedricks)
Tallant (Talent) Aaron 91,98,105,136, Edmund 138, Elizabeth 39, Josiah 93, Lott 102,136, Moses 136, Thomas 60,73,81,136,146
Taller (Tallear) John 135, Richard 135, William 46
Talley, Henry 71,84,95*,146
Talton, James 136, John 61,139, Thomas 136,139, 140, Thomas, Sr. 137, Thomas, Jr. 139
Tanner, Joseph 122,129
Tarbutton Joseph 86,108,135,146, John, Sr. 135
Tarleton, Emanuel 135, James 135
Tate, Rev. Joseph 26, John 150
Tatum, Absolem 54
Taylor, Arthur 78,90,147,148, Edmond 148, Eliz. 88, Henry 104,135,137, Jacob 33, John 146, Joshua 120, Josiah 91, Lucy 146, Nimrod 146, Stephen 122, Timothy 43,73,88,132, William 28,135,146,147
Temple, Frederick 108,109, James 136
Terrill (Terrel), Jeremiah 45,73,75,83,108,109, 133, Louisa 45, Philemon 41, William 45,50,73
Terry, Ann 117,149,153, Ann (Robards) 150, Appia 150, Benjamin 47, Calvin 154, Champ 150,154, Champness 59,153, Druscilla 154, Eli 64,125, 150*, 151,152*,153*,154*, Eli, Jr. 152, Eliz. 38,59, Fany 43, George 28*,42, James 25,28*, 30,32,38*,41,43*,47*,48,52,54,55,57,59*,60,61*, 62,73,97,109,131,133,153, James, Jr. 152, James Terry (Sav. Cr) 23,24*,29,32,46,48,51, 61*,65,66,67*,97,104,116,117,134,138,140,149*, 150*,153*, James, Sr. 151, James P. 150,152, J. Clk 150, Jeremiah 35,37, John 37,38*,41,43, 59, John K. 150, Johannah 154, Judy 154, Margaret 116, Martha 116,150, Martha Ann 150, Mary 29,32,36,52,60,116,125,127, Mary A. 150,

INDEX

Mary C. 152, Mary P. 124,125, Mary (Raiford) 149, Mathew 25*,56,58,59,92,94,104,108,132, 137,149,150*,153,154, Mathew, Sr. 151, Mourning 116, Polly 152,153, Richard Leak 59, Stephen 154, Tod R. 150, Thomas 124,125, W. 36,52,150, William, Esq. 26,27,31,32,34,36, Capt. William 27*,28*,29*, William (Sav. Cr.) 23*,24,25,29,31,32*,35,36,37,40,51,59,60,97, 99,100,104,109,111,116,125,127,149, Will (Sav. Cr) 32*, William (H. Cr) 23*,27,29,30*, 32,34,43,59,111,149,150*,153*, William, Jr. (H. Cr) 23,25,29,33,56,59,75,76,92,94,141,153, William 31,37,38,47,63,67*,80*;88,89,113,131, 132,137,153*, William (s of James) 150

Thomas, Annah 56, Avis 82, Benj. 96, 100, Charity 116, Daniel 77,89*,135,137, Edmond 142, George 44, Hannah 93, James 96,137, Jean 35, Charles 133, John 30,34,35,36,39*,45,46,49,74, 76*, 78, 81, 83,92,94,96,106,107,110,128,131, 137*, Leonard 92,142, Lewis 81,84,86,87,137, Miriam 120, Molly 76, Philemon 55,70,71,74, 77,89*,96,104,110,116, Robert 23,55,72,74,89, 96,100*,107,116,132,138, Samuel 7,139, Sarah 77, Sampson 113, Silas 93,94, Simon 55,79, 89*,137, Stephen 50,72,80,84*,87*,91,96,97, 104*,108,126,131,133,138,139, Stephen, Jr. 50, 87, Thomas 62,79,82,108,109,136,138,139, Tristam 86, Thomas 23,54,55,57,72,79*,82,83, 86,87,88*,89,90,92,93,103,104,107,108*,110, 115,116,122,131,135,137

Thomason, Alexander 45, Arnold 117, Benjamin 45, Margaret 45

Thompson, Benjamin 37, Charles 35,97,141, Elisha 37,86,91, Eliz. 37,131, Gideon 129, James 139, John 37,83,146, Joseph 106,127, 131,134,137,138*, Mary 37, Nathan 69, Sally 124, Samuel 33*, Shem 137,138, Smith 124, Sarah 37, William 27,44,73

Thoms, Joseph 139

Thomson, Elizabeth 134, Hen. 137, James 139, John 35,43,134, Samuel 131

Thorn, Robert 69,70,76

Thornton, Daniel 100

Threadgill, Elizabeth 120, John 120,129,138, John C. 68,122, Randle 66,138, Tempe (Murrel) 120, Thos. 61,62, William 50,52,56*,57,62,108*,109, 120,131,138,139, William, Jr. 118

Thurman (Thorman), John 119,128,130, Mary 119, 128,130

Tillis, Elizabeth 146, Jesse 146

Tilman, Richard 146

Tindall, J.H. 66,67, James 146, Lucy 153, Mary R. 124, Mourning, P. 153, Nancy 121, Nancy Robards 153, N. 153, The Tindalls 125

Tinnes, Robert 35,129

Tippins, Henry 36,55,134

Tisdale, Jerusha 55, Enoch 55

Tison, Jacob 63*, Jesse 66, John 54,123

Tomerlinson, Moses 120,138

Tomkins (Tompkins), Francis 108,131,139, Mary, 108,131, Stephen 72,79,106,108*, 131,139,141, Thomas 72,79,102,108*,127,131,137,139, Thomas, Jr. 102,131, William 139, Capt. William 139

Tomlin, John 140, Moses 134

Tony, John 137

Toole, Eleanor 131, Matthew 131

Touchberry, Jere 130, John 77,88, Samuel 76 (See Stouchberry)

Touchstone, Caleb 16,23*,57,94*,95,97,98*,99*, 101,102*,103,130,146,147, Christopher, 37,41, 119,142, Daniel 30, Frederick 37,41,127, Hannah 41, Henry 36,37,127*, Richard 37,41, 127*, Rose (Ashley) 119, Samuel 88, Sarah 127*, Stephen 37,41,58,74,79,82,86,95,135

Tower, Thomas 147

Townsend, Mary 34, Repentance 27,28,31,33,34, Solomon 48,49*,93,103,126,139

Travers (Travis), Charles 46,93,142,146, Edward 128,130, Henry 142, Mary 130

Treadwell, Daniel 139, Stephen 91,92,136,146

Trent, William 146, Troy, Joseph 67, More 138, Robert 67,120

Trull, Charity 128, James 146, Thomas 128,138, William 138

Truly, Thomas 134

Trysell, Chas. 91

Tucker, Andrew 138, George 136,146, John 136

Tuny, Bartho 137

Turnage, John 53,89*

Turner, Aaron 136, Charles 115, James 142,143, 151,153, John 155, Jasper 122, Jonathan 87, 134,138, Moses 137, Nathaniel 120, Thomas 103,135,137

Turpin, William 138

Turkey? James 70

Tutch, Stephen 133

Tweat, Charles Medlock 116

Tyler, Robert Gant 33

****

Umphreys, John 135

Underwood, Benjamin 134, Jacob 38,44, Hannah 44, Shadrach 44, Thomas 50,57

Usher, Samuel 134,149, Wm. 134

Ussery, Elizabeth 41,50,146, David 142,146, James 143, John 24,41,43,47,50,71,74,99, 111,133, John, Sr. 146, Joshua 134,146, Mary 111, Peter 134,142, Thomas 43,78,80, 81*,88,94,96,99,108*,130,133,134,146, Welcome 24,105,133,134,142, William 24*,41*, 44,130,135,146, William, Sr. 133

****

Vandeaver, Aaron 114
Vanderford, Benjamin 139, Bent 138, James 53*, 88*,109,118, Sarah 53, William 138,140
Vandyke, Thomas 136,147
Vanhosen (Vanhooser, Vanhoose, Vanhoese) Abraham 115, Catherine 115, Christian 115, Elizabeth 115, Jacob 71,73,77*,78,80,94,95, 96,115,141,146, John 115,148, Johannes 129, Mary 115, Valentine, 115,146,148, Yonkey 115
Vaughn (Von) Evan 138,139, Harman 117, Mary 117, Sarah 117, Stephen 117, William 117,139
Verrell, John 27
Vick Aaron 23,77,82, Isaac 51, Mary 48
Vickers, Ralph 129,139
Vickery, Joseph 136,147
Vines, Benjamin 30,44, Daniel 109,136, Elizabeth 44
Vining, Jeptha 129,139, Jane 63, John 137, Mary 117, Thomas 108,109,123,136,139, Margaret 49
Vivion, Charles 137

****

Wade, A. 63*,66, David 53, Elizabeth 63,124, George 62,117, Grizzell 62, Henry 103, Holden 49,62,63,64,97,117, Jane 63*,117, John 52,87, 103,107,109,110,112,136, Joseph 139, Judith 63,64, Judith Leak 124, Martha 52, Mary 63, 99*, Polly 63, Sarah 62,63,117, Thomas 43,49, 52,54,55,61*,62*,69,72*,73,76,77,78,79,83*,89, 90,94,95,104*,105,107*,108,109,110,116*,117, 122,124,126,136,138,139,142, Thomas, Jr. 117, 128,129,139, Col. Thos. Wade 129, Thos. Mc-Rose 124, William 70,71,109, Wm. Hambleton 63,124
Wage, William 138
Wagner, George 67
Waggoner, Samuel 33
Walker, Henry 19,33, James 90, John 85,91,92, 103,136, John, Sr. 141, Robert 73,91,115, Silvestus 133, Sylvanus 133
Wall, Henry 154, Jesse 147, John 70,72,75,76,77*, 79,90,91,92,94,97,104,106,108,130,137, John, Jr. 65 Kinchen 64, Lucy 154, Nancy 154, Polly 154, William 69,119,154, William, Jr. 65, Mr. 110
Wallace (Wallis) Jesse 69,77,78,79*,80,88,98,100, 102,134,146, John 48
Walters (Wallers), Eunice 152, John 51*,59*,7b, 83,84,89,90,104,105*,107,109,115,126,133,137, 138,152, John, Jr. 152, George 51,59*,107, 109,135,138,152, Johannah 34, Nancy 51,59, 152, Pamela 152, Robert 34
Ward, John 134,147, Mary 153,154, Thos. 78,93,97, 131,133,134,142,147, Thomas, Sr. 147, William 50
Ware, Peter 147, Roland 147, Thomas 147, William 53
Warrell (Worrell) Richard 92,95*,141
Warren, William 95

Warwick, Cummings 102
Washman, Gabriel 93
Waters, John 75
Watkins, Christopher 62,72,92,108,110, Ewel 147, George 46, Henry 154, James 142, Rachel 154, Thos. 123, William 36,70,75,76,78*,104,136
Watson, Alexander 155, Artemas 66, Elleck 137, James 36,137, John 46,103,115,136,137, Lot 137, Matthew 77,105,130, Peter 135,136, Samuel 129, William 30
Watts, Agnes 84, Andrew 133, David 47,136,137, Elleck, Jr. 137, Garrett 139, Henry 140, John 97, Malachi, 45,46,79,92,101,106,133,134,137, 139, Peter 129,136,138, William 79,84,97,136
Weaden, James 97
Weatherford, Charles 93,133,138, William 95
Weaver, Elizabeth 132, Isak 138, Jethro 134,137, Jonathan 134, Joseph 127, Joshua 43,75,132, Jothern 138, Ottwell 134, Stephen, 138, William 132,147
Webb, Elizabeth 68, George 23,44,70,77,92,96,98*, 100,103*,105,107,108,137,149,George, Jr. 98, Henley 106, James 77*,78,79*,80,104,135,137, John 25*,28,38,43,70,71,73,91,109,137, Leonard 64,133, Rachel 151, Robert 25,54,58,64*,65*, 75,77,79,81,88,91,92,97,98*,103,104,105,106, 108,109*,130*,133,135,138,141,149*, Theodoric 87,104,135,137, Theodore 123, William 68,109*, 135,137,152,106
Wells, George 138,139, James 88, Robert 138, Theoderick 88
West, John 139, Margaret 92, Onesphorus 83,92*
Westerfield, John 30
Westmoreland, John 133
White, David 30, Eleanor 129, Eliz. 73,123, Hezekiah 138, James 61, Jamima 126, Jacob 135, John 18,30,51,134,138,153, Josiah 64, 138, Joseph 27,29*,30*,31*,33*,43,46,48,54,65, 72,73,104,117,118*,119,120,133,134,135,137, 138, Joseph, Sr. 75, Joseph, Jr. 75,82, Margaret 30, Mary 119,123, Moses 73,84,105,133 Nicholas 36,38,72*,73,79,92,99,113,123, Stephen 30, Thomas 117,118,128,131, William 30, 64,72,93,126,135,136, Zedekiah 64
Whitfield, Bryant 147, James 147, Needham 147, William 147
Whitehead, Jacob 75,133, Mary 147
Whiteheart, Thomas 92
Whitly, Exodus 147, George 147,
Wild, James 99
Wilwood, George 139
Wooley, William 146
Word, Thomas
Wilkins, John 37, Joseph 38,39*, Samuel 27,29, 30,31,35,40,98, William 40,77
Wilkinson, John 142

180 INDEX

Williams, Abraham 66, Benjamin 154, Christopher 62,137, Edmund 152, Edward 110,137, 155, Elizabeth 154, Henry 39,40,46,78*,81, 82,89,90,92,95,98,99,100, Isham 147, Jacob 23* James 48,60,73,79,85, Jesse 99, John 86,139, Joseph 122, Josiah 65*, Luke 84,105,137, Nathaniel 77,90,102,141, Roland 39,40,41,47 117,133, Roger 92,100,106*,147, Sampson 7, 76,90,95*,96,99*,101,133,141, Samuel 69,76, 78,79,80*,81*,82,86*,90,91,92,94,97,98,147, 148, Seth 147, Solomon 55, 86,91,134,141,147, Stephen 147, Susannah 152, Stafford 58, Thomas Stafford 27*,32*,44,84,149,150, Thomas 33, 141, William 61,65*,109,135,147, Wilson 86,94, 102, Wincy 152

Williamson, Aquilla 139, John 128,129,138, Marling 137, Mary 129, Patty 129, Rebeckah 129, Sampson 105,135, Samuel 138

Willison, J. 40

Wilshur (Welchear), John 135,137, Jonas 137, William 37

Wilson, Andrew 64,65,117, Betsey 153, David 60, 64, George 41,43,45,48,49,56,57,58*60*,64,65, 66,70,71,72*,73,74,78,81,83,84,86,87,89,90,92, 94,97,98,102*,103*,104,105,106, George, Jr. 117, Henry 60*,137, Hugh 26*, James 33,73, Job 51,57,58,134, John 18,26,30,35,36,44,57,58*,64*, 65,71*,73,74,80,86,87,88,91,107,117,130,133,141, Martha 51,58, Mesanish 60,72*,128, Robert 65, 117,137, Samuel 27,33,36,64*,65,117,127, Sarah 127, Solomon 64*,65,117, Thomas 51,57,58,71, 77,79,80,91,101,102,103,135,141,148, William 82,136

Wimbly, Moses 147
Winfree, Charles 122, Joseph 102
Wisdom, Thoma 139, William 131,139
Wise, Jonathan 60,91, Samuel 77,86,91, Susanna 60
Wishart 99
Withrow, John 31, Mary 31
Womack, John 31
Woods, Francis 62, William 63*,77,129,138
Woodard (Woodward), Charles 97, Elizabeth 57, Henry 97, Wm. 97
Woodrow, John 62
Worthen, Richard 106,107,129*,138*, William 138
Wray, John 147
Wright, Ann 97, Carney 56,69*,71,75,107,129*, Catherine 71, Elizabeth 71, John 42,48,49,56, 71*,72,79,102,134,139*,146, John, Jr. 140, Jonathan 71,139*,140, Josias 136,147, Martha 49, Solomon 138, Stephen 71,96,122,138, Thomas 49,83,96,121,133,139, William 49,146

****

Yarbrough, Eliee (Ealie) 36,37, Frankey 62, Hum (Humphrey) 118, Joel 27, Joshua 95, May 115, Molly 120, Richard 27,28,31,32,34,36,37,116, 119, Sally 120, William 62
Yearby (Irby) Margaret 41, William 73
Yeats, Isaac 137, Peter 138
Yerkes, Samuel 50,79,85,92,98,99,101
Yoe, William 60,100,109,121,129,136,137,138, James 135
Young, Edward 146,148, James 34,36, Matthew 36, Samuel 31,33, Wm. 39

www.ingramcontent.com/pod-product-compliance
Lightning Source LLC
Chambersburg PA
CBHW051745230426
43670CB00012B/2167